Critical Thinking

Third Edition

Richard L. Epstein

with Carolyn Kernberger

Illustrations by Alex Raffi

THOMSON

™

WADSWORTH

Australia • Canada • Mexico • Singapore
Spain • United Kingdom • United States

Publisher: *Holly J. Allen*
Philosophy Editor: *Steve Wainwright*
Assistant Editors: *Lee McCracken,*
   Barbara Hillaker
Technology Project Manager: *Julie Aguilar*
Marketing Manager: *Worth Hawes*
Marketing Assistant: *Andrew Keay*

Advertising Project Manager: *Laurel Anderson*
Print/Media Buyer: *Lisa Claudeanos*
Permissions Editor: *Chelsea Junget*
Project Manager: *Jerry Holloway*
Cover Designers: *Stephen Rapley and*
   Yvo Riezebos
Printer: *Transcontinental Printing*

Printed in Canada
2 3 4 5 6 7 09 08 07

For more information about our products, contact us at:
   Thomson Learning Academic Resource Center at 1–800–423–0563
For permission to use material from this text, submit a request online at:
   http://www.thomsonrights.com
Any additional questions about permissions can be submitted to thomsonrights@thomson.com

Thomson Higher Education
10 Davis Drive
Belmont, CA 94002–3098
USA

Canada
Thomson Nelson
1120 Birchmount Road
Toronto, Ontario M1K 5G4
Canada

Asia
Thomson Learning
5 Shenton Way
#01–01 UIC Building
Singapore 068808

UK/Europe/Middle East/South Africa
Thomson Learning
High Holborn House
50–51 Bedford Road
London WC1R 4LR, United Kingdom

Australia/New Zealand
Thomson Learning Australia
102 Dodds Street
Southbank, Victoria 3006
Australia

Latin America
Thomson Learning
Seneca, 53
Colonia Polanco
11560 Mexico, D.F. Mexico

Spain (including Portugal)
Thomson Parainfo
Calle Magallanes, 25
28015 Madrid
Spain

Library of Congress Control Number: 2004110964

ISBN-13: 978-0-534-58348-4
ISBN-10: 0-534-58348-2

THE SLEEP OF REASON BEGETS MONSTERS

Dedicated to

Peter Adams

A great editor, a good friend.
With gratitude for his patience, encouragement,
and good advice that helped shape this book.

Critical Thinking
Third Edition

Cast of Characters

Preface to the Student

Preface to the Instructor

Acknowledgments

THE FUNDAMENTALS

THE STRUCTURE OF ARGUMENTS

AVOIDING BAD ARGUMENTS

ARGUMENTS for ANALYSIS

REASONING ABOUT OUR EXPERIENCE

Truth-Tables

Aristotelian Logic

Diagramming Arguments

Cast of Characters

Preface to the Student

You can read this book on your own. There are plenty of examples. The exercises illustrate the ideas you're supposed to master. With some effort you can get a lot out of this text.

But if you read this book just by yourself, you'll miss the discussion and exchanges in class that make the ideas come alive. Many of the exercises are designed for discussion. That's where your understanding will crystallize, and you'll find that you can begin to use the ideas and methods of critical thinking.

You'll get the most out of discussions if you've worked through the material first. Read the chapter through once, with a pencil in hand. Get an overview. Mark the passages that are unclear. You need to understand what is said—not all the deep implications of the ideas, not all the subtleties, but the basic definitions. You should have a dictionary on your desk.

Once the words make sense and you see the general picture, you need to go back through the chapter paragraph by paragraph, either clarifying each part or marking it so you can ask questions in class. Then you're ready to try the exercises.

You should try all the exercises. Many of them will be easy applications of the material you've read. Others will require more thought. And some won't make sense until you talk about them with your classmates and instructor. When you get stuck, look in the back where there are answers to many of the exercises.

By the time you get to class, you should be on the verge of mastering the material. Some discussion, some more examples, a few exercises explained, and you've got it.

That pencil in your hand is crucial. Reading shouldn't be a passive activity.

You need to master this material. It's essential if you want to write well. It's essential in making good decisions in your life. If you can think critically, you can advance in your work. No matter where you start in your career, whether flipping hamburgers or behind a desk, when you show your employer that you are not only responsible but can think well, can foresee consequences of what you and others do and say, you will go far. As much as the knowledge of this or that discipline, the ability to reason and communicate will speed you on your way. Those skills are what we hope to teach you here.

Preface to the Instructor

This textbook is designed to be the basis of classroom discussions. I've tried to write it so that lectures won't be necessary, minimizing the jargon while retaining the ideas. The material is more challenging than in other texts, while, I hope, more accessible.

The chapters build on one another to the end. Rely on your students to read the material—quiz them orally in class, call on them for answers to the exercises, clear up their confusions. The exercises are meant to lead to discussion, encouraging the students to compare ideas. Instead of spending lots of time grading the exercises, you can use the Quickie Exams from the Instructor's Manual. It is possible to do the whole book in one semester that way. I've chosen just the material that is essential for a one-semester course, the essentials of reasoning well.

This course should be easy and fun to teach. If you enjoy it, your students will, too.

Overview of the material

The Fundamentals (Chapters 1–5) is all one piece. It's the heart of the course. Here and throughout there is a lot of emphasis on learning the definitions. It's best to go through this in a direct line.

The Structure of Arguments (Chapters 6–8) is important. Chapter 6 on compound claims—an informal version of propositional logic—is probably the hardest for most students. There's a temptation to skip it and leave that material for a formal logic course. But some skills in reasoning with conditionals are essential. If you skip this chapter, you'll end up having to explain the valid and invalid forms piecemeal when you deal with longer arguments. It's the same for Chapter 8 on general claims—an informal introduction to quantifiers in reasoning—except that the material seems easier.

Avoiding Bad Arguments (Chapters 9–11) is fun. Slanters and fallacies give the students motive to look around and find examples from their own lives and from what they read and hear. For that reason many instructors like to put this material earlier. But if you do, you can only teach a hodge-podge of fallacies that won't connect and won't be retained. I've introduced the fallacies along with the good arguments they mock (for example, slippery slope with reasoning in a chain with conditionals, mistaking the person for the claim with a discussion of when it's appropriate to accept an unsupported claim), so that Chapter 11 is a summary and overview. Covering this material here helps students unify the earlier material and gives them some breathing room after the work in Chapters 6 and 8.

It's only at the end of this section, working through *Short Arguments for Analysis*, that students will begin to feel comfortable with the ideas from the earliest chapters. You can conclude a course for the quarter system here. Then *Complex Arguments for Analysis* introduces more about the structure of arguments and how to analyze longer, more difficult examples, with twenty-one long arguments as exercises.

The last part, *Reasoning About Our Experience* (Chapters 12–15), covers specific kinds of arguments: analogies, generalizations, and cause and effect. Chapter 13 on numerical claims could follow directly after Chapter 5.

The accompanying *Workbook for Critical Thinking* contains every exercise from the text in a format that makes students do the basic steps in argument analysis for each argument they encounter. Checking the work is much easier from the uniform answer sheets. The Workbook contains additional material, including Exercises and Examples from the Law. There is an alternative *Science Workbook* for the text that contains exercises on applying critical thinking to the sciences, with additional material on observations and experiments, models, and explanations. The Instructor's Manual CD has suggestions and a syllabus for the Science Workbook.

Writing Lessons are an integral part of the course. Included are two types of writing exercises. The *Essay Writing Lessons* require the student to write an argument for or against a given issue, where the issue and the method of argument are tied to the material that's just been presented. About midway through the course your students can read the section "Composing Good Arguments," which summarizes the lessons they should learn. In the Instructor's Manual there are suggestions for making the grading of these relatively easy.

The *Cartoon Writing Lessons* present a situation or a series of actions in a cartoon, and require the student to write the best argument possible for a claim based on that. These lessons do more to teach students reasoning than any other type of exercise. Students have to distinguish between observation and inference; they have to judge whether a good argument is possible; they have to judge whether the claim is objective or subjective; they have to judge whether a strong argument or a valid argument is called for. These deserve class time for discussion.

Together, *these exercises and a few others from the chapters provide more than enough assignments for courses that require a substantial writing component.*

Special features of this text

• The material is tied into a single whole, a one-semester course covering the basics. The text is meant to be read and studied from one end to the other.

As an example of how the ideas fit together as one piece, the Principle of Rational Discussion and the Guide to Repairing Arguments (Chapter 4) play a central role in any argument analysis and are used continuously to give shape to the analyses. They serve to organize the fallacies (Chapter 11), so that fallacies are not just a confusing list.

• There are more than a thousand exercises and hundreds of examples taken from daily life. Dialogues among cartoon characters sound like the reasoning students encounter every day. Examples from newspapers and other media are focused on the ideas in the text and on what will interest students. Philosophical issues are raised in the context of dialogues that students can imagine hearing their friends say. The text relates theory to the needs of students to reason in their own lives.

In each section the exercises move from stating a definition, to relating the various ideas, to applying the concepts. The most important ideas are reinforced with similar exercises in succeeding sections. Worked examples in the text help students see how to begin with their homework.

• Cartoons have been drawn especially for this book to reinforce the ideas, to show relationships of ideas, and to get students to convert nonverbal experience into arguments. The Cartoon Writing Lessons help students grasp the ideas much faster.

• Examples and Exercises from the Law are given in the Workbook. For example, Montana's Supreme Court ruling regarding the basic law on speeding is presented in the discussion of vagueness; a Federal Trade Commission decision on truth in advertising is linked to the discussion of when to accept an unsupported claim.

• There is a complete Instructor's Manual with suggestions for teaching and answers to the exercises in the text. An accompanying Instructor's CD contains fifty-four sample exams, answers to those, more than five hundred additional examples, and additional material ready to modify and print.

• *Five Ways of Saying "Therefore,"* also available from Wadsworth, was written to provide a theoretical framework for the ideas presented in this text. It is also suitable for an upper-division course.

• Definitions and key ideas are boxed. It's easy to find the important material.

• The text is fun to read, yet challenges the very best student.

New to the Third Edition

• Carolyn Kernberger, my co-author for *The Guide to Critical Thinking in Economics*, has collaborated in rewriting the material to make it easier to teach.

• A new section on prescriptive and descriptive claims has been added to Chapter 2. That distinction is followed through in analyses of many examples in the text. It is particularly useful in the discussion of appeals to emotions.

• A new section on graphs has been added to the chapter on numerical claims.

- A new section on advertising and the Internet has been added to the chapter on evaluating unsupported claims.

- There are 198 new exercises and 62 new examples.

> I've tried to steer between the Scylla of saying nonsense
> and the Charybdis of teaching only trivialities. I hope
> you find the journey memorable. The water is deep.

Acknowledgments

I am grateful that so many people have been willing to give their time and ideas to help me improve this text. I am indebted to:

- Tom Bittner, Jeanette Catsoulis, Vanessa Christopher, Peter Eggenberger, Stephen Epstein, Maurice Finocchiaro, Peter Hadreas, Neta Hoff, Todd Jones, Susan Kowalski, Fred Kroon, Ron Leonard, Benson Mates, and Maria Sanders for discussions on the ideas and drafts of the first edition.
- Reviewers, whose comments were crucial in clearing up confusions and shaping the text. *First edition* David Adams, Phyllis Berger, Blanche Radford Curry, Betsy Decyk, Roger Ebertz, George Gale, Kevin Galvin, James W. Garson, Don Levi, Isabel Luengo, Brian J. Rosmaita, Darlene Macomber, and Kenneth Stern. *Second edition* and the *Science Workbook* Sharon Crasnow, Brian Domino, Gary Elkins, James F. Sennett, William Tinsley, James F. Sennett, and Gina Zavota. *Third edition* Theodore Gracyk, Carol J. Nicholson, G. A. Spangler, Scot Miller, and Jim Chesher.
- Peter Adams for many good suggestions on how to organize and present the material, and for his help and encouragement throughout.
- Alex Raffi who contributed so many ideas in collaboration on the cartoons.
- My development editors, whose suggestions improved the text. *First edition* Alan Venable; *Second edition* Kara Kindstrom; *Third edition* Lee McCracken.
- Stephen Epstein, Paul Yackel, and Adriana Zuñiga for working through and correcting a draft of the Science Workbook.
- Elizabeth Ray and Mark McNellis for some excellent examples.
- Robert Epstein and Christian Fritz for help on the examples from the law.
- Mircea Dumitru and William S. Robinson for comments on the appendix on Aristotelian logic.
- Signe Wolsgård Krøyer and Rasmus Ploug for reading through the entire draft of the third edition and making many helpful comments.
- Timothy A. D. Hyde for suggestions and critiques for the third edition.
- And my students, who provided me with many examples, whose quizzical looks made me rewrite, and whose delight in the material motivated me to finish this book.

I am grateful to them all. Much of what is good in this text comes from them. What is bad is mine, all mine.

The FUNDAMENTALS

1 Critical Thinking?

A. Are You Convinced?

Everyone's trying to convince you of something: You should go to bed early. You should drop out of college. You should buy a Dodge Ram truck. You should study critical thinking . . . . And you spend a lot of time trying to decide what you should be doing, that is, trying to convince yourself: Should I take out a student loan? Is chocolate bad for my complexion? Should I really date someone who owns a cat?

Are you tired of being conned? Of falling for every pitch? Of making bad decisions? Of fooling yourself? Or just being confused?

Thinking critically is a defense against a world of too much information and too many people trying to convince us. But it is more. Reasoning is what distinguishes us from beasts. Many of them can see better, can hear better, and are stronger. But they cannot plan, they cannot think through, they cannot discuss in the hopes of understanding better.

An older student was in the spring term of his senior year when he took this course. He was majoring in anthropology and planned to do graduate work in the fall. Late in the term he brought me a fifteen-page paper he'd written for an anthropology class. He said he'd completed it, then he went over it again, analyzing it as we would in class, after each paragraph asking, "So?" He found that he couldn't justify his conclusion, so he changed it and cut the paper down to eleven pages. He showed me the professor's comments, which were roughly "Beautifully reasoned, clear. A+." He said it was the first A+ he'd ever gotten. I can't promise that you'll get an A on all your term papers after taking this course. But you'll be able to comprehend better what you're reading and write more clearly and convincingly.

1

Once in a while I'll tune into a sports talk show on the radio. All kinds of people call in. Some of them talk nonsense, but more often the comments are clear and well reasoned. The callers know the details, the facts, and make serious projections about what might be the best strategy based on past experience. They comment on what caused a team to win or lose; they reason with great skill and reject bad arguments. I expect that you can too, at least on subjects you consider important. What we hope to do in this course is hone that skill, sharpen your judgment, and show you that the methods of evaluating reasoning apply to much in your life.

In trying to understand how to reason well, we'll also study bad ways to convince, ways we wish to avoid, ways that misuse emotions or rely on deception. You could use that knowledge to become a bad trial lawyer, but I hope you will learn a love of reasoning well, for it is not just ethical to reason well; it is, as we shall see, more effective in the long run. Critical thinking is part of the study of philosophy: the love of wisdom. We might not reach the truth, but we can be searchers, lovers of wisdom, and treat others as if they are, too.

B. Claims

We'll be studying the process of convincing. An attempt to convince depends on someone trying to do the convincing and someone who is supposed to be convinced.

> • Someone tries to convince you.
> • You try to convince someone else.
> • You try to convince yourself.

Let's call an attempt to convince an "argument."

But, you say, an argument means someone yelling at someone else. When my mom yells at me and I yell back, that's an argument. Yes, perhaps it is. But so, by our definition, is you and your friend sitting down to talk about your college finances to decide whether you need to get a job. We need a term that will cover our attempts to convince. The word "argument" has become pretty standard.

Still, that isn't right. Suppose the school bully comes up to Flo and says, "Hand over your candy bar." Flo won't. She hits Flo on the head with a stick. Flo gives up her candy bar. Flo's been convinced. But that's no argument.

The kind of attempts to convince we'll be studying here are ones that are or can be put into language. That is, they are a bunch of sentences that we can think about. But what kind of sentences?

When we say an argument is an attempt to convince, what exactly is it we're supposed to be convinced of? To do something? If we are to try to reason using arguments, the point is that something is true. And what is that something? A sentence, for it's sentences that are true or false. And only certain kinds of sentences: not threats, not commands, not questions, not prayers. An attempt to convince, in order to be classified as an argument, should be couched in plain language that is true or false: declarative sentences.

You should already know what a declarative sentence is. For example:

This course is a delight.
The author of this book sure writes well.
Intelligent beings once lived on Mars.
Everyone should brush his or her teeth at least once every day.
Nobody knows the troubles I've seen.

The following are not declarative sentences:

Shut that door!
How often do I have to tell you to wipe your feet before you come into
  the house?
Dear God, let me be a millionaire instead of a starving student.

Still, not every declarative sentence is true or false: "Green dreams ride donkeys" is a declarative sentence, but it's nonsense. Let's give a name to those sentences that are true or false, that is, that have a *truth-value*.

Claim A declarative sentence used in such a way that it is either true or false (but not both).

One of the most important steps in trying to understand new ideas or new ways of talking is to look at lots of examples.

Examples   Are the following claims?

Example 1   Your instructor for this course is male.
Analysis   This is a claim. It's either true or false.

Example 2   Your teacher is short.

Analysis   Is this a claim? Probably not, since the word "short" is so vague. We'll consider problems with vagueness in Chapter 2.

Example 3   Cats are nasty.

Analysis   If when you read this you disagreed, then you are implicitly accepting the example as a claim. You can't disagree unless you think it has a truth-value.

Example 4 $2 + 2 = 4$

Analysis   This is a claim, though no one is going to disagree with you about it.

Example 5   I wish I could get a job.

Analysis   How is this being used? If Maria, who's been trying to get a job for three weeks, says it to herself late at night, then it's not a claim. It's more like a prayer or an extended sigh.

But if Dick's parents are berating him for not getting a job, he might say, "It's not that I'm not trying. I wish I could get a job." That might be true, but it also might be false, so in this context "I wish I could get a job" would be a claim.

Example 6   How can anyone be so dumb as to think that computers can think?

Analysis   As it stands this is not a claim; it is a question. But in some contexts we might rewrite it as "Someone must be dumb to think that computers can think," or perhaps "Computers can't think." The process of rewriting and reinterpreting is something we'll consider throughout this course.

Example 7   Todo cachorro pode latir.

Analysis   Is this a claim? If you don't understand Portuguese, you better say you're not prepared to accept it as one. You can't reason with it if you don't understand it.

Example 8   Every mollusk can contract myxomatosis.

Analysis   If you don't know what these words mean, you shouldn't try to reason with this as a claim. But that doesn't mean you should just dismiss any attempt to convince that uses language you don't understand. A dictionary is an important tool of a good reasoner.

C. Arguments

We're trying to define "argument." We said it was an attempt to convince someone, using language, that a claim is true. The only language that we should allow in an argument, then, should be sentences that are true or false.

> *Argument* An argument is an attempt to convince someone
> (possibly yourself) that a particular claim, called the ***conclusion***, is true.
> The rest of the argument is a collection of claims called ***premises***,
> which are given as the reasons for believing the conclusion is true.

The point of an argument is to convince that a claim—the conclusion—is true.
The conclusion is sometimes called the ***issue*** that's being debated.

> ***Critical thinking*** is evaluating whether we should be convinced that some
> claim is true or some argument is good, as well as formulating good arguments.

Examples   Are the following arguments?

Example 1

Analysis   The nurse is making an argument. She's trying to convince the doctor
that "Your patient in Room 47 is dying" is true. She offers the premise: "He's in
cardiac arrest." Sounds pretty convincing.

Example 2

Analysis   Dick is making an argument, trying to convince the police officer that the
following claim is true: "The accident was not my fault" (reworded a bit). He uses
two premises: "She hit me from the rear" and "Anytime you get rear-ended it's not
your fault."

Example 3   Out? Out? I was safe by a mile. Are you blind? He didn't even touch me with his glove!

Analysis   This was spoken at a baseball game by a runner who'd just been called out. He was trying to convince the umpire to believe "I was safe." He used only one premise: "He didn't even touch me with his glove." The rest is just noise.

Example 4   Give me that *$!#&* wrench.

Analysis   I can remember who said this to me. He was trying to convince me. But it was no argument, just a series of commands and threats. And what he was trying to convince me of wasn't the truth of some claim.

Example 5   Follow the directions provided by your doctor for using this medicine. This medicine may be taken on an empty stomach or with food. Store this medicine at room temperature, away from heat and light.

Analysis   This is not an argument. Instructions, explanations, and descriptions, though they may use declarative sentences, aren't arguments. They're not intended to convince you that some claim is true.

Example 6

Analysis   Zoe's mother is attempting to convince her, but not of the truth of a claim. So there's no argument. Perhaps we could interpret what is being said as having an unstated conclusion "You should feel guilty for not calling your mother," and premises (disguised as questions) "Anyone who doesn't call her mother doesn't love her mother" and "If you don't love your mother, then your mother did something wrong." But it would be the interpretation that is an argument, not the original. And we would have to consider whether the interpretation is faithful to what Zoe's mother intended. We'll consider the process of interpretation in Chapter 4.

Example 7   The sky is blue. That's because sunlight is refracted through the air in such a way that other wavelengths of light are diminished.

Analysis   This is not an attempt to convince you that the sky is blue—that's obvious. This is an explanation, and *an explanation is not an argument.*

Example 8   You see a chimpanzee trying to get some termites out of a hole. She can't manage it because the hole is too small for her finger. So she gets a stick and tries to pull the termites out. No success. She licks the end of the stick and puts it in the hole and pulls it out with a termite stuck to it. She eats the termite, and repeats the process. Is she convincing herself by means of an argument?

Analysis   This isn't an argument. Whatever the chimpanzee is doing, she's not using claims to convince herself that a particular claim is true.

But isn't she reasoning? That's a hard question you can study in philosophy and psychology courses.

Summary   We said that this course will be about attempts to convince. But that's too much for one course. We narrowed the topic to attempts to convince that use language. That was still too broad. An argument, we decided, should mean an attempt to convince someone that a sentence is true. We defined a claim as a declarative sentence used in such a way that it is true or false. Arguments, then, are attempts to convince that use only claims.

Now we'll begin to look at methods and make distinctions. Because your reasoning can be sharpened, you can understand more, you can avoid being duped. And, we can hope, you will reason well with those you love and work with and need to convince, and you will make better decisions. But whether you will do so depends not just on method, not just on the tools of reasoning, but on your goals, your ends. And that depends on virtue.

Key Words

truth-value	claim	premise
true	argument	issue
false	conclusion	critical thinking

Exercises for Chapter 1

These exercises are meant to help you become familiar with the basic ideas we've seen in this chapter. They should raise enough worries about the nature of claims and arguments that you'll be glad to see how we clarify those in the next few chapters.

1. What is this course about?

2. How did I try to convince you that this course is important? Pick out at least two places where I tried to convince you and decide whether they are arguments.

3. Explain how to divide up all attempts to convince in terms of who is trying to convince whom.

4. Which of the following are claims?
   a. Keanu Reeves is a woman.
   b. I am 2 meters tall.
   c. Is any teacher capable of writing a good exam?
   d. Power corrupts.

    e.   Feed Spot.

    f.   Did you feed Spot?

    g.   A friend in need is a friend indeed.

    h.   No se puede vivir sin amor.

    i.   Whenever Spot barks, Zoe gets mad.

    j.   Britney Spears wasn't married in Las Vegas.

    k.   Your instructor believes that Britney Spears wasn't married in Las Vegas.

    l. $2 + 2 = 5$

    m.   I feel cold today.

    n.   There is an odd number of stars in the universe.

5.   Write down five sentences, four of which are claims and one of which is not. Exchange with a classmate and see if he or she can spot which are the claims.

6.   What is an argument?

7.   What is the point of making an argument?

8.   What is a premise? What is a conclusion?

9.   Why isn't every attempt to convince an argument? Give an example.

10.   Bring in an example of an argument you heard or read in the last two days.

11.   Bring in a short article from the front page of a newspaper. Are all the sentences used in it claims? Is it an argument?

12.   Your friend goes outside, looks up at the sky, and sees it's cloudy. She goes back inside and gets her raincoat and umbrella. Is she making an argument? Explain.

13.   Bring an advertisement to class that uses an argument. State the premises and the conclusion.

Here are two exercises done by Tom, along with Dr. E's comments.

Tom Wyzyczy
Critical Thinking
Section 4

Sheep are the dumbest animals. If the one in front walks off a cliff, all the rest will follow it. And if they get rolled over on their backs, they can't right themselves.

Argument? (yes/no) Yes.

Conclusion: Sheep are the dumbest animals.

Premises: If a sheep walks off a cliff, all the rest will follow it.

               If a sheep gets rolled over on its back, it can't right itself.

This is good work, Tom.

> **How can you go to the movies with Sarah and not me? Don't you remember I helped you fix your car last week?**
>
> *Argument?* (yes/no) Yes.
> *Conclusion*:   You should go to the movies with me.
> *Premises*:   I helped you fix your car last week.
>
> *Is what you are given an argument? No. There are just two questions, and questions aren't claims. So it can't be an argument. And if there's no argument, there are no premises and no conclusion. Sure, it seems that we ought to interpret what's said as an argument—as you have done. But before we go putting words in someone's mouth, we ought to have rules and a better understanding of when that's justified.*

Answer each of Exercises 14–26 in the same way: State whether it is an argument. If it is an argument, identify the premises and conclusion.

14. You shouldn't eat at Zee-Zee Frap's restaurant. I heard they did really badly on their health inspection last week.

15. You liked that movie? Boy, are you dumb. I guess you just can't distinguish bad acting from good. And the photography was lousy. What a stupid ending, too.

16. If it's O.K. to buy white mice to feed a pet boa constrictor, why isn't it O.K. to buy white mice for your cat to play with?

17. If you don't take a course on critical thinking, you'll always end up being conned, a dupe for any fast-talker, an easy mark for politicians. So you should take a course on critical thinking. You'd be especially wise to take one from the instructor you've got now— he [she] is a great teacher.

18. Whatever you do, you should drop the critical thinking course from the instructor you've got now. He [she] is a really tough grader, much more demanding than the other professors that teach that course. You could end up getting a bad grade.

19. I would not live forever, because we should not live forever, because if we were supposed to live forever, then we would live forever, but we cannot live forever, which is why I would not live forever.
    (A contestant's response to the question "If you could live forever, would you and why?" in the 1994 Miss USA contest.)

20. (Advertisement) The bigger the burgers, the better the burgers, the burgers are bigger at Burger King.

21. Look Dick! Look Zoe! See Spot. See Spot run.

22. Flo has always wanted a dog, but she's never been very responsible. She had a fish once, but it died after a week. She forgot to water her mother's plants, and they died. She stepped on a neighbor's turtle and killed it.

23. Maria: Ah-choo.
    Lee: Gesundheit.
    Maria: I'm just miserable. Stuffy head and trouble breathing.
    Lee: Sounds like the allergies I get.
    Maria: No, it's the flu. I'm running a fever.

24. You may own stocks or securities which are selling at a lower price than when purchased. Tax considerations might call for a sale of such securities in order to create a currently deductible tax loss. However, if it is desired to still own the securities while producing a tax loss, you can't just sell securities at a loss and then buy them right back. Any purchase of the same securities within 30 days before or after the sale negates any losses. To get around this restriction, you can purchase similar but not identical securities to the ones sold. Or, in the case of bonds, you can achieve the same result by making a swap through a brokerage house.

    1994 Tax Guide for College Teachers

25. The light bulb is located in the upper left corner of the oven. Before replacing the bulb, disconnect electric power to the range at the main fuse or circuit breaker panel or unplug the range from the electric outlet. Let the bulb cool completely before removing it. Do not touch a hot bulb with a damp cloth as the bulb will break.

    To remove: Hold hand under lamp bulb cover so it doesn't fall when released. With fingers of same hand, firmly push down wire bail until it clears cover. Lift off cover. Do not remove any screws to remove this cover. Replace bulb with a 40-watt home appliance bulb.

    How to get the best from your range, Hotpoint

26. Letter to the editor:

    I'm 45, a mother and a postal worker. I also happen to be in a long-term relationship with a woman. We both work, pay taxes, vote, do volunteer work, and lead full, productive lives.

    My partner Sara and I have been together for over four years and we formalized our lifetime commitment to each other in a ceremony several years ago. In a fair and non-discriminating society, we would be able to obtain the same benefits for each other that heterosexual Americans obtain when they marry.

    I've worked for the postal service for 10 years, yet I can't obtain health insurance for Sara, nor can I use family leave to care for or be with her if she's ill, has had surgery or has been injured.

    Heterosexual employees who are married or get married can get benefits for a spouse and any number of children, including adopted, foster and stepchildren.

    Even when we have legal papers drawn up to protect our rights, property and relationships, it often takes lengthy and expensive court battles to get other people to honor our wishes and instructions. Sometimes we lose those battles, and some rights (like family health insurance coverage) we simply can't get.

    No one should be surprised that we want the right to marry.

    Kathy Worthington, *The Spectrum*, May 26, 1996

27. In order to choose good courses of action in our lives, we need not only knowledge of the world and the ability to reason well, but what else?

Further Study   There is much more to learn about the nature of claims, truth, falsity, and the relation of language to our experience. We'll touch on some of those in the next chapter. An introductory philosophy course goes much deeper.

Attempts to convince that use language but aren't arguments, such as fables and examples, are studied in courses in rhetoric. Courses in marketing, advertising, or psychology study both verbal and nonverbal ways to convince that aren't arguments. Convincing that uses body language is at the heart of acting classes.

A place to begin reading about whether animals can reason is *The Animal Mind*, by James and Carol Gould, Scientific American Library.

Writing Lesson 1

Write an argument either for or against the following:

> *Student athletes should be given special leniency when the instructor assigns course marks.*

Your argument should be at most one page long.

2   What Are We Arguing About?

We want to arrive at truths from our reasoning. So we need to be able to recognize whether a sentence is true or false and what kind of standards it invokes—or whether it is just nonsense.

A. Vague Sentences

1.   Too vague?

Zoe heard a radio advertisement that said "Snappy detergent gets clothes whiter." So when she went to the supermarket she bought a box. She's not very happy.

Some sentences may look like claims, or people try to pass them off as claims, but they're worthless for reasoning. If we can't understand what someone is saying, we can't investigate whether it's true or false.

> **Vague sentence**   A sentence is vague if there are so many ways to understand it that we can't settle on one of those without the speaker making it clearer.

We hear vague sentences all the time:

You can win a lot playing blackjack.
Public education is not very good in this state.
Freedom is worth fighting for.

They sound plausible, yet how can anyone tell whether they are true?

But isn't everything we say somewhat vague? After all, no two people have identical perceptions, and since the way we understand words depends on our experience, we all understand words a little differently. There has to be some wiggle room in the meaning of words and sentences for us to be able to communicate. You say, "My English professor showed up late for class on Tuesday." Which Tuesday? Who's your English professor? What do you mean by late? 5 minutes? 30 seconds? How do you determine when she showed up? When she walked through the door? At exactly what point? When her nose crossed the threshold?

That's silly. We all know "what you meant," and the sentence isn't too vague for us to agree that it has a truth-value. *The issue isn't whether a sentence is vague, but whether it's too vague, given the context, for us to be justified in saying it has a truth-value.*

Examples   Are the following too vague to be taken as claims?

Example 1 Men are stronger than women.
Analysis Don't bother to argue about this one until you clarify it, even though it may seem plausible. What's meant? Stronger for their body weight? Stronger in that the "average man" (whoever that is) can lift more than the "average woman"? Stronger emotionally?

Example 2 On the whole, people are much more conservative than they were 30 years ago.
Analysis We get into disagreements about sentences like this and make decisions based on them. But the example is too vague to have a truth-value. What does "people" mean? All adults? What does "conservative" mean? That's really vague. Is George W. Bush conservative? Pat Buchanan? Rush Limbaugh?

Example 3 Capricorn: This is the time to finalize travel and higher education plans. You are vibrant with friends and group projects. This will be a progressive period of unexpected change.   Heather Subran, *It's in the stars!,* September 18, 1997

Analysis Ever notice how vague horoscopes are? How could you tell if this horoscope was false? There's no claim here.

Example 4 *Greeks, Turks spar over islet*
Greek and Turkish warships faced off Tuesday in the Aegean Sea, escalating a dispute over a tiny barren island 3.8 miles off the Turkish coast.

   Both Greece and Turkey claim sovereignty to the uninhabited islet, called Imia in Greek and Kardak in Turkish.

   State Department spokesman Glynn Davies called the situation "hot and heavy . . . a little tense. The message we're sending to both governments is to please calm down and to draw back."   Marilyn Greene, *USA Today,* February 1, 1996

Analysis What is a situation that is "hot and heavy . . . a little tense"? What does it mean to say "warships faced off"? These are sentences masquerading as claims.

Example 5 City officials in Murfreesboro, Tenn.—about 30 miles south of Nashville— say one smelly employee is responsible for a new policy that requires all city employees to smell nice at work.

   "No employee shall have an odor generally offensive to others when reporting to work. An offensive odor may result from lack of good hygiene, from an excessive application of a fragrant aftershave or cologne or from other cause."

   The definition of body odor was left intentionally vague.

   "We'll know it when we smell it," said City Councilman Toby Gilley.
                              Knoxville News-Sentinel, August 26, 2003

Analysis Sometimes it isn't possible to make a precise distinction, yet that doesn't mean we're being too vague in the intended context.

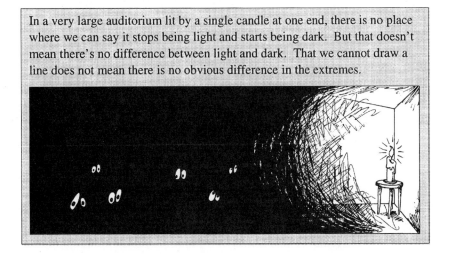

In a very large auditorium lit by a single candle at one end, there is no place where we can say it stops being light and starts being dark. But that doesn't mean there's no difference between light and dark. That we cannot draw a line does not mean there is no obvious difference in the extremes.

Throughout this text we'll often point out a common mistake in reasoning and label it a *fallacy*.

Drawing the line fallacy   It's bad reasoning to argue that if you can't make the difference precise, then there is no difference.

---

2.   Ambiguous sentences

A special case of vagueness is when there are just two, or a very few, obvious ways that a sentence could be understood as a claim.   In that case we say the sentence is **ambiguous**.

It's not always easy to see that ambiguity is infecting an argument:

Saying that having a gun in the home is an accident waiting to happen
is like saying that people who buy life insurance are waiting to die.
We should be allowed to protect ourselves.

The speaker is trading on two ways to understand "protect": physically protect vs. emotionally or financially protect.   It's easy to get confused and accept unreasonable conclusions when an ambiguous sentence is used as a premise.   We can tolerate some vagueness, but we should never tolerate ambiguity in reasoning.

Examples   Is there any ambiguity in these passages?

Example 1   There is a reason I haven't talked to Robert [my ex-lover] in seventeen years (beyond the fact that I've been married to a very sexy man whom I've loved for two-thirds of that time).   Laura Berman, *Ladies' Home Journal,* June, 1996
Analysis   The rest of the time she just put up with him?

Example 2   Your mother says you shouldn't argue with your elders. Your instructor is older than you, and he says that this course is about arguing. How can you possibly pass this course and still be a good son or daughter?
Analysis   Don't drop this course! Your mother is saying you shouldn't disagree in a rude manner with your elders, while your professor is trying to teach you how to reason. There's the colloquial understanding of "argue," and the way we understand that word in critical thinking and English composition.

Example 3   Dr. E's dogs eat over 10 pounds of meat every week.
Analysis   Is this true or false? It depends on whether it means: "Each of Dr. E's dogs eats over 10 pounds of meat every week" (big dogs!), or "Dr. E's dogs altogether eat over 10 pounds of meat every week." *It's ambiguous whether the individual or the group is meant.*

Example 4   Homosexuality can't be hereditary: Homosexual couples can't reproduce, so genes for homosexuality would have died out long ago.

Analysis   The argument appears good, but only because "Homosexual couples can't reproduce" is ambiguous. That's true if understood as "Homosexuals can't reproduce *as a couple*," but it is false in the sense needed to make the argument good: "Homosexuals, who happen to be in couples, each can't reproduce." Again there's ambiguity between the individual and the group.

Exercises for Section A

1. Give an example of a vague sentence that someone tried to pass off to you as a claim.

2. Which of the following are too vague to be considered claims?
   (You may have to suggest a context in which the sentence is spoken.)
   a. Manuel: Maria is a better cook than Lee.
   b. Lee: Manuel looks like he has a cold today.
   c. Public animal shelters should be allowed to sell unclaimed animals to laboratories for experimentation.
   d. Tuition at state universities does not cover the entire cost to the university of a student's education.
   e. All unnatural sex acts should be prohibited by law.
   f. All citizens should have equal rights.
   g. People with disabilities are just as good as people who are not disabled.
   h. Boy, are you lucky to get a date with Jane—on a scale of 1 to 10, she's at least a 9.
   i. Zoe has beautiful eyes.
   j. Dog food is cheaper at Furr's grocery store than at Smith's grocery.
   k. Alpo in cans is cheaper at Furr's grocery store than at Smith's grocery.
   l. Spot is a big dog.
   m. Cholesterol is bad for you.
   n. Parents should be held responsible for crimes their children commit.
   o. There's a good chance of rain tomorrow.
   p. There's a 70% chance of rain tomorrow.

3. Find an advertisement that treats a vague sentence as if it were a claim.

4. What's wrong with the following attempt to convince?

   Look, officer, if I were going 36 in this 35 m.p.h. zone, you wouldn't have given me a ticket, right? What about 37? But at 45 you would? Well, isn't that saying that the posted speed limit is just a suggestion? Or do you write the law on what's speeding?

5. a. Can a claim be ambiguous?
   b. Can a claim be vague?

6. How much ambiguity can we tolerate in an argument?

7. Decide whether each of the following sentences is a claim. If it is ambiguous, give at least two sentences corresponding to the ways it could be understood.

    a. Zoe saw the waiter with the glasses.

    b. Rumsfeld: Intelligence still lacking. (Headline in *The Albuquerque Tribune*, 8/7/02)

    c. Americans bicycle thousands of miles every year.

    d. If someone is under 18 years old, then he cannot vote in this country.

    e. I am over 6 feet tall.

    f. Zoe is cold.

    g. The players on the basketball team had a B average in their courses.

    h. All men are created equal.

    i. It is better to be rich than famous.

8. Give an example of an ambiguous sentence you've heard recently.

Additional Exercises

9. A special kind of ambiguity occurs when we're talking about what we say. For example, suppose I say:

    The Taj Mahal has eleven letters.

    I don't mean that the building has eleven letters, but that the name of it does. In speech we use a different tone of voice or make quote marks in the air with our fingers. In writing we use quotation marks around a word or phrase to show that we're talking about that word or phrase. I should indicate that as:

    "The Taj Mahal" has eleven letters.

    We also use quotation marks as an equivalent of a wink or a nod in conversation, a nudge in the ribs indicating that we're not to be taken literally, or that we don't really subscribe to what we're saying. We call these "scare quotes," and when used this way they allow us to get away with "murder."
    For each of the following, indicate if any quotation marks should be inserted.

    a. Suzy can't understand what argument means.

    b. Suzy can't understand the argument Dr. E gave in class.

    c. The judge let him get away with murder.

    d. O'Brien says that there are seven legal ways to never pay taxes.

10. Each of the following arguments depends on ambiguity or vagueness to sound convincing. *Rewrite* at least one of the sentences in each to eliminate the ambiguity.

    a. Zoe says that nothing is better than an ice cream cone on a hot summer's day. It's a hot summer's day. So, I'd better give Zoe nothing rather than this ice cream cone.

    b. In some places, golden eagles have used the same nesting site for hundreds of years. So golden eagles live longer than humans.

    c. Dick to Zoe: Anything that's valuable should be protected. Good abdominal muscles are valuable—you can tell because everyone is trying to get them.
        A layer of fat will protect my abs. So I should continue to be 11 pounds overweight.

11. The defense attorney in the first trial of the policemen charged with beating Rodney King argued roughly:

    If a suspect who is totally uncooperative is hit once by a policeman, then that's not unnecessary force. Nor twice, if he's resisting. Possibly three times. If he's still resisting, shouldn't the policeman have the right to hit him again? It would be dangerous not to allow that. So you can't tell me exactly how many times a policeman has to hit a suspect before it's unnecessary force. So the policeman did not use unnecessary force.

    Explain why this is bad reasoning, even though it did convince the jury.

12. *Mother defends decision to let daughter fly plane*
    Jessica Dubroff's mother Friday defended her decision to allow her 7-year-old daughter to make the flight that ended in tragedy, saying, "You've no idea what this meant to Jess."

    "She had a freedom which you can't get by holding her back," a crying Lisa Blair Hathaway told NBC's "Today" while cradling her 3-year-old daughter Jasmine.

    Jessica, in an effort to become the youngest person to fly cross-country, was killed Thursday when her single-engine plane crashed in driving rain and snow shortly after takeoff, barely missing a house. Her father and flight instructor also died.

    At the site of the crash in a commercial-residential section of north Cheyenne, an impromptu memorial was set up as people dropped off flowers, teddy bears and even framed poems. By this morning the pile of teddy bears had grown to a row about 3 feet long by 8 feet wide. Someone placed a yellow flower on the driveway where the airplane's tail section came to rest.

    "I did everything so this child could have freedom and choice and have what America stands for," Hathaway said. "Liberty comes from . . . just living your life, . . . I couldn't bear to have my children in any other position."

    Hathaway said that if children were forbidden to do anything unsafe, "they would be padded up and they wouldn't go anywhere. They wouldn't ride a bicycle. My God, they wouldn't do anything."

    Associated Press, 1996

    Show how Ms. Hathaway's argument relies crucially on the use of vague sentences.

B. Subjective and Objective Claims

Sometimes the problem with a sentence that appears to be vague is that we're not clear what standards are being used. Suppose Dick hears Harry say,

> "New cars today are really expensive."

Harry might have some clear standards for what "expensive" means, perhaps that the average price of a new car today is more than 50% of what the average person earns in a year.

Or Harry might just mean that new cars cost too much for him to be comfortable buying one. That is, Harry has standards, but they're personal, not necessarily shared by anyone else. They're how he thinks or believes or feels.

Or Harry might have no standards at all. He's never thought very hard about what it means for a car to be expensive.

It's convenient to have terms for these different possibilities.

> ***Subjective claim***   A claim is subjective if whether it is true or false depends on what someone (or something or some group) thinks, believes, or feels. A subjective claim invokes ***personal standards***.
>
> ***Objective claim***   A claim is objective if it is not subjective. An objective claim invokes ***impersonal standards***.

So Harry might have objective standards for what it means for a car to be expensive; or he might have subjective standards; or he might have no standards at all. Until we know what he meant, we shouldn't accept what he said as a claim.

An example of an objective claim is "Every car made by Volkswagen has a gasoline engine." It is false, and it doesn't depend on whether anyone thinks or believes that. But when Dick says, "Steak tastes better than spaghetti," that's subjective. Its truth-value depends on whether Dick believes or thinks that steak tastes better than spaghetti; its truth-value is relative to a personal standard.

If I say, "It's cold outside," is that objective or subjective? If it's meant as shorthand for "I feel cold when outdoors," then it's subjective, and it's a claim. But if it's meant as objective, that is, I mean to assert that it's cold independently of me or anyone, then it's too vague for us to consider it to have a truth-value. A sentence that's too vague to be an objective claim might be perfectly all right as a subjective claim, if that's what the speaker intended. After all, we don't have very precise ways to describe our feelings.

But what if it's so cold that everyone agrees that it's cold outside. Is "It's cold" still subjective? Yes, since whether it's true or false depends on what a lot of people think—no standard independent of people has been put forward. We can further classify subjective claims that (nearly) everyone agrees on as ***intersubjective***.

Examples   Are the following objective or subjective claims, or not claims at all?

Example 1   Dick weighs 215 pounds.

Analysis   This is an objective claim. Whether it's true or false doesn't depend on what anyone thinks or believes.

Example 2   Dick is overweight.

Analysis   If Dick's doctor says this, he's probably thinking of some standard for being overweight, and he intends it as an objective claim. If you or I say it, it's probably subjective, just as if we were to say someone is ugly or handsome.

Example 3   Wanda is fat.

Analysis   "Fat" isn't a technical term of a doctor. It's a term we use to classify people as unattractive or attractive, like "beautiful." The claim is subjective. If Wanda is so obese that (we suspect) everyone will agree she's fat, we could further classify the example as an intersubjective claim.

Example 4   Lee: I felt sick yesterday, and that's why I didn't come to work.

Analysis   Lee didn't feel sick yesterday—he left his critical thinking writing assignment to the last minute and had to finish it before class. So this is a false subjective claim.

Example 5   Dick: Spot eats canned dog food right away, but when we give him dry dog food, he doesn't finish it until half the day is over.

  Zoe: So Spot likes canned dog food better than dry.

Analysis   Dick makes an objective claim: It's about how Spot acts. Zoe infers from that a subjective claim about what Spot thinks or feels.

Example 6   There is an even number of stars in the sky.

Analysis   You might think it's easier to know whether objective claims are true compared to subjective ones. But this example is objective and no one has any idea how to go about finding out whether it is true. On the other hand, when it's well below freezing outside and I see my dog whining and shivering, I'm almost certain that "My dog feels cold" is true.

Example 7

Analysis   Sure, "too loud" is vague. It's subjective, too. But it serves its purpose here. We understand what he means.

Example 8   Socialism is the most efficient way to ensure that all members of a society are fed and clothed.

Analysis   There's a lot of disagreement about this, but that doesn't mean it's subjective. It's objective, assuming that "efficient" has been clearly defined.

Whether a claim is subjective or objective doesn't depend on whether it's true or false, nor on whether someone knows if it's true or false, nor on how much disagreement there is about whether it's true or false.

Subjectivist fallacy   It's a mistake to argue that because there is a lot of disagreement about whether a claim is true, it's therefore subjective.

The subjectivist fallacy is just one version of the common mistake of ***confusing objective with subjective*** claims.

Lee: I deserve a higher mark in this course.
Dr. E: No, you don't. Here's the record of your exams and papers.
        You earned a C.
Lee: That's just your opinion.

Lee is treating an objective claim, "I deserve a higher mark in this course," as if it were subjective. But if it really were subjective, there'd be no point in arguing about it with Dr. E, any more than arguing about whether Dr. E feels cold.

Often it's reasonable to question whether a claim is really objective. But sometimes it's just a confusion. All too often people insist that a claim is subjective — "That's just your opinion"—when they are unwilling to examine their beliefs or engage in dialogue.

Treating a subjective claim as objective is also a mistake.

What are Dick and Zoe arguing about? He likes the tie; she doesn't.

Exercises for Section B

1. a.   What is a subjective claim?
    b.   What is an objective claim?
    c.   Are there any claims that are neither objective nor subjective?

2. What is meant by a "personal standard"?

3. a.   Give an example of a true objective claim.
    b.   Give an example of a false objective claim.
    c.   Give an example of a true subjective claim.
    d.   Give an example of a false subjective claim.

4. Explain why a sentence that is too vague to be taken as an objective claim might be acceptable as a subjective claim.

5. Make up a list of five claims for your classmates to classify as objective or subjective.

6. State whether each of the following is objective, or subjective, or not a claim at all. In some cases you'll have to imagine who's saying it and the context. Where possible, explain your answer in terms of the standards being used.

    a.   Wool insulates better than rayon.
    b.   Silk feels better on your skin than rayon.
    c.   Pablo Picasso painted more oil paintings than Norman Rockwell.
    d.   Bald men are more handsome.
    e.   All ravens are black.
    f.   You intend to do your very best work in this course.
    g.   Murder is wrong.
    h.   Your answer to Exercise 3 in Chapter 1 of this book is wrong.
    i.   Demons caused me to kill my brother.
    j.   (In a court of law, said by the defense attorney) The defendant is insane.
    k.   He's sick. How could anyone say something like that?
    l.   He's sick; he's got the flu.
    m.   Suzy believes that the moon does not rise and set.
    n.   Dick's dog is hungry.
    o.   God exists.

7. Bring to class two advertisements, one that uses only subjective claims and another that uses only objective claims.

8. a.   Give an example of someone treating a subjective claim as if it were objective.
    b.   Give an example of someone treating an objective claim as if it were subjective.

9. Dick: If you don't slow down, we're going to get in an accident! You nearly went out of control going around that last corner!

    Zoe: That's just what you think.

    Is Zoe right? How should Dick respond?

C. Prescriptive Claims and Value Judgments

Suppose Tom says to Suzy, "Abortion is wrong." It's clear that Tom thinks "wrong" means no one should do it. Tom isn't speaking about how the world is, but how it should be.

> ***Descriptive and prescriptive claims***   A claim is descriptive if it says what is. A claim is prescriptive if it says what should be.

Compare:

Drunken drivers kill more people than sober drivers do.	*descriptive*
There should be a law against drunken driving.	*prescriptive*
Dick is cold.	*descriptive*
Dick should put his sweater on.	*prescriptive*
Selling cocaine is against the law.	*descriptive*
Larry shouldn't sell cocaine.	*prescriptive*

Often when someone says that something is "good," "better," "best," "bad," "worse," "worst," or makes some other ***value judgment***, it's meant as prescriptive, in the sense that we shouldn't do what is bad/wrong/worse, and that we should do or choose what is good/better/best.

What appears to be a moral claim or value judgment, though, is often too vague to be a claim. For example, when Tom says "Abortion is wrong," what standard is he invoking? In disagreement with the commands of the Bible? In disagreement with what a priest said? In disagreement with the Koran? In disagreement with moral principles that are not codified but are well-known? Until he and Suzy are clear about the standard, there's nothing to debate.

On the other hand, Suzy might say, "Maybe abortion is wrong to you, but it's O.K. to me." No further standard is needed then, for she views "Abortion is wrong" as a subjective claim—the standard is personal. But then there's nothing to debate.

Often when you challenge people to make things clearer, they'll say, "I just mean it's wrong (right) to me." Yet when you press them, it turns out they're not so happy that you disagree. They're being defensive, and what they really mean is "I have a right to believe this." Of course they do. But do they have a *reason* to believe it? It's rare that people intend moral views to be subjective.

> I've got a right to believe this. ≠ I have a good reason to believe this.

Examples   Are the following prescriptive or descriptive claims? What standards are being invoked?

Example 1   Omar: Eating dogs is bad.

Analysis   This is a prescriptive claim, since it carries with it the assumption that we should not eat dogs.

Zoe agreed with Omar when he said this to her, but did she really know what standard Omar had in mind? Perhaps he's a vegetarian and believes:

You should treat all animals humanely, and butchering animals is inhumane.

Or Omar might believe just:

Dogs taste bad and you shouldn't eat anything that tastes bad.

Or perhaps Omar believes:

We should not eat anything forbidden by the standard interpretation
of the Koran, and it is forbidden to eat carnivores.

Or Omar might just believe what almost all Americans believe:

Dogs should be treated as companions to people and not as food.

Until Zoe knows what Omar means by "bad," she has no reason to view what he's said as a claim.

Example 2   Harry: The Federal Reserve Board ought to lower interest rates.

Analysis   This is a prescriptive claim. Zoe's mother disagrees with Harry, since she wants to see her savings account earn more interest. Harry says the standard he's assuming is "The Federal Reserve Board should help the economy grow," which is what he and Zoe's mom should debate.

Example 3   Zoe: That's enough ice cream for you, Dick.
  Dick: What do you mean? There's no such thing as too much ice cream.

Analysis   Zoe is making a prescriptive claim, since when she says "That's enough" she means that Dick should stop eating. Dick challenges her unstated standard.

Example 4   Dick: Cats are really disagreeable animals.

Analysis   Not every value judgment is prescriptive. Here Dick is making a value judgment, but there's no "should" in it or implied by it.

Exercises for Section C

1. What is a prescriptive claim?

For each of the following, explain why you understand it as prescriptive or descriptive, providing a standard to make it clear enough to be a claim if necessary. Then say whether you think it is true or whether you think it's false.

2. Incest is evil.

3. Incest is against the law.

4. Larry shouldn't marry his sister.

5. Drinking and driving is bad.

6. It's better to conserve energy than to heat a room above 68°.

7. Risking a prison term is the wrong thing for a father to do.

8. It's about time that the government stop bailing out the farmers.

9. Dick and Zoe have a dog named "Spot."

10. It's wrong to tax the rich at the same rate as the poor.

11. (Clerk at the supermarket) Picasso is a better painter than Rembrandt.

12. (Lee's art history teacher) Picasso is a better painter than Rembrandt.

D. Definitions

We've seen that we can get into problems, waste our time, and generally irritate each other through misunderstandings. It's always reasonable and usually wise to ask people we are reasoning with to be clear enough that we can agree on what it is we are discussing.

Two general methods of making clear what we say are:

1. Replace the entire sentence by another that is not vague or ambiguous.

2. Use a definition to make a specific word or phrase precise.

> **Definition**   A definition explains or stipulates how to use a word or phrase.

"Dog" means "domestic canine."
Puce is the color of a flea, purple-brown or brownish-purple.
"Puerile" means boyish or childish, immature, trivial.

There are several ways we can make a definition. One way, as with the definition of "dog," is to give a synonym, a word or phrase that means the same and that could be substituted for "dog" wherever that's used.

Another way is to describe: A lorgnette is a kind of eyeglass that is held in the hand, usually with a long handle.

Or we can explain, as when we say a loophole is a means of escaping or evading something unpleasant.

Or we can point:

Even though pointing isn't part of language, it serves to make our language clear.

Definitions are not true or false, but good or bad. Definitions tell us what we're talking about. Claims are what we use to make assertions about that subject.

> *A definition is not a claim.* We add a definition to an argument so that we can understand each other. A definition is not a premise.

People often hide a claim that should be debated behind an apparent definition. For example, if someone defines "abortion" as "the murder of unborn children," he's made it impossible to have a reasoned discussion about whether abortion is murder and whether a fetus is a person. A ***persuasive*** or ***self-serving definition*** is a claim that should be argued for, masquerading as a definition.

> If you call a tail a leg, how many legs has a dog? Five? No, calling a tail a leg don't *make* it a leg.   attributed to Abraham Lincoln

Examples   Which of the following are definitions? Persuasive definitions?

Example 1   A donkey is an animal.
Analysis   This is not a definition. It doesn't tell us how to use the word "donkey"; it tells us something about donkeys. Not every sentence with "is" in it is a definition.

Example 2   "Coitus" means "sexual intercourse."
Analysis   Definition by synonym is the simplest, most reliable definition we can get, *if* we know the synonym.

Example 3   Getting good marks in school means that you are intelligent.

Analysis   Getting good marks in school is not what the word "intelligent" means. Here "means" is used in the sense of "If you get good marks in school, then you're intelligent."

Example 4   Meyer Friedman and Ray Rosenman . . . identified a cluster of behavioral characteristics—constant hurriedness, free-floating hostility, and intense competitiveness—that seemed to be present in most of their patients with coronary disease. They coined the term *Type A* to describe this behavior pattern; *Type B* describes people who do not display these qualities.

Daniel Goleman and Joel Gurin, Mind Body Medicine

Analysis   We often find definitions embedded in a text like this. But these are much too vague unless some standards are given for what is meant by "constant hurriedness," "free-floating hostility," and "intense competitiveness" (none were given in the text). How could you determine whether someone you know is Type A or Type B from this definition? A good definition must use words that are clearer and better understood than the word being defined.

Example 5   —Maria's so rich, she can afford to pay for your dinner.
            —What do you mean by "rich"?
            —She's got a Mercedes.

Analysis   This is not a definition, since by "rich" we don't mean "has a Mercedes." There are lots of people who are rich who don't have a Mercedes, and some people who own a Mercedes aren't rich. What we have here is an argument: "Maria has a Mercedes" is given as evidence that Maria is rich; "means" is used in the sense of "therefore."

I just tried to convince you that "has a Mercedes" is not a good definition of "rich." How? I pointed out that someone could own a Mercedes and not be rich, or be rich and not own a Mercedes.

Example 6   Microscope: an instrument consisting essentially of a lens or combination of lenses, for making very small objects, as microorganisms, look larger so that they can be seen and studied.

Webster's New World Dictionary

Analysis   This is from a dictionary, so it's got to be a good definition. But if you're trying to convince someone that what she sees through a microscope is actually there—that it's not in the lens or inside the microscope like a kaleidoscope—then this definition won't do. "See, there really are microorganisms. After all, it's part of the definition of a microscope that it's just enlarging what's there." What counts as a persuasive definition can depend on the context.

Example 7   A Pittman Elementary School teacher won a narrow Supreme Court [of Nevada] victory Tuesday allowing her to bring a service dog in training to her music class.

One dissenting justice warned, however, that the majority opinion could have far-reaching consequences for public employers ranging from hospitals to bakeries.

The majority decision, written by Justice Cliff Young, interprets a state law prohibiting a public place from refusing admittance to a person training a service dog as applying to employees as well as the public. The majority also found the school is a public place.

Las Vegas Review-Journal, September, 1996

Analysis The court has to decide the meaning of vague language by giving definitions. The definition can be explicit. Or the definition can be implicit: After enough cases have been decided it becomes pretty clear what the court thinks the words (ought to) mean.

Good definition A good definition satisfies both:

- The words doing the defining are clear and better understood than the word or phrase being defined.

- The words being defined and the defining phrase can be used interchangeably. That is, it's correct to use the one exactly when it's correct to use the other.

The key to making a good definition is to look for examples where the definition does or does not apply, in order to make sure that it is not too broad or too narrow. For example, suppose we want to define "school cafeteria." That's something a lawmaker might need in order to write a law to disburse funds for a food program. As a first go, we might try "A place in a school where students eat." But that's too broad, since that would include just a room where students can take their meals. So we might try "A place in a school where students can buy a meal." But that's too broad, too, since that would include a room where you could buy a sandwich from a vending machine. How about "A room in a school where students can buy a hot meal that is served on a tray"? But if there's a fast-food restaurant like Burger King at the school, that would qualify. So it looks like we need "A room in a school where students can buy a hot meal that is served on a tray, and the school is responsible for the preparation and selling of the food." This looks better, though if adopted as a definition in a law, it might keep schools that want money from the legislature from contracting out the preparation of their food. Whether that's too narrow will depend on how the lawmakers intend the money to be spent.

> ***Steps in making a good definition***
> - Show the need for a definition.
> - State the definition.
> - Make sure the words make sense.
> - Give examples where the definition applies.
> - Give examples where the definition does not apply.
> - If necessary, contrast it with other likely definitions.
> - Possibly revise your definition.

Exercises for Section D

1. Classify the following as a definition, a persuasive definition, or neither. If it is a definition, state why you think it is good or bad.

   a. "Dog" means "a canine creature that brings love and warmth to a human family."

   b. Domestic violence is any violent act by a spouse or lover directed against his or her partner within the confines of the home of both.

   c. A feminist is someone who thinks that women are better than men.

   d. A conservative, in politics, is one who believes that we should conserve the political structure and laws as they are as much as possible, avoiding change.

   e. A liberal is someone who wants to use your taxes to pay for what he thinks will do others the most good.

   f. Love is blind.

   g. Sexual intercourse is when a man and a woman couple sexually with the intent of producing offspring.

   h. *Less-developed countries* (LDCs) The economies of Asia, Africa, and Latin America. (From an economics textbook)

2. For each of the following, give both a definition and a persuasive definition:
   a. Homeless person.
   b. Spouse.
   c. School bus.

3. For each of the following, *replace* "believes in" with other words that mean the same:
   a. Zoe believes in free love.
   b. Dick believes in God.
   c. Zoe believes in the Constitution.
   d. Zoe believes in herself.

4. What is required of a good definition?

5. Why should we avoid persuasive definitions?

6. Bring in an example of a definition used in one of your other courses. Is it good?

7. What term is being defined in the following passage? State the definition explicitly.

> Fasting and very low calorie diets (diets below 500 calories) cause a loss of nitrogen and potassium in the body, a loss which is believed to trigger a mechanism in the body that causes us to hold on to our fat stores and to turn to muscle protein for energy instead.
>
> Jane Fonda, Jane Fonda's New Workout and Weight Loss Program

Additional Exercises

8. Verify whether the presentation of the definition of "claim" in Chapter 1 follows the steps in making a good definition.

9. Sometimes we can make an apparently subjective claim objective by making a definition. For example, "Harry is intelligent" can be objective if we define "intelligent" to mean "has a B average or better in university courses." Give definitions that make the following subjective claims objective.
   a. It's hot outside.
   b. Eating a lot of fat every day is unhealthy.

10. Find the definition of "Hispanic" from the U.S. Census Bureau. Compare it to the definition of "Latino."

Summary   In Chapter 1 we learned that arguments are attempts to convince using claims. So we need to be able to distinguish different kinds of claims and be aware of sentences that look like claims but aren't.

A sentence is *vague* if it's unclear what the speaker intended. We can learn to recognize when a sentence is too vague to use in our reasoning. It's a bad argument, though, to say that just because we can't draw a precise line, there's never any clear meaning to a word. An *ambiguous* sentence is vague in a bad way, for it has two or more clear interpretations. Ambiguous sentences should never be taken as claims.

Often the problem with a vague sentence is to determine what standards are being assumed. They could be *objective*—independent of what anyone or anything thinks/believes/feels; or they could be *subjective*; or there might not be any standard at all. A sentence that's too vague to be an objective claim might be all right as a subjective claim.

Considering whether a claim is objective or subjective can save us a lot of heartache: We won't debate someone else's feelings. Confusing subjective and objective claims leads to bad arguments.

Often we make *prescriptive* claims about what should be, not just what is. Moral claims usually are meant as prescriptive and objective, though often people retreat to saying they're subjective when they can't defend their views. Debates about prescriptive claims should be about the standard they invoke or whether they follow from that standard.

We need to eliminate ambiguity and excessive vagueness if we are to reason together. We can do so by rewriting our arguments or speaking more precisely.

Or we can define the words that are causing the problem. A definition isn't a claim, though; it's something added to an argument to clarify. Definitions shouldn't prejudge the issue by being self-serving.

Key Words

vague sentence	subjectivist fallacy
drawing the line fallacy	confusing objective with subjective
ambiguous sentence	prescriptive claim
objective claim	descriptive claim
subjective claim	value judgment
intersubjective claim	definition
personal standard	persuasive (self-serving) definition
impersonal standard	good definition

Exercises for Chapter 2

Here are a few of Tom's attempts to do exercises that use the ideas we've learned in this chapter, along with Dr. E's comments. Tom's supposed to underline the terms that apply.

Dogs bark.

<u>claim</u>	subjective	ambiguous or too vague
not claim	objective	definition persuasive definition

Yes, it's a claim. But if it's a claim, then it has to be either objective or subjective.

Cats are nasty.

claim	<u>subjective</u>	<u>ambiguous or too vague</u>
not claim	objective	definition persuasive definition

No—if it's ambiguous or too vague, then it's not a claim. This is an example of a subjective claim.

Rabbits are the principal source of protein for dogs in the wild.

<u>claim</u>	subjective	ambiguous or too vague
not claim	<u>objective</u>	<u>definition</u> persuasive definition

No—if it's a definition, it's not a claim. And this is not a definition—what word is it defining? Certainly not "rabbit."

Dogs are canines that bring warmth and love to a family.

claim	subjective	ambiguous or too vague
<u>not claim</u>	objective	definition <u>persuasive definition</u>

No. If it's a persuasive definition, then it is a claim—just masquerading as a definition.

---

1. State which of the following can together apply to a single sentence and give an example:

claim	subjective	ambiguous or too vague
not claim	objective	definition persuasive definition

For each of the following, indicate which of the terms in Exercise 1 apply. If you think your instructor might disagree, provide an explanation.

2. Donkeys can breed with other equines.

3. The manifest content of a dream is what a dream appears to be about to the dreamer.

4. A grade of A in this course means you know how to parrot what the professor said.

5. Public Health Is the Greatest Good for the Most Numbers
   (on the logo of the New Mexico Department of Health)

6. Too much TV is bad for children.

7. China has the largest land mass of any single country.

8. I've already heard the new album by Britney Spears.

9. There are five countries in North America.

10. We handled 1.6 million claims last year—many within 48 hours! (Geico advertisement)

11. I'm going to throw up.

12. "We [the United States] are the leader of the free world."
    Senator J. Rockefeller on "Day to Day," National Public Radio, July 23, 2004

13. Remember loved ones lost through Christmas concert.
    (Headline, *The Spectrum*, December 4, 1998)

Further Study   Much of philosophy is concerned with attempts to give criteria that will turn apparently subjective claims into objective claims. A course on ethics will study whether claims about what's wrong or right can be made objective. A course on aesthetics will analyze whether all claims about what is beautiful are subjective. And a course on the philosophy of law or criminal justice will introduce the methods the law uses to give objective criteria for determining what is right or wrong.

Some people believe that all there is to a claim being objective is that it is believed by enough people. That is, objectivity is just intersubjectivity. Philosophy courses deal with that debate.

Courses in nursing discuss how to deal with subjective claims by patients and vague instructions by doctors.

Some courses in English composition or rhetoric deal with definitions, particularly the correct forms and uses of definitions. Courses on the philosophy of language or linguistics study the nature of definitions, ways in which definitions can be made, and misuses of definitions. Ambiguity and vagueness are also covered in English composition and rhetoric courses.

Writing Lesson 2

We know that before we begin deliberating we should make the issue precise enough that someone can agree or disagree.

Make the following sentence sufficiently precise that you could debate it:

Student athletes should be given special leniency when the instructor assigns course marks.

Your definition or explanation should be at most one page long. (At most one page, not at least or exactly one page.)

To give you a better idea of what you're expected to do, here is the homework on another topic from Tom and Mary Ellen, along with Dr. E's comments.

Tom Wyzyczy
Critical Thinking
Section 4
Writing Lesson 2

"All unnatural sex acts should be prohibited by law."

Before we can debate this we have to say what it means. I think that "unnatural sex act" should mean any kind of sexual activity that most people think is unnatural. And "prohibited by law" should mean there's a law against it.

You've got the idea, but your answer is really no improvement. You can delete the first sentence. And you can delete "I think." We can guess that, because you wrote the paper.

Your proposed definition of "unnatural sex act" is too vague. It's reminiscent of the standard the U.S. Supreme Court uses to define obscenity: prevailing community standards. In particular, what do you mean by "sexual activity"? Does staring at a woman's breasts count? And who are "people"? The people in your church? Your neighborhood? Your city? Your state? Your country? The world?

Of course, "prohibited by law" means there's a law against it. But what kind of law? A fine? A prison sentence? A penalty depending on severity of the offense? How do you determine the severity?

Mary Ellen Zzzyzzx
Critical Thinking
Section 4
Writing Lesson 2

"All unnatural sex acts should be prohibited by law."

By "unnatural sex act" I shall mean any sexual activity involving genitals, consensual or not, *except* between a man and a woman who are both over sixteen and in a way that could lead to procreation if they wanted it to and which is unobserved by others.

By "prohibited by law" I shall mean it would be a misdemeanor comparable to getting a traffic ticket.

> *I don't really think that everything else is unnatural, but I couldn't figure out any other way to make it precise. Is that what we're supposed to do?*
> *Mary Ellen*

You did just fine. Really, the burden to make it precise would be on the person suggesting that the sentence be taken as a claim. Most attempts are going to seem like a persuasive definition. But at least you now have a claim you could debate. If the other person thinks it's the wrong definition, that would be a good place to begin your discussions.

3   What Is a Good Argument?

A. Good Reason to Believe

What makes an argument good? We don't want to say a good argument is one that actually convinces someone. Who's being convinced? Me? You? Maybe you're in a bad mood and nothing would convince you, or your friend is drunk and you can't convince him. Does that mean the argument is bad?

No, a good argument is one in which *the premises give good reason to believe the conclusion is true.* But what is "good reason"?

Certainly if we don't have good reason to believe the premises, the premises won't give us good reason to believe the conclusion. After all, from a false premise we can prove anything at all. For example:

> *False premise, false conclusion*
> All books are written by women.
> So the author of this book is a woman.

> *False premise, true conclusion*
> All books are written by women.
> So the author of this book is a human being.

An argument is no better than its least plausible premise.

> ***Plausible claims*** A claim is plausible if we have good reason to believe
> it is true. It is less plausible the less reason we have to believe it is true.
> It is ***implausible*** or ***dubious*** if we have no reason to believe it is true.

In Chapter 5 we'll look at what counts as good reason to accept a premise.
But plausibility isn't enough. Suppose you overhear:

—God exists.
—How do you know?
—Because the Bible says so.
—But why do you think that's true?
—Because God wrote the Bible.

The first person is arguing in a circle. He's given a bad argument.
Or consider:

Dogs have souls.
So you should treat dogs humanely.

Even if you agree that the premise is plausible, it's less plausible than the conclusion.

> ***Begging the question*** An argument begs the question if one of its premises
> is no more plausible than the conclusion.

Any argument that begs the question is bad.

B. The Conclusion Follows From the Premises

Even if an argument has plausible premises, that's not enough. Consider:

Dr. E teaches critical thinking.
So Dr. E is bald.

There's no connection: The conclusion does not follow from the premises. The
premises do not lead to, support, establish the conclusion.
We all have some intuition about whether a conclusion follows from some
premises. If we didn't, we'd be hopelessly confused in all our reasoning, no more
clever than a four-year old. But most folks have only some bare intuition that they
can't extend to any reasoning outside the subject they're most interested in (music,
sports, car repair, chemistry, . . .). We need to come up with a clear understanding
of what it means to say that a conclusion follows from premises, an understanding
we can use in our daily lives and in our work.

What would be the best connection between premises and conclusion? If there were no way at all—no possibility—that both the premises could be true and the conclusion false, then if the premises are true, the conclusion has to be true, too. For example,

> Every student at this school has paid tuition.
> Suzy is a student at this school.
> So Suzy has paid tuition.

It's impossible for the premises to be true and the conclusion false. If we then have good reason to believe that every student at this school has paid tuition, and also that Suzy is a student at this school, then we have good reason to believe she has paid tuition—it couldn't be otherwise.

Valid argument   An argument is valid if there is *no possible way* for its premises to be true and its conclusion false (at the same time).

An argument that is not valid is called *invalid.*

   A valid argument need not be good. For example:

> Every elected official in the United States is under thirty-four years old.
> So the President of the United States is under thirty-four years old.

This argument is valid: There is no way the premise could be true and the conclusion false at the same time. *Were* the premise true—say if tomorrow the laws were changed and enforced to prohibit people older than thirty-four from holding elective office—then it would be impossible for the president to be older than thirty-four. But the argument is bad, since after all it has a false conclusion. And that's because the premise is false.

   So some valid arguments are bad. But is every good argument valid? Does the idea of validity fully capture what we want "follows from" to mean? Dick heard this morning that there are parakeets for sale down at the mall. He knows that his neighbor has a birdcage in her garage, and he wonders if it will be big enough for one of those parakeets. He makes the following argument:

> All parakeets anyone I know has ever seen, or heard, or read about are
>   under 2 feet tall.
> Therefore, the parakeets on sale at the mall are under 2 feet tall.

Surveying all the ways the premise could be true, he thinks that, yes, a new super-grow bird food could have been formulated and the parakeets at the local mall are really 3 feet tall, he just hasn't heard about it. Or a rare giant parakeet from the Amazon forest could have been discovered and brought here. Or a UFO might have abducted a parakeet by mistake, hit it with growing rays, and it's now gigantic.

All of these ways that the premise could be true and the conclusion false are *so very unlikely* that Dick would have very good reason to believe the conclusion, even though it's still *possible* that the conclusion is false. The conclusion does *follow from* the premises, even though the argument is not valid.

> ***Strong and weak arguments*** An argument is ***strong*** if there is some way, some possibility, for its premises to be true and its conclusion false (at the same time), but every such possibility is extremely unlikely. An argument is ***weak*** if it is possible and not unlikely for its premises to be true and its conclusion false (at the same time).

We just saw a strong argument that was good. But a weak argument is always bad. For example,

Dick is a student.
So Dick doesn't drive a motorcycle.

We don't know much about Dick, but we do know that it's not unlikely he could own a motorcycle—lots of students do, and even if he doesn't, he could have borrowed one last week to use this semester. This is a bad argument.

> ***The conclusion follows from the premises*** "The conclusion follows from the premises" means that the argument is valid or strong.

An argument is either valid or it isn't; there are no degrees to it, no judgment involved. But evaluating the strength of an argument does involve judgment, for it depends on how likely certain possibilities appear. The strength of an argument is a matter of degree, and *we classify invalid arguments on a scale from strong to weak.*

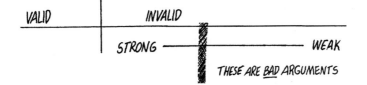

Here is the process involved in analyzing whether the conclusion follows from the premises of an argument.

To evaluate an argument, you have to imagine possible ways the premises could be true. You have to be creative. *Imagine the possibilities.*

Here are some basic points you need to remember.

- Every good argument is valid or strong.
- Not every valid or strong argument is good
  (a premise could be implausible).
- Only invalid arguments are classified from strong to weak.
- Every weak argument is bad.

C. The Tests for an Argument to Be Good

We have three tests for an argument to be good.

Tests for an argument to be good
- The premises are plausible.
- The premises are more plausible than the conclusion.
- The argument is valid or strong.

Each of these tests is *independent* of the others: Each can fail while the other two hold. So in evaluating whether an argument is good, we can start with whichever of these tests is easiest to determine.

But why should we be interested in whether the argument is valid or strong if we don't know whether the premises are true? Compare evaluating an argument whose premises we don't know to be true to applying for a home loan. A couple goes in and fills out all the forms. The loan officer looks at their answers. She might tell them right then that they don't qualify. That is, even though she doesn't know if the claims they made about their income and assets are true, she can see that even if they are true, the couple won't qualify for a loan. So why bother to investigate whether what they said is true? On the other hand, she could tell them that they'll qualify if those claims are true. Then she goes out and makes phone calls, checks credit references, and so on, and finds out if they were telling the truth.

With an argument that is valid or strong you can say about the premises: Grant me this and the conclusion follows. Good reasoning is concerned with what follows from what, as well as with what is true.

Evaluating whether an argument passes these tests requires skills, which is what this course is meant to teach you. But evaluating whether an argument is good also depends on your knowledge, for as you know more, you become better at evaluating whether premises are plausible and whether possibilities are likely.

Examples   Are the following arguments valid? If not valid, where on the scale from strong to weak does the example lie? If the argument is valid or strong, is it also good?

Example 1 Dr. E is a philosophy professor. All philosophy professors are bald. So Dr. E is bald.

Analysis The argument is valid: There is no possible way the premises could be true and the conclusion false at the same time. The conclusion is true, too. But it's a bad argument, because the second premise is false. We have no more reason to believe the conclusion than we did before we heard the argument.

Example 2   Maria (to her supervisor): I was told that I would earn a bonus if I put in 100 hours of overtime and had a perfect attendance record for two months. I have since put in 110 hours of overtime and have a perfect attendance record for the last ten weeks. So I'm entitled to a bonus.

Analysis   This is a valid argument. It's not possible for the premises to be true and the conclusion false. But we don't know if the argument is good because we don't know if the premises are true.

Example 3   Student athletes should not be given special leniency in assigning their course marks, because that wouldn't be treating all students equally.

Analysis   This is how Maria answered her first writing lesson. But what does "treating all students equally" mean? It means "treat everyone the same way." So the argument is: You shouldn't treat athletes differently, because you should treat everyone the same way. The premise may be true, but it's just a restatement of the conclusion. The argument begs the question, so it's bad.

Example 4   Dick is a bachelor. So Dick was never married.

Analysis   This is not valid: Dick *could have been* divorced. This argument is weak: Given what we know, it's not unlikely that the premise could be true and the conclusion false. So the argument is bad.

Example 5   Good teachers give fair exams, and Dr. E gives fair exams. So Dr. E is a good teacher.

Analysis   The premises of the argument are true. And the conclusion is true, too! But is it a good argument? Can we imagine a way in which the premises could be true and the conclusion false? Yes: Dr. E might bore his students to tears and just copy fair exams from the instructor's manual of the textbook. After all, the premise doesn't say that *only* good teachers give fair exams. So the argument is weak, and hence bad.

Example 6   Maria's hair is naturally black. Today Maria's hair is red. So Maria dyed her hair.

Analysis   Could the premises be true and the conclusion false? Perhaps: Maria might be taking a new medication that has a strong effect, or she might have gotten too close to the machinery when they were painting her car, or . . . . These are all extremely unlikely, but still possible. So the argument is strong, not valid. Since we know that Maria's hair is black, it's a good argument.

> How do we show an argument is weak? *We describe at least one likely way in which the premises could be true and the conclusion false.*

Example 7 Harry: Every time I can remember eating eggs I've broken out in a rash. It couldn't be the butter or oil they're fried in, 'cause I remember it happening when I had hard-boiled eggs, too. I must be allergic to eggs.

Analysis This is a strong argument, and we can trust that Harry isn't lying. So it's a good argument. But it's not valid: There could be a strange new virus that Harry caught whose only symptom is that it makes him sick when he eats eggs. In a week or two he might be fine.

Example 8 Prosecuting attorney: The defendant intended to kill Louise. He bought a gun three days before he shot her. He practiced shooting at a target that had her name written across it. He staked out her home for two nights. He shot her twice.

Analysis The argument is strong. If there's good reason to believe the premises, then the argument is good and establishes beyond a reasonable doubt "The defendant intended to kill Louise." But it's not valid: We don't know the defendant's thoughts, and the conclusion might be false.

Example 9

Analysis The defendant may be telling the truth. All he says may be true, yet the argument is weak, and hence bad. What he says shouldn't create reasonable doubt.

Example 10 Tom: You didn't have eggs in the house this morning, did you?
Dick: No. Why?
Tom: Well, you've got some in the refrigerator now.
Dick: Zoe must have bought eggs, since she knew we were out.

Analysis This isn't valid. Zoe's mom could have brought over the eggs; when they were out, the landlord might have brought them over; a guest who was staying with them might have bought them; . . . . There are so many likely possibilities for the premises to be true and the conclusion false that the argument is weak.

Example 11 Tom: You didn't have eggs in the house this morning, did you?
Dick: No. Why?
Tom: Well, you've got some in the refrigerator now.
Dick: Zoe must have bought eggs, since she knew we were out.
Tom: Are you sure?

Dick: Sure. No one else has a key to the apartment. And Zoe didn't plan to have any guests over today.

Analysis This argument is stronger than the last one, because some of the possible ways the premises could be true and the conclusion false have been ruled out. But it's still not very strong.

Example 12 Tom: You didn't have eggs in the house this morning, did you?
Dick: No. Why?
Tom: Well, you've got some in the refrigerator now.
Dick: Zoe must have bought eggs, since she knew we were out.
Tom: Are you sure?
Dick: Sure. No one else has a key to the apartment. And we never let anyone else in.
Tom: But didn't your neighbor Mrs. Zzzyzzx say she had some eggs from her cousins' farm?
Dick: Yes, but Zoe said we should only bring food into the house that we'd purchased ourselves at the health-food store. And she always keeps her word.

Analysis This argument is a lot stronger because so many of the ways in which the premises could be true and the conclusion false have been ruled out. Still, it's not valid: The landlord could have gotten a locksmith to open the door, and then before he went out put eggs in the refrigerator; or a burglar could have broken in and left some eggs behind; or Zoe could have bought a chicken and left it in the refrigerator and it laid eggs there; or . . . . These are possible ways that the premises could be true and the conclusion false, but they are all so unlikely that the argument is strong. And since we can trust Dick's word, it is good. So Tom and Dick have good reason to believe that Zoe bought the eggs.

Though we can't say exactly where Example 11 lies on the scale from strong to weak, we can say that Example 10 is weak, and Example 12 is strong. But if we can't say exactly how strong an argument is, isn't the whole business of classifying arguments worthless? That would be a drawing the line fallacy. There may be some fuzziness in the middle, but we can distinguish strong arguments from weak ones.

We've seen good arguments and we've seen bad arguments. A good argument gives us good reason to believe the conclusion. ***A bad argument tells us nothing about whether the conclusion is true or false.*** If we encounter a bad argument, we have no more reason to believe or disbelieve the conclusion than we had before.

Exercises for Sections A–C

1. What is an argument?

2. What does it mean to say an argument is valid?

3. What does it mean to say an argument is strong?

4. If an argument is valid or strong, does that mean it's a good argument? Explain.

5. a. How can you show that an argument is not valid?
   b. How can you show that an argument is weak?

6. If an argument is valid and its premises are true, is its conclusion true, too? Explain.

7. If an argument is bad, what does that show about its conclusion?

8. If an argument is strong and its premises are true, is its conclusion true, too? Explain.

9. To be classified as good, an argument must pass three tests. What are they?

10. What does it mean to say the three tests for an argument to be good are independent?

11. a. Make up an example of an argument that is valid and good.
    b. Make up an example of an argument that is valid and bad.

12. a. Make up an example of an argument that is strong and good.
    b. Make up an example of an argument that is strong and bad.

13. Make up an example of an argument that is weak. Is it good?

14. Can we show that an argument is not valid by showing that its conclusion is false? Give an example or explanation.

15. To decide whether an argument is good, does it depend on whether it convinced anyone?

16. Can an argument be both valid and strong?

17. What do we call an argument with a clearly false premise?

18. Which of the following uses of the words "valid" and "invalid" accord with the definition in this chapter?
    a. Your parking sticker is invalid.
    b. That's not a valid answer to my question.
    c. Your reasoning is invalid.
    d. I can't believe the referee made that decision. It's completely invalid.
    e. Tom has a valid excuse for showing up late to football practice.

For Exercises 19–24, select the claim that makes the argument valid. *You're not supposed to judge whether the claim is plausible, just whether it makes the argument valid.* These examples may seem artificial, but we need simple practice on the definition of "validity."

19. The dogs are drinking a lot of water today. It must be hot.
    a. Dogs always drink when they are hot.
    b. Every dog will drink when the weather is hot.
    c. Hot weather means dogs will drink.
    d. Only on hot days do dogs drink a lot of water.
    e. None of the above.

20. Every color monitor I've had either was defective and had to be returned, or else burned out in less than two years. So you'd be foolish to buy a color monitor.
    a. You should do what I tell you to do.
    b. Every color monitor will be defective or go bad.
    c. All monitors that are reliable are not color.
    d. None of the above.

21. Puff is a cat. So Puff meows.
    a. Anything that meows is a cat.
    b. Dogs don't meow.
    c. All cats meow.
    d. Most cats meow.
    e. None of the above.

22. Suzy is a cheerleader. So Suzy goes to all the football games.
    a. Cheerleaders get in free to the football games.
    b. Cheerleaders are expected to attend all football games.
    c. Suzy is dating Tom, who is the football captain.
    d. All cheerleaders attend all football games.
    e. None of the above.

23. If Spot gets into the garbage, Dick will hit him with a newspaper. So Dick will hit Spot.
    a. The garbage is a bad thing for Spot to get into.
    b. Whenever Spot gets into the garbage, Dick hits him.
    c. Whenever Dick hits Spot, Spot was in the garbage.
    d. Spot got into the garbage.
    e. None of the above.

24. The President is on every channel on television. So he must be making an important speech.
    a. Only Presidents make important speeches on television.
    b. When the President makes an important speech on television, he's on every channel.
    c. When the President is on every channel on TV, he's making an important speech.
    d. Presidents only make important speeches.
    e. None of the above.

D. Strong vs. Valid Arguments

Last week Lee said:

> Every garbage can issued by this city that I or anyone I know has seen is blue.
> Therefore, all city-issued garbage cans in this city are blue.

This is a good strong argument. Compare that to a valid argument with the same conclusion:

> This city issues only blue garbage cans.
> Therefore, all city-issued garbage cans in this city are blue.

This one begs the question.

> A strong argument with true premises is sometimes better than a valid one with the same conclusion.

Folks often indicate when they make an argument that they think that it's valid or that it's strong. For example,

> Manuel says he visited Mexico. He speaks Spanish and he described the towns he visited. So Manuel really visited Mexico.

> Manuel says he visited Mexico. He speaks Spanish and he described the towns he visited. So maybe Manuel visited Mexico.

These are the *same argument*: They have the same premises, and the conclusion of both is "Manuel visited Mexico." The words "maybe" and "really" just tell us the speaker's attitude toward the argument: "so really" instead of "so maybe" lets us know the speaker thinks the argument is valid or strong, but that doesn't make the argument valid or strong. You can't make an argument valid by calling it valid, any more than Zoe can make Dick a pig by calling him a pig. *These words are a comment on a claim, not part of the claim.*

> Whether an argument is valid or strong does *not* depend on:
> - Whether the premises are true.
> - Whether we know the premises are true.
> - Whether the person making the argument thinks the argument is valid or strong.

Summary   We said a good argument is one that gives good reason to believe the conclusion is true. But we needed a standard for "good reason."
     We saw that if we have no good reason to believe the premises of an argument, or one of the premises is no more plausible than the conclusion, the argument is bad.

A good argument also needs that the conclusion of the argument follows from the premises. We determined that meant the argument is valid or strong: Either there is no possible way for the premises to be true and the conclusion false, or if there is such a way, it is very unlikely.

In all, then, there are three tests an argument must pass to be good: There should be good reason to believe its premises; it must be valid or strong; its premises must be more plausible than its conclusion.

Depending on the conclusion we're trying to prove and the evidence we have, we have to decide whether it's best to make a valid argument or a strong argument.

Key Words	good argument	valid argument
	plausible claim	strong argument
	dubious (implausible) claim	weak argument
	begging the question	tests for an argument to be good

Exercises for Chapter 3

1. If an argument is bad, what does that tell us about the conclusion?

2. Consider the strong argument that Dick gave that we saw above:

   > All parakeets anyone I know has ever seen, or heard, or read about are under 2 feet tall.
   > Therefore, the parakeets on sale at the mall are under 2 feet tall.

   Explain why this is better or worse than the valid argument:

   > All parakeets are under 2 feet tall.
   > Therefore, the parakeets on sale at the mall are under 2 feet tall.

3. If we want to give a good argument with a subjective claim as its conclusion, would it be better for it to be valid or strong? Explain.

4. To prove an objective claim, should we always give an argument that is valid? Explain or give an example.

5. Which subjects in your school would employ only valid arguments? Which would employ primarily strong arguments? Which would rely on a mix of the two?

Here are some of Tom's answers to exercises that require all the ideas we've learned in this chapter. He's supposed to fill in the italicized parts. Dr. E has corrected his work.

Ralph is a dog. So Ralph barks.
Argument? (yes or no) Yes.
Conclusion: Ralph barks.
Premises: Ralph is a dog.
Classify: <u>valid</u> strong ————— weak
If not valid, show why:

Good argument? (Choose one)
- It's good (passes the three tests). ✓
- It's bad because a premise is false.
- It's bad because it's weak.
- It's bad because it begs the question.
- It's valid or strong, but you don't know if the premises are true, so you can't say if it's good or bad.

No! This isn't valid. Ralph might be a basenji (a kind of dog that doesn't bark). But it's strong, so a good argument if the premise is true—which you don't know for sure.

Whenever Spot barks, there's a cat outside. Since he's barking now, there must be a cat outside.

Argument? (yes or no)   Yes.

Conclusion: Whenever Spot barks, there's a cat outside.

Premises: Spot's barking now. There must be a cat outside.

Classify: valid   strong ————————X— weak

If not valid, show why: Maybe he's barking at the garbageman outside.

Good argument? (Choose one)
- It's good (passes the three tests).
- It's bad because a premise is false.
- It's bad because it's weak. ✓
- It's bad because it begs the question.
- It's valid or strong, but you don't know if the premises are true, so you can't say if it's good or bad.

No. The conclusion is "There is a cat outside." Ask yourself where you could put "therefore" in the argument. Which claims are evidence for which others? The argument is valid but bad: The premise "Whenever Spot barks, there's a cat outside" is implausible. As you point out, what about the garbageman? So it's not good.

Alison is Kim's sister, right? So Alison and Kim have the same mother and father.

Argument? (yes or no)   Yes.

Conclusion: Alison and Kim have the same mother and father.

Premises: Alison is Kim's sister.

Classify: valid   strong ————————X— weak

If not valid, show why: They might be half sisters, or stepsisters, or adopted. It depends on what the speaker means by "sister."

Good argument? (Choose one)
- It's good (passes the three tests).
- It's bad because a premise is false.
- It's bad because it's weak. ✓
- It's bad because it begs the question.
- It's valid or strong, but you don't know if the premises are true, so you can't say if it's good or bad.

Good work!

> **Bob has worked as a car mechanic for twenty years. Anyone who works that long at a job must enjoy it. So Bob enjoys being a car mechanic.**
>
> *Argument?* (yes or no) Yes.
>
> *Conclusion:* Bob enjoys being a car mechanic.
>
> *Premises:* Bob has worked as a car mechanic for twenty years. Anyone who works that long at a job enjoys it.
>
> *Classify:* valid   strong ————————X— weak
>
> *If not valid, show why:* Bob might not be able to get any other job.
>
> *Good argument?* (Choose one)
> - It's good (passes the three tests).
> - It's bad because a premise is false.
> - It's bad because it's weak. ✓
> - It's bad because it begs the question.
> - It's valid or strong, but you don't know if the premises are true, so you can't say if it's good or bad.
>
> *Wrong! The argument is <u>valid</u>. What you showed is that the second premise is false or at least very dubious. So the argument <u>is</u> bad, but not for the reason you gave.*

For the exercises below answer the following questions:

Argument? (yes or no)

Conclusion:

Premises:

Classify: valid   strong ———————— weak

If not valid, show why:

Good argument? (choose one)
- It's good (passes the three tests).
- It's bad because a premise is false.
- It's bad because it's weak.
- It's bad because it begs the question.
- It's valid or strong, but you don't know if the premises are true, so you can't say if it's good or bad.

6. Flo's hair was long. Now it's short. So Flo must have gotten a haircut.

7. Intelligent students study hard. Zoe studies hard. So Zoe is intelligent.

8. All cats meow. Puff is a cat. So Puff meows.

9. All licensed drivers in California have taken a driver's test. Dick has taken a driver's test in California. So Dick is a licensed driver in California.

10. No dog meows. Puff meows. So Puff is not a dog.

11. Lee: I didn't get mail today and neither did Manuel or Maria. So there must not have been any mail deliveries today.

12. No cat barks. Spot is not a cat. So Spot barks.

13. Lee: My friend Judy manages a local bookstore. She drives a new Jaguar. So bookstore managers must make good money.

14. Dick missed almost every basket he shot in the game. He couldn't run, he couldn't jump. He should give up basketball.

15. Dick: I got sick after eating at the school cafeteria this week.
    Zoe: Me, too. What happened?
    Dick: Runs and dizziness.
    Zoe: Exactly the same for me.
    Dick: You know, the same thing happened to me last week.
    Zoe: It must be the food at the school cafeteria that's making us sick.

16. Suzy: You're mean.
    Tom: What? Why do you say that?
    Suzy: Because you're not nice.

17. What do you want to eat for dinner? Well, we had fish yesterday and pasta the other day. We haven't eaten chicken for a while. How about some chicken with potatoes?

18. Maria: Almost all the professors I've met at this school are liberals.
    Manuel: So to get a teaching job here it must help to be a liberal.

19. Tom: If Dick bought a new car, then he must have had more money than I thought.
    Harry: Well, look, there's the new hatchback he bought.
    Tom: So Dick must have had more money than I thought.

20. Zoe: Spot got out of the yard somehow.
    Dick: He must have got out under the fence.
    Zoe: No way he got out under the fence. There's no sign of new digging.

21. Zoe: Spot got out of the yard somehow.
    Dick: He must have got out under the fence.
    Zoe: No way he got out under the fence. There's no sign of new digging. And we blocked all the old ways he used to get out under the fence.

22. Zoe: Spot got out of the yard somehow.
    Dick: He must have got out under the fence.
    Zoe: No way he got out under the fence. There's no sign of new digging. And we blocked all the old ways he used to get out under the fence.
    Dick: But he pulled down that chicken wire last week.
    Zoe: (*later*) I checked—all the wire and rocks we put up are still there, and there's no sign that the fence has been disturbed at the bottom.
    Dick: I hope he hasn't learned how to jump over the fence.

23. Suzy: Every student who has ever taken a course from Professor Zzzyzzx has passed. So if I take his composition course, I'll pass, too.

24. Tom: See that guy over there? He's a Muslim.
    Suzy: And he has a beard. He must be a terrorist.

25. There are 30 seconds left in the football game. The 49ers have 35 points. The Dolphins have 7 points. So the 49ers will win.

Writing Lesson 3

We've been learning how to analyze arguments. Now it's time to try to write one.

You know what tests a good argument must pass. It must be composed of claims, and claims only. It shouldn't contain any ambiguous or excessively vague sentences. It must be valid or strong. And the premises should be plausible, more plausible than the conclusion.

Write an argument in OUTLINE FORM either for or against the following:

Everyone should use a bicycle as his or her main form of transportation.

- Just list the premises and the conclusion. Nothing more.
- Your argument should be at most one page long.
- Check whether your instructor has chosen a different topic for this assignment.

It doesn't matter if you never thought about the subject or whether you think it's terribly important. This is an exercise, a chance for you to sharpen your skills in writing arguments. It's the process of writing an argument that should be your focus.

If you have trouble coming up with an argument, think how you would respond if you heard someone say the claim at a city council meeting or if someone in class said it. Make two lists: *pro* and *con*. Then write the strongest argument you can. And in this case, remember to make clear what standards you're invoking for that "should."

Don't get carried away. You're not expected to spin a one-page argument into three pages. You can't use any of the literary devices that you've been taught are good fillers. List the premises and conclusion—that's all. And remember, premises and conclusion don't have those words "therefore" or "I think" attached. Once you can write an argument in this outline form, you can worry about making your arguments sound pretty. It's clarity we want first.

To give you a better idea of what you're expected to do, below I've included Tom's argument on a different topic.

Tom Wyzyczy
Critical Thinking
Section 4
Writing Lesson 3

Issue: Students should be required to take a course on critical thinking.

Definition: I'll understand the issue as "College students should be required to take a course on critical thinking before graduating."

Premises:

1. A critical thinking course will help students to write better in their other courses.

2. A critical thinking course will help students to read assignments in all their other courses.

3. A critical thinking course will make students become better informed voters.

4. Most students who take a critical thinking course appreciate it.

5. Professors will be able to teach their subjects better if they can assume their students know how to reason.

6. Critical thinking is a basic skill and should be required, like Freshman Composition.

Conclusion: College students should be required to take a course on critical thinking before graduating.

Tom, it's good that you began by making the issue precise. Even better is that you realized the definition wasn't a premise. You've learned a lot from the last assignment.

Your argument is pretty good. You've used claims for your premises. Some of them are a bit vague. But only the fourth is so vague you should delete it or make it more precise. All of your premises support your conclusion. But the argument's not strong as stated. You're missing some <u>glue</u>, something to fill the gap. You're piling up evidence, but to what end? To your third premise, I'd just say "SO?" We really don't know what standard you have in mind for that "should." And you never used in your argument that you're talking about <u>college</u> students. Won't your argument work just as well for high school? Is that what you want?

We'll look at how to fill in what you've missed in the next chapter.

Cartoon Writing Lesson A

Here is a chance to reason as in your everyday life with six scenes in cartoons.

Imagine seeing the scene depicted in the cartoon. Do you believe the claim that accompanies the cartoon? Why? Or why not? How would you convince someone to agree with you who hasn't witnessed the scene?

Here are the steps you can go through:

1. Write down what you see—nothing else.
   (Refer to the cast of characters at the front of the book.)
   We can assume that those claims are true.

2. Ask yourself whether it's possible for everything you've listed to be true, yet the claim in question to be false.

3. If the answer is no, you've already got a valid argument for the claim in question. Since the premises are true, it's also good.

4. If the answer is yes and such a possibility isn't all that unlikely, you know that you can't get a good argument for the claim in question.

5. The last case is if each such possibility—where what you see is true but the claim in question is false—is very unlikely. Then look for a claim or claims that will rule out all or almost all such possibilities to get a valid or strong argument. That's the *glue*. But don't make up a story; the claim(s) should be common knowledge, something we all know is true.

Steps (2)–(5) are exactly what's pictured on p. 41, except that here you can add the glue.

In summary, then, for each cartoon write the best argument you can that has as its conclusion the claim that accompanies the cartoon. List only the premises and conclusion. If you believe there is no good argument, explain why.

To give you a better idea of what to do, I've included on the next page an example of what Tom did with his homework.

Name ___Tom Wyzyczy___ Section ___4___

The fellow stole the purse.

> The guy is in the room and he spots a purse on the table.
> He looks around pretty shiftily and thinks that he can get away with
>   taking the purse.
> So he grabs it and goes.

This isn't a course in creative writing! How do you know he thinks that he can get away with it? That's just making up a story. How do you know he grabbed it? You didn't <u>see</u> that. And what makes you say he looks around shiftily? You need to distinguish what you see from what you deduce. If I didn't have the cartoon in front of me, I could never have imagined what you saw. You need to use the <u>observation</u> that almost no time passed from the time he saw it to the time the purse was gone, and that there was no one else around. Then you can conclude he took the purse.

Also, be sure to put in the conclusion. "So he grabs it and goes" is only a step along the way. You need some glue to get from that to the conclusion "The fellow stole the purse," something like, "Almost anytime a guy looks around quickly and takes a purse, he's stealing it." But that's false: Maybe he just recognized that it belonged to his girlfriend or his mother, and when he didn't see her he decided to take it to her. It looks like there is no good argument you can make for the conclusion.

This was your first try, and I'm sure that next time you'll know better. Describe what you saw, and try to get from that to the conclusion.

1.

Spot chased a cat.

2.

Professor Zzzyzzx is cold.

3.

Dick didn't wash his hands properly.

4.

Dick broke his leg skiing.

5.

Flo isn't really sick.

6.

Dick should not drink the coffee.

4   Repairing Arguments

A. We Need to Repair Arguments

Lee: Tom wants to get a dog.

Maria: What kind?

Lee: A dachshund. And that's really stupid, since he wants one that will catch a Frisbee.

Lee has made an argument, if we interpret what he said as: Tom wants a dog that will catch a Frisbee, so Tom shouldn't get a dachshund. After the last chapter, you're probably thinking this is a bad argument. There's no *glue*, no claim that gets us from the premise to the conclusion. We just ask "So?". But Maria knows very well, as do we, that a dachshund would be a lousy choice for someone who wants their dog to catch a Frisbee. Dachshunds are too low to the ground, they can't run fast, they can't jump, and the Frisbee is bigger than they are, so they couldn't bring it back. Any dog like that is a bad choice for a Frisbee partner. Lee just left out these obvious claims, but why should he bother to say them?

Folks normally leave out so much that if we look only at what's said, we'll be missing too much in trying to determine what we should believe. We can and must rewrite many arguments by adding an **unstated premise** or an **unstated conclusion**.

When are we justified in adding an unstated premise? How do we know whether we've rewritten an argument well or just added our own prejudices? And how can we recognize when an argument is beyond repair?

59

B. The Principle of Rational Discussion

What assumptions are we entitled to make about anyone with whom we wish to reason?

The Principle of Rational Discussion We assume that the other person who is discussing with us or whose arguments we are reading:

1. Knows about the subject under discussion.
2. Is able and willing to reason well.
3. Is not lying.

What justification do we have for invoking this principle? After all, not everyone fits these conditions all the time.

Consider condition (1). Dr. E leaves his car at the repair shop because it's running badly, and he returns later in the afternoon. The mechanic tells him that he needs a new fuel injector. Dr. E asks, "Are you sure I need a new one?" That sounds like an invitation for the mechanic to give an argument. But she shouldn't. Dr. E doesn't have the slightest idea how his engine runs, and the mechanic might as well be speaking Greek. She should try to educate Dr. E, or she'll have to ask Dr. E to accept her claim on trust.

Consider condition (2). Sometimes people intend not to reason well. Like the demagogic politician or talk-show host, they want to convince you by nonrational means and will not accept your arguments, no matter how good they may be. There's no point in deliberating with such a person.

Or you may encounter a person who is temporarily unable or unwilling to reason well, a person who is upset or in love. Again, it makes no sense at such a time to try to reason with that person. Calm him or her, address his or her emotions, and leave discussion for another time.

Then again, you might find yourself with someone who wants to reason well but just can't seem to follow an argument. Why try to reason? Give them a copy of this book.

What about condition (3)? If you find that the other person is lying—not just a little white lie, but continuously lying—there's no point in reasoning with him or her, unless perhaps to catch that person telling lies.

The Principle of Rational Discussion does not instruct us to give other people the benefit of the doubt. It summarizes the necessary conditions for us to be reasoning with someone. Compare it to playing chess with someone: What's the point if your opponent doesn't understand or won't play by the rules?

Still, you say, most people don't follow the Principle of Rational Discussion. They don't care if your argument is good. Why should you follow these rules and assume them of others? If you don't:

• You are denying the essentials of democracy.

• You are not going to know what to believe yourself.

• You are not as likely to convince others.

A representative democracy is built on the idea that the populace as a whole can choose good men and good women to write laws by which they can agree to live. If any appeal to the worst in people succeeds, then a democracy will degenerate into the rule of the mob, as it did in ancient Athens. It is only by constantly striving to base our political discussions on good arguments that we have any hope of living in a just and efficient society.

And how can you know what to believe yourself if you've adopted methods of convincing that appeal to the worst in people? Abandoning the standards of good reasoning, you'll soon be basing your own life on illusions and false beliefs.

But most of all, you're wrong if you think that in the long run convincing with clever ads, sound bites, or appeals to prejudice work better than good arguments. They don't. I've seen the contrary in my city council meetings. I've seen it with my friends. I've seen it with my students. With a little education, most people, most of the time, prefer to have a sensible, good argument to think about.

> If you once forfeit the confidence of your fellow citizens, you can never regain their respect and esteem. It is true that you may fool all the people some of the time; you can even fool some of the people all the time; but you cannot fool all of the people all the time.
>
> Abraham Lincoln

Still, there are times when an argument appears good, but you think the conclusion is false. Then if you are a good reasoner, you should try to show the argument isn't good: The conclusion doesn't really follow from the premises, or one of the premises is false, or it begs the question.

What if you hear arguments for both sides, and you can't find a flaw in either? Then you should *suspend judgment* on whether the claim is true until you can investigate more.

> ***The mark of irrationality*** If you recognize that an argument is good, then it is irrational not to accept the conclusion.

C. The Guide to Repairing Arguments

With the Principle of Rational Discussion, we can formulate a guide to help us evaluate and interpret arguments. Since the person is supposed to be able to reason well, we can add a premise to his or her argument only if it makes the argument stronger or valid and doesn't beg the question. Since the person isn't lying and knows the subject under discussion, any premise we add should be plausible, and plausible to that person. We can also delete a premise if it doesn't make the argument worse.

The Guide to Repairing Arguments   Given an (implicit) argument that is apparently defective, we are justified in adding a premise or conclusion if it satisfies all three of the following:

1. The argument becomes stronger or valid.
2. The premise is plausible and would seem plausible to the other person.
3. The premise is more plausible than the conclusion.

If the argument is then valid or strong, we may delete a premise if doing so doesn't make the argument worse.

For example, suppose we hear:

Lee: I was wondering what kind of pet Dick has. It must be a dog.
Maria: How do you know?
Lee: Because I heard it barking last night.

Maria shouldn't dismiss Lee's reasoning just because the link from premises to conclusion is missing. She should ask what claim(s) are needed to make it strong, since by the Principle of Rational Discussion we assume Lee intends to and is able to reason well. The obvious premise to add is "All pets that bark are dogs." But Maria knows that's false (seals, foxes, parrots) and can assume that Lee does, too, since he's supposed to know about the subject. So she tries "Almost all pets that bark are dogs." That's plausible, and with it the argument is strong and good.

We first try to make the argument valid or strong, because we don't need to know what the speaker was thinking in order to do that. Then we can ask whether that claim is plausible and whether it would be plausible to the other person. *By first trying to make the argument valid or strong, we can show the other person what he or she needs to assume to make the argument good.*

It's the same when you make your own arguments. You have premises and a conclusion, and you ask yourself: Is it possible for the premises to be true and the conclusion false? When you find a possible way for the premises to be true and the conclusion false, you try to eliminate it by adding a premise—of course a plausible one. As you eliminate ways in which the premises could be true and the conclusion false, you make the argument better.

But why go to all this bother when we hear a defective argument and can see how to make a better one for the same conclusion? Why not just use what we can from it and ignore the rest in order to come up with a good argument? After all, we're trying to learn what's true about the world. Fine, but first you should take seriously what the other person said. You can't learn if you don't listen. The Guide to Repairing Arguments is a method to hear and understand better by paying attention to what's actually said.

One aid we have in following what someone actually said is to note certain words such as "so" or "therefore," which tell us a conclusion is coming up, and "since" or "because," which introduce premises.

Indicator word An indicator word is a word or phrase added to a claim to tell us the role of the claim in an argument or what the speaker thinks of the claim or argument.

Indicator words are flags put on claims—they are not part of a claim. Here are some common ones:

conclusion indicators	*premise indicators*
so	since
therefore	because
hence	for
thus	in as much as
consequently	given that
we can then derive	suppose that
it follows that	it follows from

These are good to use in our own arguments to structure our writing and help others understand us. But most arguments we encounter won't have such clear signposts.

Other indicator words tell us what a speaker thinks of a claim or argument, as we saw in Chapter 3 (p. 48).

Examples   Are the following good arguments? Can they be repaired?

Example 1 No dog meows. So Spot does not meow.
Analysis "Spot is a dog" is the only premise that will make this a valid or strong argument. So we add that. Then since that's true, the argument is good.

We don't add "Spot barks." That's true, too, and certain to seem obvious to the person who stated the argument, but it doesn't make the argument any better. So adding it violates requirement (1) of the Guide. *We repair only as needed.*

Example 2 All professors teach. So Ms. Han is a professor.
Analysis The obvious claim to add is "Ms. Han teaches." But then the argument is

still weak: Ms. Han could be an instructor, or a part-time lecturer, or a graduate student. *The argument can't be repaired because the obvious premise to add makes it weak.*

Example 3 Dr. E has a dog named "Anubis." So Anubis barks.

Analysis We can't make this valid by adding "All dogs bark," because that's false.

We could make it stronger by adding "Anubis is not a basenji" and "Anubis didn't have her vocal cords cut." Those would rule out a lot of possibilities where Anubis is a dog but doesn't bark. And why not add "Anubis scares away the electric meter reader every month"? Or we could add . . . . But this isn't a course in creative writing. We can't make up just anything to add to the argument to make it stronger or valid. We have no reason to believe those claims are true.

The only premise we can add here is a blanket one that rules out lots of possibilities without specifying any one of them: "Almost all dogs bark." That's the *glue* that links the premise to the conclusion. Then the argument is good.

Example 4 Dr. E is a good teacher because he gives fair exams.

Analysis The unstated premise needed to make this valid or strong is "Almost any teacher who gives fair exams is a good teacher." That gives a strong argument. But it's not plausible: A teacher could copy fair exams from the instructor's manual. (If you thought the claim that's needed is "Good teachers give fair exams," then reread Example 2.) *The argument can't be repaired because the obvious premise to add to make the argument strong or valid is false or dubious.*

But can't you make it strong by adding, say, "Dr. E gives great explanations," "Dr. E is amusing," "Dr. E never misses class," . . . ? Yes, all those are true, and perhaps obvious to the person. But adding those doesn't repair this argument—it makes a whole new argument. *Don't put words in someone's mouth.*

Example 5   Dick: Dogs are loyal. Dogs are friendly. Dogs can protect you from intruders.
Maria: So?
Dick: So dogs make great pets.
Maria: Why does that follow?

Analysis Maria's right. Dick's argument is missing the "glue," the link between premises and conclusion that rules out other possibilities, in this case, something like "Anything that is loyal, friendly, and can protect you from intruders is a great pet." But it's exactly that which Maria thinks is false: Dogs need room to run around, they need to be walked every day, it costs more to take care of a dog than a goldfish, ... *Just stating a lot of obvious truths doesn't by itself get you a conclusion.*

Example 6 You shouldn't eat the fat on your steak. Haven't you heard that cholesterol is bad for you?

Analysis The conclusion is the first sentence. But what are the premises? The speaker's question is rhetorical, meant to be taken as an assertion: "Cholesterol is bad for you." But that alone won't give us the conclusion. We need something like "Steak fat has a lot of cholesterol" plus the obvious standard for that "should": "You shouldn't eat anything that's bad for you." Premises like these are so well known that we don't bother to say them. This argument is O.K.

Example 7 I totally don't support prohibiting smoking in bars—most people who go to bars do smoke and people should be aware that a bar is a place where a lot of people go to have a drink and smoke. There are no youth working or attending bars and I just don't believe you can allow people to go have a beer but not to allow people to have a cigarette— that's a person's God-given right.

Gordy Hicks, City Councilor, Socorro, N.M., reported in *El Defensor Chieftain*, 7/24/2002

Analysis *The conclusion here needs to be stated*: "Smoking should not be prohibited in bars."

That prescriptive claim needs some standard. The unstated one here seems to be that society should not establish sanctions against any activity that doesn't corrupt youth or create harm to others who can't avoid it. The argument is just as good without the appeal to God, so we can ignore that. If it turns out that Hicks really does think the standard is theological, then the argument he gave isn't adequate.

> You can't get a prescriptive conclusion from only descriptive premises: *"is" does not imply "ought."*

Example 8 You're going to vote for the Green Party candidate for President? Don't you realize that means your vote will be wasted?

Analysis Where's the argument here? These are just two questions.

If you heard this, you'd certainly think that the speaker is trying to *convince* you to believe "You shouldn't vote for the Green Party candidate for President." And the speaker is giving a reason to believe that: "Your vote will be wasted." This is an implicit argument.

The argument sounds pretty good, though something is missing. A visitor from Denmark may not know "The Green Party candidate doesn't have a chance of winning." But even then, she could ask "So?". The argument is missing the glue that links the premises to the conclusion. We'd have to fill in the argument further: "If you vote for someone who doesn't have a chance of winning, then your vote will be wasted." And when we add that premise, we see the argument that used such "obvious" premises is really not very good. Why should we believe that if you vote for someone who doesn't stand a chance of winning then your vote is wasted? If that were true, then who wins is the only important result of an election, rather than, say, making a position understood by the electorate. At best we can say that when the unstated premises are added in, we get an argument one of whose premises needs a substantial argument to convince us that it is true. *Trying to repair arguments can lead us to unstated assumptions about which the real debate should be.*

Example 9   Cats are more likely than dogs to carry diseases harmful to humans. Cats kill songbirds and can kill people's pets. Cats disturb people at night with their screeching and clattering in garbage cans. Cats leave paw prints on cars and will sleep in unattended cars. Cats are not as pleasant as dogs and are owned only by people who have satanic affinities. So there should be a leash law for cats just as much as for dogs.

Analysis   This letter to the editor is going pretty well until the next to last sentence. *That claim is a bit dubious, and the argument will be better without it. So we should delete it.* Then, by adding some obvious claims that glue the premises to the conclusion by ruling out other possibilities, we'll have a good argument.

Example 10   In a famous speech, Martin Luther King Jr. said:

> "I have a dream that one day this nation will rise up and live out the true meaning of its creed: 'We hold these truths to be self-evident—that all men are created equal.' . . . I have a dream that one day even the state of Mississippi, a desert state sweltering with the heat of injustice and oppression, will be transformed into an oasis of freedom and justice. I have a dream that my four little children will one day live in a nation where they will not be judged by the color of their skin but by the content of their character."
>
> . . . King is also presenting a logical argument . . . the argument might be stated as follows; "America was founded on the principle that all men are created equal. This implies that people should not be judged by skin color, which is an accident of birth, but rather by what they make of themselves ('the content of their character'). To be consistent with this principle, America should treat black people and white people alike."

David Kelley, *The Art of Reasoning*

Analysis   The rewriting of this passage is too much of a stretch—putting words in someone's mouth—to be justified. Where did David Kelley get "This implies . . ."? Stating my dreams and hoping others will share them is not an argument. Martin Luther King, Jr. knew how to argue well and could do so when he wanted. We're not going to make his words more respectable by pretending they're an argument. *Not every good attempt to persuade is an argument.*

Example 11   Alcoholism is a disease, not a character flaw. People are genetically predisposed to be addicted to alcohol. An alcoholic should not be fired or imprisoned, but should be given treatment.

Treatment centers should be established, because it is too difficult to overcome the addiction to alcohol all by oneself. The encouragement and direction of others is what is needed to help people, for alcoholics can find the power within themselves to fight and triumph over their addiction.

Analysis On the face of it, "Alcoholism is a disease, not a character flaw" contradicts "Alcoholics can find the power within themselves to fight and triumph over their addiction." Both these claims are important premises for the conclusion "Treatment centers should be established." *When premises contradict each other and can't be deleted, there's no way to repair the argument.*

Example 12 U.S. citizens are independent souls, and they tend to dislike being forced to do anything. The compulsory nature of Social Security therefore has been controversial since the program's beginnings. Many conservatives argue that Social Security should be made voluntary, rather than compulsory. Brux and Cowen, *Economic Issues and Policy*

Analysis The first two sentences look like an argument. But the first sentence is too vague to be a claim. And even if it could be made precise, we'd have an explanation, not an attempt to convince. *Don't try to repair what isn't an argument.*

Example 13 It is only for the sake of profit that any man employs capital in the support of industry; and he will always, therefore, endeavour to employ it in the support of that industry of which the produce is likely to be of greatest value, or to exchange for the greatest quantity either of money or of other goods. Adam Smith, *The Wealth of Nations*

Analysis The argument is valid, but *its single premise is false.* Lots of other considerations about where to invest money matter to many people: convenience, social responsibility, ... So there's no way to repair it, and it's bad.

Example 14 When Dick put out the dry dog food that Spot usually won't eat, Spot ran over and right away ate it. So Spot was hungry.

Analysis The conclusion is subjective. To have a good argument, we also need a premise such as "When a dog races to eat food that he normally doesn't eat, then he is hungry," which is plausible and makes this a good argument. That subjective claim is the link between the observed behavior and the inferred state of mind. Often *an assumption linking behavior to thoughts is needed to make an argument good.*

Example 15 None of Dr. E's students are going to beg in the street. 'Cause only poor people beg. And Dr. E's students will be rich because they understand how to reason well.

Analysis This is a superb argument!

We've seen how to repair some arguments. And just as important, we've seen that some arguments can't be repaired.

Unrepairable arguments We don't repair an argument if:

- There's no argument there.
- The argument is so lacking in coherence that there's nothing obvious to add.
- A premise it uses is false or dubious and cannot be deleted.
- Two of its premises are contradictory, and neither can be deleted.
- The obvious premise to add would make the argument weak.
- The obvious premise to add to make the argument strong or valid is false.
- The conclusion is clearly false.

D. Relevance

Tom is making an argument (the second question is rhetorical):

> Environmentalists should not be allowed to tell us what to do.
> The federal government should not be allowed to tell us what to do.
> Therefore, we should go ahead and allow logging in old-growth forests.

When the argument is put this way, it seems obvious to us that Tom has confused whether we have the *right* to cut down the forests with whether we *should* cut them down. Tom's proved something, just not the conclusion.

Sometimes people say an argument like Tom's is bad because his premises are irrelevant to the conclusion. They say an argument is bad if in response to one or more premises your reaction is "What's that got to do with anything?" or "So?"

What would you do if someone told you a claim you made is irrelevant? You'd try to show that it is relevant by adding more premises to link it to the conclusion.

The trouble is that the premises needed to make the claim relevant are not obvious to the other person. When we say that a premise is irrelevant to the conclusion, all we're saying is that it doesn't make the argument any better, and we can't see how to add anything plausible that would link it to the conclusion. And when we say that all the premises are irrelevant, we're saying that we can't even imagine how to repair the argument.

> A premise is *irrelevant* if you can delete it and the argument isn't any weaker.

Exercises for Sections A–D

1. Why add premises or a conclusion? Why not take arguments as they are?

2. State the Principle of Rational Discussion and explain why we are justified in adopting it when we reason with others.

3. What should you do if you find that the Principle of Rational Discussion does not apply in a discussion you are having?

4. You find that a close friend is an alcoholic. You want to help her. You want to convince her to stop drinking. Which is more appropriate, to reason with her or take her to an Alcoholics Anonymous meeting? Explain why.

5. Since many people often don't satisfy the Principle of Rational Discussion, why not just use bad arguments to fit the circumstances?

6. State the guide we have in judging when to add or delete a premise, and then what would count as a suitable unstated premise.

7. When can't we repair an argument?

8. When you show an argument is bad, what does that tell you about the conclusion?

9. a. What is an indicator word?
   b. List at least five words or phrases not in the chart that indicate a conclusion.
   c. List at least five words or phrases not in the chart that indicate premises.
   d. List five more words or phrases that show an attitude toward a claim or argument.
   e. Bring in an argument from some source that uses indicator words.

10. Mark which of the blanks below would normally be filled with a premise (P) and which with a conclusion (C).
    a. (i)_____, (ii)_____, (iii)_____, therefore (iv)_____.
    b. (i)_____, since (ii)_____, (iii)_____, and (iv) _____.
    c. Because (i)_____, it follows that (ii)_____ and (iii)_____.
    d. Since (i)_____ and (ii)_____, it follows that (iii)_____, because (iv)_____.
    e. (i)_____ and (ii)_____, and that's why (iii)_____.
    f. Due to (i)_____ and (ii)_____, we have (iii)_____.
    g. In view of (i)_____, (ii)_____, and (iii)_____ we get (iv)_____.

   h. From (i)_____ and (ii)_____, we can derive (iii)_____.
   i. If (i)_____, then it follows that (ii)_____, for (iii)_____ and (iv)_____.

11. How should we understand the charge that a premise is irrelevant?

Here are some of Tom's homeworks on repairing arguments.

Anyone who studies hard gets good grades. So it must be that Zoe studies hard.

Argument? (yes or no) Yes.

Conclusion (if unstated, add it): Zoe must study hard.

Premises: Anyone who studies hard gets good grades.

Additional premises needed to make it valid or strong (if none, say so):
     Zoe gets good grades.

Classify (with the additional premises): <u>valid</u>   strong ——————— weak

Good argument?   (Choose one and give an explanation.)
   • It's good (passes the three tests). ✓   with the added premise.
   • It's valid or strong, but you don't know if the premises are true,
     so you can't say if it's good or bad.
   • It's bad because it's unrepairable (state which of the reasons apply).

*No! First, "must" is an indicator word. The conclusion is "Zoe studies hard."
Even then, Zoe could get good grades and not study hard if she's very bright.
It's the obvious premise to add, all right, but it makes the argument weak.
The argument is unrepairable. It's just like Example 2 on p. 63.*

Celia must love the coat Rudolfo gave her. She wears it all the time.

Argument? (yes or no) Yes.

Conclusion (if unstated, add it): Celia loves the coat Rudolfo gave her.

Premises: She wears it all the time.

Additional premises needed to make it valid or strong (if none, say so):
     Anyone who wears a coat all the time loves it.

Classify (with the additional premises): valid   strong ——X——— weak

Good argument? (Choose one and give an explanation.)
   • It's good (passes the three tests). ✓   with the added premise.
   • It's valid or strong, but you don't know if the premises are true,
     so you can't say if it's good or bad.
   • It's bad because it's unrepairable (state which of the reasons apply).

*You've confused whether an argument is valid or strong with whether it's good.
With your added premise, the argument is indeed valid. But the premise you
added is clearly false. Weakening it to make the argument only strong won't
do—the person making the argument intended it to be valid (that word "must" in
the conclusion). So the argument is unrepairable because the obvious premise
to add to make it valid is false.*

I got sick after eating shrimp last month. Then this week again when I ate shrimp, I got a rash. So I shouldn't eat shellfish anymore.

Argument? (yes or no) Yes.

Conclusion (if unstated, add it): I shouldn't eat shellfish anymore.

Premises: I got sick after eating shrimp last month. This week again when I ate shrimp I got a rash.

Additional premises needed to make it valid or strong (if none, say so):
   None.

Good argument? (Choose one and give an explanation.)
   • It's good (passes the three tests).
   • It's valid or strong, but you don't know if the premises are true, so you can't say if it's good or bad. ✓   Sounds very strong to me. I sure wouldn't risk eating shrimp again.
   • It's bad because it's unrepairable (state which of the reasons apply).

First, a prescriptive claim is needed as premise—see p. 65. Then I agree that I wouldn't risk eating shrimp again. But that doesn't make the argument strong—there are lots of other possibilities for why the person got a rash. The argument is only moderate. <u>Risk may determine how strong an argument we're willing to accept, but it doesn't affect how strong the argument actually is.</u>

Our congressman voted to give more money to people on welfare. So he doesn't care about working people.

Argument? (yes or no) Yes.

Conclusion (if unstated, add it): Our congressman doesn't care about working people.

Premises: Our congressman voted to give more money to people on welfare.

Additional premises needed to make it valid or strong (if none, say so):
   I can't think of any that are plausible.

Classify (with the additional premises):   valid   strong ————X weak

Good argument? (Choose one and give an explanation.)
   • It's good (passes the three tests).
   • It's valid or strong, but you don't know if the premises are true, so you can't say if it's good or bad.
   • It's bad because it's unrepairable (state which of the reasons apply). ✓ The only premise I can think of that would even make the argument strong is something like "Almost anyone who votes to give more money to people on welfare doesn't care about working people." And I know that's false. So the argument is unrepairable, right?

Right! Excellent work. You've clearly got the idea here. I'm sure you can do more of these now if you'll just remember that sometimes the correct answer is that the argument is unrepairable. Review those conditions on p. 68.

Analyze Exercises 12–34 by answering these questions:

Argument? (yes or no)
Conclusion (if unstated, add it):
Premises:
Additional premises needed to make it valid or strong (if none, say so):
Classify (with the additional premises):   valid   strong ———————— weak
Good argument? (Choose one and give an explanation.)
- It's good (passes the three tests).
- It's valid or strong, but you don't know if the premises are true, so you can't say if it's good or bad.
- It's bad because it's unrepairable (state which of the reasons apply).

12. Dr. E is a teacher. All teachers are men. So Dr. E is a man.

13. George walks like a duck. George looks like a duck. George quacks like a duck. So George is a duck.

14. If you're so smart, why aren't you rich?

15. You caught the flu from me? Impossible! I haven't seen you for two months.

16. You caught the flu from me? Impossible! You got sick first.

17. Mary Ellen just bought a Mercedes. So Mary Ellen must be rich.

18. All great teachers are tough graders. So Dr. E is a great teacher.

19. No dog meows. So Spot will only eat canned dog food.

20. No cat barks. So Ralph is not a cat.

21. You're blue-eyed. So your parents must be blue-eyed.

22. Dick: Can you stop at the grocery and buy a big bag of dog food when you're out?
    Zoe: You know I'm riding my bike today.

23. Dick: Harry got into college because of affirmative action.
    Suzy: Gee, I didn't know that. So Harry isn't very bright.

24. They should fire Professor Zzzyzzx because he has such a bad accent that no one can understand his lectures in his English literature course.

25. (Advertisement) The bigger the burgers, the better the burgers, the burgers are bigger at Burger King.

26. Suzy: Did you see how that saleslady treated Harry?
    Tom: Yeah, she just ignored him.
    Suzy: She must be racist.

27. —That masked man saved us.
    —Did you see he has silver bullets in his gunbelt?
    —And he called his horse Silver.
    —Didn't he call his friend Tonto?
    —He must be the Lone Ranger.

28. These exercises are impossible. How do they expect us to get them right? There are no right answers! They're driving me crazy.

29. These exercises are difficult but not impossible. Though there may not be a unique right answer, there are definitely wrong answers. There are generally not unique best ways to analyze arguments you encounter in your daily life. The best this course can hope to do is make you think and develop your judgment through these exercises.

30. What!? Me sexually harass her? You've got to be kidding! I never would have asked her out for a date. Look at her—she's too fat, and besides, she smokes. I'm the boss here, and I could go out with anyone I want.

31. (From the Associated Press, July 8, 1999, about a suit against tobacco companies for making "a defective product that causes emphysema, lung cancer, and other illnesses.")
    The industry claimed there is no scientific proof that smoking causes any illness and that the public is well aware that smoking is risky.

32. Flo has always wanted a dog, but she's never been very responsible. She had a fish once, but it died after a week. She forgot to water her mother's plants, and they died. She stepped on a neighbor's turtle and killed it.

33. This book will be concerned exclusively with abstract decision theory and will focus on its logical and philosophical foundations. This does not mean that readers will find nothing here of practical value. Some of the concepts and methods I will expound are also found in business school textbooks.
    Michael Resnik, *Choices*

34. (An advertisement that Dr. E found in his e-mail)

    Click Here to Spice Up Your Sex Life Today!

    Do you want to improve your Sex Life?
    IMPULSE is an all Natural Herbal formula that is guaranteed to increase your sexual performance! Remember, it's all natural so your body doesn't get harmful side effects.

    IMPULSE HERBAL BENEFITS:
    1. Gives Long-Lasting and Powerful Erections!
    2. You Don't Need a Prescription to buy IMPULSE!
    3. Very Affordable PRICE! (1/10 the cost of Viagra!)
    4. Revitalizes the sex interest in both partners
    5. Sex plays a vital part in any relationship! Bring back that missing piece!
    6. Never Any Negative Side Effects! (All Natural Ingredients)
    7. Helps women with a sexual response dysfunction

    Ordering is very simple and completely anonymous. You don't have to wait another day to improve your sex life, you now have an all natural solution!

    The #1 best selling 100% all natural aphrodisiac in America!

    Increase Your Sex Life Today! IMPULSE!

Additional Exercises

35. Find a letter to the editor with an argument that depends on at least one unstated premise.

36. Find a letter to the editor with an argument that has an unstated conclusion.

37. a. Make up an argument against the idea that lying is a good way to convince people.
    b. Convert your argument in (a) to show that reasoning badly on purpose is not effective or ethical.

38. Read the Gettysburg Address and explain why it is or is not an argument.

E. Inferring and Implying

Suppose your teacher says in class, "All of my best students hand in extra written arguments for extra credit." She hasn't actually said you should hand in extra work. But you infer that she has implied "If you want to do well in this class, you'd better hand in extra-credit work." The words "imply" and "infer" are not synonyms.

> ***Inferring and implying***   When someone leaves a conclusion unsaid, he or she is implying the conclusion. When you decide that an unstated claim is the conclusion, you are inferring that claim.
>
> We can also say someone is implying a claim if in context it's clear he or she believes the claim. In that case we infer that the person believes the claim.

Implying and inferring is risky business. If you complain to the department head that your teacher is demanding more than she asked on the syllabus, your teacher could reply that you just inferred incorrectly. She might say, "I've observed that my best students hand in extra-credit work—that's all I was saying. I had no intention of making an argument." You, however, could say that in the context in which she made the remark it was fairly obvious she was implying that if you wanted her to believe you are a good student, you should hand in extra work.

When Suzy was home for vacation, her father said to her before she went out Saturday night, "Don't forget we're going to be leaving very early for the beach tomorrow." Suzy got home at 3:30 a.m., and the next morning her father was livid when she said that she was too tired to help with the driving. "I *told* you we were leaving very early," he said. To which Suzy replied, "So?" Her father believes he clearly implied, "You should get home early and rest enough to help with the driving." Suzy says he should have been more explicit.

The trouble is, we aren't always explicit; we often leave the conclusion unstated because it seems so obvious. And what is obvious to you may not be obvious to someone else. One person's intelligent inference is another's jumping to conclusions.

Examples   What's being implied? What's being inferred?

Example 1   I'm not going to vote, because no matter who is President nothing is going to get us out of this war.

Analysis   An unstated claim is needed to make this into a strong or valid argument: "If no matter who is President nothing is going to get us out of this war, then you shouldn't vote for President." We infer this from the person's remarks; he has implied it.

Example 2   Lee is working in the computer lab at school. He's been there for an hour and a half. He looks up and notices that all the students who have come in lately are wearing raincoats and are wet. He figures it must be raining outside.

Analysis   We can say that Lee inferred "It is raining outside." But where's the argument? This is the kind of inferring that psychologists and scientists and lawyers do all the time. They have evidence, but not stated verbally, and proceed as if they had an argument.

We often infer from our experience, but we can't analyze those inferences nor discuss them with others until we have verbalized them into arguments.

Example 3   Lee's teacher makes a sexual innuendo the first day of class. He figures she must have meant something harmless, and he just didn't get it. But it happens again. And again. Lee starts taking notes on all the remarks. Finally, after four weeks Lee is fed up and goes to the head of the department. He says, "My teacher is making sexually suggestive remarks in class. It's not an accident. It's intentional."

Analysis   The argument Lee would need to make to the department head might be "My teacher made many remarks over a long period of time that could be taken sexually. This could not be an accident, because it happened too often. Therefore, she intended to make sexually suggestive comments."

This may or may not be a strong argument, depending on exactly what remarks were said. It has a subjective claim as a conclusion, one Lee inferred from the teacher's actions.

Exercises for Section E

1. Suzy says, "I find fat men unattractive, so I won't date you."
   a. What has Suzy implied?
   b. What can the fellow she's talking to infer?

2. The following conversation is ascribed to W. C. Fields at a formal dinner party. What can we say he implied?

   W. C. Fields: Madame, you are horribly ugly.

   Lady: Your behavior is inexcusable. You're drunk.

   W. C. Fields: I may be drunk, but tomorrow I'll be sober.

3. What can we infer when Dr. E says, "I always keep about 15 pounds extra on me because I heard that women are intimidated by a man with a perfect body"?

4. In July 2002, the famous race-car driver Al Unser was arrested on allegations by his girlfriend that very late one night he hit her and forced her out of the car in a deserted area. His uncle, Bobby Unser, was quoted in the *Albuquerque Journal* as saying:

    > What Little Al and Gina Sota did that night was the most nothing thing I've ever heard of . . . . He didn't use a gun or a knife or a stick. What's the big deal about that? This girl is a topless dancer. She's been down that road 100 times.

    What can we infer that Bobby Unser believes?

5. [State Senator Manny Aragon] has complained that New Mexico's population is 42 percent Hispanic but the state has no Hispanic representative in Congress.

    That sentiment was echoed Thursday by state House Majority Whip James Taylor, an Albuquerque Democrat, who, like Aragon, represents the South Valley in Bernalillo County. "It's embarrassing that New Mexico currently has no Hispanic representative in Congress, especially being a majority-minority state," Taylor said in an interview, meaning that the sum of all non-Anglo residents is larger than the Anglo population. "We need to make sure all people of the state are represented."

    What has James Taylor implied?   Associated Press, June 1, 2001

6. Jean Bottomley, 81, had a radical mastectomy in July and received radiology treatments for several weeks after that. Bottomley also suffers from macular degeneration, Parkinson's disease, and Alzheimer's disease. Unable to drive more than a couple of miles from her home, Bottomley called the cancer society's local office and requested help.

    Albuquerque Tribune, November 14, 2002

    What can we infer about Bottomley's driving habits?

7. Give a recent example where you inferred a claim.

Summary Most arguments we encounter are flawed. But they aren't necessarily bad. They can often be repaired by adding claims that are common knowledge.

By reflecting on the conditions for us to enter into a rational discussion, we can formulate a guide for how to repair apparently defective arguments. We assume the other person is knowledgeable about the subject, is able and willing to reason well, and is not lying. So we add premises that make the argument stronger or valid and that are plausible to us and to the other person.

Of course, not everyone can reason well, or wishes to reason well. And lots of arguments can't be repaired, which is something we can discover when we try to add premises. That, too, helps us evaluate arguments.

Our actions, as well as our words, can lead people to think we believe some claims. People imply claims by their actions or words, and others infer claims from them.

Key Words   unstated premise   indicator word
                    unstated conclusion   unrepairable argument
                    The Principle of Rational Discussion   irrelevant premise
                    mark of irrationality   imply
                    suspend judgment   infer
                    The Guide to Repairing Arguments

Further Study   To follow up on the idea that rational discussion is necessary for a democracy, you can read Plato's *Gorgias*, in which Socrates castigates those who would convince without good arguments.

An interesting article about the moral and the utilitarian values of reasoning well, especially for how that may or may not be a "Western" value, is "East and West: The Reach of Reason," by Amartya Sen in the *New York Review of Books*, vol. XLVII, no. 12 (July 20, 2000), pp. 33–38.

A full discussion of rationality, both in terms of arguments and inferring beliefs from actions, can be found in my *Five Ways of Saying 'Therefore'*, also published by Wadsworth. That book gives a foundation for all of critical thinking.

Writing Lesson 4

Write an argument in outline form either for or against the following:

No one should receive financial aid their first semester at this school.

- Just list the premises and the conclusion—nothing more.
- Your argument should be at most one page long.
- Check whether your instructor has chosen a different topic for this assignment.

Remember that with a prescriptive conclusion you need at least one prescriptive premise that establishes the standard.

To give you a better idea of what you're expected to do, I've included Manuel's argument on a different issue on the following page.

Manuel Luis Andrade y Castillo de Pocas
Critical Thinking
Section 2
Writing Lesson 4

Issue: The chance of contracting AIDS through sexual contact can be significantly reduced by using condoms.

Definition: "AIDS" means "Acquired Immunodeficiency Syndrome"
"significantly reduced" means by more than 50%
"using condoms" means using a condom in sexual intercourse rather than having unprotected sex

Premises:

- AIDS can only be contracted by exchanging blood or semen. *A*

- In unprotected sex there is a chance of exchanging blood or semen.

- Condoms are better than 90% effective in stopping blood and semen.*

- 90% is bigger than 50%.

- AIDS has never been known to have been contracted from sharing food, using a dirty toilet seat, from touching, or from breathing in the same room with someone who has AIDS. *B*

- If you want to avoid contracting AIDS you should use a condom. *C*

Conclusion: The chance of contracting AIDS through sexual contact can be significantly reduced by using condoms.

*I'm not sure of the exact figure, but I know it's bigger than 90%.

Good. Your argument is indeed valid. But it could easily be better. You don't need "only" in A, which is what makes me uneasy in accepting that claim. And without a reference to medical literature, I'm not going to accept B. But you don't need it. You can delete it and your argument is just as good.

And the last claim, C, is really irrelevant—delete it. This isn't an editorial: You're not trying to convince someone to <u>do</u> something; you're trying to convince them an objective claim is true.

Cartoon Writing Lesson B

Here is a chance to reason as you might in your everyday life.

For each cartoon write the best argument you can that has as its conclusion the claim that accompanies the cartoon. List only the premises and conclusion. If you believe the best argument is only weak, explain why. Refer back to Cartoon Writing Lesson A on p. 55 for suggestions about how to do this lesson.

Remember that with subjective claims, you may need to have a premise that links actions to thoughts, beliefs, or feelings.

To give you a better idea of what you're expected to do, I've included Maria's writing lesson for a different cartoon below the ones you're to do.

1.

Spot ran away.

2.

Dr. E shaved.

3.

The dog is trying to catch the Frisbee.

4.

The mother is scolding her child for breaking the flower pot.

5.

Spot is afraid of being punished.

6.

Suzy hit Puff with the car.

Name   Maria Schwartz Rodriguez   Section   6

Restaurant

New Mexico's best chile!

123 LTD

In New Mexico cars are required to have only one license plate, in the rear.

1. Some of the cars don't have license plates in the front.
2. All of the cars have license plates in the back.
3. So probably the rear license plate is required, and no front plate is required in New Mexico, since it is pretty unlikely all the front plates just fell off.

You've only proved part of the conclusion with your argument. How do you know these are New Mexico cars?

First, this is a restaurant parking lot, so these are normal cars, not cars for sale in a used car lot, where of course many of them wouldn't have license plates.

Second, the restaurant is advertising New Mexico's best chile, and so it must be in New Mexico. It would be absurd for a restaurant to advertise like that in another state.

Third, if it's in New Mexico, it's likely that most of the cars there are from New Mexico—not certain, but likely.

Now you can use the argument you gave to get the conclusion. But you could have gotten a much stronger argument using the following general claim:

It would be extremely unlikely for three drivers at the same time and place to have lost their front plates and to risk a serious penalty for not having a front plate.

Overall, this is pretty good. You're only using what you see, not making up a story. But you're not using enough of what you see—remember to prove all of the conclusion. Also, it's really good how you put in the glue, the last part of #3 that shows how you got from what you saw to the conclusion. But #3 is two claims, not one, as you recognized by using that indicator word "since." Be sure to list each claim separately so you can judge the plausibility of each and see how it links to the others.

5   Is That True?

A. Evaluating Premises

Recall the tests that an argument must pass to be good:

> There is good reason to believe the premises.
> The premises are more plausible than the conclusion.
> The argument is valid or strong.

In the last two chapters we looked at how to evaluate whether the conclusion follows from the premises. Now we'll consider what is good reason to believe the premises.

    But why simply believe a premise? Shouldn't every claim be backed up with an argument? We can't do that. If we want a justification for every claim, we'd have to go on forever. We'd never get started. Sometimes when someone makes a claim we just have to decide if we believe it.

> ### Three choices we can make about whether to believe a claim
> - Accept the claim as true.
> - Reject the claim as false.
> - Suspend judgment.

We needn't pretend to be all wise, nor force ourselves to make judgments. Sometimes it's best to suspend judgment and evaluate the argument as well as we can. If we find that it's valid or strong, we can then worry about whether the premise is true. Rejecting a claim means to say that it is false.

not believe it ≠ believe it is false

lack of evidence ≠ evidence it is false

B. Criteria for Accepting or Rejecting Claims

There are no absolute rules for when to accept, when to reject, and when to suspend judgment about a claim. It's a skill, weighing up the criteria in this section, as presented in their order of importance.

1. Personal experience

What would you think of an adult who never trusted his own experience, who always deferred to authority? He goes to a priest and asks him if it's daytime. He looks up in an atlas whether his hometown is in Nevada. He asks his wife whether the room they're standing in is painted white. You'd say he's crazy.

> Our most reliable source of information about the world is our own experience.

We need to trust our own experience because that's the best we have. Everything else is second-hand. Should you trust your buddy, your spouse, your priest, your professor, the President, the dictator, when what they say contradicts what you know from your own experience? That way lies demagoguery, religious intolerance, and worse. Too often leaders have manipulated the populace: All Muslims want the overthrow of the West? But what about my neighbor who's Muslim and a city councilor? You have to forget your own experience to believe the Big Lie. They repeat it over and over and over again until you begin to believe it, even when your own experience says it isn't so.

Oh, we get the idea. Don't trust the politicians. No. It's a lot closer to home than that. Every rumor, all the gossip you hear, compare it to what *you* know about the person or situation. Don't repeat it. Be rational, not part of the humming crowd.

Still, there are times we shouldn't trust our own experience. Sometimes our memory is not reliable. As Sgt. Carlson of the Las Vegas Police Department says, "Eyewitnesses are terrible. You get a gun stuck in your face and you can't remember anything." The police do line-ups, putting a suspect to be identified by a witness among other people who look a bit similar. The police have to be very careful not to say anything that may influence the witness, because memory is malleable.

The state of the world around us can also affect our observations and make our personal experience unreliable. You could honestly say you were sure the other driver didn't put on a turn signal, when it was the rain and distractions that made you not notice.

But even then, there are times we're right not to trust our own experience. You go to the circus and see a magician cut a lady in half. You *saw* it, so it has to be true. Yet you don't believe it. Why? Because it contradicts too much else you know about the world.

Or stranger still: Day, after day, after day we see the sun rise in the east and set in the west, yet we say the sun isn't moving, the earth is. We don't accept our own experience because there's a long story, a theory of how the earth turns on its axis and revolves around the sun. And that story explains neatly and clearly so many other phenomena, like the seasons and the movement of stars in the skies, that we accept it. A convincing argument has been given for us to reject our own experience, and that argument builds on other experiences of ours.

> • We accept a claim if we know it is true from our own experience.
> • We reject a claim if we know it is false from our own experience.
> *Exceptions*
>   —We have good reason to doubt our memory or our perception.
>   —The claim contradicts other experiences of ours, and there is a
>   good argument (theory) against the claim.

But too often we remember what we deduced from our experience, not what we actually experienced. Look at Tom's cartoon writing lesson on p. 56. He said he saw the guy grab the purse. But he didn't see that; he inferred it.

Exercises for Sections A and B.1

1. Why can't we require that every claim be backed up?

2. What three choices can we make about whether to believe a claim?

3. If the conclusion of a valid argument is false, why must one of the premises be false?

4. Give an example of a rumor or gossip you heard in your personal life recently that you believed. Did you have good reason to believe it? Why?

5. We can tell that a rumor or gossip is coming up when someone says, "Guess what I heard." Give five other phrases that alert us similarly.

6. Shouldn't you trust an encyclopedia over your own experience? Explain.

7. Give an example of a claim that someone made this week that you knew from your own experience was false.

8. Give an example of a claim that you believed was true from memory, but really you were making a deduction from your experience.

9. When is it reasonable for us to accept a claim that disagrees with our own experience? Give an example (not from the text) of a claim that it is reasonable for you to accept even though it seems false from your own experience.

10. Remember the last time this class met? Answer the following about your instructor.
a. Male or Female?	f. Did he/she bring a backpack to class? Describe it.
b. Hair color?	g. Did he/she use notes?
c. Eye color?	h. Did he/she get to class early?
d. Approximate height?	i. Did he/she wear a hat?
e. Approximate weight?	j. Is he/she left-handed or right-handed?

11. Remember the last time this class met? Answer the following about the room.
a. How many windows?	g. How many students showed up?
b. How many doors?	h. Chalkboard?
c. How many walls?	i. Lectern?
d. Any pictures?	j. Wastebasket?
e. How high is the ceiling?	k. What kind of floor (concrete, tile, linoleum, carpet)?
f. How many chairs?	l. Did you get out of class early?

12. Which of your answers to Exercises 10 and 11 were from actual memory and which were inferences?

13. List five ways that the physical conditions around us can affect our observations.

14. List five ways that your mental state could affect your observations.

15. Our personal observations are no better than _____ .

16. What does a bad argument tell us about its conclusion?

17. If a strong argument has one false premise and thirteen true premises, what choice should we make about whether to believe its conclusion?

2. Other sources

What about claims from other sources?

> We can accept a claim made by someone we know and trust who is an authority on this kind of claim.

Zoe tells Harry to stay away from the area of town around South 3rd. She's seen people doing drugs there and knows two people who have been held up in that neighbor-hood. He'll believe those premises and likely accept the conclusion that follows from those (and other unstated) premises. It makes sense. Zoe is reliable, and the claims she's making are the sort about which her knowledge would matter.

On the other hand, your mother tells you that you should major in business so you can get ahead in life. Should you believe her? She can tell you about her friends' children. But what are the chances of getting a good job with a degree in business? It would be more reasonable to check with the local colleges where they keep records on the hiring of graduates. Don't reject her claim. Suspend judgment until you get more information.

Other authorities we don't know as well are sometimes reliable, too. For example, the Surgeon General announces that smoking is bad for your health. She's got no axe to grind. She's a physician. She's in a position to survey the research on the subject. It's reasonable to believe her.

> We can accept a claim made by a reputable authority whom we can trust as an expert on this kind of claim and who has no motive to mislead.

The doctor hired by the tobacco company says there's no proof that smoking is addictive or causes lung cancer. Is he an expert on smoking-related diseases or a pediatrician? It matters in deciding whether to trust his ability to interpret the epidemiological data. And he has a motive to mislead, being paid by the tobacco companies. There's no reason to accept his claim, and some motive to reject it.

And when the Surgeon General says that marijuana should not be legal, we should ask what kind of authority she is on this subject. Is she a politician? What kind of expertise does she have on matters of law and public policy? She's an authority figure, but not an expert on *this* kind of claim. No reason to accept her claim just because she said so.

Which authorities we trust and which we disregard change from era to era. It was the lying by Presidents Nixon and Johnson that led many of us to distrust pronouncements from the government. It was the Chicago police killing the Black Panthers in their beds and calling it self-defense that convinced many of us not to accept what big city police say. I remember when I visited Denmark in 1965 as an exchange student, they asked me who I thought killed President Kennedy. I said, "Oswald." They asked me why I believed that. I said because the FBI said so. They all shook their heads in sadness, right after they stopped laughing.

The moral is that some authorities are more trustworthy than others, even in their own areas of expertise. Some may have motive to mislead. The more you tell the truth, the more likely you are to be believed; but even one lie can ruin your reputation for reliability.

What are you to do if the authorities disagree? Suspend judgment. Except that you don't always have that option. If you're on a jury where two ballistics experts disagree on whether the bullet that killed the victim came from the defendant's gun, what should you do? You have to make a decision. Even if you think an authority has the expertise to speak on a subject and has no motive to mislead, you'll still have to use your judgment.

Up to this point we've considered whether to believe people who claim to be knowledgeable. But sometimes we can rely on the quality and reputation of an organization or reference work. For example, *The New England Journal of Medicine* is regularly quoted in newspapers, and for good reason. The articles in it are subjected to peer review: Experts in the subject are asked to evaluate whether the research was done to scientific standards. That journal is notable for having high scientific standards, and its official website is similarly reliable.

The National Geographic has less reliable standards, since they pay for their own research. But it's pretty reliable about natural history.

What about the *Dictionary of Biography*? There's probably no motive for bias in it, though it may be incomplete. Yet it's often hard to get a better source of information about, say, a 19th century physician.

> We can accept a claim in a reputable journal or reference source.

On the Internet you're likely to come across sites with very impressive names. But anyone can start up an organization called the "American Institute for Economic Analysis," or any other title you like, and get an address that ends with ".org". A name is not enough to go by.

There are good sources for checking about the history and reputation of an institute, for example, *Research Centers Directory* in your library and on the Internet, or the *Encyclopedia of Medical Organizations and Agencies* in the library. There's no reason to accept a claim made by an "institute" you don't know about.

Most remote from our experience and least reliable is what we hear and read from what is called "the media." That includes newspapers, television, radio, magazines. Remember, what you read on the Internet is not personal experience.

With these sources it's partly like trusting your friend and partly like trusting an authority. The more you read a particular newspaper, for instance, the better you'll be able to judge whether to trust its news gathering as reliable or not. The more you read a particular magazine, the better you'll be able to judge whether there's an editorial bias.

> We can accept a claim in a media outlet that's usually reliable.

Here are three factors that are important in evaluating a news report.

• *The outlet has been reliable in the past.*
A local paper seems to get the information correct about local stories most of the time. It's probably trustworthy in its account of a car accident. *The National Enquirer* gets sued a lot for libel, so it may not be reliable about the love life of a movie star.

• *The outlet doesn't have a bias on this topic.*
A television network consistently gives a bias against a particular presidential candidate. So when it says that the candidate contradicted himself twice yesterday, you should take it with a grain of salt. That may be true, but it may be a matter of interpretation. Or it may be plain false.

Bias often follows the money. Try to find out who owns the media outlet or who its principal advertisers are. If you hear NBC saying what a good job General Electric Co. is doing in the "reconstruction" of Iraq, it's worth knowing that GE owns NBC.

• *The source being quoted is named.*
Do you know who wrote the articles you read in your newspaper? "From our sources" or no byline at all often means that the article is simply a reprint of a publicity handout from a company.

Remember those Department of Defense unnamed sources? Don't trust them. "Usually reliable sources" are not even as reliable as the person who is quoting them, and anyway, they've covered themselves by saying "usually." And when someone is unwilling to admit being a source, it's a sign he or she may have a motive to mislead. An unnamed source is no better than a rumor. *There's never good reason to accept a claim from an unnamed source.* That's particularly important to remember when you're looking at sites on the Internet.

In summary, we have our personal experience and what we learn from other sources. And we have to weigh that against what new claims are presented to us. For example, a buddy tries to convince you that you shouldn't go to a restaurant with a friend because she has AIDS and you could catch it from eating at the same table with her. You reject the claim that you can catch AIDS in that manner, because you've read in a public health pamphlet that AIDS can be transmitted only through contact with bodily fluids. You make your own argument: AIDS can only be transmitted through contact with bodily fluids; when eating at a restaurant with a friend it is extremely unlikely that you'll share bodily fluids with her; so it's safe to go to a restaurant with a friend who has AIDS.

> We can reject a claim that contradicts other claims we know to be true.

Sometimes, though, it isn't that we know one claim is true and the other false, but that two *contradictory* claims are offered to us as premises, as in Example 11 of Chapter 4, on p. 66. In that case, all we can do is suspend judgment.

Here, then, are the criteria we can use in evaluating unsupported claims.

Summary: When to accept and when to reject a claim

PERSONAL EXPERIENCE

Accept: We know the claim is true from our own experience.

Reject: We know the claim is false from our own experience.
(Exceptions: We have good reason to doubt our memory or our perception; the claim contradicts other experiences of ours, and there is a good argument against the claim.)

Reject: The claim contradicts other claims we know to be true.

OTHER SOURCES

Accept: The claim is made by someone we know and trust, and the person is an authority on this kind of claim.

Accept: The claim is made by a reputable authority whom we can trust as an expert about this kind of claim and who has no motive to mislead.

Accept: The claim is put forward in a reputable journal or reference.

Accept: The claim is in a media source that's usually reliable and has no obvious motive to mislead, and the original source is named.

We don't have criteria for when to **suspend judgment** on a claim. That's the default choice when we don't have good reason to accept or reject a claim.

Remember that these criteria are given in order of importance. Regardless of how good the source may seem to be, you still need to trust your own experience.

> "Who are you going to believe, me or your own eyes?"   Groucho Marx

Teacher Deb Harris could hardly believe what she was reading to her fourth-grade class. Whales in Lake Michigan?

But that's what it said in her "Michigan Studies Weekly," a newspaper distributed to 462 teachers statewide. Harris called Utah-based Studies Weekly, Inc., which puts out the teaching aid, but she said an editor stood behind the story. "I've lived here all my life—there are no whales in Lake Michigan," Harris recalled telling the editor.

A retraction was later posted on the company's Web site with an explanation that the false information came from a different Internet site intended as a joke. "We at Studies Weekly want this to be a lesson to you," the apology said. "Not all Web sites are true, and you cannot always believe them. When researching, you should always look for a reliable site that has credentials (proof of truthfulness)." Studies Weekly publications have a circulation of 1.2 million readers in third through sixth grades nationwide.

The article read: "Every spring, the freshwater whales and freshwater dolphins begin the 1300-mile migration from Hudson Bay to the warmer waters of Lake Michigan." In reality, the closest whales get to Michigan is the salty estuary at the mouth of the St. Lawrence River, which is home to beluga whales.

Associated Press, November 17, 2002

Exercises for Section B

1. When should we suspend judgment on a claim?

2. a. Give five criteria for accepting an unsupported claim.
   b. Give two criteria for rejecting an unsupported claim.

3. Explain why we should apply the criteria listed in the summary in the order in which they are listed.

4. a. Describe two people you encounter regularly whose word you trust and say why you believe them.
   b. Give an example of a claim that one of them made that you shouldn't accept because the knowledge or expertise he or she has does not bear on that claim.

5. List three *categories* of authorities you feel you can trust. State for which kind of claims those kinds of authorities would be experts.

6. Give a recent example from some media outlet of an authority being quoted whose claims you accepted as true.

7. Give an example from some media outlet of an authority being quoted whose expertise does not bear on the claim being put forward, so you have no reason to accept the claim.

8. Give an example of an authority who made a claim recently that turned out to be false. Do you think it was a lie? Or did the person just not know it was false?

9. Give an example of a claim you've heard repeated so often you think it's true, but which you really have no reason to believe.

10. Look at the front page of your local newspaper and the first page of the local section of your newspaper and see if you can determine who wrote each article. Can you do the same with your local TV newscast?

11. Which section of your local newspaper do you think is most reliable? Why?

12. Choose a magazine you often read and tell the class what biases you expect from it. That is, for what kinds of claims in it should you suspend judgment rather than accept?

13. a. What part of a national newscast do you think is most likely to be true? Why?
    b. Which part do you think is least reliable? Why?

14. Give an example of a news story you heard or read that you knew was biased because it didn't give the whole story.

15. Find an article that has quotes from some "think tank" or "institute." Find out what bias that group would have.

16. Here is part of an article from the Associated Press, Nov. 2, 2004. Should you believe it?
    Militants given $500,000 for hostages' release
    Militants [in Iraq] released seven foreign hostages Wednesday after their employer paid $500,000 ransom, while France mustered support from Muslims at home and abroad to push for the release of two French journalists still held captive in Iraq. . . .

    Militants waging a violent 16-month-old insurgency have turned to kidnapping foreigners in recent months as part of their campaign to drive out coalition forces and contractors. Other groups have taken hostages in hopes of extorting ransom, sometimes masking their greed under a cloak of politics.

17. Choose one of the large national news broadcasting outlets and find out who owns the company and what companies it owns or are owned by the same company.

18. Bring to class an article that praises some business or type of business that comes from a magazine that has lots of advertising from that business or type of business.

19. Find an example of an argument that uses claims you know to be false, though not from personal experience. (Letters to the editor in a newspaper are a good source.)

20. You tell your friend who's experimenting with heroin he should stop. It's dangerous. He says you're no expert. Besides, you've never tried it. How do you respond?

21. Your friend who's an avid fan tells you that the basketball game on Saturday has been cancelled. Five minutes later you hear on the radio that tickets are on sale for the game on Saturday. Whom do you believe? Why?

22. Your doctor tells you that the pain in your back can't be fixed without surgery. You go to the health-food store, and the clerk tells you they have a root extract that's been made especially for back pain that'll fix your back. Whom do you believe? Why?

23. Tom: I'm going to start taking steroids.
    Zoe: What? Are you crazy? They'll destroy your body.
    Tom: No way. My coach said it will build me up. And my trainer at the health club said he could get them for me.
    Comment on Tom's reasons for believing that steroids won't harm his body.

24. The old adage "Where there's smoke, there's fire" is a license to believe any rumor. During the initial stages of the war in Kosovo and Yugoslavia, the following appeared in *USA Today* (April 12, 1999). Is the following an example of that adage?

> While it is impossible to independently verify the accounts [of human rights abuses in Kosovo by Serbs] because human rights officials, aide workers and journalists are not allowed to travel freely in Kosovo, the refugees on opposite sides of Macedonia provided similar dates, times and locations of incidents involving Serb soldiers. They also provided identical names of the victims, as well as such details as scars and other physical attributes on the Serb soldiers who took them.

Lee was asked to decide whether to accept, reject, or suspend judgment on some claims, with an explanation of what criteria he's using. Dr. E didn't make any comments on his homework, since Lee's answers are good.

Suzy prefers to go out with athletes.

accept   reject   *suspend judgment*

criteria: Personal experience. She told me so.

Japanese are good at math.

accept   *reject*   *suspend judgment*

criteria: I know everyone thinks this is so, but it's just a stereotype, isn't it? I know a couple who aren't <u>real</u> good at math, but maybe they mean "almost all"? It just seems so unlikely.

Crocodiles are found only in Asia and Africa.

accept   reject   *suspend judgment*

criteria: I think this is true. At least I seem to remember hearing it. Crocodiles are the ones in Africa and alligators in the U.S. But I'm not sure. So I guess I should suspend judgment.

---

25. Evaluate the following claims by saying whether you accept, reject, or suspend judgment, citing the criteria you are using to make that decision.

    a. Toads give you warts. (said by your mother)
    b. Toads give you warts. (said by your doctor)
    c. The moon rises in the west.
    d. The Pacers beat the Knicks 92–84 last night. (heard on your local news)
    e. They're marketing a new liposuction machine you can attach to your vacuum cleaner. (in the weekly supplement to your Sunday paper)
    f. You were speeding. (said by a police officer)
    g. Boise-Cascade has plans to log all old-growth forests in California. (said by a Sierra Club representative)
    h. The United States government was not involved in the recent coup attempt in Venezuela. (unnamed sources in the Defense Department, by the Associated Press)
    i. Cats are the greatest threat to public health of any common pet. (said by the author of this book)

j. Cats are the greatest threat to public health of any common pet.
(said by the Surgeon General)

k. Crocodiles weep after eating their victims, hence the term "crocodile tears."
(in the travel section of your local newspaper)

l. They've started serving sushi at KFC. (said by your friend)

m. State Representative Hansen-Fong: The streets aren't safe. We need to get tougher on crime. We should lock up more of those drug-pushers and scare people into obeying the law. Get more police, lock the criminals up, and throw the key away. And we also need to reduce taxes. We can't afford the bond proposition to build a new prison.

C. Advertising and the Internet

1. Advertising

The truth-in-advertising laws weren't written because all the advertisers were always telling us the truth. Many advertisements are arguments, with the (often unstated) conclusion that you should buy the product, or frequent the establishment, or use the service. Sometimes the claims are accurate, especially in print advertising for medicines. But sometimes they are not. There's nothing special about them, though. They should be judged by the criteria we've already considered.

If you think there should be more stringent criteria for evaluating ads, you're not judging other claims carefully enough.

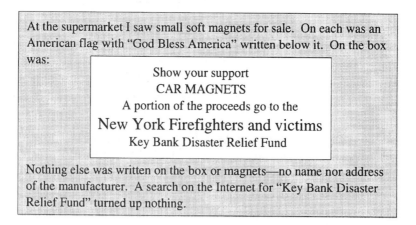

At the supermarket I saw small soft magnets for sale. On each was an American flag with "God Bless America" written below it. On the box was:

> Show your support
> CAR MAGNETS
> A portion of the proceeds go to the
> New York Firefighters and victims
> Key Bank Disaster Relief Fund

Nothing else was written on the box or magnets—no name nor address of the manufacturer. A search on the Internet for "Key Bank Disaster Relief Fund" turned up nothing.

2. The Internet

Re-read the discussion about advertising. Now ask yourself what reason you have to believe something you read on the Internet. Next time you're ready, mouth agape, to swallow what's up there on the screen, imagine Zoe saying to you, "No, really, you believed *that*?" Don't check your brain at the door when you go online.

> *E-mail regarding W.'s IQ gets F*
>
> You may have seen the forwarded and reforwarded e-mail by now. "President Bush Has Lowest IQ of all Presidents of past 50 years." The note, claiming to summarize a report compiled by the Lovenstein Institute of Scranton, Penn., shows that George W. Bush is the possessor of an intelligence quotient of a pitiful 91, the lowest such rating of any man to hold the position of U.S. President in the past 70 years. According to the e-mail, the Lovenstein Institute rated the presidents based on scholarly achievements, speaking ability, and "several other factors."
>
> Believable, right? Not so fast, retort urban legend-debunking Websitessnopes2.com and urbanlegends.about.com. Though no doubt many political lefties will find the study both credible and satisfying (the Dems outscore their GOP counterparts by an average of 39.5 points), there's one minor problem: the Lovenstein Institute doesn't even appear to exist. The barebones site at http://lovenstein.org offers a copy of the "study" and not much else, save for a lone photo of an iceberg. That didn't stop at least six newspapers, including the Russian *Pravda* and the U.K.'s *Guardian*, from reporting the story as actual fact.
>
> *The Alibi* (Albuquerque), November 15, 2001
>
> Now ask yourself why you should believe this article.

And speaking of the Internet, avoid those sites that sell you essays—if you want your instructor to assume that you can and want to reason well, that you're knowledgeable about what you write, and that you're not lying. "Plagiarism," after all, is just a fancy name for "lying."

Exercises for Section C

1. Fill in the blanks: A _____ and his (or her!) _____ are soon _____ .

2. What difference is there between how we evaluate an advertisement and how we evaluate any other (implicit) argument?

3. Find an advertisement from some magazine or newspaper and evaluate the claims in it.

4. Identify a website whose claims you believe, and explain why you consider it to be a reliable source. (Don't use a personal website of friends or family—or yourself.)

5. a. Print out a page of a website devoted to UFOs.
   b. Evaluate it: Are any sentences too vague to be claims? Are the claims plausible? Contradictory? Is there an argument? Is the argument good?
   c. Trade with a classmate to comment on each other's evaluation.

Exercises 6–8 are real advertisements. Evaluate them in terms of the criteria in this chapter.

6. Maxell media—offers 100 years of archival life! Delivers quality you can trust! (MacMall catalogue, 2003)

7. *Pet Healer* Pet Healer with psychic abilities to communicate with pets that have left

this earthly plane. Contact 292–xxxx.   Suggested donation: $25–$100.
(*Crosswinds Weekly*, Albuquerque)

8.   *$250,000* is what you can make per year playing CRAPS
   Finally: a two-part video and book written by a top Las Vegas
      gaming expert that is easy to follow. In fact it's
                     CRAP$ MADE EASY
   You do not need a large bankroll to get started.
   Order toll free 1-800-xxx-xxxx and receive
   • 1 hour instructional video   • Regulation dice and playing chips
   • 150 page book with graphs charts, and inside tips
   • Pocket-sized game card for quick reference   . . . $59.95 . . .
   • Felt layout for home play

9.   Evaluate the website of McWhortle Enterprises at <www.McWhortle.com>.

D. Common Mistakes in Evaluating Premises

1. Arguing backwards

Someone gives an argument that sounds pretty reasonable, the conclusion of which
we're pretty sure is true. So we think it must be a good argument with true premises.

> Dick had to break up a fight between Puff and Spot, and then he had to
>   take Puff home.
> Dick is allergic to cats.
> So Dick has been sneezing like crazy.

Suzy saw Dick sneezing, and she saw the fight. So she reckons that Dick is allergic
to cats. But she's wrong: Dick is allergic to the weeds at the house where Puff lives.
Suzy is arguing from the truth of the conclusion back to the truth of the premises.
That's backwards.

It's easy to think that when someone gives reasons to believe a claim is true,
and the claim is true, and the reasons sound O.K., it must be that those reasons are
true. But they needn't be; the argument may be defective. *An argument is supposed
to convince us that its conclusion is true, not that its premises are true.*

> *Arguing backwards*   It's a mistake to reason that because we have a strong
> or valid argument with a true conclusion, its premises must be true.

When can we go from the conclusion to the premises? When the conclusion is
false and the argument is valid, we know that one of the premises is *false*.

2. Confusing possibility with plausibility

> The Green Party's just a front to take votes away from the Democrats. The
> Republican party puts a lot of cash into the Green's coffers. And the
> Republicans are behind Ralph Nader, bankrolling his Presidential campaign.
> That's why he ran even though he knew he had no chance to win.

It all sounds so good and it would explain a lot. But don't confuse possibility
with plausibility. Yes, sometimes there are conspiracies, like when the U.S. soldiers
and military tried to cover up their My Lai massacre in Vietnam. But an interesting
explanation is at most a good reason to investigate whether its claims are true.
We need evidence, not just a theory, before we should believe. And for conspiracies,
reckoning what Ben Franklin said, we can be pretty sure evidence will eventually
come out: "Three may keep a secret, if two of them are dead."

3. Bad appeals to authority

When we accept a claim because of who said it, we call that an ***appeal to authority***.
But as in some of the examples we've already seen, folks often accept claims from
people who aren't authorities on the subject or who have a motive to mislead. That's
a ***bad appeal to authority***.

We often treat our friends as authorities. We accept their claims because they
sound like they know what they're talking about, or because we'd be embarrassed
not to. "How can you not believe Senator Domenici about the good intentions of the
oil companies? All of us think he's right." Sometimes it's the conviction that if
everyone else believes it or does it, it must be true or right, as when Harry's buddies
said to him Friday night, "Come on, have a drink. Everyone's doing it."

> ***Bad appeal to common belief*** It's usually a mistake to accept a claim as true
> solely because a lot of other people believe it.

If we have further evidence, an appeal to common belief can be good. For
example, when Harry went to Japan he reasoned that since everyone there was
driving on the left-hand side, he should, too.

4. Mistaking the person for the claim

We can sometimes accept a claim because of who said it. But it's always a mistake
to reject a claim as false because of who said it.

> ***Mistaking the person for the claim*** It's a mistake to reject a claim
> solely because of who said it.

> George Orwell and his colleagues detested the British minister in charge of foreign affairs, Lord Halifax. But Orwell agreed with Halifax that atrocities were being committed by foreign governments. In exasperation he said to his colleagues, "They happened even though Lord Halifax said they happened."

5. Mistaking the person for the argument

Suppose Dr. E gives an argument in class that a critical thinking course should be required of every college freshman. His students are not convinced. So he makes the same argument tap-dancing on his desk while juggling beanbags, between each claim whistling "How much is that doggy in the window?" Is the argument any better? Suppose someone in class just found out that Dr. E lost his temper and threw Puff back over the hedge to his neighbor's yard. Is the argument any worse?

We have standards for whether an argument is good or bad. It may be more memorable if Dr. E stands on his head; you may be repulsed by him if you know he threw Puff over a hedge. But the argument is good or bad—independently of how Dr. E or anyone presents it and independently of their credentials.

To *refute* an argument is to show it is bad. Just as we don't reject a claim because of who said it, we don't refute an argument because of who said it.

> **Mistaking the person (or group) for the argument**   It's a mistake to reject an argument solely because of who said it.

Maria: I went to Professor Zzzyzzx's talk about writing last night. He said that the best way to start on a novel is to make an outline of the plot.
Lee: Are you kidding? He can't even speak English.

Lee makes an (implicit) argument: "Don't believe what Professor Zzzyzzx says about writing a novel because he can't speak English well." To make that argument strong you'd need the implausible premise "(Almost) any argument that someone who doesn't speak English gives about writing a novel is bad."

We can also mistake a *group* for an argument:

Dick: This proposed work corps program for the unemployed is a great idea.
Tom: Are you kidding? Wasn't that on the Green Party platform?

Mistaking the group for the argument is a favorite ploy of demagogues. It's an important tool in establishing stereotypes and prejudice.

Often we think we can refute an argument by showing that the person who made it doesn't believe one of the premises or even the conclusion itself.

Harry: We should stop logging old-growth forests. There are very few of them left in the U.S. They are important watersheds and preserve wildlife. And once cut, we cannot recreate them.

Tom: You say we should stop logging old-growth forests? Who are you kidding? Didn't you just build a log cabin on the mountain?

Tom's rejection of Harry's argument is understandable: It seems Harry's actions betray the conclusion he's arguing for. But whether they do or not (perhaps the logs came from the land Harry's family cleared in a new-growth forest), Tom has not answered Harry's argument. Tom is not justified in ignoring an argument because of Harry's actions.

If Harry were to respond to Tom by saying that the logs for his home weren't cut from an old-growth forest, he's been suckered. Tom got him to change the subject, and they will be deliberating an entirely different claim than he intended. It's a phony refutation.

> ***Phony refutation*** It's not a real refutation of an argument to point out that the person who made the argument has done or said something that shows he or she does not believe one of the premises or the conclusion of the argument.

We have a desire for consistency in actions and words. We don't trust hypocrites. But when you spot a contradiction between actions and words, at most you can lay a charge of hypocrisy or irrationality. Sincerity of the speaker is not one of the criteria for an argument to be good, and insisting on that is just mistaking the person for the argument. Besides, the contradiction is often only apparent, not real.

Whether a claim is true or false is not determined by who said it.

Whether an argument is good or bad is not determined by who said it.

> First, realize that it is necessary for an intelligent person to reflect on the words that are spoken, not the person who says them. If the words are true, he will accept them whether he who says them is known as a truth teller or a liar. One can extract gold from a clump of dirt, a beautiful narcissus comes from an ordinary bulb, medication from the venom of a snake.
> Abd-el-Kader, Algerian Muslim statesman, 1858

Exercises for Section D

1. What do we mean when we say that someone is arguing backwards?

2. a. What is an appeal to authority?
   b. Give an example of a bad appeal to authority you heard recently.

3. When are we justified in rejecting a claim because of who said it?

4. Give an example of a bad appeal to common belief you heard recently.

5. Why should you never mistake the person for the argument?

6. Hypocrisy is bad. So why shouldn't we reject anything that smacks of hypocrisy?

7. What does it mean to say that a person has made a phony refutation?

8. Print out a conspiracy theory presented on the Web. Explain why you do or do not believe it is true.

Here are some more of Tom's exercises. He's trying to see if he can distinguish between good and bad reasons for accepting or rejecting claims. You can see Dr. E's comments, too.

Doctor Ball said that for me to lose weight I need to get more exercise, but he's so obese. So I'm not going to listen to him.

This person is mistaking the person for the claim. Looks like a phony refutation to me.

You're right that it's mistaking the person for the claim. But it's not a phony refutation, because we don't know of any argument that Dr. Ball said.

Lucy said I shouldn't go see Doctor Williams because he's had problems with malpractice suits in the past. But Lucy also believes in herbs and natural healing, so she's not going to like any doctors.

Looks O.K. to me. The speaker is just questioning the authority of Lucy and deciding not to accept her claim.

Perhaps. But it might be a case of mistaking the person for the argument. It isn't clear whether the speaker is suspending judgment on a claim or is rejecting Lucy's argument.

Zoe: **Everyone should exercise. It's good for you. It keeps you in shape, gives you more energy, and keeps away depression.**

Dick: **Are you kidding? I've never seen you exercise.**

Phony refutation.   *Right!*

For Exercises 9–20 answer the following:

    a. What, if any, classifications of this section does this fit?

    b. Is it a bad argument?

9. Suzy: I played doubles on my team for four years. It is definitely a more intense game than playing singles.

   Zoe: Yesterday on the news Michael Chang said that doubles in tennis is much easier because there are two people covering almost the same playing area.

   Suzy: I guess he must be right then.

10. Mom: You shouldn't stay out so late. It's dangerous, so I want you home early.

    Son: But none of my friends have curfews and they stay out as long as they want.

11. Manuel: Barbara said divorce'll hurt her kids' emotions.

     Maria: But she goes out with her boyfriend every night leaving the kids and her husband at home. She won't divorce, but she's already hurt her kids. So it doesn't matter if she gets divorced or not.

12. Zoe: You should be more sensitive to the comments you make around people.

     Dick: Of course you'd think that—you're a woman.

13. Zoe: The author of this book said that bad people always make wrong decisions. You need to have virtue to make good use of critical thinking.

     Suzy: What does he know about virtue?

14. Zoe: That program to build a new homeless shelter is a great idea. We need to help get poor people off the streets so they can eventually fend for themselves.

     Suzy: How could you say that? You don't even give money to the homeless who beg on street corners.

15. Zoe: That new law against panhandling is terrible. People have a right to ask for money so long as they aren't really bothering anyone.

     Tom: Sure. And I suppose you believe everything else the ACLU says.

16. Prof. Zzzyzzx: Mine doctor told me cigarettes I should be giving up. He said bad lungs they will give me and my skin wrinkle and my blood pressure to increase. But I do not listen to his talk because he is always smoking like the chimney.

17. Zoe: Don't throw that candy wrapper out of the window. That's terrible. It makes a mess someone else will have to clean up.

     Dick: What are you talking about? Everyone does it. Do you want to reform the whole world?

18. Tom: What do you think about requiring kids at school to wear uniforms?

     Lee: My mom said it was great, so I'm behind it.

19. Manuel: We should tax cigarettes much more heavily.

     Maria: I can't believe you said that. Don't you smoke two packs a day?

20. Maria: What do you think about the new book on financial independence?

     Lee: It must be good; it's on the New York Times Best Seller list.

Summary We can't prove everything. We must take some claims as given or we'd never get started. But when should we accept a claim someone puts forward without proof, and when should we suspend judgment?

     We don't have hard and fast rules, but we can formulate some guidelines. Most important is experience: We can accept a claim that from experience we know is true; we can reject a claim that we know from experience is false. But we need to be sure that it is from our experience and not a faulty memory or a deduction. And there are some times when we can reject what we seem to know from experience because it contradicts other claims that we know are true and explain a lot.

     We are inclined to accept claims from people we trust who know what they're talking about, and to accept claims from respected authorities, though we can give too much deference to an authority. But it's wrong to think a claim is false because of the source. We can argue badly by rejecting anything that a particular person or group says. Worse is when we reject an argument because of who said it. Arguments are good or bad regardless of who made them.

Key Words

accept	bad appeal to authority
reject	bad appeal to common belief
suspend judgment	mistaking the person for the claim
personal experience	mistaking the person for the argument
arguing backwards	refuting an argument
	phony refutation

Further Study   Courses in psychology deal with the reliability of witnesses and the nature of memory. Courses in journalism or communications discuss the reliability of various sources in the media and bias in the media. A short course on how to use the library is offered at most schools in order to help you find your way through reference sources.

A book about the psychology of why people believe claims for bad reasons is *How We Know What Isn't So*, by Thomas Gilovich, The Free Press.

You can look up the Federal Trade Commission's guidelines against deceptive pricing in advertising at <http://www.ftc.gov/bcp/guides/decptprc.htm>.

Writing Lesson 5

Write an argument in outline form either for or against the following:

No unmanned spacecraft landed on Mars; the photos are faked.

- Just list the premises and the conclusion. Nothing more.
- Your argument should be at most one page long.
- Check whether your instructor has chosen a different topic for this assignment.

You know whether you believe this claim. But why do you believe it or doubt it? Make your argument based on the criteria we studied in Chapter 5.

What if you're unsure? You write pro and con lists, yet you can't make up your mind. You're really in doubt. Then write the best argument you can for why someone should suspend judgment on the claim. That's not a cop-out; sometimes suspending judgment is the most mature, reasonable choice to take. But you should have good reasons for suspending judgment.

To give you an idea of what to do, here are arguments by Tom and Suzy on other topics.

Issue: Elvis is still alive.

Definition: By "Elvis" I understand Elvis Presley.

Premises:

Elvis Presley was reported to have died a number of years ago.

All the reputable press agencies reported his death.

Many people went to his funeral,^{A} which was broadcast live.^{B}

His doctor signed his death certificate, according to news reports.

There have been reports that Elvis is alive.

No such report has been in the mainstream media, only in tabloids.^{C}

No physical evidence that he is alive has ever been produced.

No one would have anything to gain by faking his death.^{D}

If Elvis were alive, he would have much to gain by making that known to the public.

Conclusion: Elvis is not alive.

Good. But it could be better. First, split the third premise into two (A and B). I don't know if it was broadcast live, yet I can accept part A.

Second, the sentence C is too vague—what's "mainstream media"? What counts as a "tabloid"? You should cite real sources if you want someone to accept your argument.

And premise D is dubious: Any of his heirs had lots to gain.

Finally, you take for granted that the reader knows why some of your premises are important. But it isn't obvious. Why is A important? To explain, you need to add the glue, a premise or premises linking it to the conclusion. You're still leaving too much unstated. Don't rely so much on the other person making your argument for you. Review Chapters 3 and 4.

Still, I think you have the idea from Chapter 5 and won't be suckered by the conspiracy theorists.

Suzy Queue
Critical Thinking
Section 2
Writing Lesson 5

Issue: The CIA started the cocaine epidemic in the ghettos in order to
control and pacify African-Americans.

Premises:

The CIA has lied to us a lot in the past.

Riots in the past in the ghettos have been a serious problem in the U.S.

The government wants to control African-Americans, so they won't make any
trouble.

African-American people in the ghetto had too much to ~~loose~~ *lose* to start.

Many people in the ghettos believe that the CIA introduced cocaine to the U.S.

It was reported on national news that the CIA was involved with drug running
from Latin America.

Conclusion: The CIA started the cocaine epidemic in the ghettos in order to
control and pacify African-Americans.

*At best you've given reason to <u>suspend judgment</u>. You haven't given me any reason
to believe the claim is <u>true</u>, only that it isn't obviously false.*

*Some of your premises are way too vague ("national news," "serious problem"). And
I can't see how they link to the conclusion. Are you suggesting that if the CIA lied to us
in the past, that makes it highly probable that they introduced cocaine into the ghettos?
That's pretty weak. And big deal that a lot of people in the ghettos believe the CIA
introduced cocaine there. A lot of people think the moon doesn't rise or that it rises in
the West—that doesn't make it true. Are they authorities?*

Review the criteria in Chapter 5.

Review Chapters 1–5

Let's review what we've done.

We began by saying we would study attempts to convince. But that was too broad, so we restricted ourselves to convincing through arguments: collections of claims used to show a particular claim is true.

We said a claim was any declarative sentence that we can view as true or false. But to use that definition took practice. We learned to recognize sentences that posed as claims but were ambiguous or too vague for us to deliberate. Definitions were one way to clear up confusions. And we differentiated among claims, noting that unstated standards could make a claim objective or subjective, and the need for standards for most prescriptive claims.

We saw that there are three tests for an argument to be good: There should be good reasons to believe the premises, and we looked at criteria for that. And the premises should be more plausible than the conclusion. But even if the premises are plausible, it might not be enough to convince. The conclusion should follow from the premises. We decided that means the argument must be either valid or strong.

Often there's a gap between the premises and conclusion. We needed a guide for when it's reasonable to repair an argument and when an argument is unrepairable. We based the guide on the assumptions we need in order to deliberate with someone. Along the way, we also saw various types of bad arguments that are common mistakes in reasoning.

You should now be able to analyze an attempt to convince.

Steps in evaluating an argument

- Is it an argument?
- What's the conclusion?
- What are the premises?
- Are any further premises needed?
- Is it valid? If not, where is it on the scale from very strong to weak?
- Is it a good argument?
- Can it be repaired?

You'll get a lot more practice in analyzing arguments in the following chapters. The review exercises here are designed to make sure you know the *definitions*. You can't apply ideas you only half-remember.

Steps in understanding a definition

- Know what the words mean and be able to recall the definition.
- Know an example of the definition.
- Know an example of something that doesn't fit the definition.
- Practice classifying with the exercises.
- Relate the definition to other concepts you've learned.

The last step is crucial in putting this material together. You may have learned the definition of "valid" and know how to recognize whether an argument is valid, but you don't really understand that definition until you know how it relates to other terms, such as "strong" and "good argument."

Review Exercises for Chapters 1–5

1. What is an argument?

2. What is a claim?

3. a. What is an objective claim?
   b. Give an example of an objective claim.
   c. Give an example of a subjective claim.

4. Can a vague sentence be a claim? Explain.

5. a. What is a prescriptive claim?
   b. Give an example.
   c. What standard, if any, is presupposed by your example?

6. Is a definition a claim? Explain.

7. a. What is a persuasive definition?
   b. Give an example.

8. What is the drawing the line fallacy?

9. What three tests must an argument pass for it to be good?

10. a. What is a valid argument?
    b. Give an example of a valid argument that is good.
    c. Give an example of a valid argument that is bad.

11. a. What does it mean to say an argument is strong?
    b. Give an example of a strong argument that is good.
    c. Give an example of a strong argument that is bad.

12. Is every weak argument bad? Give an explanation or example.

13. How do you show an argument is weak?

14. If a strong argument has eight true premises and one false premise, should we accept the conclusion? Explain.

15. If an argument is bad, what does that tell us about its conclusion?

16. Is every valid or strong argument with true premises good? Give an explanation or example.

17. Should we always prefer valid arguments to strong arguments? Give an explanation or example.

18. State the Principle of Rational Discussion.

19. What is the mark of irrationality?

20. State the Guide to Repairing Arguments.

21. List the circumstances in which we shouldn't repair an argument.

22. a. What is an indicator word?
    b. Is an indicator word part of a claim?

23. What is our most reliable source of information about the world?

24. What three choices can we make about whether to believe a claim?

25. Give five criteria for accepting an unsupported claim.

26. Give two criteria for rejecting an unsupported claim.

27. When should we suspend judgment on a claim?

28. What does it mean to say that someone is arguing backwards?

29. What does it mean to say that someone is mistaking the person for the argument?

30. When are we justified in rejecting a claim because of who said it?

31. When are we justified in rejecting an argument because of who said it?

32. What is a phony refutation?

The STRUCTURE
of ARGUMENTS

6   Compound Claims

A. Consider the Alternatives

1. Compound claims and "or" claims

Some words can link two or more claims together to make a new, compound claim whose truth-value depends on the truth-values of the claims that are part of it. For example, suppose your neighbor says,

> "I'll return your lawn mower or I'll buy you a new one."

Has he promised to return your lawn mower? No. Has he promised to buy you a new lawn mower? No. He's promised to do one or the other. We have one claim, not two.

Compound claim   A compound claim is one composed of other claims, but which has to be viewed as just one claim.

In this chapter we'll look at different kinds of compound claims and see how to reason with them. One word that can link two claims to make a compound is "or":

> Either a Democrat will win the election or a Republican will win.
> Either some birds don't fly or penguins aren't birds.
> Columbus landed in South Carolina or on some island near there.

Each is just one claim, though made up of two claims. The last one, for instance, contains:

> Columbus landed in South Carolina.
> Columbus landed on some island near South Carolina.

> *Alternatives* Alternatives are the claims that are the parts of an "or" claim.

But not every sentence with two or more claims is compound. For example,

> Dr. E is a professor because he teaches critical thinking.

This is an argument, not a claim: the word "because" is an indicator word.

2. The contradictory of a claim

Because a compound claim is made up of other claims, it's easy to get confused about how to say it's false.

> *Contradictory of a claim* The contradictory of a claim is one that has the opposite truth-value in all possible circumstances. Sometimes a contradictory is called the *negation* of a claim.

The contradictory of "Spot is a doberman" is "Spot is not a doberman." But the contradictory of "Spot will never learn to fetch" is "Spot will learn how to fetch," and "not" doesn't appear in it.

Claim	*Contradictory*
Spot is barking.	Spot isn't barking.
Dick isn't a student.	Dick is a student.
Suzy will go to the movies or she will stay home.	Suzy won't go to the movies and she won't stay home.
Tom or Suzy will pick up Manuel for class today.	Neither Tom nor Suzy will pick up Manuel for class today.

In order to discuss the forms of compound claims, we'll use the letters A, B, C, D, . . . to stand for any claims, and "not A" to stand for the contradictory of a claim.

> ***Contradictory of an* or *claim***   A *or* B has contradictory *not* A *and not* B.

For example, the following fits into this form:

Either Lee will pick up Manuel, or Manuel won't come home for dinner.
   contradictory:
Lee won't pick up Manuel, and Manuel will come home for dinner.

We can also use *neither* A *nor* B for the contradictory of A *or* B.

Using "and" to join two claims creates a compound, but it's simpler to consider each claim independently. For example,

Pigs can catch colds, and they can pass colds on to humans.

When is this true? Exactly when both "Pigs can catch colds" is true and "Pigs can pass colds on to humans" is true. So in an argument we'd have to treat each of those claims separately anyway. It's the same with "but."

Pigs can catch colds, but dogs can't.

This is true when both parts are true. So we might as well view each claim independently, as if the sentence is just a list of claims. "But" works the same as "and" in an argument—it's just a stylistic variation.

> ***Contradictory of an* and *claim***   A *and* B has contradictory *not* A *or not* B.

Pigs can catch colds, but dogs can't.
   contradictory: Pigs can't catch colds, or dogs can catch colds.

Exercises for Sections A.1 and A.2

1. What is a compound claim?
2. What do we call the parts of an "or" claim?
3. What is the contradictory of a claim?
4. How do you say the contradictory of "A or B"?
5. How do you say the contradictory of "A and B"?
6. Why can we take both A and B to be premises when someone says "A and B"?

For each of the following, write the contradictory of the claim. If it is an "or" claim, identify the alternatives.

7.   Inflation will go up or interest rates will go up.

8.   Manuel can go everywhere in his wheelchair.

9.   Maria or Lee will pick up Manuel after classes.

10. Neither Maria nor Lee has a bicycle.

11. You're either for me or against me.

12. You'd better stop smoking in here or else!

13. AIDS cannot be contracted by touching nor by breathing air in the same room as a person infected with AIDS.

14. Maria will go shopping, but Manuel will cook.

15. Zoe (to Dick): Will you take the trash out or do I have to?

3. Reasoning with "or" claims

Often we can determine that an argument is valid or weak by looking at the role a compound claim plays in it. For example,

> Either there is a wheelchair ramp at the school dance, or Manuel stayed home.
> But there isn't a wheelchair ramp at the school dance.
> Therefore, Manuel stayed home.

The argument is valid: There's no possible way for the premises to be true and the conclusion false at the same time.

This is just one example of lots of arguments that have the same form and are valid. In order to illustrate that form in a diagram, I'll use an arrow (⟶) to stand for "therefore," and the symbol "+" to indicate an additional premise.

Excluding possibilities
A or B

not A   *Valid*

So B

$$\underline{A \text{ or } B \; + \; not\,A}$$
↓
B

This form of argument is sometimes called the *disjunctive syllogism.*

We also have the valid argument form: A or B, not B, therefore A.
Or there may be more than two alternatives:

Somebody's cat killed the bird that always sang outside. *1*
Either it was Sarah's cat or the neighbor's cat or some stray. *2*
Sarah says it wasn't her cat, *3* because hers was in all day. *4*
My neighbor says her cat never leaves the house. *5*
So it must have been a stray. *6*

From *3* and *4* we get:

Sarah's cat didn't kill the bird. *a*

(Lowercase letters mark claims that are added to an argument.) And from *5* we get:

My neighbor's cat didn't kill the bird. *b*

With *2* rewritten as "Either Sarah's cat killed the bird, or the neighbor's cat killed the bird, or some stray cat killed the bird," we now have:

A or B or C
not A, not B
Therefore C.

Sometimes we can only reduce the possibilities, not exclude all but one:

Either all criminals should be locked up forever, or we should put more
    money into rehabilitating criminals, or we should accept that our
    streets will never be safe, or we should have some system for
    monitoring ex-convicts. *1* (*this is all one claim*)
We can't lock up all criminals forever, *2* because it would be too expensive. *3*
We definitely won't accept that our streets will never be safe. *4*
So either we should put more money into rehabilitating criminals, or we
    should have some system for monitoring ex-convicts. *5*

The argument is valid, because *2* and *4* eliminate some of the possibilities given in *1*. But even if *1* is true (it really lists all the possibilities), all we get from this argument is another "or" claim—we've reduced the possibilities.

> A or B or C or D
>   not A, not C
> Therefore, B or D.

Arguments like this are valid, too.

4. False dilemmas

Zoe has made a valid argument, but not a good one. She's posed a false dilemma: "You're either going to have to stop smoking those nasty expensive cigars or we'll have to get rid of Spot" is false. Dick could respond that Zoe could give up talking to her mother long distance every day. Excluding possibilities is a valid form of argument. But valid arguments need not be good. We get a bad argument when the "or" claim doesn't list all the possibilities.

> ***False dilemma***   A false dilemma is a bad use of excluding possibilities where the "or" claim is false or implausible. Sometimes just the dubious "or" claim itself is called a "false dilemma."

For example,

> Society can choose high environmental quality but only at the cost of lower tourism or more tourism and commercialization at the expense of the ecosystem, but society must choose. It involves a tradeoff.
>
> Robert Sexton, *Exploring Economics*

The alternatives are claimed to be mutually exclusive. But Costa Rica has created a lot of tourism by preserving almost 50% of its land in parks. When you see a *versus*-claim, think, "Is this a false dilemma?"

To avoid false dilemmas, we have to imagine other possibilities.

Exercises for Section A

1. Give an "or" claim that you know is true, though you don't know which of the alternatives is true.

2. a. State the form of valid arguments called "excluding possibilities."
   b. Give two other forms of valid arguments that use "or" claims.

3. What is a false dilemma?

4. Give an example of a false dilemma you've used or which was used on you recently.

5. Why is using a false dilemma so good at making people do what you want them to do? Is it a good way to convince?

6. Show that the argument about Manuel going to the dance on p. 116 is a false dilemma.

7. Sometimes a false dilemma is stated using an "if . . . then . . ." claim:

    > If you don't stop smoking, you're going to die.
    >   (Either you stop smoking or you will die.)

    > Mommy, if you don't take me to the circus, then you don't really love me.
    >   (Either you take me to the circus or you don't love me.)

    > If you can't remember what you wanted to say, it's not important.
    >   (Either you remember what you want to say or it's not important.)

    Give two examples of false dilemmas stated using "if . . . then . . .".
    Trade with a classmate to rewrite them as "or" claims.

8. A particular form of false dilemma is the *perfectionist dilemma,* which assumes:

    > Either the situation will be perfect if we do this, or we shouldn't do it.
    > (*All or nothing at all.*)

    > — I'm voting for raising property taxes to pay for improvements to the schools.
    > — Don't be a fool. No matter how much money they pour into the schools, they'll never be first-rate.

    a. Give the unstated premise that shows that this argument is a false dilemma.
    b. Give an example of a perfectionist dilemma you've heard or read.

Evaluate Exercises 9–13 by answering the following:

Argument? (yes or no)
Conclusion (if unstated, add it):
Premises:
Additional premises needed (if none, say so):
Classify (with the additional premises):   valid   strong ——————— weak
Good argument? (choose one—if it's a false dilemma, say so)
   • It's good (passes the three tests).
   • It's valid or strong, but you don't know if the premises are true, so you can't say if it's good or bad.
   • It's bad because it's unrepairable (state which of the reasons apply).

9. Tom: Look, either you'll vote for the Republican or the Democratic candidate for president.

   Lee: No way I'll vote for the Democrat.

   Tom: So you'll vote for the Republican.

10. Lee: Manuel and Tom went to the basketball game if they didn't go to the library.

    Maria: I know they're not at the library because I was just there.

    Lee: So they must have gone to the basketball game.

11. Tom: Both Lee and I think they should allow logging on Cedar Mountain. You do, too—don't you, Dick?

    Dick: Actually, no, . . .

    Tom: I didn't know you were one of those environmentalist freaks.

12. Dick: Somebody knocked over our neighbor's trash can last night. Either our neighbor hit it with her car when she backed out again, or a raccoon got into it, or Spot knocked it over.

    Zoe: Our neighbor didn't hit it with her car, because she hasn't been out of her house since last Tuesday.

    Dick: It wasn't a raccoon, because Spot didn't bark last night.

    Zoe: Spot! Bad dog! Stay out of the trash!

13. Zoe: We should get rid of Spot. He keeps chewing on everything in the house.

    Dick: But why does that mean we should get rid of him?

    Zoe: Because either we train him to stop chewing or we get rid of him. And we haven't been able to train him.

    Dick: But I love Spot. We can just make him live outdoors.

    (Evaluate what Zoe says as an argument. Consider Dick's answer in doing so.)

B. Conditionals

1. Conditionals and their contradictories

Suppose your instructor says to you:

> If you do well on the final exam, then I'll give you an A in this course.

This is *one* claim. If it shows up in an argument, we don't say one premise is "You do well on the final exam" and another is "I'll give you an A in this course." Rather *if* you do well, *then* your instructor will give you an A in this course. There is no promise to give you an A, only a *conditional* promise. If you do poorly on the final exam, your instructor is not obligated to give you an A.

Sometimes "then" is left unsaid, or the order of the two parts is reversed:

a. If Dick loves Zoe, he will give her an engagement ring.

b. I'll meet you at the cafeteria if they're not serving beef stroganoff.

And sometimes neither "if" nor "then" is used, yet it's clear the claim makes sense as an "if . . . then . . ." claim. For example,

c. Bring me an ice cream cone and I'll be happy.

> **Conditional claim**   A claim is a conditional if it can be rewritten as an "if . . . then . . ." claim that must have the same truth-value.
>
>   In a conditional (rewritten as) "If A, then B", the claim A is the **antecedent**, and the claim B is the **consequent**.

In (a), the antecedent is "Dick loves Zoe," and the consequent is "He will give her an engagement ring."

In (b), though the order is reversed, it is the part that follows "if" that is the antecedent, "They're not serving beef stroganoff," and the consequent is "I'll meet you at the cafeteria."

In (c), the antecedent is "Bring me an ice cream cone," and the consequent is "I'll be happy."

How do we form the contradictory of a conditional? Yesterday Manuel said, "If Maria called in sick today, then Lee had to go to work." To decide whether this is true, we ask whether Lee was obligated to work if Maria called in sick. He wasn't: She called in sick and he didn't have to go to work.

> **Contradictory of a conditional**   *If* A, *then* B has contradictory A *but not* B.

Zoe: I'm so worried. Spot got out of the yard. If he got out of the yard, then the dogcatcher got him, I'm sure.

Suzy: Don't worry. I saw Spot. He got out of the yard, but the dogcatcher didn't get him.

Contradictory

The contradictory of a conditional is not another conditional.

Sometimes, when we reason about how the world might be, we use a conditional with a false antecedent:

If cats had no fur, they would not give people allergies.

We could form the contradictory as for any conditional. But more commonly we use words like "although" or "even if":

Even if cats had no fur, they would still give people allergies.

"Even if" does *not* make a conditional. "Even if" is used in much the same way as "although" or "despite that."

Exercises for Section B.1

1. a. What is a conditional?
    b. Is a conditional a compound claim?

2. Make a conditional promise to your instructor that you believe you can keep.

3. What is the antecedent of a conditional?

4. What is a contradictory of a claim?

5. Make up five examples of conditional claims that don't use the word "if" or don't use the word "then." At least one should have the consequent first and antecedent last. Exchange with a classmate to identify the antecedents and consequents.

6. How do you say the contradictory of "If A, then B"?

7. a. Give a contradictory of:

    (*) If Suzy studies hard, then she'll pass Dr. E's class.

    Show that each of (b)–(d) is not a contradictory of (*) by giving for each a possibility where both it and (*) could be true or both of them could be false at the same time.
    b. If Suzy doesn't study hard, then she'll pass Dr. E's class.
    c. If Suzy doesn't study hard, then she won't pass Dr. E's class.
    d. If Suzy studies hard, then she won't pass Dr. E's class.

8. Make up two conditionals and two "or" claims. Exchange them with a classmate to write the contradictories.

Here are two examples of Tom's work on conditionals.

Getting an A in critical thinking means that you studied hard.
Conditional? (yes or no) Yes.
Antecedent: You get an A in critical thinking.
Consequent: You studied hard.
Contradictory: You got an A in critical thinking, but you didn't study hard.
   (or Even though you got an A in critical thinking, you didn't study hard.)
Good work.

Spot loves Dick because Dick plays with him.
Conditional? (yes or no) No.
Antecedent: Spot loves Dick. *No*
Consequent: Dick plays with him. *No*
Contradictory: Spot loves Dick but Dick doesn't play with him.. *No*

You're right, it's not a conditional: the word "because" tells you it's an argument. But if it's not a conditional, then there is no antecedent and no consequent. And there can't be a contradictory of an argument.

For each exercise below, answer the following. Remember that even though it might not be a conditional, it could still have a contradictory.

Conditional? (yes or no)
Antecedent:
Consequent:
Contradictory:

9. If Maria goes shopping, then Manuel will cook.

10. Lee will take care of Spot next weekend if Dick will help him with his English exam.

11. If you don't apologize, I'll never talk to you again.

12. Flo's mother won't go to the movie if she can't get someone to watch Flo.

13. Loving someone means you never throw dishes at them.

14. Since 2 times 2 is 4, and 2 times 4 is 8, I should be ahead $8, not $7.

15. Get me some cake mix at the store and I'll bake a cake.

16. Tuna is good for you even though they say you shouldn't eat it more than once per week.

17. Tom: Being late for football practice will make the coach really mad.

18. If it's really true that if Dick takes Spot for a walk Dick will do the dishes, then Dick won't take Spot for a walk.

19. If Manuel went to the basketball game, then he either got a ride with Maria or he left early to wheel himself over there.

20. When there's a raccoon in the yard, you can be sure that Spot will bark.

21. Lee didn't go to the lecture because he knew Maria would take notes.

2. Necessary and sufficient conditions

We say that two claims are *equivalent* if each is true exactly when the other is. For example, the following are equivalent:

> If interest rates go down, then unemployment will go down.
>
> If unemployment doesn't go down, then interest rates won't go down.

Contrapositive The contrapositive of *If* A, *then* B is *If not* B, *then not* A. A claim and its contrapositive are equivalent.

Sometimes it's easier to understand a conditional via its contrapositive:

> If you get a speeding ticket, then a policeman stopped you.
> *Contrapositive*: If a policeman didn't stop you, then you didn't get a ticket.

Conditionals are crucial for understanding what we mean by necessary or sufficient conditions. For example, what's necessary for getting a driver's license? Well, you've got to pass the driving exam. That is, if you don't pass the driving exam, you won't get a driver's license. There's no way you'll get a driver's license if you don't pass the driver's exam.

What's sufficient for getting money at the bank? Well, cashing a check there will do. That is, if you cash a check at the bank, then you'll get money at the bank.

A is *necessary* for B means *If not* A, *then not* B is true.

A is *sufficient* for B means *If* A, *then* B is true.

For example, passing an eye test is necessary but not sufficient for getting a driver's license. This is the same as saying: "If you don't pass an eye test, you can't get a driver's license" is true, but "If you pass an eye test, then you get a driver's license" is false.

But lots of times we get confused. Here's what Lee and Manuel were saying last week:

Manuel: It's just wrong that Betty didn't make the basketball team.

Lee: Yeah. I watched the tryouts and she was great. She hit a couple three-pointers, and she can really jump.

Manuel: And the coach chose only girls who could jump well and hit three-pointers.

Lee: She had everything you need to get on the team.

Lee thinks that jumping well and hitting three-pointers are sufficient for getting on the team. But what Manuel said is that they're necessary. Lee's got it backwards. This kind of mistake is easy enough to avoid if you translate statements about necessary or sufficient conditions into conditionals.

Here's another example heard on National Public Radio:

Interviewer: So, will we continue to see home schooling in America?

Interviewee: As long as there are parents who love their kids and are willing to work hard, yes.

The last person has said that love and willingness to work hard are enough for home schooling to continue. That may be necessary, but it's certainly not sufficient. Also needed are laws allowing home schooling, a cultural climate encouraging it, ...

Exercises for Section B.2

1. State the contrapositive of:
   a. If Flo plays with Spot, then she has to take a bath.
   b. If Manuel doesn't get his wheelchair fixed by Wednesday, he can't attend class Thursday.
   c. If Maria goes with Manuel to the dance, then Lee will be home alone on Saturday.

2. We know that the following are equivalent claims:
   - If Dick went to the movies, then he got home before 6 p.m.
   - If Dick didn't get home before 6 p.m., then he didn't go to the movies.
   - For Dick to go to the movies, it's necessary for him to get home before 6 p.m.

   Similarly, rewrite each of the following in two ways (using "necessary" or "sufficient" as appropriate):
   a. Suzy will go with Tom to the library if he gets out of practice by 6.
   b. For Dick to take Spot for a walk, it's necessary that it not be raining.
   c. If Spot got out of the yard, then the gate was unlatched.

3. State which of the following hold:

   (i) is necessary for (ii)   (i) is both necessary and sufficient for (ii)

   (i) is sufficient for (ii)   (i) is neither necessary nor sufficient for (ii)

   a. (i) Dr. E had his annual physical examination.
      (ii) Dr. E had an appointment with his physician.

b. (i) Manuel opened a checking account. (ii) Manuel wrote his first check.

c. (i) Zoe won $47 at blackjack. (ii) Zoe was gambling.

d. (i) Maria is divorced. (ii) Maria has an ex-husband.

e. (i) Suzy is over 21. (ii) Suzy can legally drink in this state.

4. Often we say one condition is necessary or sufficient for another, as in "Being over 16 is necessary for getting a driver's license." That means that the general conditional is true: "If you can get a driver's license, then you're over 16."

State which of the following hold:

(i) is necessary for (ii)   (i) is both necessary and sufficient for (ii)

(i) is sufficient for (ii)   (i) is neither necessary nor sufficient for (ii)

a. (i) visiting City Hall   (ii) leaving home

b. (i) having the ability to fly   (ii) being a bird

c. (i) being a U.S. citizen   (ii) being allowed to vote in the U.S.

d. (i) losing at the lottery   (ii) buying a lottery ticket

5. What is a necessary condition for there to be a fire?

6. What is a sufficient condition for you to be happy? Is it necessary?

7. Rewrite each of the following as an "if . . . then . . ." claim if that is possible. If it is not possible, say so.

a. Paying her library fines is required in order for Zoe to get a copy of her transcript.

b. Dick: Since I'm on the way to the store anyway, I'll pick up some dog food.

c. Suzy loves Puff even though he isn't her cat.

d. Of course, Suzy loves Tom despite the coach suspending him for a game.

e. For Tom to get back on the team, he has to do 200 push-ups.

f. Dick apologizing is enough for Zoe to forgive him.

8. The phrase *only if* does not mean the same as *if*:

> Harry will get into graduate school only if his grades place him in the top 10% of his graduating class.

> Harry will get into graduate school if his grades place him in the top 10% of his graduating class.

These are not equivalent. The first gives a necessary condition for Harry to get into graduate school, and it's true. The second gives a sufficient condition, and it's false.

> A *only if* B means the same as *if not* B, *then not* A.

Since we know the right-hand side is equivalent to *if* A, *then* B, we have:

> A *only if* B is equivalent to *if* A, *then* B.

Rewrite each of the following as a conditional and as a statement of a necessary or sufficient condition.

a. Maria will buy a new dress only if she gets a bonus this month.

b. Flo will go over to play with Spot only if her mother lets her.

c. Lee: Only if Tom is back on the team can we win this weekend.

9. From Exercise 8 we have that "A only if B" is equivalent to "if A then B".

> A *if and only if* B means *if* A, *then* B; *and if* B, *then* A.

We use "if and only if" to show that two claims are *equivalent*: each is necessary and sufficient for the other. For example,

> Suzy will marry Tom if and only if he remains faithful to her until graduation.

This means that it is necessary for Tom to stay faithful to Suzy for her to marry him. But it is also sufficient for Tom to stay faithful to Suzy to ensure that she will marry him.

> Give an example of an "if and only if " claim from your own life you know is true.

3. Valid and weak forms of arguments using conditionals

> If Spot barks, then Dick will wake up.
> Spot barked.
> So Dick woke up.

That's valid. It's impossible for the premises to be true and the conclusion false.

> If Suzy calls early, then Dick will wake up.
> Suzy called early.
> So Dick woke up.

This is valid, too.

Notice that these arguments are similar. They have the same *form*:

If <u>Spot barks,</u> *then* <u>Dick will wake up</u>.	*If* <u>Suzy calls early,</u> *then* <u>Dick will wake up</u>.
A B	A B
<u>Spot barked</u>.	<u>Suzy called early</u>.
A	A
So <u>Dick woke up</u>.	*So* <u>Dick woke up</u>.
B	B

Any argument of this form is valid (though not necessarily good, since a premise could be false).

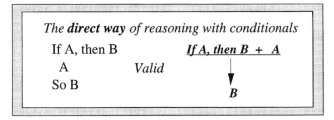

> *The **direct way** of reasoning with conditionals*
>
> If A, then B   *If A, then B + A*
>   A   *Valid*
>   So B   *B*

This way of reasoning is sometimes called *modus ponens*.

We can also reason:

If Spot barks, then Dick will wake up.
Dick didn't wake up.
So Spot didn't bark.

That's valid. After all, if Spot had barked, Dick would have woken up. Similarly:

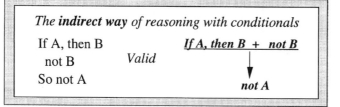

If <u>Suzy calls early</u>, *then* <u>Dick will wake up</u>.
       A   B

<u>Dick didn't wake up</u>.
    not B

So <u>Suzy didn't call early</u>.
     not A

The *indirect way* of reasoning with conditionals

If A, then B   ***If A, then B + not B***
  not B   *Valid*
So not A   ***not A***

This way of reasoning is sometimes called *modus tollens*. Here, again, "not A" and "not B" are shorthand for "the contradictory of A" and "the contradictory of B." For example, this argument also uses the indirect way:

If Suzy doesn't call early, then Zoe won't go shopping.
Zoe went shopping.
So Suzy called early.

Recognizing this form can be hard if "not" occurs in the antecedent or consequent, or if their order is reversed. For example, this uses the indirect way:

Zoe won't go shopping if Dick comes home early.
Zoe went shopping.
So Dick didn't come home early.

<u>Zoe won't go shopping</u> *if* <u>Dick comes home early</u>.
       B   A
<u>Zoe went shopping</u>.
    not B
So <u>Dick didn't come home early</u>.
     not A

To help us see how reasoning with conditionals involves possibilities, look at what Dick has to face every morning:

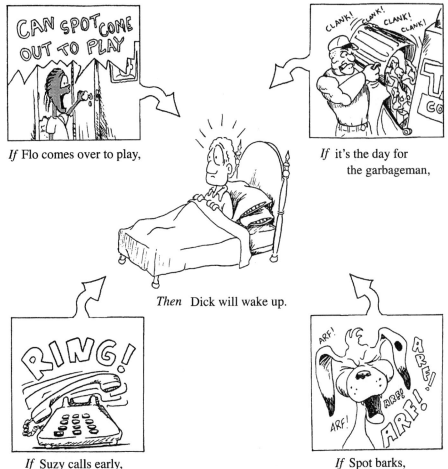

If Flo comes over to play,

If it's the day for
the garbageman,

Then Dick will wake up.

If Suzy calls early,

If Spot barks,

There are many ways that Dick could be awakened. And if he doesn't wake up, then we know that none of those happened.

But it's wrong to reason that if Dick did wake up, then Spot barked. Maybe Suzy called early. Or maybe Flo came over to play. It's reasoning backwards, overlooking possibilities, to reason: If A, then B, B, so A. Yet it's easy to get confused and use this way of reasoning as if it were valid, because it's so similar to the direct way of reasoning with conditionals.

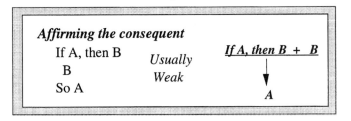

Affirming the consequent

If A, then B   *Usually*   <u>*If A, then B* + *B*</u>
  B   *Weak*   ↓
So A   **A**

Just as there's a weak form that's easy to confuse with the direct way, there's a weak form that's easy to confuse with the indirect way.

> If it's the day for the garbageman, then Dick will wake up.
> It's not the day for the garbageman.   So Dick didn't wake up.

This, too, is overlooking other possibilities. Even though the garbageman didn't come, maybe Flo came over to play, or Spot barked.

Denying the antecedent

If A, then B	*Usually*	*If A, then B* + *not A*
not A	*Weak*	↓
So not B		*not B*

With this form, too, we have to be alert when "not" shows up in the conditional.

If Dick doesn't wake up,	*If* <u>Dick doesn't wake up,</u> *then* <u>Dick will miss his class</u>.
then he'll miss his class.	A B
Dick woke up.	<u>Dick did wake up</u>. *So* <u>Dick didn't miss his class</u>.
So Dick didn't miss his class.	not A not B

But if Dick woke up, can't we at least say that one of those four claims from the picture are true? No, there could be another possibility:

Here's a chart to summarize the valid and weak forms we've seen.

Valid	*Usually Weak*
If A, then B + *A*	*If A, then B* + *B*
↓	↓
B	*A*
If A, then B + *not B*	*If A, then B* + *not A*
↓	↓
not A	*not B*

These weak forms of arguing with conditionals are clear confusions with valid forms, mistakes a good reasoner doesn't make. *When you see one, don't bother to repair the argument.* For example, suppose you hear:

Maria: If Suzy called early, then Dick woke up.
Lee: So Dick didn't wake up.

The obvious premise to add is "Suzy didn't call early," and probably Lee knows that. But it makes the argument weak. So Lee's argument is unrepairable.

Exercises for Section B.3

1. Assume that all of the following conditionals are true:

    * If Dick and Zoe get another dog, then Spot will be happy.
    * If Dick buys Spot a juicy new bone, then Spot will be happy.
    * If Dick spends more time with Spot, then Spot will be happy.
    * If Spot finally learns how to catch field mice, then Spot will be happy.

    Using them:
    a. Give two examples of the direct way of reasoning with conditionals.
    b. Give two examples of the indirect way of reasoning with conditionals.
    c. Give two examples of affirming the consequent. Explain why each is weak in terms of other possibilities.
    d. Give two examples of denying the antecedent. Explain why each is weak in terms of other possibilities.

2. Give an example (not from the text) of the direct way of reasoning with conditionals.

3. Give an example (not from the text) of the indirect way of reasoning with conditionals.

4. Give an example (not from the text) of affirming the consequent. Show that it is weak.

5. Give an example (not from the text) of denying the antecedent. Show that it is weak.

For Exercises 6–11, if there's a claim you can add to make the argument valid according to one of the forms we've studied, add it. If the argument is unrepairable, say so.

6. If Flo comes over early to play, then Spot will bark. So Spot barked.

7. Whenever Flo comes over to play, Spot barks. So Flo didn't come over to play.

8. Tom: Suzy will fail Dr. E's class for sure if she doesn't study hard.
    Harry: So she'll have to repeat that class, right?

9. Zoe will wash the dishes if Dick cooks. So Dick didn't cook.

10. Suzy: Dr. E won't give an exam today if he doesn't finish grading by this afternoon.
    Maria: So Dr. E will give an exam today.

11. If Flo does her homework, then she can watch TV. So Flo did her homework.

12. Here's another valid form of reasoning with conditionals:

> **No matter what**
> If A, then B   ___If A, then B___ + ___If not A, then B___
> If not A, then B   *Valid*
> So B   B

Dick: If I study for my math exam this weekend, we won't be able to have a good time at the beach.

Zoe: But if you don't study for your exam, you'll worry about it like you always do, and we won't be able to have a good time at the beach. So it looks like this weekend is shot.

Give another example of a no-matter-what argument.

4. Reasoning in a chain and the slippery slope

Suppose we know that if Dick takes Spot for a walk, then Zoe will cook dinner. And if Zoe cooks dinner, then Dick will do the dishes. Then we can conclude that if Dick takes Spot for a walk, he'll do the dishes. We can set up a chain of reasoning, a chain of conditionals.

Here's another example:

> If Manuel's wheelchair isn't fixed tomorrow, then he can't go to classes.
> If Manuel can't go to classes, then Lee will have to take notes for him.
> If Lee takes notes for Manuel, then Manuel will have to cook dinner.
> So if Manuel's wheelchair isn't fixed tomorrow, then Manuel will have to cook dinner.

The conclusion is another conditional.

> **Reasoning in a chain** *with conditionals*
> If A, then B   ___If A, then B___ + ___If B, then C___
> If B, then C   *Valid*
> So if A, then C   If A, then C

Reasoning in a chain is important: We go by little steps. Then if A is true, we can conclude C.

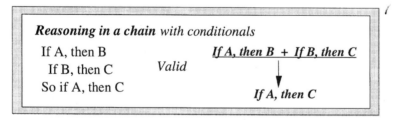

> If A, then B   ___If A, then B___ + ___If B, then C___ + A
> If B, then C   *Valid*
>   A
> So C   C

But this valid form of argument can be used badly. As Lee said to Maria:

> Don't get a credit card! If you do, you'll be tempted to spend money you
> don't have. Then you'll max out on your card. Then you'll be in real
> debt. And you'll have to drop out of school to pay your bills. You'll
> end up a failure in life.

This isn't stated as a series of conditionals, but it's easy to rewrite it that way (that's
Exercise 6 below). Then it will be valid. But it's not a good argument. If you take
the first step (accept the antecedent of the first conditional), then the chain of
conditionals forms a slippery slope for you to slide all the way to the conclusion.
But you can stop the slide: Just point out that one of the conditionals is dubious.
The second one is a good candidate. Or perhaps each one is only a little dubious,
but your reason to believe the conclusion becomes thinner and thinner as the doubt of
each one adds to the doubt of the previous ones.

Slippery slope argument   A slippery slope argument is a bad argument
that uses a chain of conditionals, at least one of which is false or dubious.

Zoe: Don't go out with a football player.
Suzy: Why not?
Zoe: You're crazy about football players, and if you go out with one you're sure
       to sleep with him.
Suzy: So?
Zoe: Then you'll get pregnant. And you'll marry the guy. But those guys are
       such jerks. You'll end up cooking and cleaning for him while he and his
       buddies watch football on TV. In twenty years you'll have five kids, no
       life, and a lot of regrets.
Suzy: Gosh. I guess you're right. I'll go out with a basketball player instead.

5. Reasoning from hypotheses

Lee: I'm thinking of doing a nursing degree.
Maria: That means you'll have to take summer school.
Lee: Why?
Maria: Look, you're in your second year now. To finish in four years like
         you told me you need to, you'll have to take all the upper-division
         biology courses your last two years. And you can't take any of those
         until you've finished the three-semester calculus course. So you'll
         have to take calculus over the summer in order to finish in four years.

Maria has not shown that Lee has to go to summer school. Rather, Maria has shown on the assumption (hypothesis) that Lee will do a nursing degree, Lee will have to go to summer school. That is, Maria has proved: If Lee does a nursing degree, then he'll have to go to summer school.

> ***Reasoning from hypotheses***   The following are equivalent:
> - Start with an hypothesis A and make a good argument for B.
> - Make a good argument for *If* A, *then* B.

Summary   Some claims are made up of other claims. We need to recognize that such claims must be treated as just one claim.

We looked at two kinds of compound claims in this chapter that involve possibilities for how things could be: "or" claims and conditionals. There are lots of confusing issues to master with conditionals: How to say they are false; necessary and sufficient conditions; valid and weak forms. But we need to do that work, because conditionals are the way we talk about how things could turn out under certain conditions.

We found that compound claims are an important way to construct valid arguments. We can reason with "or" claims by excluding possibilities. We can reason with conditionals the direct or indirect way, or with a chain of conditionals. We can reason from hypotheses.

There are typical mistakes people make using these valid forms. Some use dubious or false premises, like false dilemmas or slippery slope arguments. Others overlook possibilities by affirming the consequent or by denying the antecedent.

Key Words

compound claim	sufficient condition
"or" claim	direct way of reasoning
alternative	with conditionals
contradictory of a claim	indirect way of reasoning
excluding possibilities	with conditionals
false dilemma	affirming the consequent
conditional	denying the antecedent
antecedent	reasoning in a chain
consequent	with conditionals
contrapositive	slippery slope argument
necessary condition	reasoning from hypotheses

Exercises for Chapter 6

1. Make a list of the valid argument forms we studied in this chapter.

2. Make a list of the weak argument forms we studied in this chapter.

3. Make a list of the bad argument types we studied in this chapter.

4. What does it mean to say someone is reasoning in a chain with conditionals?

5. What is a slippery slope argument?

6. Rewrite the credit card argument on p. 133 to show that it is reasoning in a chain.

7. Assume these three claims are true:
   - If Dr. E wins the lottery, then Dr. E will be rich.
   - If Dr. E's book sells one million copies, then Dr. E will be rich.
   - If Dr. E marries a rich woman, then Dr. E will be rich.

   a. Write an equivalent contrapositive for each.
   b. Write the contradictory of each.
   c. Give an example of each of the valid and weak forms of arguments using conditionals, except reasoning in a chain.
   d. State which claims are sufficient for which others.
   e. State which claims are necessary for which others.

8. Make flash cards to practice recognizing the forms of arguments we saw in this chapter.
   - On the back of a card, put the form (for example, If A then B; not A; so not B).
   - Write whether it's valid or weak. On the front, put an example you've made up.
   - Make three cards for each form, each card showing a different example. Some of the examples should have a conditional that isn't already in "if . . . then . . ." form.
   - Practice with your own cards.
   - Trade with a fellow student.
   - If you're not sure that your examples illustrate the forms, ask your instructor.

Here's some more of Tom's homework, with Dr. E's comments.

Suzy: **If you apologize to Zoe, I'm sure she'll help you look for Spot.**
Dick: **It's her fault he got loose. I won't apologize.**
Suzy: **Then she won't help you look for Spot.**

Argument? (the whole dialogue) (yes or no) Yes.

Conclusion (if unstated, add it): Zoe won't help Dick look for Spot.

Premises: If you apologize to Zoe, she'll help you go look for Spot.
        It's Zoe's fault Spot got loose. Dick won't apologize to Zoe.

Additional premises needed (if none, say so): None.

Classify (with the additional premises): Valid.

Form: It's the direct way of reasoning with conditionals.

Good argument? (yes or no, with an explanation) Good.

No. It's a case of denying the antecedent. The premises are true, all right, but Zoe did go help Dick. She felt guilty.

> **If you don't give to charity, you're selfish. If you pay all your bills on time with nothing left over, you can't give to charity. Since you don't want to be selfish, you shouldn't pay all your bills on time.**
>
> *Argument?* (yes or no) Yes.
>
> *Conclusion* (if unstated, add it): You shouldn't pay all your bills on time.
>
> *Premises*: If you don't give to charity, you're selfish. If you pay all your bills on time with nothing left over, you can't give to charity. You don't want to be selfish.
>
> *Additional premises needed* (if none, say so): When you pay your bills, you have nothing left over.
>
> *Classify* (with the additional premises): Valid.
>
> *Form*: Reasoning in a chain and indirect way.
>
> *Good argument?* (yes or no, with an explanation) It looks O.K. if the premises apply to the person, but something seems wrong.
>
> *Good. You recognized the form, and you're getting good at spotting what unstated premises are needed. What's wrong here is that "selfish" is too vague. The first premise isn't true. What is true, perhaps, is "If you don't give to charity when you have more money than you need for your essentials, then you're selfish."*

For Exercises 9–26, answer the questions below.

> *Argument?* (yes or no)
> *Conclusion*:
> *Premises*:
> *Additional premises needed to make it valid or strong* (if none, say so):
> *Classify*: valid   very strong ——————— weak
> *One of the forms we studied in this chapter?* (state which one)
> *Good argument?* (check one)
> - It's good (passes the three tests).
> - It's valid or strong, but you don't know if the premises are true, so you can't say if it's good or bad.
> - It's bad because it's unrepairable (state which of the reasons apply).

9. If Suzy breaks up with Tom, then she'll have to return his letter jacket. But there is no way she'll give up that jacket. So she won't break up with Tom.

10. Steve Pearce is a congressman who meets with his constituents regularly. If someone is a good congressman, he meets with his constituents regularly. So Mr. Pearce is a good congressman.

11. To take issue with current Israeli policy is to criticize Israel. To criticize Israel is to be anti-Israel. To be anti-Israel is to be anti-Semitic. So if you take issue with current Israeli policy, you're an anti-Semite.

12. Dr. E (on an exam day): If students don't like me, they won't show up. But all of them showed up today. So they must really like me.

13. Manuel: Look here in the paper. People in Uganda are dying of some fever where they hemorrhage a lot.

    Maria: If people in Uganda are dying of hemorrhagic fever, it must be the ebola virus.

    Manuel: So it's the ebola virus!

14. Maria: Professor, professor, why wouldn't you answer my question in class?

    Professor Zzzyzzx: Questions in my class I do not allow. If one student I am allowing to ask a question, then others I must allow. Und then I will have lots and lots of questions to answer. Und time I won't have for my lecture.

15. Maria: Lee will take care of Spot Tuesday if Dick will help him with his English paper.

    Manuel: (*later*) Dick didn't help Lee with his English paper, so I guess Lee didn't take care of Spot on Tuesday.

16. Dick: If Freud was right, then the only things that matter to a man are fame, riches, and the love of beautiful women.

    Zoe: But Ralph is poor, single, never married, and uninterested in women. And he's certainly not famous. Yet he's happy. So Freud was wrong.

17. Only if Columbus landed in a place with no people in it could you say that he discovered it. But the Americas, especially where he landed, were populated. He even met natives. So Columbus didn't discover America. He just discovered a route to America.

18. Tom: If Dick loves Zoe, he'll give her an engagement ring.

    Harry: But Dick loves Spot a lot more than Zoe.

    Suzy: So Dick won't give Zoe an engagement ring.

19. Every criminal either is already a hardened repeat offender or will become one because of what he'll learn in jail. We don't want any hardened criminals running free on our streets. So if you lock up someone, he should be locked up forever.

20. Mary Ellen: If I go on Jane Fonda's workout and diet plan, I'll lose weight.

    Suzy: (*later*) Did you see how much weight Mary Ellen lost?

    Zoe: She must have gone on that workout plan by Jane Fonda.

21. Dick: I heard that Tom's going to get a pet. I wonder what he'll get?

    Zoe: The only pets you're allowed in this town are dogs or cats or fish.

    Dick: Well, I know he can't stand cats.

    Zoe: So he'll get a dog or fish.

    Dick: Not fish. He isn't the kind to get a pet you just contemplate.

    Zoe: So let's surprise him and get him a leash.

22. Mom: For a marriage to work, people have to have a lot in common.

    Zoe: Wrong! I know lots of miserable marriages where the people had a lot in common.

23. Lee: If Maria's paycheck comes in on time, she can pay the rent this month.

    Manuel: I saw Maria at the bank this afternoon. She said she was depositing her paycheck.

    Lee: Great! So the rent will be paid!

24. Aid to third-world countries? Why should we care more about starving children there than here?

25. Zoe: I can't believe you let Spot run away on your walk.

    Dick: We'll just have to wait for him to come home. I searched everywhere for him.

    Zoe: (*later*) Did you let Spot back in the yard?

    Dick: No.

    Zoe: So someone else must have let him in. The gate's latched.

    Dick: Maybe he got back in by himself.

    Zoe: No. If he could get in, he could get out. And if he could get out, he would, because he loves to run around the neighborhood. But he never gets out anymore when the gate is latched.

26. Maria: Listen to this argument I read in Steen's *Practical Philosophy for the Life Sciences,* "If the population density of a species is high in some area, then the species will not reproduce in that area. If a species doesn't reproduce in some area, it will go extinct in that area. Therefore, if the population density of a species is very high in some area, it will go extinct in that area."

    Lee: Gosh, that explains why there aren't any alligators in New York: there used to be too many of them.

27. You've worked hard enough. Take some time off. Go to a bar or a party or a church gathering. Listen. And bring back examples of the valid and weak forms of reasoning we studied in this chapter.

Additional Exercise

28. Assume that all the claims below are true:
    - If a 250 ton meteor crashes into earth, then mankind will become extinct.
    - If scientists are put in charge of nuclear weapons, then mankind will become extinct.
    - If the ebola virus breaks out in Africa, then mankind will become extinct.
    - If an ice age freezes all the seas, then mankind will become extinct.

    Using them:
    a. Write the contradictory of each "if . . . then . . ." claim.
    b. Write the contrapositive of each "if . . . then . . ." claim.
    c. Give an example of each of the valid and weak forms of arguments using conditionals, except reasoning in a chain.
    d. State which claims are sufficient for which others.
    e. State which claims are necessary for which others.

Further Study   Propositional logic is the study of how to analyze arguments solely in terms of their structure as composed of compound claims using "and," "or," "not," "if . . . then . . .". The appendix on truth-tables is a short introduction to it. A course on formal logic will spend several weeks on the subject.

Writing Lesson 6

You've learned about filling in unstated premises, indicator words, what counts as a plausible premise, and reasoning with compound claims.

Write an argument either for or against the following:

For any course at this school, if a student attends every class, takes all the exams, and hands in all the assignments, then the professor should give the student a passing mark.

Check whether your instructor has chosen a different topic for this assignment.

In order to improve your new skills, the directions for this assignment are a little different. You should hand in two pages:

First page: A list of premises and the conclusion.

Second page: The argument written as an essay with indicator words.

We should be able to see at a glance from the list of premises whether your argument is good. The essay form should read just as clearly, if you use indicator words well. Remember, there should be no claims in the essay form that aren't listed as premises.

Note that the topic is a conditional. You need to understand how to form the contradictory in order to make up your pro and con lists and to write your argument. Be very clear in your mind about what you consider to be necessary as opposed to sufficient conditions to get a passing mark.

To show you some of the problems students have, I'm including Suzy's argument on a different topic, as well as Tom's. Lee wrote a better one, so I've included his, too.

Suzy Queue
Critical Thinking

Issue: If a professor's colleagues do not consider his exams to be well written, then marks for the course should be given on a curve, not on percentage.

Premises:
1. A grade on a test reflects just how students are doing on that subject. If a test is not clearly understood, then the reflection of the scores will be lower.

2. Every student deserves to be treated fairly if the test is not clearly written the opportunity is not equal.

3. Due to the unclear test, the grading should start with the highest scored test in the class and the other test scores behind that.

4. Unclear tests should not be given in the first place, so to compensate for the strain on your brain for trying to decipher the test, grades should be curved to compensate.

5. The test is a direct reflection of how the teacher is getting through to his students, so in order to have an accurate idea, grading on the curve would show him the relation of all the students scores together.

Conclusion: Teachers who give poorly written exams should grade on the curve.

The essay's on the next page like you asked.

A grade on a test reflects just how students are doing on that subject. If the test is not clearly understood, then the reflection of the scores will be lower. Every student deserves to be treated fairly if the test is not clearly written the opportunity is not equal. Due to the unclear test, the grading should start with the highest scored test and the other test score behind that. Unclear tests should not be given in the first place, so to compensate for the strain on your brain for trying to decipher the test, grades should be curved to compensate. The test is a direct reflection of how the teacher is getting through to his students, so in order to have an accurate idea, grading on a curve would show him the relation of all the students scores together. Teachers who give poorly written exams should grade on the curve.

Some serious problems here. For (1), what does "reflect" mean? And "clearly understood"? By whom? That's the point. Besides, it's not one premise—it's two claims. For (2) you apparently have two claims, but it's incoherent. Your (4) is an argument (that word "so" is the clue), not a premise. And (5) is two claims, too.

You almost proved the conclusion you've stated. But you missed the point. It's a lot easier to prove what you stated than the issue you were supposed to write on. Who decides what "poorly written" means? Where is anything about his colleagues?

It's pretty clear to me that you wrote the essay first, and then tried to figure out what you said.

Tom Wyzyczy
Critical Thinking
Section 4
Writing Lesson 6

Issue: Every student should be required to take either critical thinking or freshman composition, but not both.

Definition: I'll understand the issue as "University students should be required to take either a freshman course on critical thinking or freshman composition, but not both."

Premises:

Critical thinking courses teach how to write. *1*

Freshman composition teaches how to write. *2*

Critical thinking courses teach how to read an essay. *3*

Freshman composition teaches how to read an essay. *4*

Credit should not be given for taking two courses that teach roughly the same material. *5*

If credit shouldn't be given for taking a course, students shouldn't be required to take it. *6*

Conclusion: Every student should be required to take either critical thinking or freshman composition, but not both.

continued on next page

This is sloppy work compared to what you've done in the past. You've shown, more or less, that a student should not have to take both courses. But you haven't shown that he should take one or the other, which is also part of the issue [(A or B) and not C]. So you've established neither the original claim nor its contradictory.

   You need a claim that links 1–4 with 5 and 6, like "Freshman composition and critical thinking courses teach the same material." (I see on the next page you do have that claim.)

   But worse is that 6 is at best dubious: How about those students who have to take remedial math for which no credit is given? And 1 and 2 are too vague. Both courses teach "how to write," but quite different aspects of that. Ditto for 3 and 4.

Tom Wyzyczy, Writing Lesson 6, page 2

Both critical thinking courses and freshman composition courses teach how to write. Both critical thinking courses and freshman composition courses teach how to read an essay. Since they both teach roughly the same material, they shouldn't both be required, because credit should not be given for taking two courses that teach roughly the same material. And if credit shouldn't be given for taking a course, students shouldn't be required to take it.

Good use of indicator words. It was O.K. to put two claims together in the first sentence as you did, since you recognized in your list of premises that they were two claims.

But you did what I specifically asked you not to do. You added a claim here you didn't have on the previous page: "Both courses teach roughly the same material."

The argument looks good when it's written this way, but the previous page shows its weaknesses.

You should re-do this whole assignment.

Lee Hong-Nakamura O'Flanagan

Issue: If critical thinking were not a required course, a lot fewer people would take it.

Definition: I assume that "a lot fewer" is purposely vague.

Premises: ‡ Critical thinking is required of all students now.
‡ Critical thinking is one of the harder core requirement courses.
‡ A lot of students prefer to take easy courses, rather than learn something.
‡ Students in engineering and architecture have more courses to take than they can finish in four years.
‡ Students don't want to spend more time at their studies than they have to. *1*
‡ Money is a problem for many students. *2*
‡ For most students, if they have more courses to take than they can finish in four years, they will not take courses that aren't required. *3*
‡ Students think they already know how to think critically. *4*
‡ If critical thinking weren't required, then students who prefer easy courses and students who want to finish as quickly as they can, which are a lot of students, will not take it.

Conclusion: If critical thinking were not a required course, a lot fewer people would take it.

Critical thinking is required of all students now. And critical thinking is one of the harder core requirement courses. A lot of students prefer to take easy courses, rather than learn something. So many of them won't take critical thinking. *5* Besides, students in engineering and architecture have more courses than they can finish in four years. Why would they take critical thinking if they didn't have to? After all, we all know that students don't want to spend more time at their studies than they have to. After all, money is a problem for most students. So for most students, if they have more courses to take than they can finish in four years, they will not take courses that aren't required. Anyway, students think they already know how to think critically. Thus we can see that if critical thinking weren't required, then students who prefer easy courses and students who want to finish as quickly as they can, which are a lot of students, will not take it. That is, if critical thinking were not a required course, a lot fewer people would take it.

This is good, but there are a few problems. 1 isn't tied into 3, though the unstated premise is pretty clear. But 2 definitely needs to be tied into 3 better. And 4 is left dangling—what's the connection you intend? Finally, you use 5 and it should be on the list of premises. Nonetheless, this is pretty good work.
But it was supposed to be on 2 pages!

Cartoon Writing Lesson C

For each cartoon write the best argument you can that has as its conclusion
the claim that accompanies the cartoon. List only the premises and conclusion.
If you believe the best argument is only weak, explain why. Refer back to Cartoon
Writing Lesson A on p. 55 for suggestions about how to do this lesson.

1.

There are searchlights behind the hill.

2.

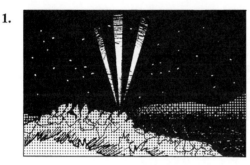

Someone has walked here since the snow began falling.

3.

Spot took the steak.

4.

Spot escaped by digging a hole under the fence.

5.

Crows ate Farmer Hong's corn.

6.

The fellow standing between Harry and Manuel is or was in the military.

7   Counter-arguments

A. Raising Objections

> Everyone should ride a bicycle for transportation. *1*
> Cars are expensive to buy and maintain and cause a lot of pollution. *2*
> A bicycle is better for your health and also for everyone else's. *3*
> Bicycles also look better than cars. *4*

When asked to evaluate this argument, most students think it's good—to which I respond, "Why do you drive a car?" Remember, it is irrational to say that an argument is good and then deny its conclusion.

Some students, rather than evaluating the argument directly, raise objections:

> Bicycles aren't good for people who are handicapped or weak. *5*
> Bikes aren't useful for carrying groceries or lots of kids. *6*

Then they say that the argument is bad. They have good reason not to believe the conclusion (*1*).

Raising objections is a standard way to show that an argument is bad. In doing so, we are making another argument that either calls into question one of the premises, or shows that an unstated premise is dubious, or illustrates why the argument is weak.

In this example, *5* shows that *3* is dubious, while *6* makes us doubt the unstated premise needed to make the argument good: "Anything that's cheaper to buy and maintain than a car, causes less pollution than a car, and is better for your health and everyone else's should be the form of transportation for everyone." (We might as well ignore *4*, since it's subjective and there's no sense to debate it.)

Raising objections is common.

Dick: Zoe, we ought to get another dog.
Zoe: What's wrong with Spot?
Dick: Oh, no, I mean to keep Spot company.
Zoe: Spot has us. He doesn't need company.
Dick: But we're gone a lot. And he's always escaping from the yard,
        'cause he's lonely. And we don't give him enough time.
        He should be out running around more.
Zoe: But think of all the work! We'll have to feed the new dog.
        And think of all the time necessary to train it.
Dick: I'll train him. We can feed him at the same time as Spot,
        and dog food is cheap. It won't cost much.

Dick is trying to convince Zoe to believe "We should get another dog." But he has to answer her objections.

We ought to get another dog.
        (*objection*) We already have Spot.
The other dog will keep Spot company.
        (*objection*) Spot already has us for company.
We are gone a lot. (*answer*)
He's always escaping from the yard. (*answer*)
He's lonely. (*answer*)
We don't give him enough time. (*answer*)
He should be out running around more. (*answer*)
        (*objection*) It will be a lot of work to have a new dog.
        (*objection*) We will have to feed the new dog.
        (*objection*) It will take a lot of time to train the new dog.
Dick will train him. (*answer*)
We can feed him at the same time as Spot. (*answer*)
Dog food is cheap. (*answer*)

Argument. Counterargument. Counter-counterargument. This is how we reason every day. Objections are raised: Someone puts forward a claim that, if true, makes one of our claims false or at least doubtful. We then have to answer that challenge to sustain our argument. *Knocking off an objection is a mini-argument within your argument—if it's not a good (though brief) argument, it won't do the job.*

Or you could say, "I hadn't thought of that. I guess you're right."

Or you could say, "I don't know. I'll have to think about that."

In making an argument of your own, you'll want to make it strong. You might think you have a great one. All the premises seem obvious, and they glue together to get the conclusion. But if you imagine someone objecting, you can see how to give better support for doubtful premises. And answering counterarguments in your own writing allows the reader to see you haven't ignored obvious objections. All you have to do, as in the earlier writing lessons, is make a list of the pros and cons. Then answer the other side.

B. Refuting an Argument

1. Refuting directly

Zoe can't let it pass. But how do you refute an argument?

Zoe might object to one of the premises, saying Dick won't be killing the slowest, but only the ones that happen to come into their house.

Or she could agree with the premises, but note that "over time" could be thousands of years, so the conclusion doesn't follow.

Or she could attack the conclusion, saying that it's not useless to kill flies, because she does it all the time and it keeps their home clean.

All the ways that we can show an argument is unrepairable are useful in refuting an argument. We pick out three as fundamental.

> ### Direct ways of refuting an argument
> - Show that at least one of the premises is dubious.
> - Show that the argument isn't valid or strong.
> - Show that the conclusion is false.

2. Refuting indirectly

Sometimes you can't point to any one premise that is false or dubious, but you know there's something wrong with the premises. They might get the conclusion that's argued for, but they get a lot more, too—so much that you can see the premises are inconsistent or lead to an absurdity. For example,

> You complain that taxes are already too high and there is too much crime. And you say we should permanently lock up everyone who has been convicted of three felonies. In the places where this has been instituted, it hasn't reduced the crime rate. So we will have many, many more people who will be incarcerated for their entire lives. We will need more prisons, many more, because these people will be in forever. We will need to employ more guards. We will need to pay for considerable healthcare for these people when they are elderly. Thus, if we lock up everyone who has been convicted of three felonies, we will have to pay substantially higher taxes. Since you are adamant that taxes are too high, you should abandon your claim that we should permanently lock up everyone who has been convicted of three felonies.

Here the speaker isn't refuting an argument. He's showing that the other person's beliefs lead to an unwanted conclusion: You'll have to raise taxes.

> **Reducing to the absurd**   To reduce to the absurd is to show that at least one of several claims is false or dubious, or collectively they are unacceptable, by drawing a false or unwanted conclusion from them.

If a valid argument has a false conclusion, one of the premises is false. If a strong argument has a false conclusion, one of the premises is very likely false. If the conclusion is absurd, the premises aren't what you want. *You have to be sure the argument you use to get the false or absurd conclusion is really strong or valid and doesn't use any other dubious claims.* Only then is there good reason to believe that there's a problem with the original collection of claims.

One particular form of reducing to the absurd is called ***refuting by analogy***: Vary only some of the premises while retaining the crucial ones to get an absurd conclusion.

> LOOK, YOUR ARGUMENT AGAINST KILLING FLIES IS BAD. I COULD USE THE SAME ARGUMENT AGAINST KILLING BACTERIA, OR AGAINST KILLING CHICKENS FOR DINNER FROM AUNT MARGERY'S HENHOUSE. THOSE CONCLUSIONS WOULD BE ABSURD.

We'll look more at analogies in Chapter 12.

3. Attempts to refute that are bad arguments

Some attempts to refute are just bad arguments.

In Chapter 5 we studied **phony refutations**. They're bad versions of reducing to the absurd: Here's the conclusion, here's what the speaker believes, they're contradictory, so the argument is bad.

Or an attempt to reduce to the absurd can lead to a **slippery slope**:

> Gun control should not be allowed. If laws requiring registration of all guns
> are passed, then they'll start investigating people who have guns. They'll
> tap our phones. They'll look at what we check out of the library. They'll
> tap our Internet records. They'll come gunning for us. It'll be a police state.

This person has argued that gun control legislation is the first step on a slippery slope that will end in a disaster for us all. But this doesn't refute, because the slippery slope adds false or dubious premises.

Then there's **ridicule**:

> Dr. E: I hear that your department elected a woman as chairman.
> Professor Zzzyzzx: Jah, jah, dat is right. Und now we is trying to decide
>   what we should be calling her—"chairman" or "chairwoman" or
>   "chairperson."
> Dr. E: "Chairperson"? Why not use a neutral term that's really
>   appropriate for the position, like "chaircreature"?

In rational discussion, ridicule is a worthless device: It ends arguments, belittles the other person, and makes enemies. No argument has been given for why "chairman" shouldn't be replaced by "chairperson," though Dr. E thinks he's shown the idea's absurd.

In theory there's a big difference between reducing to the absurd and ridicule, but in practice it's difficult to distinguish them. Often, not enough of an argument is given to see how the absurd conclusion follows, so it sounds like ridicule.
*If someone wants us to see his or her comments as an argument, it's their
responsibility to make that clear.* Otherwise, let's classify it as ridicule.

REDUCE TO THE ABSURD

{A, B, ..., C} — THE OTHER PERSON'S CLAIMS

(OTHER PLAUSIBLE CLAIMS)

D - CONCLUSION, FALSE OR ABSURD

RIDICULE

A — THE OTHER PERSON'S CLAIM

HA! HA! HA! HA! HA!

When judging whether something is ridicule, an attempt to reduce to the absurd, a slippery slope, or an unwillingness to acknowledge distinctions because they're a bit vague, think less of rejecting what the other person says and more of taking his or her comments as a challenge to make your own argument clearer.

The worst of the bad ways to refute, though, is to attack an argument the other person didn't even say. When someone makes a claim, and the other person tries to refute it by putting words in that person's mouth, that's a ***strawman*** (because it's easier to knock down a strawman). It often shows up in political discourse:

> The incumbent congressman is against gun control. Clearly, he doesn't care about violence on the streets.

Excuse me? What's the connection here? The congressman never said he wasn't against violence in the streets.

The only reasonable response to a strawman is to say calmly that that isn't what you said:

> Tom: Unless we allow the logging of old-growth forests in this county, we'll lose the timber industry and these towns will die.
> Dick: So you're saying that you don't care what happens to the spotted owl and to our rivers and the water we drink?
> Tom: I said nothing of the sort. You've misrepresented my position.

Note that Tom did not say, "You've misrepresented my position, you jerk." Let's keep alive some hope of rational discourse.

Summary   When we make an argument, we should be prepared to defend it. Think ahead and imagine what objections might be raised, then answer them.

There are direct ways to refute an argument: Show a premise is false, show the argument isn't valid or strong, or show the conclusion is false.

We can also refute an argument by showing that a false or absurd conclusion follows from the premises. To do that, we must be sure that any other claims we use to get the false or absurd conclusion are plausible, and that the argument we give is strong or valid.

But remember: Refuting an argument does not show that the conclusion is false.

There are four bad ways to reason that imitate reducing to the absurd: phony refutation, slippery slope arguments, and ridicule. And then there's a strawman—which is just putting words in someone's mouth.

Key Words   direct ways of refuting   ridicule
                   reducing to the absurd   strawman
                   refuting by analogy

Exercises for Chapter 7

1. In my first comment after the argument about bicycling on p. 147, I challenge the student. Have I shown the argument is bad? Explain.

2. What is a counterargument?

3. If you show an argument is bad, what have you shown about its conclusion?

4. How should you respond to a counterargument?

5. a. Why are counterarguments useful in your own writing?
   b. Give three phrases you can use to introduce objections to your own argument in your writing.

6. Find an article in which the author answers a counterargument. Good places to look are in other textbooks and in editorial opinions in the newspaper.

7. Explain the role of each claim in the following discussion.

   Zoe: I think sex is the answer to almost everyone's problems.
   Dick: How can you say that?
   Zoe: It takes away your tension, right?
   Dick: Not if you're involved with someone you don't like.
   Zoe: Well, anyway, it makes you feel better.
   Dick: Not if it's against your morals. Anyway, heroin makes you feel good, too.
   Zoe: But it's healthy and natural, just like eating and drinking.
   Dick: Sure, and you can catch terrible diseases. Sex should be confined to marriage.
   Zoe: Is that a proposal?

8. Write a short argument against drinking alcohol that acknowledges why some people want to drink alcohol.

9. If you can show that a collection of claims leads to a false conclusion, do you know that the claims are inconsistent or one of them is false? Explain.

10. Refuting an argument directly is just showing that the argument is _____ .

11. What is reducing an argument to the absurd?

12. Which of the ways of refuting an argument is best? Why?

13. What's the difference between ridicule and reducing to the absurd?

14. Why isn't a phony refutation really a refutation of an argument?

15. Why won't a slippery slope argument do as a way to reduce to the absurd?

16. a. What is a strawman?
    b. Bring in an example.

Evaluate the attempts to refute arguments in Exercises 17–22 by answering the following questions:

What is the method of refutation?
Is the refutation a good argument? (Explain)

17. There is no value at all in Heidegger's philosophy, especially his ethics, since he collaborated with the Nazis in running German universities in the 1930s and fired all the Jews.

18. You say you want to raise tuition again? Why not raise the parking fees, too? And the dorm contracts. And raise prices at the cafeteria, while you're at it. Or maybe even charge students for using the library. You could balance the school's budget for sure that way.

19. Look, I agree with you. We have too much violence in the streets, too many drug pushers, too little respect for the law. But our prisons are overflowing, and that's costing us a fortune. So we've got to reduce our prison population. Yet you say we should be even tougher on crime. The answer is simple: Institute a lottery among all convicted felons in jail and execute one of them every month—no appeals. That'll instill a real fear of being arrested. And it'd be fair, too.

20. Lee: I'm going to vote for that initiative to eliminate discrimination against homosexuals in hiring and getting places to live. They should be treated like everyone else. They deserve a chance to get jobs and homes.

    Tom: Are you kidding? I'm voting against it. You should, too. They don't deserve any preference over the rest of us.

21. (Complete letter to the editor from Vern Raburn, CEO, Eclipse Aviation, in *Crosswinds Weekly*, 7/11/02, in response to an article "Eclipse Aviation's Money Troubles".)

    Should you decide you are interested in supplying your readers with something other than lies and bullshit, I suggest you spend more time fact checking for yourself. This will help prevent you from the embarrassment of propagating others' inaccuracies.

22. Zoe: You should eat less red meat. Red meat has lots of cholesterol which blocks up the arteries and leads to an increased risk of heart disease.

    Dick: Mankind has been eating red meat since the dawn of time, and we have still survived as a species. If we stopped eating everything that was bad for us, we would be left with nothing to consume but small white tasteless pills, which would later be discovered to cause a new type of deadly cancer.

Refute the following arguments. Say whether you are showing a premise is dubious, attacking an unstated premise, showing the argument is weak, or reducing to the absurd.

23. Mrs. Wang is a great marriage therapist. She really cares about her clients.

24. Multiple-choice examinations are the best way to examine students. The grading is completely objective. Students know how to prepare for them. And professors don't have to spend a lot of time grading them.

25. You should keep a gun in your home. This is a dangerous neighborhood, and a gun is the best protection you can get. Think of what could happen if someone broke in.

26. Single parents should get special assistance from the government. After all, a two-parent family has two paychecks and twice the attention to give to their children. Some single-parent families end up having to use the welfare system because they can't afford child care. Therefore, the government should give free child care to single-parent families.

Writing Lesson 7

Now you know that you should include the other side when arguing for a controversial claim. Argument, counterargument, counter-counterargument. Remember that to knock off an objection you need a mini-argument that will be judged by the same standards as any argument.

Write an argument either for or against the following:

Peer-to-peer sharing of songs on the Internet is theft.

Check whether your instructor has chosen a different topic for this assignment.

In order to make sure you use your new skills, the directions for this assignment are the same as for Writing Lesson 6. You should hand in two pages:

First page: A list of premises and the conclusion.

Second page: The argument written as an essay with indicator words.

We should be able to see at a glance from the list of premises whether your argument is good. The essay form should read just as clearly, if you use indicator words well. Remember, there should be no claims in the essay form that aren't listed as premises. And you should include the other side.

For this issue, and generally, there is a trade-off:

You can make your argument very strong, but perhaps only at the expense of a rather dubious premise. Or you can make all your premises clearly true, but leave out the dubious premise that is needed to make the argument strong. Given the choice, *opt for making the argument strong*. If it's weak, no one should accept the conclusion. And if it's weak because of unstated premises, it is better to have those premises stated so they can be the object of debate.

Tom is so embarrassed about his last writing assignment that he's asked me not to include any more. But he's doing much better now, and I'm sure he'll do well in the course. Maria has done such a good job, though, that I'm including her essay on a different issue.

Maria Schwartz Rodriguez
Critical Thinking, Section 6
Writing Lesson 7

Issue: If a woman has a baby, then she should not work outside the home until the child reaches the age of four.

Definition: I take "work outside the home" to mean the woman takes a job that requires her to be away from her home and child at least 15 hours/week.

Premises:

1. Some women who have a child under the age of four are single mothers.

2. Some women who have a child under the age of four have husbands who do not earn enough money to support them and the child.

3. Some women who have children have careers from which they cannot take time without stopping them permanently or for a very long time from advancing.

4. Some women who have children do not have extended families or lots of friends.

5. A woman who has only her family can go stir-crazy if she is just with her child all the time.

6. A woman who is going stir-crazy, or who is too poor to provide for her child, or who is unsatisfied because her child is stopping her from getting along in her career will make a bad mother and companion for her child who is under four.

7. Mothers who are not with their children do not deserve to have children.

8. Whether they deserve to have them or not, they do have them.

9. Children who are not with their mothers will not develop proper intellectual and emotional skills.

10. What studies I have seen contradict that claim. Until reliable studies are produced for it, we should not accept it.

11. Day-care can be dangerous.

12. The mother can screen day-care providers, and besides, a bitter, unsatisfied mother can be dangerous, too.

Conclusion: Under some circumstances it is acceptable for a woman to work outside the home when she has a child under the age of four.

Maria Schwartz Rodriguez
Critical Thinking, Section 6
Writing Lesson 7, page 2

Under some circumstances it is acceptable for a woman to work outside the home when she has a child under the age of four. After all, some women who have a child under the age of four are single mothers. And other women who have a child under the age of four have husbands who do not earn enough money to support them and the child. We can't forget women who have children and have careers from which they cannot take time without stopping them permanently or for a very long time from advancing. And think of the women who have children who do not have extended families or lots of friends. She could go stir-crazy if she is just with her child all the time. These women should be allowed to take work outside the home, for a woman who is going stir-crazy, or who is too poor to provide for her child, or who is unsatisfied because her child is stopping her from getting along in her career will make a bad mother and companion for her child who is under four.

But lots of people say that mothers who are not with their children do not deserve to have children. Well, whether they deserve to have them or not, they do have them.

But children who aren't with their mothers will not develop proper intellectual and emotional skills, it is said. Well, what studies I have seen contradict that claim. Until reliable studies are produced for it, we should not accept it.

One objection is that mothers who work outside the home often need day-care.*A* And day-care can be dangerous. But the mother can screen day-care providers, and besides, a bitter, unsatisfied mother can be dangerous, too.

So despite the obvious objections, we can see that under some circumstances it is acceptable for a woman to work outside the home when she has a child under the age of four.

This is really excellent. Bravo! A few points where you could improve:

You must include the definition in the essay, right after the first sentence giving the conclusion.

The grammar on premise (3) is not right.

You missed a possible response to (8) that the state or a church should take the child, and you'd need to come up with a response to that.

Some variety in putting in the objections might be good—for example, stating (9) as a question.

You left A out of your list of premises. And (12) is two premises, not one.

I see you avoided entirely the issue of welfare. Have you asked other students to look at your paper to see if they can think of objections or support because of that?

If you can write like this in your other courses, you'll do great all through college!

8   General Claims

A. General Claims and Their Contradictories

We need to know how to reason using *general claims* that assert something in a
general way about all or a part of a collection. For example,

> All good teachers give fair exams. Professor Zzzyzzx gives fair exams.
> So Professor Zzzyzzx is a good teacher.

This may seem valid, but it's not. The premises could be true, yet Professor Zzzyzzx
could be a terrible teacher and give fair exams from an instructor's manual.

> Some dogs like cats. Some cats like dogs.
> So some dogs and cats like each other.

This seems valid, too. But it's not. It could be that all the dogs that like cats are
abhorred by the cats as too wimpy.

These arguments sound right, but they're bad. How are we to avoid getting
lured into belief? We first need to be clear about what "all" and "some" mean.

"All" means "every single one, no exceptions." But then is the following true?

> All polar bears in Antarctica can swim.

There are no exceptions: There's not one polar bear in Antarctica that can't swim. Of course, there aren't any polar bears in Antarctica that can swim either. There aren't any polar bears at all in Antarctica.

Some people say the claim is false: There has to be at least one object for us to be right when we say "all" in ordinary conversation. Others say the claim is true.

There's disagreement about "some", too. Consider:

Dr. E: At the end of this term, some of my students will get an A.

At the end of the term one student in all of Dr. E's classes got an A. Was Dr. E right? If you don't think so, then how many is "some students"? At least 2? At least 8? At least 10%? More than 18%?

"Some" is purposely vague. We use it when we can't or don't want to be precise. When we say "some," we are only guaranteeing that there is at least one.

Dr. E: Some of my students will pass my next exam.

All Dr. E's students pass the exam. Was Dr. E right? For this claim to be true, don't some students also have to fail? With "some" we usually mean "at least one, but not all." But not always. "Some" and "all" can be ambiguous.

All means "Every single one, no exceptions." Sometimes *all* is meant as "Every single one, and there is at least one." Which reading is best may depend on the argument.

Some means "At least one." Sometimes *some* is meant as "At least one, but not all." Which reading is best may depend on the argument.

There are lots of different ways to say "all" in English. For example, the following are equivalent claims:

All dogs bark.   Dogs bark.
Every dog barks.   Everything that's a dog barks.

There are lots of ways to say the reading of "some" in the sense of "at least one." For example, the following are equivalent claims:

Some foxes are affectionate.   At least one fox is affectionate.
There is a fox that's affectionate.   There exists an affectionate fox.

There are also lots of ways of saying that nothing or no part of a collection satisfies some condition. For example, the following are equivalent claims:

No dog likes cats.   Nothing that's a dog likes cats.
All dogs do not like cats. Not even one dog likes cats.

> *No* means "not even one," "every single one is not."

Another word used in general claims is "only." Consider:

Only postal employees deliver U.S. mail.
Ralph is a postal employee.
So Ralph delivers U.S. mail.

This is not valid. Only postal employees deliver U.S. mail does not mean that all postal employees deliver U.S. mail. It means that anyone who delivers U.S. mail has got to be a postal employee. To clarify the meaning of "only," and for other analyses in this chapter, we'll use the letter S, P, Q, R for parts of a sentence.

> *Only*   "Only S are P" means "All P are S."

It's easy to get the contradictory of a general claim wrong. Recall that a *contradictory* of a claim is one that always has the opposite truth-value. For example, here's an advertisement that's on TV:

Zocor is a cholesterol medicine. Zocor is not right for everyone.

Why are they advertising medicine that no one should use? They've got the contradictory of "Zocor is right for everyone" wrong. It should be: "Zocor is not right for some people."
And the contradictory of "All dogs bark" isn't "All dogs don't bark." Both claims are false. The contradictory is "Some dogs don't bark."
The contradictory of "Some students are athletes" isn't "Some students are not athletes." Both claims are true. Rather it's "Not even one student is an athlete" or "All students are not athletes." Or better still, "No student is an athlete."
Here are some examples of claims and their contradictories:

Claim	*Contradictory*
All dogs bark.	Some dogs don't bark.
Some dogs bark.	No dogs bark.
Some dogs don't bark.	All dogs bark.
No women are philosophers.	Some women are philosophers.
Every Mexican likes vodka.	Some Mexicans don't like vodka.
Some Russians like chile.	No Russian likes chile.
Some whales eat fish.	Not even one whale eats fish.

The contradictory of "Only S are P" can be made in two ways:

Not every P is S.
Some P are not S.

So "Only postal employees deliver mail" is contradicted by "Some people who deliver mail are not postal employees." If we want to say that just exactly postal employees and no one else delivers U.S. mail, we should say that. Or we can say:

All postal employees and only postal employees deliver U.S. mail.
    Contradictory Either some postal employees don't deliver U.S. mail, or some people who deliver U.S. mail aren't postal employees.

Because there are so many ways we can make general claims, it's hard to give set formulas for contradictories. With some practice you ought to be able to use your common sense to get the contradictory right. As an aid, here is a rough guide:

Claim	*Contradictory*
All —	Some are not — Not every —
Some —	No — All are not — Not even one —
Some are not —	All are —
No —	Some are —
Only S are P	Some P are not S Not every P is S

Exercises for Section A

1. Give two other ways to say "All dogs eat meat."

2. Give two other ways to say "Some cats can swim."

3. Give two other ways to say "All computers are powered by electricity."

4. Give two other ways to say "Some state governors are women."

5. Give another way to say "Only birds fly."

6. Give two other ways to say "No police officer is under 18 years old."

7. Give another way to say "Everything that's a dog is a domestic canine, and everything that's a domestic canine is a dog."

8. Give two other ways to say "No pig can fly."

9. Judging from your experience, which of the following claims are true? Be prepared to defend your answer.
    a. Only dogs bark.
    b. All blondes are dumb.
    c. Some textbooks are designed to fall apart after one semester.
    d. Crest toothpaste is not for sale in all stores.
    e. Some English professors are women.
    f. Dictionaries are the only way to learn the meaning of new words.
    g. No student can register for this course after the first week of classes.

10. For each of the following, give a contradictory claim.
    a. All students like to study.
    b. No women are construction workers.
    c. Every CEO of a Fortune 500 company is a man.
    d. This exam will be given in all of the sections of critical thinking.
    e. No exam is suitable for all students.
    f. Some exams don't really test a student's knowledge.
    g. Not all drunk drivers get in accidents.
    h. Donkeys eat carrots.
    i. Only the good die young.
    j. All teachers and only teachers are allowed to grade exams.
    k. Nothing both barks and meows.
    l. Tom will start every football game if he's not suspended.
    m. If some football player is a vegetarian, then his coach will hate him.
    n. All decisions about abortion should be left to the woman and her doctor.
    o. The Lone Ranger was the only cowboy to have a friend called "Tonto."

11. There are general claims about time, too. Give a contradictory for each of the following:
    a. Dr. E always gives an exam when he is irritated with his students.
    b. It never rains in Seattle in July.
    c. Sometimes Spot will not chase Puff.
    d. Only during the winter are there flocks of birds along the river.

B. Some Valid and Invalid Forms

Recall the first argument in this chapter:

> All good teachers give fair exams. Professor Zzzyzzx gives fair exams.
> So Professor Zzzyzzx is a good teacher.

We saw that it's weak: Professor Zzzyzzx could be among the bad teachers who give fair exams. Here's a diagram that summarizes the discussion:

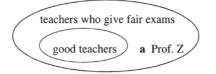

This argument sounds good because it's similar to a valid form of argument. Schematically, where "a" stands for the name of someone or something:

*The **direct way** of reasoning* *with* **all**	*Arguing backwards* *with* **all**
All S are P	All S are P
a is S *Valid*	a is P *Usually*
So a is P	So a is S *weak*
All S are P + *a is S*	*All S are P* + *a is P*
↓	↓
a is P	*a is S*

Valid: All dogs bark.   *Weak:*   All dogs bark.
         Ralph is a dog.   Ralph barks.
         So Ralph barks.   So Ralph is a dog.

The argument on the right is overlooking possibilities. One way to be something that barks is to be a dog, but there may be other ways (seals and foxes).

The diagram on the previous page is an example of a way to check whether certain kinds of arguments that use general claims are valid.

Checking for validity with diagrams

- A collection is represented by an enclosed area.

- If one area is entirely within another, then everything in the one collection is also in the other.

- If one area overlaps another, then there is something that is common to both collections.

- If two areas do not overlap, then there is nothing common to both collections.

- An "a" or a dot in an area marks that a particular object is in that collection.

- Draw the areas to represent the premises as true while trying to represent the conclusion as false. If you can, then the argument is invalid. If there's no way to represent the premises as true and the conclusion as false, the argument is valid.

For example, we can use diagrams to check whether the following is valid:

All dogs bark. Everything that barks is a mammal.
So all dogs are mammals.

We first draw the diagram to represent the premises as true.

The "dogs" area is completely inside the
"things that bark" area: All dogs bark.

The "things that bark" area is completely
inside the "mammals" area: All things that
bark are mammals.

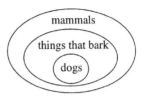

So the "dogs" area ends up being inside the "mammals" area. There's no way it
couldn't be. That represents that all dogs are mammals. So if we represent the
premises as true, we are forced to represent the conclusion as true. The argument
is valid, reasoning in a chain with "all."

Compare that to a similar argument:

Some kangaroos are tame. Some creatures that are tame
live in New Zealand. So some kangaroos live in New Zealand.

Is the argument valid? What do we need to have in a diagram?

The "kangaroos" area must overlap the
"tame" area: Some kangaroos are tame.

The "tame" area must overlap the
"New Zealand" area: Some creatures
that are tame live in New Zealand

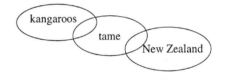

We were able to draw the diagram to represent both premises as true, yet there's
no overlap between the "kangaroos" area and the "New Zealand" area, so the
conclusion is false: It's possible that no kangaroos live in New Zealand. Thus, the
argument is invalid. Even though its conclusion is true (there are some kangaroos in
zoos there), it's weak.

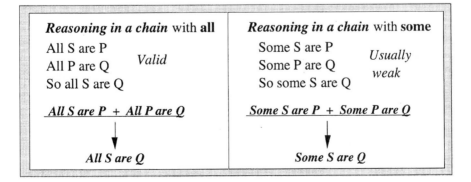

Reasoning in a chain with **all**	*Reasoning in a chain* with **some**
All S are P	Some S are P
All P are Q *Valid*	Some P are Q *Usually weak*
So all S are Q	So some S are Q
All S are P + All P are Q	*Some S are P + Some P are Q*
↓	↓
All S are Q	*Some S are Q*

Here's an argument with "no":

> All dogs bark. No professor is a dog.
> So no professor barks.

How do we check if this is valid? We do what we've always done: Look for all the possible ways that the premises could be true. Only now we can use diagrams to represent those possibilities. We know that the "dogs" area must be entirely within the "things that bark" area (All dogs bark). So we just have to figure out where to put the "professors" area. We know that there must be no overlap of the "professors" area and the "dogs" area (No professor is a dog). Here are three possibilities:

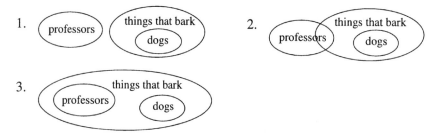

These (schematically) represent all the ways the premises could be true. Yet in both (2) and (3) the conclusion is represented as false. It's possible for there to be a professor who barks, even though he (she?) isn't a dog. The argument is invalid. It mimics a valid form of argument.

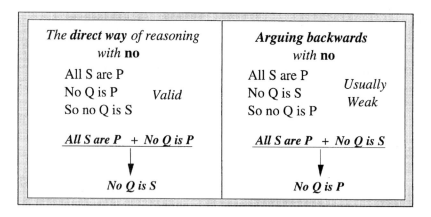

Drawing diagrams to check validity is just another way to look for possibilities that make the premises true and the conclusion false. The method works for some arguments that use general claims, but not for all. Even the simple argument about dogs that like cats with which we began the chapter can't be analyzed using diagrams this way. You'll have to think your way through all possible ways the premises could be true when you do some of the exercises.

Here is how Lee and Maria have been using diagrams to check for validity.

The Workbook has two more examples of Lee and Maria using this method.

Exercises for Section B

Which of the argument forms in Exercises 1–6 are valid? Justify your answer. Then give an argument of that form.

1. All S are P.
   No Q is S.
   So some Q aren't P.

2. All S are P.
   a is S.
   So *a* is P.

3. Some S are P.
   All P are Q.
   So some S are Q.

4. Only S are P.
   a is S.
   So *a* is P.

5. Some S aren't P.
   So no P are S.

6. All S are P.
   No Q is P.
   So no Q is S.

Exercises 7–14 are simple examples for you to develop some skill in analyzing general claims. For each, select the claim that makes the argument valid—you're not asked to judge whether the claim is plausible, just whether it makes the argument valid.

7. All turtles can swim. So turtles eat fish.
    a. Anything that eats fish swims.
    b. Fish swim and are eaten by things that swim.
    c. Anything that swims eats fish.
    d. None of the above.

8. Anyone who plagiarizes is cheating. So Ralph plagiarizes.
    a. Ralph wrote three critical thinking essays in two days.
    b. Ralph cheated last week.
    c. Both (a) and (b).
    d. None of the above.

9. Pigs are mammals. So pigs eat apples.
    a. Anything that eats apples is a mammal.
    b. Pigs don't eat meat.
    c. Anything that is a mammal eats apples.
    d. None of the above.

10. All professional dancers cannot hold a day job. So no lawyer is a professional dancer.
    a. Lawyers don't usually like to dance.
    b. Dancers aren't interested in making money.
    c. Being a lawyer is a day job.
    d. Professional dancers can't write essays.
    e. None of the above.

11. Every voter must have a legal residence. So no sex-offender has a legal residence.
    a. No sex-offender is a voter.
    b. No sex-offender can register to vote.
    c. If you're a sex-offender, then no one will want to live near you.
    d. None of the above.

12. Some cats chase songbirds. So some songbirds are eaten by cats.
    a. Some cats catch songbirds.
    b. Some things that chase songbirds eat them.
    c. Some songbirds attack cats.
    d. None of the above.

13. Every dog chases cats. So Spot chases Puff.
    a. Spot is a dog.
    b. Puff is a cat.
    c. Puff irritates Spot.
    d. Both (a) and (b).
    e. None of the above.

14. Manuel is sweating. So he must be hot.
    a.   Manuel sweats when he is hot.
    b.   Anyone who is hot sweats.
    c.   Only Manuel sweats when he is hot.
    d.   Only people who are hot sweat.
    e.   None of the above.

Which of Exercises 15–32 are valid arguments? You're not asked to determine whether the argument is good, only whether it is valid. Check by doing *one* of the following:

- Give a possible way in which the premises could be true and the conclusion false to show it's invalid.
- Draw a diagram.
- Point out that the argument is in one of the forms we have studied.
- Explain in your own words why it's valid.

15. Not every student attends lectures. Lee is a student. So Lee doesn't attend lectures.

16. No professor subscribes to *Rolling Stone* magazine. Maria is not a professor. So Maria subscribes to *Rolling Stone* magazine.

17. No professor subscribes to *Rolling Stone* magazine. Lou subscribes to *Rolling Stone* magazine. So Lou is not a professor.

18. Some dogs bite postal workers. Some postal workers bite dogs. So some dogs and postal workers bite each other.

19. Everyone who is anxious to learn works hard. Dr. E's students work hard. So Dr. E's students are anxious to learn.

20. All CEOs of Fortune 500 companies earn more than $400,000. Ralph earns more than $400,000. So Ralph is a CEO of a Fortune 500 company.

21. All students who are serious take critical thinking in their freshman year. No one who smokes marijuana every week is a serious student. So no one who smokes marijuana every week takes critical thinking his or her freshman year.

22. No student who cheats is honest. Some dishonest people are found out. So some students who cheat are found out.

23. Only ducks quack. George is a duck. So George quacks.

24. Everyone who likes ducks likes quackers. Dick likes ducks. Dick likes cheese. So Dick likes cheese and quackers.

25. No dogcatcher is kind. Anyone who is kind loves dogs. So no dogcatcher loves dogs.

26. Some things that grunt are hogs. Some hogs are good to eat. So some things that grunt are good to eat.

27. Dogs are loyal. Dogs are friendly. Anything that is friendly and loyal makes a great pet. Hence, dogs are great pets.

28. Every newspaper Dr. E reads is published by an American publisher. All newspapers published by an American publisher are biased against Muslims. So Dr. E reads only newspapers that are biased against Muslims.

29. Some paraplegics can't play basketball. Belinda is a paraplegic. So Belinda can't play basketball.

30. Every dog loves its master. Dr. E has a dog. So Dr. E is loved.

31. Only janitors have access to this building after midnight. Paul is a janitor. So Paul has access to the building after midnight.

32. All mammals have both a heart and a liver. The fossil remains of this animal show that it had a heart and a liver. So it must have been a mammal.

33. Arguing backwards with "all" and arguing backwards with conditionals are related. We can rewrite:

All dogs bark.		If anything is a dog, then it barks.
Ralph barks.	as	Ralph barks.
So Ralph is a dog.		So Ralph is a dog.

Rewrite the following claims as *conditionals*:
a. All cats cough hair balls.
b. Every donkey eats hay.
c. Everything that's made of chocolate is good to eat.
d. Ducks like water.

C. Between One and All

1. Precise generalities

There are a lot of quantities between one and all. For example,

> 72% of all students who take critical thinking from Dr. E think he's the best teacher they've ever had. Harry took Dr. E's critical thinking course last year. So Harry thinks Dr. E is the best teacher he's ever had.

This is not valid. Where does it land on the strong–weak scale? We can say exactly: There's a 28% chance the premises could be true and the conclusion false, which is not strong. If the percentages are very high or very low, though, we can get a strong argument, assuming we know nothing more about the people or things involved:

> 95% plus-or-minus 2% of all cat owners have cat-induced allergies. Dr. E's ex-wife has a cat. So Dr. E's ex-wife has cat-induced allergies.

> Only 4 of the 123 students who take Dr. E's classes failed his final exam. Mary Ellen took Dr. E's class. So Mary Ellen passed Dr. E's final exam.

2. Vague generalities

There are a lot of ways we talk about all or a part of a collection without specifying a precise number:

> *All* dogs bark.
> *Almost all* dogs bark.
> *Many* students at this school will vote.
> *Most* dogs bark.
> *A lot of* students at this school will vote.
> *Some* students study hard.
> *A few* students study hard.
> *Very few* students dislike Dr. E.

Despite the ambiguity of the words "all" and "some," we can analyze whether arguments using those are valid. We have enough precision.

The rest of these quantity words are too vague to figure in valid arguments. Most of them are too vague even to be used in a claim. How could we tell if "A few students dislike Dr. E" is true? Or "A lot of students will vote"?

There are two vague generalities, though, that we can use in *strong* arguments:

> *Almost all* parakeets are under 2 feet tall.
> So the parakeets at Boulevard Mall are under 2 feet tall.

> *Very few* dogs don't bark.
> Spot is a dog.
> So Spot barks.

The premises give us good reason to believe the conclusion of each, even though the conclusion doesn't follow with no exceptions. The following are the "almost all" versions of the forms for "all":

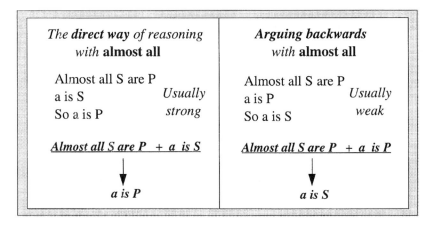

*The **direct way** of reasoning* *with **almost all***		*Arguing backwards* *with **almost all***	
Almost all S are P		Almost all S are P	
a is S	*Usually*	a is P	*Usually*
So a is P	*strong*	So a is S	*weak*
Almost all S are P + *a is S*		**_Almost all S are P_** + *a is P*	
↓		↓	
a is P		*a is S*	

But reasoning in a chain with "almost all" is usually weak. For example:

Almost all dogs like peanut butter. Almost all things that like peanut butter don't bark. So almost all dogs don't bark.

The premises are true and the conclusion false.

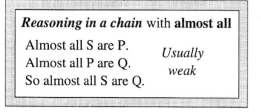

Reasoning in a chain with **almost all**

Almost all S are P.   *Usually*
Almost all P are Q.   *weak*
So almost all S are Q.

An argument of this form might be strong if you could specify exactly which S aren't P, and which P aren't Q. But that's just to say you need further premises to make it strong.

Exercises for Section C

1. Give two other ways to say "Almost all teenagers listen to rock music."

2. Give two other ways to say "Only a few adults listen to rock music."

Which of the argument forms in Exercises 3–6 are strong? Justify your answer.

3. Very few S are P.   5. Most S are P.
    a is S.   Most P are Q.
    So *a* is not P.   So most S are Q.

4. Very few S are P.   6. Almost all S are P.
    a is P.   Every P is Q.
    So *a* is not S.   So almost all S are Q.

Which of the following arguments are strong? Check by doing one of the following:

- Give a not unlikely possible way in which the premises are true and the conclusion false to show the argument is weak.
- Point out that the argument is in one of the forms we have studied.
- Explain in your own words why it's strong or weak.

7. Very few college students use heroin. Zoe is a college student. So Zoe doesn't use heroin.

8. Almost no students read *The New York Review of Books*. Martha reads *The New York Review of Books*. So Martha is not a student.

9. Only a very few dogs like cats. Almost no cats like dogs. So virtually no dogs and cats like each other.

10. No student who cheats is honest. Almost all dishonest people are found out. So almost all students who cheat are found out.

11. Almost all people who are vegetarians like pizza. Almost all vegetarians will not eat eggs. So all but a few people who like pizza will not eat eggs.

12. Most newspaper columnists have a college degree. Almost everyone who has a college degree is not self-employed. So most newspaper columnists are not self-employed.

13. Very few paraplegics can play basketball. Belinda is a paraplegic. So Belinda can't play basketball.

14. All but a few members of Congress have a college degree. Mr. Ensign is a member of Congress. So Mr. Ensign has a college degree.

15. Almost every dog loves its master. Dr. E has a dog. So Dr. E is loved.

Summary General claims are how we assert something about all or part of a collection. We studied ways to use "all," "some," "no," and "only" in arguments. We first tried to get clear about how to understand those words, and then noted that there are lots of equivalent ways to say them and to form their contradictories. Then we looked at a few valid and invalid forms of arguments using those words. We also saw that we could sometimes use diagrams to decide if an argument is valid.

Other precise general claims that lie between "one" and "all" normally don't figure in valid arguments, but we saw that sometimes they can figure in strong arguments.

Then we looked at vague generalities. Most don't figure in good arguments. Most don't even belong in claims. But "almost all" and "a few" can be used in strong arguments. We looked at some strong and weak argument forms using them.

Key Words

all	reasoning in a chain with "some"
some	direct way of reasoning with "no"
no	arguing backwards with "no"
only	precise generalities
contradictory	vague generalities
direct way of reasoning with "all"	direct way of reasoning with "almost all"
arguing backwards with "all"	arguing backwards with "almost all"
reasoning in a chain with "all"	reasoning in a chain with "almost all"

Further Study My book *Predicate Logic*, also published by Wadsworth, is an introduction to the role of general claims in arguments. An introductory course on formal logic will cover that, too.

Writing Lesson 8

Write an argument either for or against the following:

No one should be allowed to ride in the back of a pickup truck.

Check whether your instructor has chosen a different topic for this assignment.

As for Writing Lessons 6 and 7, you should hand in two pages:

First page: A list of premises and the conclusion.

Second page: The argument written as an essay with indicator words.

We should be able to see at a glance from the list of premises whether your argument is good. The essay form should read just as clearly, if you use indicator words well. Remember, there should be no claims in the essay form that aren't listed as premises.

The issue is simple. There's nothing subtle that you're supposed to do here that you haven't done on the previous assignments. You just need to know how to argue for or against a general claim. And for that you must be sure you can form the contradictory of it.

By now you should have learned a lot about writing arguments. You don't need more examples, just practice using the new ideas presented in the chapters. As a guide you can use the section *Composing Good Arguments* on p. 345, which summarizes many of the lessons you've learned.

Review Chapters 6–8

In Chapters 1–5 we established the fundamentals of critical thinking. In this part we looked at the structure of arguments.

Compound claims have their own structure. We saw that a compound claim, though made up of other claims, has to be viewed as just one claim. We saw that some arguments are valid and others typically weak due to their form relative to the compound claims in them.

For example, excluding possibilities is a form of valid argument using "or" claims. But if the "or" claim doesn't list all the possibilities, we get a bad argument, a false dilemma.

Conditionals took more care. We saw how to form their contradictories and considered how conditionals that are always true express necessary or sufficient conditions.

We noted the direct and indirect ways to make valid arguments using conditionals. Two forms are similar to valid conditional arguments but are usually weak: affirming the consequent and denying the antecedent. We decided that any argument using those shouldn't be repaired.

Reasoning in a chain with conditionals is valid, too. But if some of the conditionals are false or enough of them are dubious, the result can be a bad argument, a slippery slope.

Counterarguments are important to distinguish in the structure of arguments. Counterarguments are useful in our own writing because they help us see what assumptions we may have missed. Looking at counterarguments led us to consider the ways we can refute an argument: directly or by reducing to the absurd. We also saw four bad ways to attempt to refute an argument: phony refutations, slippery slopes, ridicule, and the worst, putting words in someone's mouth.

General claims are how we assert something about all or a part of a collection, and they lead to a lot of common mistakes in reasoning. We made sure how to understand the words "all," "some," "no," and "only". Then we considered how to form contradictories of general claims. We looked at a few valid and weak forms using general claims, finding that sometimes we could use diagrams to check for validity. But with vague generalities we had less scope. They don't figure in valid arguments, and only "almost all" and "a very few" seemed to yield strong argument forms.

You should now be able to use the methods of Chapters 1–5 on arguments that have more complicated structures. In the next part we'll work on spotting bad arguments. Then you can try your hand at evaluating lots of real arguments.

Review Exercises for Chapters 6–8

1. What is an argument?

2. What are the tests for an argument to be good?

3. What is a valid argument?

4. What does it mean to say an argument is strong?

5. Is every valid argument good? Explain.

6. How do you show an argument is weak?

7. Is every valid or strong argument with true premises good? Explain.

8. What is a compound claim?

9. Give a conditional, then rewrite it three ways.

10. a. What is a contradictory of a claim?
    b. Give an example of an "or" claim and its contradictory.
    c. Give an example of a conditional and its contradictory.

11. Give an example of arguing by excluding possibilities. Is it valid?

12. What is a false dilemma? Give an example.

13. Give an example of the direct way of reasoning with conditionals. Is it valid?

14. Give an example of the indirect way of reasoning with conditionals. Is it valid?

15. Give an example of affirming the consequent. Is it valid?

16. Give an example of denying the antecedent. Is it valid?

17. Is every argument that uses reasoning in a chain with conditionals good? Explain.

18. a. What does it mean to say that A is a necessary condition for B?
    b. Give examples of claims A and B such that:
        i.   A is necessary for B, but A is not sufficient for B.
        ii. A is sufficient for B, but A is not necessary for B.
        iii. A is both necessary and sufficient for B.
        iv. A is neither necessary nor sufficient for B.

19. Why is it a good idea to include a counterargument to an argument that you are writing?

20. What are the three ways of directly refuting an argument?

21. When you use the method of reducing to the absurd to refute an argument, does it show that one of the premises is false? Explain.

22. How does a slippery slope argument differ from reducing to the absurd?

23. How does ridicule differ from reducing to the absurd?

24. Give an example of an "all" claim and a contradictory of it.

25. Give an example of a "some" claim and a contradictory of it.

26. Give an example of a "no" claim and a contradictory of it.

27. Give an example of arguing backwards with "all." Is it valid?

28. Give an "only" claim and rewrite it as an "all" claim.

29. Give an example of a strong method of reasoning with vague generalities.

30. Give an example of a weak method of reasoning with vague generalities.

31. List the valid forms of arguments we studied in Chapters 6–8.

32. List the weak forms of argument in Chapters 6–8 that we said indicated an argument is unrepairable.

AVOIDING BAD ARGUMENTS

9   Concealed Claims

A. Where's the Argument?

Someone tries to convince us by a choice of words rather than by an argument—
the subtleties of rhetoric in place of reasoned deliberation.

    We've already seen an example: persuasive definitions. Someone tries to close
off the argument by making a definition that should be the conclusion. When a
person defines "abortion" to mean "the murder of an unborn child," he or she has
made it impossible to debate whether abortion is murder and whether a fetus is a
human being. Those conclusions are built into the definition.

    There are lots of ways we conceal claims through our choice of words.

> **Slanter**   A slanter is any literary device that attempts to convince by using
> words that conceal a dubious claim.

    Slanters are bad because they try to get us to assume a dubious claim is true
without reflecting on it. Let's look at some.

B. Loaded Questions

"When are you going to stop drinking and driving?"

Don't answer. Respond, instead, by pointing out the concealed claim: "What makes you think I have been drinking and driving?"

Loaded question A loaded question is a question that conceals a dubious claim that should be argued for rather than assumed.

When are you going to start studying in this course?

Why don't you love me anymore?

Why can't you dress like a gentleman?

What Do Dogs Dream About? (the title of an actual book)

The best response to a loaded question is to point out the concealed claim and begin discussing that.

C. What Did You Say?

1. Making it sound nasty or nice

President Reagan called the guerillas fighting against the Nicaraguan government in the 1980s "freedom fighters." The Nicaraguan government called them "terrorists." The labels they chose slanted the way we viewed any claim about those people. Each label concealed a claim:

"Freedom fighter"—The guerillas are good people, fighting to liberate their country and give their countrymen freedom.

"Terrorist"—The guerillas are bad people, inflicting violence on civilians for their own partisan ends without popular support.

Euphemism (yoo´-fuh-mizm) A euphemism is a word or phrase that makes something sound better than a neutral description.

Dysphemism (dis´-fuh-mizm) A dysphemism is a word or phrase that makes something sound worse than a neutral description.

In 1985 a State Department spokesman explained why the word "killing" was replaced with "unlawful or arbitrary deprivation of life" in its human rights report: "We found the term 'killing' too broad."

The descriptions in the personals ads are full of euphemisms, like "full-figured" or "mature." But not every description involves a euphemism. One man described himself as "attractive, fun, and fit." He may have lied, but he didn't use a nice word in place of a neutral one. Nor is every euphemism bad. We don't want to get rid of every pleasant or unpleasant description in our writing and speech. We just want to be aware of misuses where we're being asked to buy into dubious concealed claims.

Sometimes people use complicated sounding terms to make their work sound more "scientific." In *Nursing Process and Nursing Diagnosis* the authors talk about "diversional activity deficit"; when you read on, you realize they mean "boredom."

2. Downplayers and up-players

> The President and Congress managed to ensure that only two million jobs were lost in the economy from 2001–2004.

"Only"? That's downplaying the significance of a very disagreeable outcome. And "managed to" is up-playing the significance of the effort.

A *downplayer* is a word or phrase that minimizes the significance of a claim, while an *up-player* exaggerates the significance.

> "Yes, I have cheated in a class although it has never been off someone else. Just crib notes." *U. The National College Magazine,* November, 1996

The extreme version of an up-player is called *hyperbole* (hi-purr´-buh-lee):

Zoe: I'm sorry I'm late for work. I had a terrible emergency at home.
Boss: Oh, no. I'm so sorry. What happened?
Zoe: I ran out of mousse and had to go to the store.

> Chilly 58-degree days normally happen in December and January, but they blew in early to make Sunday teeth-chattering. *Las Vegas Review-Journal*

One way to downplay is with words that restrict or limit the meaning of others, what we call *qualifiers*—as in my promise that if you buy this book you will certainly pass this course.* Here's another example.

> The city will install stop signs this week for a four-way stop at the corner of St. George Boulevard, attempting to cut down accidents and prepare motorists for a stoplight at the intersection.
>
> "The city has recorded six accidents at the intersection in the past four months, and there may have been more that were not reported," said city traffic engineer Aron Baker. *The Spectrum,* September 23, 1996

---

* Purchaser must agree to study this material at least four hours per day during the term.

What did he say? Were there more accidents? No. There *may have been* more. But then there may not have been more. Or aliens may have landed at that intersection. The qualifiers "may" and "might" allow someone to suggest what he's not willing to say. In a badly written history book you'll find those words too often: "Thomas Jefferson may have thought that . . .".

> Zoe (to her boss): I am truly sorry that it has taken so long for you to understand what I have been saying.

Zoe isn't sorry at all. A *weaseler* is a claim that's qualified so much that the apparent meaning is no longer there.

People also downplay by using quotes or a change in voice:

> He got his "degree" from a beauty school.

The hidden claim is "A degree from a beauty school is not really something worth calling a degree."

3. Where's the proof?

By now you must be convinced what a great textbook writer I am. It's obvious to anyone. Of course, some people are a little slow. But surely you see it.

In the last paragraph I didn't prove that I was a great textbook writer, though I made it sound as if I were proving something. I was just reiterating the claim, trying to browbeat you into believing it with the words "obvious," "some people are a little slow," "surely," "must be convinced."

> **Proof substitute**   A proof substitute is a word or phrase that suggests the speaker has a proof, but no proof is actually offered.

When I was an undergraduate, I had a famous teacher for an upper-division mathematics course, Professor Fröelich. One day he wrote a claim on the board and said, "So the following is obvious." Then he stopped and looked puzzled. He went to the end of the blackboard and looked at the wall for a few minutes. Then he returned and said, "Yes, it is obvious," and continued.

I always say I prefer a student who asks questions. It's better to be thought dumb and learn something than to sit on your ignorance. If someone tells you it's obvious, or conceals a lack of proof with flowery language, don't be cowed—ask for the proof.

Ridicule, which we looked at before, is a particularly nasty form of proof substitute: That's so obviously wrong it's laughable.

> Rats can reason? Sure, and the next thing you know you'll be inviting them over to play poker.

No argument has been given for why rats can't reason.

Another way to conceal that you have no support for your claim is to ***shift the burden of proof***.

Zoe: Rats can reason.
Dick: You've got to be joking.
Zoe: O.K. then, mister smarty-pants, tell me why you think they can't.

The burden of proof is on the person putting forward the claim. The implausible assumption here is "I don't have to support my assertions; you have to show why they aren't true." This is a variation on the theme that whatever's plausible must be true (Section D.2 of Chapter 5).

4. Innuendos

Any concealed claim is an ***innuendo***. But usually we use that term for concealed claims that are really unpleasant.

Zoe: Where are you from?
Harry: New York.
Zoe: Oh, I'm sorry.

Just to belabor the point, the concealed claim is "You deserve pity for having had to live in New York." Innuendos imply nasty claims (Section D of Chapter 4), as politicians know well: "I agree. My opponent is telling the truth this time."

D. Slanters and Good Arguments

You may be tempted to use slanters in your own writing. Don't. Slanters turn off those you want to convince—you'll only be preaching to the converted. Worse, though they may work for the moment, they don't stick. Without reinforcement, the other person will remember only the joke or jibe. A good argument can last and last—the other person can see the point clearly and reconstruct it. And if you use slanters, your opponent can destroy your points not by facing your real argument but by pointing out the slanters.

> If you reason calmly and well you will earn the respect of the other, and may learn that the other merits your respect, too.

When evaluating someone else's argument, acknowledge that he or she may have been a bit emotional. Get rid of the noise—ignore the slanting, interpret the claims neutrally, and see if there is a good argument.

If there are just too many slanters, though, used time and again, then it's clear the other person can't or won't reason well. The Principle of Rational Discussion doesn't apply.

Summary   The point is to recognize slanters. Labels and classifications like
"downplayer," "weaseler," or "innuendo" are aids to help you learn how to
recognize that something bad is going on in an argument. Often not just one,
but two or more labels apply.

You know the material in this chapter when you can take an argument and
point out the concealed claims in it, rewriting to eliminate slanted language. The
labels are just shorthand for explanations you can give in your own words.

Key Words

slanter	downplayer	weaseler
loaded question	up-player	proof substitute
euphemism	hyperbole	burden of proof
dysphemism	qualifier	innuendo

Exercises for Chapter 9

1. Come up with a loaded question you might pose to an instructor to try to make him or
    her give you a better grade.

2. Give a loaded question you might ask a police officer who stops you.

3. Give an example of "politically correct" language and rephrase it in neutral language.

4. Give a euphemism and a dysphemism for each of the following. Be sure your word or
    phrase can be used in a sentence in place of the original.
    a. Used car.
    b. Sexually explicit books.
    c. Mentally handicapped person.
    d. Unemployed person.

5. Find an example of a euphemism from a network news broadcast.

6. Find an example of a dysphemism from a network news broadcast.

7. Find an example of a downplayer. Say what the hidden claim is.

8. Find an example of hyperbole from a network news broadcast.

9. Typical proof substitutes are "obviously," and "everyone knows that . . .". List six more.

10. Find an example from *another* textbook in which it sounds like the author is giving
    an argument, but there's really no proof.

11. Find an example from a political speech in which it sounds like the speaker is giving
    an argument, but there's really no proof.

12. Write a neutral description of someone you know well, one that a third party could use to
    recognize him or her. Now write a slanted version by replacing the neutral terms with
    euphemisms or dysphemisms, adding downplayers or up-players.

13. Rewrite the following actual quotes in neutral language:
    a. "Our operatives succeeded with the termination with extreme prejudice."
        (Reported by the CIA)
    b. "There was a premature impact of the aircraft with the terrain below."
        (Announced by the FAA)

Say what, if anything, is wrong with the following. Make any concealed claim explicit.

14. Dick: That was really rotten, making me wait for an hour.
    Zoe: I'm sorry you feel that way.

15. I was only three miles over the speed limit, Officer.

16. Thousands of words from U.S. officials, it appears, have proved no match for the last week's news, which produced a barrage of pictures of wounded Afghan children and of Israeli tanks rolling into Palestinian villages.
    "Talking heads just can't compete," a Western diplomat in Cairo said. "The images touch emotions, and people in this part of the world react according to their emotions."
    New York Times News Service, October 19, 2001

17. "In a way, we're a kind of a Peace Corps."
    A training director of the Fort Bragg Green Beret Center, 1969

18. How many years in prison should someone get for sending a virus out on the Internet that infects thousands of machines?

19. It seems fairly safe to assume that foreign-exchange dealers are human and hence more intelligent than ants. We may occasionally have our doubts, but broadly speaking this is true.   Paul Ormerod, *Butterfly Economics*

20. U.S. Air Force Colonel David Opfer, air attaché in Cambodia, complained to reporters about their coverage of the Vietnam War, "You always write bombing, bombing, bombing. It's not bombing; it's air support."

21. Did you hear that the lumber company is planning to cut down the forest?

22. Students should be required to wear uniforms in high schools. It has been well documented that wearing uniforms reduces gang violence.

23. A book on Hopi prophecies by a former Lutheran minister [Rev. Thomas Mails] has reignited a battle between tribal members and the author about the sanctity of his actions.
    Mails claims he and Evehema recently deciphered a symbol on an ancient Hopi stone tablet that revealed the next world war will be started by China at an undisclosed time.
    "If what they told me is true, it's the most important message in the world today," Mails said.   Associated Press, September 30, 1996

24. Despite the fact that [Benjamin] Franklin was out of touch with the centers of European thought, his ideas on electricity were truly original and fundamental.
    Gordon S. Wood, *The New York Review of Books*, September 26, 2003

25. Maria: Wanda's so sad. It looks like she's in another bout of blues.

26. The gaming industry in Nevada recorded another record year of profits.

27. (In a review of a book that contains descriptions of leaders of the Soviet Union)
    Even for politicians, they spend a disproportionate amount of their time drinking, plotting, lying, swearing, and insulting one another.
    Robert Cottrell, *The New York Review of Books*, May 1, 2003

28. Manuel: Hey, Dr. E, I read in the *New Scientist* that in Queensland, Australia, you can
buy free-range eggs endorsed by the Australian humane society, where the
egg boxes say, "These eggs come from hens that are: Free from hunger and
thirst; Free from pain, injury and disease; Free from fear and distress; Free
from discomfort; Free to express themselves."
    Dr. E: Great. I should apply for a job as a free-range hen.

29. "It's not a matter of life and death. It's more important than that."
Lou Duva on the fight of his boxer against Mike Tyson

30. The U.S. economy shed 1.4 million jobs over the 12 months ended in March.
USA Today, March 24, 2002

31. Tom: Hey, Dr. E, did you read in the newspaper what Madonna said after she had her
first child this week? "This is the greatest miracle that's ever happened to me."
    Dr. E: The greatest miracle that ever happened to Madonna is that she had a career in
music.

32. Charles Barkley played for the Houston Rockets against the Utah Jazz in the 1997
NBA playoffs. Speaking before the Lakers' loss to the Jazz in those playoffs, he said,
"We're not like the Lakers. We try to use our brains."

33. That corporation wants to erect a hotel in an unspoiled wilderness area.

34. "We didn't turn him down. We didn't accept him." President of Springdale Country
Club (Princeton, N.J.), concerning an African-American applicant for membership.

35. (A written response by a female department chair to a male professor who complained
that she had interfered with the teaching of his course by giving a student a grade the
professor hadn't authorized without telling the professor)

    I should have spoken to you before I took my action, and I apologize. I am an
inexperienced administrator, and also a woman who often doesn't "get" the
hierarchical, dominance-based way that males perceive situations.
Barbara Hannan

36. The proposed ban on bulk shipments [of tequila to the United States] would not take
place until January 2005, and Greisser said the year's delay was to provide Mexican
companies time to expand their bottling plants.
    "This proposal could have a grave effect on consumers worldwide through higher
prices, fewer choices and the significant potential for serious product shortages," said
Peter Cressy, president of the Distilled Spirits Council of the United States.
Albuquerque Journal, Sept. 26, 2003

37. In Pittsburgh, Steve Finley's sixth-inning homer struck a woman in a wheelchair located
behind a protective railing . . . .
    Several fans rushed immediately to assist the woman in the right-field stands before
a paramedic arrived. She received several stitches in her head but otherwise was not
seriously injured.   Associated Press, May 15, 2002

38. [Malcolm] Sharbutt [co-star of the current production and two-year veteran] attributes
the staying power [of the Vortex theater] to the plays on the program. "It's because we

offer a different venue than the other places in town," he says. "You can see 'Arsenic and Old Lace' or a play by Neil Simon anywhere in town, but we're going to do plays about junkies and rape and bad families. We try to keep it real."

Albuquerque Tribune, January 10, 2003

39. A ghost is a translucent being that lives in abandoned houses.

40. The United States has no plans at present for invading Cuba.

41. At last our government has decided to give compensation to the Japanese who were resettled in internment camps during World War II.

42. *Blondes aren't dumb—they're just slow*
Berlin—Blonde women are not dumber than brunettes or redheads, a reassuring study shows—they are just slower at processing information, take longer to react to stimuli and tend to retain less information for a shorter period of time than other women.
   "This should put an end to the insulting view that blondes are airheads," said Dr. Andrea Stenner, a blonde sociologist who studied more than 3,000 women for her doctoral research project.
Weekly World News, October 15, 1996

43. On the day that Wislawa Symborski was awarded the Nobel Prize for Literature, there were orders for 12,000 copies of her most recent book. Dori Weintraub, the publicist for Symborski's American publisher, Harcourt Brace, said, "For a Polish poet, that's not bad."

44. *One injured in one-car rollover*
A West Valley, Utah, woman was injured Sunday when she apparently fell asleep at the wheel on Interstate 15.
   Utah Highway Patrol dispatch reports that 18-year-old Jennifer Gustin was heading north on I-15 Sunday morning about 7:30 a.m. when she fell asleep at the wheel.
   Gustin drifted off to the right and then over-corrected to the left. The vehicle rolled and then came to rest on its top in the median. Gustin was not wearing a seat belt and was partially ejected from the vehicle.
   UHP reports state she suffered from internal injuries.
   She was taken to Valley View Medical Center in Cedar City following the accident and was later transferred to Pioneer Valley hospital in West Valley, Utah.
   Nancy Camarena, 19, also of West Valley, was in the car, but received no injuries despite not wearing a seat belt.
Tyson Hiatt, The Spectrum, April 30, 1996

45. The slayings of four Army wives at Fort Bragg in the past six weeks, all allegedly by their husbands, has prompted the Army to re-evaluate the base's family counseling program. . . .
   "It's mind boggling," said Henry Berry, manager of family advocacy programs at Fort Bragg. "To be absolutely honest, I was completely caught off guard. We're going to look at these cases to prevent them from happening in the future." . . .
   Until the recent murders, base officials said no domestic abuse deaths involving base personnel had occurred in the past two years.
Associated Press, July 27, 2002

46. Long the subject of human rights criticism from the United States, China shot back today with a rebuttal, saying the U.S. government continually denounces other nations while "turning a blind eye to its own human-right-related problems." . . .

    Among the report's many assertions, which it buttressed with a flurry of statistics:

    • The United States is "wantonly infringing upon human rights of other countries" with military and political actions.

    • American mass media are "inundated with violent content," which in turn encourages more violence. "A culture beautifying violence has made young people believe that the gun can 'solve' all problems," the report says.

    • Police brutality, torture and forced confession are common, and death row is full of "misjudged or wronged" inmates. Prisons are overcrowded and inhumane.

    • Americans living in poverty are "the forgotten 'third world' within this superpower," and the gap between rich and poor is growing.

    • Violence against women and sexual abuse of children are common.

Ted Anthony, Associated Press, March 11, 2002

Additional Exercises

47. Identify every slanter in the following letter to the editor, either eliminating it or rewriting neutrally. Then evaluate the argument.

I am writing this letter to complain about the stupid, ridiculous $4 fee they are trying to impose on people using Snow Canyon [a large state park recreational area near St. George, Utah where there had previously been no fee]. It is getting harder and harder to find forms of recreation that don't cost money in this area. Now you have to pay $4, even if it's just to sit on the sand for a few minutes and collect some rays.

    I've never really had a problem paying $5 to get into Zion's Park [a national park nearby], because going to Zion is an all day event. However, going to Snow Canyon is not. It's a place you go to after work or school when you only have a couple of free hours and a case of spring fever. Being charged for it would be comparable to charging $4 to enter the city park.

    I don't feel that my presence in Snow Canyon is costing the state any extra expense that needs to be covered. The only facility I ever use is the road that goes through the park. It is my understanding that the fee isn't new, but they haven't had the staff to collect it until now. So in other words, they need the $4 to pay for the bigger staff, and the reason they need a bigger staff is to collect the $4 (a slight case of circular logic).

    It just seems like we are losing more and more freedom all the time. Next they'll probably start charging us $4 to go on to the Sugar Loaf on the red hill. Who knows, maybe some day they will have government officials waiting on the streets to collect money from us every time we leave the house—to pay for the air we breathe—or has that already happened?

Shawn Williams, *The Spectrum*, March 24, 1996

48. Bring to class a letter to the editor. Read it to the class. Then replace all the slanters and read it again.

Further Study   Courses on rhetoric and on advertising spend a lot of time looking at slanters in non-argumentative persuasion.

10 Too Much Emotion

Appeals to Emotion

Emotions do and should play a role in our reasoning: We cannot even begin to make good decisions if we don't consider their significance in our emotional life. But that does not mean we should be swayed entirely by our emotions.

An *appeal to emotion* in an argument is just a premise that says, roughly, you should believe or do something because you feel a certain way. Often we call the entire argument in which such a premise appears an appeal to emotion.

Here's an example from when Suzy and Tom were watching TV:

Suzy: Did you see that ad? It's so sad, I cried. That group says it will help those poor kids. We should send them some money.

To construe this as a good argument, we need to add "If you feel sorry for poor kids, you should give money to any organization that says it will help them." That's an *appeal to pity*, and it's simply implausible, since some drug cartels help kids, too.

Compare that to what Zoe said to Dick last week:

We should give to the American Friends Service Committee. They help people all over the world help themselves, and they don't ask those they help whether they agree with them. They've been doing it well for nearly a century now, and they have very low overhead: almost all the money they get is given to those who are in need. All those people who don't have running water or health care deserve our help. Think of those poor kids growing up malnourished and sick. We've got enough money to send them at least $50.

This requires an unstated premise appealing to pity, too. But it isn't just "Do it because you feel sorry for someone." What's needed is something like "If you feel sorry for people, *and* you have a way to help them that is efficient and morally upright, *and* you have enough money to help, then you should send the organization money." That seems plausible, though whether this is the best use of Zoe and Dick's money needs to be addressed.

Appealing to fear is a way politicians and advertisers manipulate people. For example, on the cover of a free three-minute video mailed to voters' homes in Las Vegas there is a picture of a bearded young man in a sweatshirt, pointing a gun directly at the reader with the following text:

At 14 Years Old He Stole A Car.
At 16 He Raped.
At 17 He Killed.
And He Still Doesn't Have A Record.
We Cannot Continue To Allow Violent Criminals To Terrorize Our Neighborhoods.

Las Vegas Review Journal Tuesday, June 25, 1996	Reuter News Service Friday, June 18, 1996	Reno Gazette Journal Sunday, July 14, 1996
Living in Fear	Nevada Rated Most Dangerous State	Youth-Crime Increase Alarms Officials
"*. . . By many measures, the threat of youth related crime and its fallout are on the rise in Las Vegas Valley . . .*"	"*. . . Nevada is the most dangerous state in the nation this year . . .*" *according to an independent midwest research firm.*	"*The rise in violent crime young people commit is the most serious issue confronting the juvenile system today . . .*"

Elect COBB Nevada State Senate

This is an argument. The unstated conclusion is "You should vote for Cobb." It is a bad argument. The only reason it gives for electing Cobb is fear. And in this particularly egregious example it doesn't even link the fear to the conclusion. An appeal to fear is bad if it substitutes one legitimate concern for all others, clouding our minds to alternatives.

Often it requires some thought to see whether an appeal to fear is good. Consider the advertisement:

A lonely road. Your car breaks down. It's dark. Aren't you glad you bought a Dorkler brand cellular phone?

The implicit argument here is "Because your car might break down at night on a lonely road, you should buy a Dorkler brand cellular phone." What's needed to make it a strong argument is a premise like "Dorkler brand cellular phones will save you from the dangers of the night." That's not so implausible. But it isn't enough.

Also needed is "Your only consideration in deciding whether to buy *this* brand of cellular phone is your concern about your safety." That's implausible.

But sometimes an appeal to fear can be the sole legitimate factor in making a decision:

> Zoe: You shouldn't drive so fast in this rain.
> Dick: Why not?
> Zoe: The roads are very slippery after the first rain of the season,
>   and we could get into a serious accident.

There's nothing wrong here. The argument appeals to Dick's fears, but appropriately so. The unstated and quite plausible appeal to emotion is "You should slow down driving in the rain if you are afraid of getting into a serious accident."

An *appeal to spite*, the hope of revenge, is invariably rejected as bad by some people on moral grounds. In some cultures, though, it's not only acceptable, but a moral imperative to "get even," to preserve one's "honor." We encounter this kind of argument often enough:

> Dick: Hi, Tom. What's wrong with your car?
> Tom: The battery's dead. Can you help me push it? Harry will steer.
> Dick: Sure.
> Zoe: (whispering) What are you doing, Dick? Don't you remember
>   that Tom wouldn't help you fix the fence last week?

What Zoe said isn't an argument, but we can construe it as one: "You shouldn't help Tom start his car, because he wouldn't help you last week." The premise needed to make this a strong argument is "You shouldn't help anyone who has refused to help you (recently)." We'll leave to you whether that's plausible.

An appeal to spite often invokes the "principle" that *two wrongs make a right*. For example, when a new national monument was declared in Utah just before the 1996 presidential election, some who were opposed to it complained there was no consultation before the decision, no "due process." Here's what the Southern Utah Wilderness Alliance, strong lobbyists for the monument, said in their November 1996 *Bulletin*:

> Q: What about due process?
> A: Due process meant nothing to Utah politicians last year when they tried to
>   ramrod their anti-wilderness proposal down the throat of not only Utahns,
>   but all Americans; their intransigence only proved to the President that
>   rational negotiation on land protection issues in southern Utah is not possible.

An argument that *calls in your debts* appeals to the opposite of spite: "You should believe or do something if you owe someone a favor." For example,

How can you go to the movies with Harry and not watch the game with me? Don't you remember how I helped you wash your car last week?

Calling in your debts as a motive is often nothing more than milking guilt.

It isn't only the negative emotions that are played on in trying to convince. A *feel-good argument* is one that appeals to our wanting to feel good about ourselves. Yesterday Suzy said to Dr. E,

> I really deserve a passing grade in your course. I know that you're a fair grader, and you've always been terrific to everyone in the class. I admire how you handle the class, and I've enjoyed your teaching so much that it would be a pity if I didn't have something to show for it.

"Gee," Dr. E thinks, "I guess I should pass her . . . No, wait, she hasn't given me any reason to change her grade." The premise that's missing is "You should give a passing mark to anyone who thinks you're a great person." This *apple polishing* is an *appeal to vanity*.

But not every comment on what seems to be vanity is a bad argument:

> *To Have and to Hold*
> Get healthy, shiny hold with Pantene® Pro-V® Hairspray. The pro-vitamin formula penetrates to make your hold strong and your shine last. Now, spray your way to all-day hold and all-day shine. With Pantene Pro-V Hairsprays. PANTENE PRO-V For Hair So Healthy It Shines

This attempt to convince you to buy their hairspray isn't necessarily bad. It requires an unstated premise that you want to look good with shiny, well-kept hair. That may be true. Whether to believe the other claims, though, and whether to believe the unstated premise that this hairspray is the best to satisfy your desire to look good, are the real issues.

Yet sometimes invoking our wish to feel good is all that's needed. As Zoe said to Dick:

> We should go to the Zoe Austen movie tonight. I've always liked her novels, and I'm sure I'll enjoy it, and you said it was my turn to pick.

After all, what besides feeling good is there in making a choice of which movie to attend?

Each appeal to emotion we've looked at has a prescriptive conclusion; each is an attempt to convince someone that he or she should do something.

> An appeal to emotion in an argument with a *prescriptive* conclusion can be good or can be bad. Being alert to the use of emotion helps clarify the kinds of premises needed in such an argument, so we can more easily analyze it.

Labeling an argument as an appeal to emotion, then, is not an analysis of the argument, but only a helpful start to seeing whether the argument is good or bad. Except in some cases, . . .

This is an appeal to emotion with a *descriptive* conclusion, an example of *wishful thinking*. It's bad. Why should we believe some description of the world is true just because we are moved by our emotions? Wanting it so doesn't make it so.

> Any appeal to emotion with a *descriptive* conclusion is bad,
> if the appeal cannot be deleted as premise.

Exercises for Chapter 10

1. Write a *bad* argument in favor of affirmative action whose only premises appeal to pity.

2. Find an advertisement that uses apple polishing. Is it a good argument?

3. Find an advertisement that uses an appeal to fear. Is it a good argument?

4. Make up an appeal to some emotion for the next time a traffic officer stops you.

5. Report to the class on a "calling in your debts" argument you've heard.

6. Give an example of an appeal to spite that invokes what someone believes. (Hint: Look at political speeches.) Is it a good argument?

7. Give an example of an *appeal to patriotism*. Is it a good argument? (Samuel Johnson: "Patriotism is the last refuge of a scoundrel.")

For each of the following, decide if it is an argument. If it is, decide if it is an appeal to an emotion, and if so, which emotion(s). Then decide whether it is a good argument.

8. Zoe: We should stop all experimentation on animals right now. Imagine, hurting those poor doggies.
   Dick: But there's no reason why we shouldn't continue experimenting with cats. You know how they make me sneeze.

9. Vote for Senator Wong. He knows how important your concerns are.

10. Before you buy that Japanese car, ask whether you want to see some Japanese tycoon get rich at your expense, or whether you'd prefer to see an American kid get a meal on his plate next week.

11. Dear Dr. E,
I was very disappointed with my grade in your critical thinking course, but I'm sure that it was just a mistake in calculating my marks. Can I speak with you this Tuesday, right before I have lunch with my uncle, Dr. Jones, the Dean of Liberal Arts, where we plan to discuss sexual harassment on this campus?

Sincerely, *Wanda Burnstile*

12. Mom: Go ahead, Zoe. Live with your boyfriend, Dick. Who am I to say no? I'm just your mother. Break my heart.

13. Sunbathing does not cause skin cancer. If it did, how could I enjoy the beach?

14. Democracy is the best form of government, otherwise this wouldn't be the greatest country in the world.

15. Smoking can't cause cancer or I would have been dead a long time ago.

16. (Advertisement)
Impotent? You're not alone.
Men naturally feel embarrassed about any sexual problem, but the fact is, impotence is a treatable medical symptom. Virtually every one of the twenty million men in America struggling with this problem could overcome it with the proper treatment from our physician, David Owensby, MD, The Diagnostic Center for Men in Las Vegas. We offer:

–Medically effective, nonsurgical treatment in over 95% of all men.
–Trained and certified male physicians and staff.
–Strictly confidential & personalized care.
–Coverage by most private insurance and Medicare.
–More than 25,000 successfully treated men nationwide.

When men find out how effectively we treat impotence, their most frequent comment is, "If I would have known, I would have worked up the courage to call sooner."
Call us. We can help.

17. Dear Senator:
Before you make up your mind on how to vote on the abortion bill, I'd like to remind you that those who support abortion rights usually have small families. A few years from now all my six children, and the many children of my friends, all of whom believe abortion is morally wrong, will be voting.

18. You mean that after we flew you here to Florida, paid for your lodging, showed you a wonderful time, all for free, you aren't going to buy a lot from us?

19. You shouldn't vote for gun control. It'll just make it easier for violent criminals to take advantage of us.

20. Wanda: I know this diet's going to work because I have to lose 20 pounds by the end of this month.

21. In Dr. E's class, if a student has to miss an exam, then he or she has to petition to be excused. If the petition is granted for a midterm, then the final counts that much more. If the petition is denied, the student fails the exam. Here's an excuse petition from one of his students, written before the exam. Is it a good argument? Should Dr. E grant the petition?

> October seventeenth through the twenty-first I will be out of town due to a family function. I am aware that my philosophy midterm falls on the 17th and, unfortunately, my flight leaves at 7 a.m. that morning. I am asking to please be excused from the midterm.
>
> My boyfriend of two and a half years is standing as the best man in his brother's wedding. Being together for two years, I have become as much a part of his family as he is. This wedding is a once in a lifetime event and I want to be there to share it with him.
>
> I am a 100% devoted student and would never intentionally miss an exam. However, this is something beyond my control. I understand that if my request is granted I will have to put forth extra effort and prepare myself for the final. With the only other alternative being to drop the course, I am fully prepared to do whatever it takes.
>
> I have attached a copy of my flight reservation as well as a copy of the wedding invitation for verification. I am aware that many teachers would not even give me the opportunity to petition to be excused when the midterm is the case, but I would more than appreciate it if you would grant my request.

Further Study   *Descartes' Error: Emotion, Reason, and the Human Brain* by Antonio R. Damasio is a good discussion of how emotions are essential to good reasoning.

11 Fallacies

A summary of bad arguments

A. What is a Fallacy?

We've seen lots of bad arguments. Each fits *at least* one of the conditions for not repairing an argument (p. 68) or else directly violates the Principle of Rational Discussion. We labeled a few kinds of these as the sort that typically are unrepairable.

> *Fallacy* A fallacy is a bad argument of one of the types that have been agreed to be typically unrepairable.

There are three kinds of fallacy types: structural fallacies, content fallacies, and violations of the Principle of Rational Discussion. For some fallacy types every single argument of that type is bad; for others, most, though not all, are bad. Even taking shortcuts in analyzing arguments requires judgment.

B. Structural Fallacies

Some arguments are bad just because of their form. It doesn't matter if they are about dogs and cats, or numbers, or truth and beauty. The form alone tells us the person isn't reasoning well. These are the bad arguments we learned about when we studied compound claims and general claims. Each, unless there are other claims as premises, is weak and unrepairable.

Fallacy type	*Similar type of valid or strong argument*
affirming the consequent If A, then B. B Therefore, A.	*direct way of reasoning* If A, then B. A Therefore, B.
denying the antecedent If A, then B. not A Therefore, not B.	*indirect way of reasoning* If A, then B. not B Therefore, not A.
arguing backwards with all All S are P. a is P. Therefore, a is S.	*direct way of reasoning with* all All S are P. a is S. Therefore, a is P.
reasoning in a chain with some Some S are P. Some P are Q. Therefore, some S are Q.	*reasoning in a chain with* all All S are P. All P are Q. Therefore, all S are Q.
arguing backwards with no All S are P. No Q is S. Therefore, no Q is P.	*direct way of reasoning with* no All S are P. No Q is P. Therefore, no Q is S.
arguing backwards with almost all Almost all S are P. a is P. Therefore, a is S.	*direct way of reasoning with* almost all Almost all S are P. a is S. Therefore, a is P.

reasoning in a chain with almost all
Almost all S are P.
Almost all P are Q.
Therefore, almost all S are Q.

When someone presents an argument that fits one of these fallacy types, we assume he or she is confused about how to reason. We don't try to repair it.

C. Content Fallacies

Many arguments are bad because they use or require for repair a false or dubious premise. Usually we have to spend some time analyzing the argument, isolating the dubious premise.

But some arguments look like ones we're always suspicious of. When we spot one of those, we look for the *generic premise* the argument uses or needs for repair. An argument that uses one of these generic premises isn't necessarily bad. Sometimes the premise is plausible or even clearly true. *The argument is a fallacy only if the premise is dubious and no other premises support the conclusion.*

- *Confusing objective and subjective*

    This claim is subjective. / This claim is objective.

- *Drawing the line*

    If you can't make this difference precise, there is no difference.

- *Mistaking the person (group) for the claim*

    (Almost) anything that _____ says about _____ is (probably) false.

- *Mistaking the person (group) for the argument*

    (Almost) any argument that _____ gives about _____ is bad.

- *Bad appeal to authority*

    (Almost) anything that _____ says about _____ is (probably) true.

- *Bad appeal to common belief (or practice)*

    If (almost) everyone else (in this group) believes it (or does it),
    then it's true (good to do).

- *Phony refutation*

    1. _____ has done or said _____, which shows that he or she
       does not believe the conclusion of his or her own argument.
    2. If someone does not believe the conclusion of his or her own
       argument, the argument is bad.

- *False dilemma*

    (This is the use of any "or" claim that is false or dubious.
    Sometimes an equivalent conditional is used.)

- *Slippery slope*

    (This is reasoning in a chain with conditionals where at least
    one of them is false or dubious.)

- *Appeal to emotion*

    You should believe or do _____ because you feel _____ .
    (This is always bad if the conclusion is a descriptive claim.)

D. Violating the Principle of Rational Discussion

Sometimes it seems the other person doesn't understand what's involved in rational discussion or is intending to mislead. And sometimes there's not even an argument.

- *Begging the question*

    The point of an argument is to convince that a claim is true. So the premises of an argument have to be more plausible than the conclusion.

- *Strawman*

    It's easier to knock down someone's argument if you misrepresent it, putting words in the other person's mouth.

- *Shifting the burden of proof*

    It's easier to ask for a disproof of your claims than to prove them yourself.

- *Relevance*

    Sometimes people say a premise or premises aren't relevant to the conclusion. But that's not a category of fallacy, just an observation that the argument is so weak you can't imagine any way to repair it.

There are two other bad ways to try to convince that we've considered. Though they aren't arguments, and thus aren't fallacies, they're worth noting as violations of the Principle of Rational Discussion.

- *Slanters*

    Concealing claims that are dubious by misleading use of language.

- *Ridicule*

    Making someone or something the butt of a joke in order to convince.

E. Is This Really a Mistake?

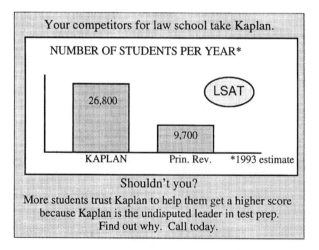

Your competitors for law school take Kaplan.

NUMBER OF STUDENTS PER YEAR*

26,800

LSAT

9,700

KAPLAN   Prin. Rev.   *1993 estimate

Shouldn't you?

More students trust Kaplan to help them get a higher score because Kaplan is the undisputed leader in test prep. Find out why. Call today.

This advertisement is an attempt to convince. Its unstated conclusion is "If you plan to take the LSAT, you should enroll at Kaplan."

It can be seen as a bad appeal to fear, with an unstated premise: "If you are afraid that your competitors will gain an advantage by enrolling at Kaplan, then you should enroll at Kaplan."

Or it can be seen as a bad appeal to common practice: "If this is the most popular way to prepare for the LSAT, and you wish to prepare for the LSAT, then you should enroll at Kaplan."

Either way the unstated premise is dubious. So the argument is bad. It's a fallacy no matter which analysis you use.

Often an unstated premise is required to make an argument valid or strong. And the richness of most arguments will allow for various choices. The argument is a fallacy only if for *each* (obvious) choice of premise, the premise is one of the generic kinds and is clearly false or dubious. *There is no reason to believe that a bad argument is bad in only one way.*

Sometimes an argument can be one of the types we call a fallacy while there is still some more or less obvious premise that will save it. But that's so rare we feel confident that arguments of the types we've labeled here are normally unrepairable.

The labels you've learned here are like names that go on pigeonholes: This bad argument can go in here. That argument there. This one fits into perhaps two or three of the pigeonholes. This argument, no, it doesn't fit into any, so we'll have to evaluate it from scratch. If you forget the labels, you can still remember the style of analysis, how to look for what's going wrong. That's what's important.

> *If you can describe what's wrong, then you understand.*
> The labels are just shorthand for doing the hard work of
> explaining what's bad in an argument.

F. So It's Bad, So What?

You've learned a lot of labels and can manage to make yourself unbearable to your friends by pointing out the bad arguments they make. That's not the point.

We are seekers of wisdom—or at least we're heading in that direction. We want to learn, to exchange ideas, not to stifle disagreements. We want to convince and educate, and to that end we must learn to judge bad arguments.

Some arguments are so bad there's no point trying to repair them. Start over.

Some arguments are bad because the other person intends to mislead you. In that case the Principle of Rational Discussion is violated. There's no point continuing the discussion, except perhaps to point out the other person's failings. These labels and analyses are then prophylactics against being taken in.

But often enough the person making the bad argument isn't aware that he or she has changed the subject or brought in emotions where they don't belong. Be gentle. Point out the problem. Educate. Ask the other person to fill in the argument, to add more claims. Then you can, perhaps, learn something, and the other person can, too.

Key Words   fallacy   generic premise
                structural fallacy   violating the Principle of
                content fallacy   Rational Discussion

Exercises for Chapter 11

The exercises here are a review of this chapter and some of the basic parts of earlier ones. Your real practice in using this material will come in evaluating the arguments for analysis that follow in the next section.

1. What are the three tests an argument must pass to be good?

2. State the Guide to Repairing Arguments.

3. State the conditions under which an argument is unrepairable.

4. Is every valid or strong argument with true premises good? Give an explanation and/or counterexample.

5. If a very strong argument has twelve true premises and one dubious one, should we accept the conclusion?

6. What does a bad argument tell us about its conclusion?

7. What is our most reliable source of information about the world?

8. Why isn't a slippery slope argument classified as a structural fallacy?

9. Why isn't a false dilemma classified as a structural fallacy?

10. How can we distinguish between ridicule and an attempt to reduce to the absurd?

11. Give an example of affirming the consequent.

12. Give an example of denying the antecedent.

13. Give an example of arguing backwards with "all."

14. Give an example of arguing backwards with "almost all."

15. Give an example of reasoning in a chain with "some." Is it valid?

16. Give an example of arguing backwards with "no."

17. Give an example of confusing objective and subjective. Is it a bad argument?

18. Give an example of drawing the line. Is it a bad argument?

19. Give an example of mistaking the person for the claim. Is it a bad argument?

20. Give an example of mistaking the person for the argument. Is it a bad argument?

21. Give an example of an appeal to authority that is *not* a bad argument.

22. Give an example of a phony refutation. Is it a bad argument?

23. Give an example of a false dilemma. Is it a bad argument?

24. Give an example of an appeal to pity. Is it a bad argument?

25. Give an example of an appeal to fear. Is it a bad argument?

26. Give an example of an argument that uses the generic premise of one of the types of content fallacies but which is *not* a bad argument.

27. Give an example of begging the question. Is it a bad argument?

28. Give an example of an argument that someone might criticize as having an irrelevant premise or premises.

29. What is a strawman? Give an example.

30. Why are slanters included in this chapter on fallacies?

Writing Lesson 9

Here is your chance to show that you have all the basic skills to write an argument. Compose an argument either for or against the following:

Cats should be legally prohibited from roaming freely in cities.

Check whether your instructor has chosen a different topic for this assignment.

This time, write only a (maximum) one-page argument. It should be clear and well structured, since you will have written out the premises and conclusion for yourself first. You can recognize slanters and fallacies, so don't use any in your argument. And you know to include possible objections to your argument.

By now you should have learned a lot about writing arguments. You don't need more examples, just practice. As a guide you can use the section *Composing Good Arguments* on p. 345, which summarizes many of the lessons you've learned.

Cartoon Writing Lesson D

For each cartoon write the best argument you can that has as its conclusion
the claim that accompanies the cartoon. List only the premises and conclusion.
If you believe the best argument is only weak, explain why. Refer back to Cartoon
Writing Lesson A on p. 55 for suggestions about how to do this lesson.

1.

Manuel is in an Olympic race for the handicapped.

2.

Flo is lying.

3.

Professor Zzzyzzx hit the wasps' nest.

4.

An adult who is not a city employee opened the fire hydrant.

5.

Spot made the boy go away.

6.

The professor is boring.

ARGUMENTS for ANALYSIS

Short Arguments
for Analysis

Here's a chance for you to put together all the ideas and methods of the previous chapters. Below are 75 short passages you might hear or read any day. Before you start analyzing them, take a look at how Tom is doing.

Dick: I can't stand Siamese cats. Ugh. They have those strange blue eyes.
Suzy: Mary Ellen has a kitten with blue eyes. I didn't know it was Siamese.

Argument? (yes or no) Yes.
Conclusion (if unstated, add it): Mary Ellen's cat is a Siamese.
Premises: Siamese cats have blue eyes. Mary Ellen's cat has blue eyes.
Additional premises needed to make it valid or strong (if none, say so): None.
Classify (with the additional premises): valid   strong ————X– weak
Good argument? (yes or no, with an explanation—possibly just the name
     of a fallacy) No. It's just arguing backwards with "all."
Excellent!

I hear that Brigitte Bardot is campaigning for animal rights. But she's the one who used to do advertisements for fur coats.

Argument? (yes or no) Yes—when rewritten.
Conclusion (if unstated, add it): You shouldn't listen to Brigitte Bardot
     about animal rights.
Premises: Brigitte Bardot used to do advertisements for fur coats.
Additional premises needed to make it valid or strong (if none, say so):
     Don't listen to anything Brigitte Bardot says about fur coats.
Classify (with the additional premises): valid   strong ————X– weak
Good argument? (yes or no, with an explanation—possibly just the name
     of a fallacy) No. I think it's mistaking the person for the argument.

At least you spotted that something was wrong. But the premise you added was just restating the conclusion. That would have made it valid all right, but also would have been begging the question.
       This is an example of mistaking the person for the claim. Review p. 97.

—**Kelly is a moron.**
—**Why do you say that?**
—**Because she's so stupid.**

Argument? (yes or no) Yes.
Conclusion (if unstated, add it):
Premises:
Additional premises needed to make it valid or strong (if none, say so):
Classify (with the additional premises):   valid   strong ————X— weak
Good argument? (yes or no, with an explanation—possibly just the name
        of a fallacy)   This is just begging the question and a bad argument. Do
I really need to fill in all the blanks in your form when it's this obvious?

*No, you don't need to fill in all the steps—as long as you're sure you've got it
right. And you almost do: It's begging the question, all right, but that's __valid__.
You've confused "bad argument" with "weak argument."*

**Wash your car? Sure, and the next thing you know you'll want me to vacuum the
upholstery, and fill up the gas tank, and maybe even make a car payment for you.**

Argument? (yes or no) Yes.
Conclusion (if unstated, add it): I shouldn't wash your car for you.
Premises:
Additional premises needed to make it valid or strong (if none, say so):
Classify (with the additional premises):   valid   strong ————X— weak
Good argument? (yes or no, with an explanation—possibly just the name
        of a fallacy)   This is a bad argument. I could rewrite it as a slippery
        slope, but it's pretty clear that the premises aren't plausible. It really
        borders on ridicule.

Good.

For each exercise, answer the following:

   Argument? (yes or no)
   Conclusion (if unstated, add it):
   Premises:
   Additional premises needed to make it valid or strong (if none, say so):
   Classify (with the additional premises):   valid   strong ———————— weak
   Good argument? (yes or no, with an explanation)

1. Wanda: I'm going to go on that Atkins diet. It's got to be safe and effective, with so
    many people doing it now.

2. Suzy: I know that there is ESP.
    Dick: How?
    Suzy: If there wasn't, there'd be too much left unexplained.

3. Suzy: I can't believe Dr. E got so angry about Ralph getting his essay from the Internet. Next thing you know, he's going to tell us we can't work on our homework together.

4. Zoe: The reason girls can't throw balls as well as boys is because their elbows are constructed differently.

   Dick: Sure, that explains it. And the reason men can't wash dishes well is because their wrists are constructed differently.

5. Dan was clever, but he couldn't go to college. His father disappeared leaving lots of debt, and his mother was ill. So Dan had to take care of his mother and work full-time.

6. Of course it's good for you—it's got all natural ingredients.

7. Lee: Maria and Manuel and I are thinking about getting a pet. What do you think?

   Dick: Get a dog.

   Tom: Get one of those small pigs. They're very intelligent animals. They make great pets. They learn to do tricks as well as any dog can. They can be housetrained too. And they're affectionate, since they like to cuddle. Pigs are known as one of the smartest animals there are. And if you get bored with it or it becomes unruly, you can eat it.

   Dick: Don't listen to him. The only pet he ever had was a turtle, and it died after two weeks. Kaput. Unless you call Suzy a pet.

   Tom: Geez, Dick, you're harsh. Zoe get on you about the dishes again?

8. Zoe: I'm going to go to City Hall to show my support for the gays who are trying to get marriage licenses.

   Mom: What? Don't you know that homosexuals getting married is wrong? Ask any of our family. Ask Uncle Stephen—he'll tell you that we all think it's wrong.

   Zoe: Uncle Stephen? He hasn't been right about anything since he said the Beatles would never get back together.

9. Manuel: Where is Maria? I'm counting on her for a ride to my early class.

   Lee: She must be asleep.

   Manuel: Then her alarm didn't go off.

10. From an interview with Vladimir Putin, President of Russia, on Russian national television, as reported in *The New York Review of Books,* May 25, 2000:

   Putin: We had a dog, true it was a different one . . . unfortunately, it died, run over by a car. . . . But the kids wanted a little dog, and they finally convinced me. Now it's not clear whose dog it is more—mine, my wife's, the kids' . . . . The dog just sort of lives here on its own.

   Interviewer (*jokingly*): Like a cat.

   Putin: (*not laughing at the joke, coldly*) No, no, don't insult our dog. It doesn't work as a cat. A dog is a dog. We really love it.

11. Unprotected sex is O.K. I know lots of people who do it, and what's the worst that can happen? You get pregnant.

12. Candidate for the Senate: My opponent doesn't even believe that inflation is a serious risk in this country. So how is he going to protect you from it?

13. Maria: I can't believe you bought a lottery ticket!
    Dick: Why not? Someone's got to win.
    Maria: The lottery's just a tax on people who don't understand mathematics.

14. [After a chemical explosion at a plant, where one man was killed by the explosion and four were injured, a man was interviewed who worked in that section of the plant. He had been on vacation at the time.]

    Powell said the idea of working every day in a plant filled with toxic chemicals hasn't worried him, and he plans to return when his vacation is over.

    "There are toxic chemicals in your house under your sink," he said. "There is constant training on how to handle them, and if you follow those guidelines, you're O.K. Every job has a potential hazard."   Tyson Hiatt, *The Spectrum,* July 31, 1997

15. Mary Giovanni, 83, was hunched over, weeding dandelions from her lawn, when informed that the atheists would be moving in down the street.

    She sat down on her front steps and lit a cigarette. A cross hung over the front door.

    She said God had taken two good men from her—her second husband, who died of asbestosis, and the fiancé who would have been her third, who died of a heart attack in the shower.

    But she doesn't hold that against God, and doesn't see how anyone could be an atheist.

    "God is everything. He's responsible for all this," she said, her left arm fanning out, her voice the sound of New Jersey gravel.

    She squinted up from the stoop at her visitor. "God makes it all happen. If *He* doesn't, who the hell does? I'd like them to tell me that."   *USA Today,* May 25, 1999

16. Tom: Everyone in the U.S. should have to speak English. Everyone's got to talk the same, so we can communicate easily, and it'll unify the country.
    Lee: Sure. But I have real trouble understanding people from New York. So why not make everyone speak just like me, with a Midwestern accent?

17. Zoe: We shouldn't go to the fair this year. You always get sick and I never have any fun. So what if it is a tradition?

18. Zoe: Dick, I can't believe you got goldfish at the fair. No goldfish from the fair will live longer than two weeks. So don't bother to buy a bowl for them.

19. Maria: Some of these cookies were baked by Mary Ellen.
    Zoe: And I know that some of the stuff Mary Ellen bakes is awful. So, thanks, but I won't eat any.

20. Dick: I've got to find a lawyer.
    Tom: Why?
    Dick: It's about that accident where the lady rear-ended me.
    Tom: Check out Mr. Abkhazian. He's been doing accident cases for 20 years.

21. Tom: It says in the paper they're going to start requiring all ATV owners to register their ATVs and display a license. That's crazy. Next thing you know they'll require us to wear helmets, and then make it illegal to drive near the lake in the national forest.

22. Suzy: Why don't you do something about Dick's smoking?

 Zoe: I don't want to give him a hard time.

 Suzy: The difference between you and me is that I care about people.

23. Reggie: Look, I deserve at least a C in this course. Here, I did all my homework and contributed in class, just like you said. I know I only got a D+ on the final, but our other work was supposed to be able to outweigh that.

 Ms. F: Perhaps I did say that, but I can't go back and change your grade. I'd have to change a lot of grades.

 Reggie: That's unfair and unethical. I'll take it to the department head.
 (Later in the head of department's office)

 Ms. F: So this student is going to come in and see you to complain about his grade. He thinks that just because he showed up regularly and handed in some homework he should get a good grade.

24. Psychiatrist: You are suffering from delusions of grandeur.

 Dr. E: What? What? There's nothing wrong with me.

 Psychiatrist: It is not normal to think that you are the smartest man in the world.

 Dr. E: But I am.

 Psychiatrist: Certainly you think so.

 Dr. E: Look, if Arnold Schwarzenegger came in and said he was the strongest man in the world, would you think he's crazy?

 Psychiatrist: Crazy? I did not say you were crazy. You are suffering from delusions of grandeur.

 Dr. E: O.K. Would Arnold Schwarzenegger be suffering from delusions of grandeur?

 Psychiatrist: Possibly not.

 Dr. E: So someone has to be the smartest person in the world.

 Psychiatrist: That's true.

 Dr. E: Why not me?

 Psychiatrist: Because you are not.

 Dr. E: How do you know?

 Psychiatrist: Trust me.

 Dr. E: You can't even define "delusions of grandeur," can you?

 Psychiatrist: I am trained to spot it when it occurs.

25. Dick: Now you're in for it. I told you the police would stop you if you didn't slow down.

 Zoe: Oh, no. If that police officer gives me a ticket, I'll get three points taken off my driver's license. And I'll lose my license if I get more than two points taken off.

 Dick: So let's hope you get off with a warning. Because if that police officer gives you a ticket, I'll have to drive you everywhere.

26. Lee: Hey! Our neighbors have a kid! I just saw Mrs. Goldenstone with a brand new baby, really tiny. She says its name is Louis.

 Maria: What? I never saw her pregnant. They must have adopted the child.

27. Tom: Everyone I know who's passed the critical thinking course has really liked it.
    Dick: Suzy liked that course.
    Harry: So she must have passed it. Amazing.

28. Israeli troops used Palestinian civilians as human shields and forced them to participate in dangerous military operations during the Israel sweep through a refugee camp in Jenin last month, according to a report released Friday by Human Rights Watch. . . .

    "When the Israeli army decided to go into this densely populated refugee camp, they had an obligation under international law to take all possible precautions to protect the civilian population," said [Peter] Bouckaert [senior researcher for HRW]. "Clearly the Israeli army failed to take the necessary precautions during its attack."

    Israel disputes that conclusion, noting that 23 of its own soldiers died in the fiercest urban warfare the [Israeli Defense Forces] has experienced in 30 years. "The extent of Israeli casualties and the duration of the combat are proof of the great efforts made by the IDF to conduct the operation carefully in an effort to bring to an absolute minimum the number of Palestinian civilian casualties," said an IDF statement.   CNN, 5/4/02

29. Manuel: Did you hear? Larry just got back from the Dead Kittens concert in Buffalo.
    Maria: Buffalo? Last month he went to Florida to hear them. And Wanda says he's planning to go to Atlanta next week for their big show there.
    Manuel: He must really like their music.

30. Lee: My calculus course is killing me. There's so much homework.
    Maria: Everyone who takes calculus complains about too much homework.
    Manuel: So Wanda must be taking calculus.

31. You should take your cousin to the dance because she's shy, and doesn't go out much, and is really sad since her dog died. It would make her feel good.

32. The U.S. Attorney General said that there was no need to investigate the President's campaign financing. So the President didn't do anything wrong.

33. *Saudi official blames Jews for Sept. 11 attack*

    The Saudi police minister [Nayef] has claimed Jews were behind the Sept. 11 attacks on the United States because they have benefited from subsequent criticism of Islam and Arabs, according to media reports.

    Interior Minister Prince Nayef made the remarks in the Arabic-language Kuwaiti daily Assyasah last month. The latest edition of Ain al-Yaqueen, a weekly Internet magazine devoted to Saudi issues, posted the Assyasah interview and its own English translation.

    In the interview, Nayef said he could not believe that Osama bin Laden and his network, including Saudi participants, worked alone.

    He was quoted as saying he believed terrorist networks have links to "foreign intelligence agencies that work against Arab and Muslim interests, chief among them is the Israeli Mossad [intelligence agency]."

    Albuquerque Tribune, December 5, 2002

34. You're good at numbers. You sort of like business. You should major in accounting—accountants make really good money.

35. Said by the CEO of a tobacco company at a U.S. Senate hearing questioning whether tobacco is a drug: "Would you prefer to be in a plane with a pilot who just drank or one who just smoked?"

36. Lee: Amazing. Did you see that Maria got a tattoo?
    Manuel: You're kidding. Well, if she did, then she must have gone to a professional. She's railed at the crazy kids who do it to each other.
    Lee: I've got to get the name of the guy she went to.

37. Dick: If Suzy doesn't pass her critical thinking class, she can't be a cheerleader unless she goes to summer school.
    Zoe: She's going to fail that course for sure.
    Dick: Looks like she'll be going to summer school.

38. Dick: Is this plate clean?
    Zoe: It's been through the dishwasher, so yes, it's clean.

39. Letter to the editor:
    Governor Pete Wilson signed a law making California the first state to require chemical castration of repeat child molesters. . . . This is one law that should be enacted in every state in the United States. I see the American Civil Liberties Union has called this procedure barbaric. However, the ACLU doesn't consider how barbaric it is when an adult molests a child.   Roger E. Nielsen, *The Salt Lake Tribune,* October 6, 1996

40. Tom: Either Suzy shows up in 10 minutes or I'll have to go to the game alone.
    Lee: I just saw her sit down with Zoe at the Dog & Duck coffeehouse on 3rd St.
    Tom: Guess I'm going to the game alone, then.

41. Suzy: There is no life on other planets. If there were, then there'd be some evidence.
    Lee: Many people have evidence of UFOs—pictures, videos, all that stuff.
    Suzy: Then I was wrong. There must be life on other planets.

42. Lee: Our kids should be allowed to pray in schools.
    Maria: What? If they're not allowed to pray, maybe God won't exist?

43. Zoe: It's not healthy to eat a lot of cholesterol.
    Dick: Why?
    Zoe: Because it's not good for your body.

44. Dick: The stupid ball went over the fence, Spot. Let's ask Harry to let us in. He's a tenant here, and I know that only tenants have a key to that gate.

45. Suzy: Either Dr. E doesn't like me or he misgraded my test, because I got a D.

46. Maria: I read that some of the cheerleaders were invited to try out for a movie they're going to film in that little town north of here.
    Lee: Tom said that some of the people at the auditions are going to get a real contract. Big money—like $900 a week.
    Maria: So maybe Suzy can finally pay me that $50 she's owed me since October. She'll get a part, or she can borrow it from one of her friends on the squad.

47. Maria: Dr. E's course is just great.
   Suzy: It's easy for you to say—you just got an A on the midterm.

48. Sixty-two of Utah's 134 credit unions—46 percent—are led by women CEOs, many of whom began their careers in entry-level positions and lack formal business education. . . .

   By comparison, none of the three-dozen banking companies operating in Utah have women CEOs, although women do hold numerous high-level positions within those organizations. . . .

   "Diversity is a priority for banks as it is with credit unions," said Howard Headlee, president of the Utah Bankers association. "But too few women meet the stringent qualifications boards of directors and banking regulators demand in top-level banking executives at publicly held companies," he said.

   "The regulatory environment does not allow a bank to look past safety and soundness issues for the sole purposes of achieving diversity," Headlee said.

   The Salt Lake Tribune, August 12, 2001

49. Adolescents who are emotionally unprepared engage in sex with serious consequences for their ability to form normal attachments later in life. Young people who are ignorant of sexually transmitted disease risk not only their immediate health but their lives by engaging in sexual intercourse. Over half of young women in America become pregnant before they are 20. For these reasons we should not only teach the mechanics of sexuality but also encourage young people to refrain from sexual intercourse.

50. Zoe: Dr. E, you have to pass Suzy.
   Dr. E: Why?
   Zoe: She said if you don't she's going to light herself on fire in the student union.

51. How can you doubt Dan's advice about getting a Jeep? He's only 25 and he already has an income over $150,000 a year.

52. (Contributed by a student)
   Student athletes should not be given special leniency in assigning course marks. Student athletes who do receive special leniency turn out to be failures. They are not given the mental challenge that regular students are given. All student athletes that I have ever met or seen that have received special leniency have not graduated from college. In order to make something of yourself, you must first graduate from college. Everyone that I have ever met or seen wants to make a good living and make something of themselves. On the other hand, all of the student athletes I know that do not receive special leniency have graduated and have been successful in life. Therefore, student athletes that want to be successful in life must not receive special leniency.

53. Smoking is disgusting. It makes your breath smell horrid. If you've ever kissed someone after they smoked a cigarette, you feel as though you're going to vomit. Besides, it will kill you.

54. Lee: Every computer science major is a nerd.
   Maria: None of the cheerleaders are majoring in computer science.
   Lee: Exactly—none of them are nerds.

55. I resent that. Our company is not racist. We give a donation to the NAACP every year.

56. Suppose this patient really does have hepatitis. Well, anyone who has hepatitis will, after a week, begin to appear jaundiced. Yellowing of the eyeballs and skin will proceed dramatically after two weeks. So if he has hepatitis now, since he's been feeling sick for two weeks, he should be jaundiced. But he isn't. So he doesn't have hepatitis.

57. (Summarizing a discussion heard on National Public Radio)
An experiment is being conducted to study temperature changes in the ocean using very low-frequency sound waves that will be generated in the South Pacific and picked up near the Arctic Circle. The sound waves will be generated two times a day for ten years.
   The interviewer, speaking to one of the people involved in the experiment, said that perhaps we shouldn't do this, since we don't know the effect of the sound on whales. The experimenter replied that the ocean is already so full of sound, if you count all the acousticians vs. all the supertankers, the supertankers would win hands down.

58. Zoe: (*Monday*) If you eat that candy bar, then you'll gain weight.
    Dick: (*Friday*) I gained weight again this week.
    Zoe: So you ate that candy bar on Monday.

59. Lee: It's odd. None of the bartenders here have ever been women.
    Zoe: But this is a union shop—all of them have been union members. So it looks like the union won't accept women.

60. Zoe: If you don't start helping around the house, doing the dishes and cleaning up, then you don't really understand what it means to be a part of a couple.
    Dick: O.K., O.K., look, I'm vacuuming. I'll do the dishes tonight.
    Zoe: So you do understand what it means to be part of a couple.

61. Professor Zzzyzzx: A dentist I am needing. My teeth they are killing me. That Dr. Bears, he is O.K., no? I read his advertising all the time.
    Dr. E: Don't go to him. I went to get a chipped front tooth fixed, and he kept me waiting an hour in the chair, and then wanted to sell me teeth whitening and a very expensive cap for the tooth. I got up and left. I ended up going to Dr. Hay, and he just filed the tooth down and it cost $60. It's been just fine.

62. Zoe: Boy, is Suzy down about her fight with Tom. If she goes out tonight, she'll get drunk. Why not call her and invite her for dinner?
    Dick: Too late. Manuel told me on the phone that she's already blotto.
    Zoe: So she did go out.

63. Lee: All felines cough up hair balls.
    Manuel: But ferrets don't cough up hair balls.
    Lee: Which is just what I thought. Ferrets aren't felines. They're more like dogs.

64. Tom: I can't believe you're an hour late!
    Suzy: What are you talking about?
    Tom: You said you'd meet me here at 7 to work on the English assignment.
    Suzy: I am not late.
    Tom: It's almost 8.
    Suzy: I said I'd be here a little after 7.

65. Manuel: There's Sam. Let's ask him to get us a drink.
    Maria: Only bartenders and managers are allowed behind the bar in this restaurant.
    Manuel: But Sam's a manager, so he's allowed behind the bar.

66. Maria: That's awful. How can you eat a steak?
    Suzy: Huh?
    Maria: You should be a vegetarian. I've been to those factory farms where they "raise" cattle and pigs. They're awful.
    Suzy: But I like steak. I just won't visit any factory farms.

67. You should not take illegal drugs. They can kill you. If you overdose, you can die. If you share a needle, you could get AIDS and then die. If you don't die, you could end up a vegetable or otherwise permanently incapacitated. By using drugs you run the risk of getting arrested and possibly going to jail. Or at least having a hefty fine against you. Although some think the "high" from drugs is worth all the risks, the truth is that they are addicted and are only trying to justify supporting their habit.

68. Doctor: You're going to have some serious heart problems if you don't start watching your fat intake, learn to relax, and get more exercise.
    Professor Zzzyzzx: That is just your opinion.

69. Beer has lots of vitamins and protein, so it can't be bad for my liver.

70. Lee: I read that almost all people who graduate from college end up earning more than $38,000 per year.
    Tom: So the guy in charge of maintenance who gets such a great salary must have graduated from college.

71. Lee: Every cat sheds hair on its master's clothes. No question about it.
    Suzy: Dr. E doesn't have a cat. So he doesn't have cat hair shed on his clothes.

72. To some Afghan commanders, the recent U.S. offensive against the Al-Qaida fighters in eastern Afghanistan failed because most of them got away. . . .
    "Operation Anaconda . . . is an incredible success," said Maj. Bryan Hilferty, spokesman of the 10th Mountain Division. "It took only 20 terrorists to kill 3,000 of the world's citizens in the World Trade Towers. We've killed hundreds and that means we've saved hundreds of thousands of lives. This is a great success."
                       Kathy Gannon, Associated Press, March 17, 2003

73. Mom: Well, what do you think? Did man evolve from cells and apes, or did God create man?
    Zoe: I don't know.
    Mom: Come on. You've got to have thought about it.
    Zoe: Oh, I guess I have, just never very hard. Beats me.
    Mom: You've got to believe one side or the other. Which is it?

74. Driving without wearing a seat belt is not dangerous or I would have been hurt a long time ago.

75. Dick: I can't believe that *Failing in Atlanta* didn't win an Oscar.
    Zoe: Nobody understands what art is.

Complex Arguments for Analysis

The Structure of Arguments

In this section we'll first look at the structure of more complex arguments than the ones you've seen so far. Then we'll analyze some longer passages. This will lead to a general outline of how to proceed in analyzing more complex arguments.

In many arguments, we support one premise from which we derive others, leaving as little as possible to be taken without support, creating a *subargument*. But it's not always obvious what the structure of the argument is. For example:

> Whatever you do, don't take the critical thinking course from Dr. E. *1*
> He's a really tough grader, *2* much more demanding than the other professors who teach that course. *3*   You could end up getting a bad grade. *4*

I've numbered every sentence or clause that might be a claim. But *1* isn't a claim, so we rewrite it as "You shouldn't take the critical thinking course from Dr. E." We can rewrite *3* as "He's much more demanding than the other professors who teach that course." Now what is the structure of this argument? There aren't any indicator words.

It seems to me that *1* is the conclusion. Why? If someone believed *2*, *3*, and *4*, then he or she would have some reason to believe *1*. Not awfully good reason, since some unstated premise(s) is needed to make the argument strong or valid. But it makes sense to say, "You shouldn't take the critical thinking course from Dr. E *because* he's a really tough grader"; while it seems silly to say, "You shouldn't take the critical thinking course from Dr. E, *therefore* he's a really tough grader."

When there are no indicator words ask:
- If I believed this claim, would I have more reason to believe that one?
- Can I put one of *therefore* or *because* between these two claims?

If it's not clear which claim is meant to support which other, that's a fault of the argument. In this argument, even with the conclusion identified, we still have two ways to interpret it:

(X)   Dr. E is more demanding than the other professors who teach that course.
Therefore, he's a really tough grader.
Therefore, you could end up getting a bad grade.
Therefore, you shouldn't take the critical thinking course from Dr. E.

(Y)   Dr. E is more demanding than the other professors who teach that course, and he's a really tough grader.
Therefore, you could end up getting a bad grade.
Therefore, you shouldn't take the critical thinking course from Dr. E.

To choose between these, we can use the Guide to Repairing Arguments to make the argument valid or strong. For (X) we'd need an unstated premise like:

(Almost) anyone who's more demanding than other professors who teach critical thinking is a really tough grader.

That's plausible. For (Y) we'd need something like:

If you take critical thinking from someone who's more demanding than other professors who teach that course and who is a really tough grader, then you could end up getting a bad grade. *a*

(We can use numbers for claims in the original argument and lowercase letters for claims we add.) That's a lot more plausible. It looks like (Y) is a better choice, though we still need a prescriptive claim to get from *4* to *1*. We can use:

You shouldn't take any course in which you might get a bad grade. *b*

That's what we need, even though it's not obviously true. In the end, then, this argument is only as good as the unsupported prescriptive premise *b*.

Even if there's no one right way to interpret this argument, that doesn't mean there aren't wrong ways. If you said that *4* supports *2*, that would be wrong.

Sometimes people use several premises hoping the combined weight of them will somehow bring about the conclusion. For example:

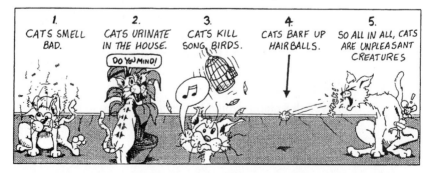

These are separate premises meant to support the conclusion. But someone who likes cats could just say "So?" after each of *1* through *4*. Compare:

Cats smell bad. *1*
Anything that smells bad is unpleasant. *a*
Cats kill songbirds. *3*
Anything that kills songbirds is nasty. *b*
Thus, cats are nasty and unpleasant creatures. *5*

Here it's not just piling up "facts" to support the conclusion. Claim *a* is the glue that links *1* to the conclusion; claim *b* is the glue that links *3* to the conclusion.

Some people think it's fine to give an argument with many independent premises supporting the conclusion: Here are lots of reasons to believe the conclusion—if you don't like this one, take that one. I've got a bag full of 'em.

That may convince some folks, but it shouldn't convince you. You're sharp enough to spot that after each independent premise you could ask, "So?" If it's not linked to the conclusion, the argument is still weak. When someone keeps piling up reasons with no glue, it just means you have to ask "So?" more often. It doesn't make the argument strong.

Here's how Tom analyzed the structure of two arguments in his homework.

The dogcatcher in this town is mean. *1*   **He likes to kill dogs.** *2*   **He is overzealous, picking up dogs that aren't really strays.** *3*   **Some people say he beats the dogs.** *4*   **So the position of dogcatcher should be eliminated.** *5*

Argument? (yes or no) Yes.

Conclusion: The position of dogcatcher should be eliminated.

Additional premises needed? If someone likes to kill dogs, picks up dogs that
      aren't really strays, and beats dogs, then he is mean. <u>*a*</u>
   If someone is mean, he shouldn't be dogcatcher. <u>*b*</u>

Identify any subargument: 2, 3, and 4 are independent and support *1*.
   Then *1* supports the conclusion, *5*.

  Good argument? Looks good to me.

You haven't been critical enough. The argument is really pretty bad. First, I agree that 2, 3, and 4 are independent. You can say they support 1, but 1 is vague and no improvement on 2, 3, and 4. I think it's too vague to be a claim. We do need something like your a. But for that we need a further premise, one you're always overlooking: "If people say that the dogcatcher beats dogs, then he does beat dogs." And that's pretty dubious. So instead of a, let's take: "If someone likes to kill dogs and picks up dogs that aren't strays, then he should not be a dogcatcher." That's true. But that doesn't get you the conclusion. What you then need is "If the person who is now dogcatcher shouldn't be dogcatcher, then the position of dogcatcher should be eliminated." And that is implausible. — Still, it's just your first try.

Today, education is perhaps the most important function of state and local governments. *1* Compulsory school attendance laws and the great expenditures for education both demonstrate our recognition of the importance of education to our democratic society. *2* It is required in the performance of our most basic public responsibilities, even service in the armed forces. *3* It is the very foundation of good citizenship. *4* Today it is a principal instrument in awakening the child to cultural values, in preparing him for later professional training, and in helping him to adjust normally to his environment. *5* In these days, it is doubtful that any child may reasonably be expected to succeed in life if he is denied the opportunity of an education. *6* Such an opportunity, where the state has undertaken to provide it, is a right which must be made available to all on equal terms. *7*

> From Justice Warren's opinion in *Brown v. Board of Education* 347 U.S. 483 (1954), ending racial segregation in public schools

Argument? (yes or no) Yes.

Conclusion: When the state undertakes to provide education, it must be made available to all on equal terms.

Additional premises needed? Something like "If 1, 2, 3, 4, 5, 6, then 7."

Identify any subargument: 1, 2, 3, 4, 5 and 6 are independent and support the conclusion, 7.

Good argument? All the premises look plausible, and it's valid with the new premise. So it's good. Anyway, it was good enough for the Supreme Court.

A good job of rewriting the conclusion to make it clear. But these premises aren't all independent. Here 2, 3, 4, and 5 are meant to support 1, and they need an additional premise: "If school attendance is mandatory and a lot of money is spent on education, and if education is the foundation of good citizenship, and if it is a principal instrument in awakening the child to cultural values and preparing him for professional training and adjusting him to his environment, then education is the most important function of state and local governments." It pays to write out the additional premise in full to see if it's really plausible. Don't get lazy when the argument gets long—that's a sure way to get conned.

That argument for 1 is pretty good. But how does he get from 1 to 7? Well, he adds 6. Then 6 + 1, together with some glue will get him 7. But what does he need? Something like "If education is the most important function of state and local government, and if it is doubtful that any child may reasonably be expected to succeed in life if he is denied the opportunity of an education, then when the state undertakes to provide education, it must be made available to all on equal terms." That isn't obvious. But you can see how Justice Warren supported that claim with the 14th Amendment in the full decision at: <http://www.nationalcenter.org/brown.html>.

Exercises on the Structure of Arguments ————————————————

For each exercise below, analyze the structure by answering the following:

Argument? (yes or no) If an argument, number each part that might be a claim.
Conclusion:
Additional premises needed?
Identify any subargument:
Good argument?

1. My neighbor should be forced to get rid of all the cars in his yard. People do not like living next door to such a mess. He never drives any of them. They all look old and beat up and leak oil all over the place. It is bad for the neighborhood, and it will decrease property values.

2. I'm on my way to school. I left five minutes late. Traffic is heavy. Therefore, I'll be late for class. So I might as well stop and get breakfast.

3. Las Vegas has too many people. There's not enough water in the desert to support more than a million people. And the infrastructure of the city can't handle more than a million: The streets are overcrowded, and traffic is always congested; the schools are overcrowded, and new ones can't be built fast enough. We should stop migration to the city by tough zoning laws in the city and county.

4. Dr. E: I took my dogs for a walk last night in the fields behind my house. It was very dark. They started to chase something—I could hear it running in front of them. It seemed like it was big because of the way the bushes were rustling, and they came back towards where I was in a U-turn, which suggests it wasn't a rabbit. Rabbits almost always run in more or less one direction. I think they killed it, because I heard a funny squeaky "awk" sound. It didn't sound like a cat, but it didn't sound like a big animal either. And I don't think rabbits make that kind of sound. I'm puzzled what it was, but one thing I am sure of after the dogs returned: It wasn't a skunk.

5. Maria: Really it was Einstein's wife who was the great genius. She was the one who had the ideas that went into those early papers "he" wrote about relativity. They were working together. But he got the honors because he was a man. And she had the child and had to keep the house.

   Harry: Look, there weren't two geniuses like Einstein. That's beyond probability. And after those earlier papers, he continued to make incredible scientific break-throughs. He would have been considered one of the greatest minds of all time for just the work that came after those early papers. While his wife never did anything scientifically important again.

   Maria: That was because she was keeping house, 'till that chauvinist pig divorced her.

   Harry: I don't doubt that she had some input into those early works, maybe even did equal work with him at the beginning. But it was Einstein who saw the ideas through and made them real to people and who continued to do great work. It wasn't his wife.

Examples of Analysis

Here's an example from a letter to the editor:

> Pet owners need to take responsibility for their animals. *1*   Not only is it unsafe for these pets to wander, *2*   it is very inconsiderate to other neighbors. *3* Many of us are tired of the endless, nauseating piles we have to shovel from our lawns and dead flowers caused by dogs passing by. *4*   Children in our neighborhoods cannot walk to a friend's house to play for fear of aggressive dogs. *5*   Pets should be in a fenced yard or on a leash, *6* not just to protect pets, *7* not just out of consideration for your neighbors, *8* but also because it is the law. *9*
>
> Claudia Empey, *The Spectrum*, 1996

I've labeled every clause that might be a claim.

First we need to identify the conclusion, though there's no indicator word. The choice seems to be between *1* and *6*. Looking at all the other claims, it seems to me they best support *6*. If I believed all the others, I'd have more reason to believe *6*. Indeed, *1* supports *6*, though weakly.

We have the conclusion, but that doesn't give us the structure. First, let's see if there's any noise or problematic sentences.

Sentence *2* is ambiguous: Does it mean "unsafe for the pets" or "unsafe for people"? Those two readings are made separately in *5* and *7*, so we can ignore *2*. Also *3* and *8* are the same, so let's ignore *8*.

What do we have? Just lots of independent premises. But the weight of them doesn't give the conclusion. We are missing the glue. Why should we care about our neighbors? Why protect the pets? Each of these needs some further premise to help us get *6*. I'll let you finish this analysis by trying to repair the argument.

A debate about affirmative action between Betsy Hart and Bonnie Erbe that appeared in newspapers gives a much more complex example. Here is the introduction and Betsy Hart's argument. Bonnie Erbe's reply is one of the arguments you can try below.

> *Affirmative action debate heads for ballot box*
> Question: Affirmative action is under attack. In California and Texas, such programs have been largely ended in state university systems–pending court challenges–by school regents or the lower courts. A fall ballot initiative will determine whether other such programs in California should go. Affirmative action will be a hot topic everywhere on the campaign trail. What's going on? (Bonnie Erbe and Betsy Hart provide differing views on current issues. Erbe is host of the PBS program "To the Contrary." Hart is a frequent commentator on CNN and other national public affairs shows.)
>
> *Betsy Hart*: What's going on is that affirmative action is counterproductive or useless, *1* and it's time for it to end. *2*
>
> First, consider its legacy for blacks. Since the civil rights laws of 1964

were passed, aggregate black-white unemployment gaps haven't contracted, and they've expanded in some markets! *3* That's because holding a space open at Yale or a prestigious law firm for a minority doesn't help the people who need help most—the inner-city drop-out with no future. *4*

Why not fight the real problems instead? *5* For instance, rampant crime in the inner-city. *6* Studies repeatedly show crime is one of the biggest inhibitors to business and job creation where it's most needed. *7* But liberals are loath to truly fight this insidious destroyer of lives and futures. *8*

Solid education is fundamental to helping disadvantaged minorities. *9* That means early on in life, as well as at the college level. *10* Yet today, the publicly run inner-city schools, which the education establishment refuses to honestly reform, *11* are rarely anything but violence-ridden cesspools. *12*

Families, too, have to be repaired. *13* The No. 1 indicator of crime rate in any neighborhood is not income or education, but the level of single-parent headed households. *14* The high rates of such families in the inner city show why many such kids are prepared for a life of violence, not a life of achievement. *15*

All the affirmative action programs in the world can't fix these problems. *16* But focusing on affirmative action allows the liberal do-gooders to avoid doing anything about the real issues facing the disadvantaged. *17*

Middle-class minorities and women no longer need affirmative action programs, if they ever did. *18* Black college educated women, for instance, make more than their white counterparts in the aggregate. *19* When factors such as age and their own parental status are controlled for, women make 98 percent of what men do. *20* And disadvantaged minorities are hurt by these programs *21* because their real problems are overlooked. *22*

Yes, it's time for affirmative action programs to go. *23*

Scripps Howard News Service, March, 1996

The first thing to do in analyzing this passage is decide if it's an argument. It seems to be, with conclusion, "It's time to end affirmative action." So we need to number every sentence or clause that might be a claim.

But what exactly does Betsy Hart mean by "affirmative action"? Does it mean different standards for entrance into university? Does it mean that some places should be reserved for minorities in universities and businesses? Does it mean that contracts should be set aside for minority people in business? Unless we are clear about that, she's whistling in the wind. What exactly are we encouraged to end? This is a problem that is fatal to her argument, unless we can infer how we should interpret those words from the rest of what she says.

1 Affirmative action is counterproductive or useless.

This is a claim. If she can prove this, then the conclusion, 2, will follow with an additional prescriptive claim like "We should end any government or private program that is counterproductive or useless." But we have to ask "Counterproductive to what?" Let's hope she makes that clear.

3 Since the civil rights laws of 1964 were passed, aggregate black-white unemployment gaps haven't contracted, and they've expanded in some markets.

This is a claim, and if true would be some support for affirmative action being useless or counterproductive, if we add as a premise "One of the goals of affirmative action is to lessen the unemployment gap between blacks and white." Do we have any reason to believe *3*? Betsy Hart doesn't back it up. Maybe it's true, maybe not. We should suspend judgment.

4 Holding a space open at Yale or a prestigious law firm for a minority doesn't help the people who need help the most—the inner-city drop-out with no future.

This is a claim. It sounds plausible, but what reason do we have to believe it? For it to be true, the word "help" must be understood as "help immediately financially" or something like that. Is that the goal of affirmative action?

5 We should fight the real problems instead.

I've taken the rhetorical question as a claim. I guess from context and *6* we can understand "real problems" to be the financial and crime problems of minorities in the ghettos. But are those the only problems we should deal with? This is an implicit *false dilemma*: We can fight the real problems or continue affirmative action, but not both.

Claim *7* we can dismiss because we don't know what studies she's talking about. And *8* is just noise: Who are these liberals?

Claims *9* and *10* are highly plausible. But then we have *11*: "The education establishment refuses to honestly reform inner city-schools." This is just noise: What is the "education establishment"? What does "honestly reform" mean? And *12*, highly overstated, is what a lot of people believe. But how does that support the conclusion? Its only value is through the false dilemma, just as with *13–15*.

But now we come to the crucial part. Betsy Hart is going to show that her argument isn't based on a false dilemma. First, affirmative action can't fix these "real" problems (*16*) (as if the problems that affirmative action can fix are not "real"). And then the most important part of her argument:

17 Focusing on affirmative action allows the liberal do-gooders to avoid doing anything about the real issues facing the disadvantaged.

This is supposed to show that there isn't a false dilemma. But who are these "liberal do-gooders"? Can she name anyone who avoids trying to deal with these "real" problems because he or she supports affirmative action? That's implausible, and without some serious support for this very vague sentence, we shouldn't even consider it a claim.

Finally, Betsy Hart tries to show affirmative action isn't needed anyway (*18*), assuming as an unstated premise, "The *only* goal of affirmative action is immediate financial equality." (*a*) The "immediate" came earlier; now it's beginning to look like a perfectionist dilemma. But she doesn't tell us where the statistics in *19* and *20* come from, and she's not an unbiased source. Finally, *21* and *22* rehearse what she's already said, and *23* restates her conclusion.

In summary, much of what Betsy Hart has said is too vague to be taken as a claim, is unsupported, or relies on a false dilemma. Nor do we ever find out what she means by "affirmative action," though it seems to be *a*. It's a weak argument, if it's an argument at all.

By taking the effort to see if there is a good argument here, we have uncovered what appears to be Betsy Hart's unstated assumption, which will help us read not only what she says here, but also see whether similar assumptions lie behind other writings on this subject. Here's the steps we've gone through.

The steps in analyzing complex arguments

1. Read the entire passage and decide if it's an argument. If so, identify the conclusion, then number every sentence or clause that might be a claim.

2. For each numbered part:
   a. Is it ambiguous or too vague to be a claim?
   b. If it's vague, could we clear that up by looking at the rest of the argument? Are the words implicitly defined?
   c. If it's too vague, scratch it out as noise.
   d. If it uses slanters, reword it neutrally.

3. Identify the claims that lead directly to the conclusion.

4. Identify any subarguments that are meant to support the claims that lead directly to the conclusion.

5. See if the obvious objections have been considered.
   a. List ones that occur to you as you read the passage.
   b. See if they have been answered.

6. Note which of the claims in the argument are unsupported, and evaluate whether they are plausible.

7. Evaluate each subargument as valid or on the scale from strong to weak.
   a. Note if the argument is a valid type or fallacy we've seen.
   b. If it is not valid or strong, can it be repaired?
   c. If it can be repaired, do so and evaluate any added premises.

8. Evaluate the entire argument as valid or on the scale from strong to weak.
   a. Note if the argument is a valid type or fallacy we've seen.
   b. If it is not valid or strong, can it be repaired?
   c. If it can be repaired, do so and evaluate any added premises.

9. Decide whether the argument is good.

That's a lot to do. But not all the steps are always needed. If you spot that the argument is one of the bad types we've discussed, you can dismiss it. If key words are too vague for the conclusion or crucial parts to be claims, you can dismiss the argument. But often you will have to go through all these steps.

Before you start analyzing the complex arguments offered below, look at how Maria used this method.

Morass of value judgments
Well-intentioned DUI law chips away at individual rights
Editorial, *Las Vegas Review-Journal*, October 1, 1995

When a new state law goes into effect today, police will be allowed to use "reasonable force" to obtain blood samples from first-time drunken driving suspects who refuse to take a breath test. *1*

Defense attorneys plan to challenge this law, citing the potential for unnecessary violence resulting from attempts to enforce it. *2* The law's proponents say it is necessary to obtain adequate evidence to lock up violators of drunken driving laws and force is already allowed against repeat offenders. *3* One supporter of the law was quoted on television recently saying that people who are suspected of driving drunk give up their rights. *4*

There is a hidden danger with laws that chip away at the Fourth Amendment prohibition against unreasonable searches and seizures. *5*

Yes, we need to vigorously fight drunken driving, take away driver's licenses of those who refuse breath tests, and lock up repeat offenders who are obviously impaired according to eyewitness testimony. *6* But our hard-won individual rights, freedoms and protections should not be flippantly squandered, even in the name of public safety. *7*

The danger is that once we begin to buy into the concept that the rights of society as a whole are superior to the rights of the individual, then we begin to slide into a morass of value judgments. *8* If it is more important for society to stop drunken driving than for the suspected driver to be free from unreasonable search of his blood veins and seizure of his blood, then might it not be argued that it is more important for elected officials and sports heroes to get organ transplants than mere working stiffs? *9*

If rights can be weighed against societal imperatives, what next? *10* Our rights against self incrimination? *11* Freedom of religion? *12* Speech? *13* Fair trial? *14* The vote? *15*

Having personally experienced the heavy hand of tyranny, the Founding Fathers wrote: "The right of the people to be secure in their persons, houses, papers, and effects, against unreasonable searches and seizures, shall not be violated, and no Warrants shall issue, but upon probable cause, supported by

Oath or affirmation, and particularly describing the place to be searched, and the person or things to be seized." *16*

Rather than slug it out in the courts, we would hope that our various police forces would give a second thought or more before resorting to constitutionally questionable exercises. *17* What difference is there between a hypodermic needle and a battering ram? *18*

If we vigilantly guard and revere the rights of individuals, society in general will be better off. *19*

Conclusion: Police should not be allowed to use reasonable force to obtain blood samples from first-time drunken driving suspects who refuse to take a breath test.

Premises: 1. This is just stating the background. The editor uses a downplayer in putting quotes around "reasonable force."

2. I suppose this is true. It shows that someone other than the editors think there's a problem. But so what?

3. Gives the other side. Counterargument.

4. Big deal. So one nut said that. Doesn't really contribute to the argument. He'd have to show that a lot of people thought that. Otherwise it's probably a strawman.

5. "Chip away" is a slanter. Dysphemism. Anyway, he hasn't shown that this law goes against the Fourth Amendment. Apparently the lawmakers didn't think so. If it does, it'll be declared unconstitutional, and that's that. Doesn't really help his conclusion. Waving the flag, sort of.

6. Sets out his position. Sort of a counterargument to the supporters of the bill. Shows he's not unreasonable. Giving a bit to the other side, I guess. Doesn't seem to help get to his conclusion.

7. "Hard-won" is there without proof. Perhaps it was hard-won. Possibly adds to the argument by adding a premise: "Whatever is hard-won should not be given up." But that's false. "Flippantly squandered" is a dysphemism, and he hasn't shown that they are flippantly squandered. But worst is when he talks about rights, protections, etc. It's not clear what "right" he is talking about. If it's the one in the Fourth Amendment, he's got to prove that this law is giving that up, which he hasn't. Otherwise he's just waving the flag.

8. He's got to prove this. It's crucial to his argument.

9. This is supposedly support for 8, but it doesn't work. I think the answer is "No." He's got to show it's "Yes." And 10 is just a question, not a claim.

11.–15. These are rhetorical questions, too. As premises they seem very dubious. Altogether they're a slippery slope.

16. The first part is just there like "hard-won" was before. Quoting the Fourth Amendment doesn't make it clear to me that this law violates it.

17. "Slug it out in the courts" is a dysphemism. He hasn't shown that the law is constitutionally questionable.

18. Another rhetorical question with a stupid comparison. My answer is "Plenty." He's got to convince me that there's no difference. The old slippery slope again.

19. Vague and unproved. Can't be support for the conclusion, and it's not the conclusion, either. Does nothing.

It's a bad argument. Too many slanters, and there's really no support for the conclusion.

Very, very good. Only you need to expand on why it's a bad argument. What exactly are the claims that have any value in getting the conclusion?

First, in 1 it's not a downplayer. It's a quote. It might also show that he doesn't believe the words have a clear meaning.

All that 2 elicits is "So?" We can't guess what the missing premise is that could save this support. He doesn't knock off 3 (perhaps 4 is intended to do that, sort of reducing to the absurd?). The support for 8 is a worthless slippery slope (9–15), plus one person's comments that we'd have to take to be exemplary of lots of people (there's a missing premise: "If one person said this on television, then lots of people believe it," which is very dubious). Number 16 is crucial, but he hasn't shown that 7 follows from it. That's the heart of the argument that he's left out (as you noted): He's got to show that this law really violates the Fourth Amendment and, for 19, that it isn't a good trade-off of personal rights vs. society's rights. So there's really no support for his conclusion. That's why it's bad. The use of slanters is bad, but it doesn't make the argument bad. We can eliminate them and then see what's wrong. I'd give B+/A– for this. Incorporate this discussion in your presentation to the class and you'll get an A.

Complex Arguments for Analysis

1. *Reply to Betsy Hart by Bonnie Erbe* (from the same article on pp. 226–227 above)

   Bonnie Erbe: Before my colleague takes off on such wild tangents, she needs to define affirmative action. The term has come to mean different things to different people, ranging from strict, unbending quotas to mild incentive programs.

   My definition of affirmative action is as follows: institutions and corporations that have extremely small percentages of women and/or minority group members among their ranks should take gender and race into account, along with a panoply of other factors (i.e., intelligence, job or grade performance, geographic distribution, economic disadvantage) when recruiting new talent.

   Using that definition, affirmative action will undoubtedly be outmoded in some institutions, but decidedly necessary in others.

   For example, there's clearly no need to pay special attention to admit more Chinese- or Japanese-Americans to the University of California at Berkeley.

   But blacks and Hispanics are still underrepresented on some campuses in the University of California system.

   Similarly, some federal agencies–most notably the FBI, the CIA and the State Department–are woefully short on women agents and diplomats. Yet the Justice Department's No. 1 and No. 2 lawyers (Janet Reno and Jamie Gorelick) are women. Hence, affirmative action for women is unneeded in some federal agencies, while not in others.

   Besides, if we are going to eliminate affirmative action entirely, we ought to eliminate all preferences throughout society.

   No more special admissions to Harvard for the young man with a B minus average just because his grandfather's name is on a Harvard dorm.

   Fathers should no longer be able to hire sons (or sons-in-law) to help run the family company simply because they're related.

   I'm being hyperbolic, but my point is this: Preferences (based on who you know and how much money you have) are still rampant in society. If we eliminate one, in fairness we should eliminate them all.

   If we actually, really eliminated preferences—all forms of affirmative action— upper-class white children would be much more thoroughly vitiated than lower-class minority children.

2. *Howard Stern's investment in tobacco/cigarette industry stocks*
   (brought in by a student who said he heard it on the Howard Stern show)

   Caller: Howard, how can you invest in killing people?
   Stern: What do you mean? I made a good business investment.
   Caller: You invested in killing kids.
   Stern: Listen, buddy, there are laws that say you have to be eighteen to buy cigarettes. If store owners sell to underage kids, that's their own greedy fault; that's not my fault or the fault of the tobacco company.
   Caller: But you invested in the tobacco company that lies to the government, and cigarettes kill.

Stern: What's this lie to the government? . . . I don't care—everybody lies—you lie. If someone is so stupid they want to smoke, that's their problem, we all know it's bad to smoke. That's why I don't smoke, I'm not stupid. But if someone else wants to smoke, that's his right, he has the right to be stupid, and I have the right to invest my money in a company that will make me money.

Caller: Howard, it's not right, next thing you know you'll be investing in AIDS.

Stern: You idiot, you can't invest in disease. I invested in a company. You don't know what you're talking about, get off my phone line, you jerk. (Hangs up)

3. *Pascal's wager*

(Pascal was a 17th Century mathematician and philosopher who had a religious conversion late in his life. His argument is roughly as follows.)

We have the choice to believe in God or not to believe in God. If God does not exist, you lose nothing by believing in Him. But if He exists, and you believe in Him, you have the possibility of eternal life, joyous in the presence of God. If you don't believe in Him, you are definitely precluded from having everlasting life. Therefore, a prudent gambler will bet on God existing. That is, it is better to believe that God exists, since you lose nothing by doing so, but could gain everlasting life.

4. *Proof that God does not exist*

(Several philosophers have become famous for their proofs that God exists. All those proofs have been theoretical. Here is a practical proof supplied by Dr. E that God does not exist. It can be repeated—try it yourself!)

I go into the Sahara Hotel and Casino in Las Vegas, Nevada. I go up to the Megabucks slot machine at which you can win at least five million dollars on a $3 bet if you hit the jackpot. I put in three $1 coins. I pull the handle. I win nothing, or just a little, and when I continue, I lose that, too. Therefore, God does not exist.

5. *On the plans being made to move some of the nearly extinct condors that have been bred in captivity to a wild area in the south of Utah*

Letter to the editor:

I do not know why we do not leave things alone. Probably environmentalists must have something to show for their reason to exist; often as stupid as wilderness laws by government to make us think they care, for what? Easy money? Now they intend to move condors to Utah. Our over-taxed taxpayers should be getting weary of financing so much for the amusement of idiots.

As long as I can remember, the wolves, elk and now the condor and other nonhuman species have been pawns on the environmental checkerboard for no reason except the whim of a loon to change the order of the universe. I would think all creatures have the instinct to move if they so desired without any help. I am sure the place of their choice would be better for them if not made by us. Let us grow up and leave the elk, wolves and condors alone and mind our own business.

Kenneth S. Frandsen, *The Spectrum,* March, 1996

6. *Ban trapping in New Mexico*

Eight states (Washington, California, Massachusetts, Colorado, Arizona, New Jersey, Florida, and Rhode Island) have banned the use of leg-hold traps. It is unconscionable that less than 1 percent of the population uses traps, and approximately 75 percent of the population opposes trapping, yet this barbarism is still legal in New Mexico.

The only justification for trapping animals is to skin them, process the skin and them make them into coats and stoles for narcissistic little twits to wear when they go out on Saturday night. All of the fur coats in the world are not worth the bone-wrenching screams of a single animal caught in these mindless traps. Many trappers admittedly don't trap for the money because it isn't a money-making business. They do it for fun. They capture, mangle, mutilate, kill and skin animals for fun!

The National Trappers Association is trying to defend the insidious activity of trapping on public land and it is lobbying various state agencies to allow this to go on.

Trappers like to lump themselves in with hunters because they know that without the hunters, they cannot win.

But hunting is fundamentally different from trapping. The hunter must be present throughout the stalk. The trapper can be home drinking beer while the trap is destroying the heart and soul of a helpless animal.

It is illegal for hunters to sell the meat of the animals they kill. The purpose of trapping is the sale of the skin.

It is illegal for hunters to use a scent-attractant to get an unfair advantage over their prey. Trappers use these to attract the animals to their traps.

Hunters have bag limits. Trappers can kill and kill and kill without a limit of any kind on any species.

Hunters, if they are ethical, will identify their target and take careful aim to insure [sic]a quick and clean death. Trapping is indiscriminate and anything but quick and clean. A helpless animal, in excruciating pain will get his skull bashed in, usually with a pipe or shovel. Then the trapper stands on his chest to be sure he is dead.

The New Mexico Department of Game and Fish thinks this is a suitable activity for children and gives them a bargain on a license fee if they are between the ages of 12 and 17. If this is considered family values by our government agencies, we are in trouble.

In states where leg-hold traps are illegal, it became illegal because of ballot initiatives. Unfortunately, in New Mexico we don't have ballot initiatives because our legislators don't want the citizens to get in the way of the special issue groups that parasitize us. If we had ballot initiatives, leg-hold traps would be banned as well as the other anti-American, satanic sport, cockfighting, which is opposed by approximately 80 percent of New Mexicans.

However, we do have ballot initiatives. We vote on the first Tuesday in November and we can choose to not elect politicians who are too cowardly to oppose trapping (and cockfighting).

Ask the candidates running for the legislature in your district whether or not they support abject animal cruelty in the form of trapping or cockfighting. Make them go on record. If they don't have the courage to declare how they stand, then vote for the other person. Ask them if they would support a constitutional amendment to give the people of New Mexico the right to have ballot initiatives, as they should. We have to get rid of these barbaric, anti-Christian and bloodthirsty activities in New Mexico.

> Richard "Bugman" Fagerlund and Holly Kern, Corrales, *El Defensor Chieftain*, August 25, 2004

7. *No to ballot initiatives* (reply to Argument 6 above)
I have to respond to the anti-trapping, anti-cockfighting, pro-California-ballot-initiative letter sent by two residents of Corrales.

They described cockfighting and trapping as "barbaric, anti-Christian and bloodthirsty." I know several people who participate in both activities and they are some of the finest people there are and certainly are not "anti-American" or "satanic."

Holly and "Bugman's" idea of forcing ballot initiatives on us by threatening our candidates is scary. In their letter, they list states that allow ballot initiatives, where if you can get enough signatures you can force a vote on anything. Why have an elected government at all? If ballot initiatives are such a good idea, why didn't Jefferson and Mason include them in the U.S. Constitution?

The Corrales couple should just come out and say what they really want: a meatless, petless, non-hunting, non-ranching society. A country where people like them make the decisions as to how the rest of us live our lives.

> Jim Nance, *El Defensor Chieftain*, August 28, 2004

8. *Other side of trapping* (reply to Argument 6 above)
Mr. Fagerlund and Ms. Kern, I admire your passion for wildlife, but do believe you're only looking at half of the debated matter.

When I was a little boy, my grandfather, who was a trapper, told me that "there are two sides to all matters." I would like to tell my side of this heavily debated matter.

Let us start with New Jersey, one of the eight states you mention that have banned trapping. New Jersey was the first to ban the trapping of all fur-bearing animals and the hunting of bears in 1994, which gave the bear population ample time to overpopulate. Because of this overpopulation, the bears start showing up on city streets and in local backyards. Last year, to fix the problem of overpopulation, the New Jersey legislature passed a bill to allow bear hunting. How convenient?

In California (another state mentioned) last year, two joggers were killed by a mountain lion. Is this the result we have to have in New Mexico before people start respecting the job that the Personnel in the Game and Fish Department is doing on a daily basis for our safety? Do we need those results for people to start supporting the Game and Fish physically and financially like hunters, fisherman and trappers do? If you don't want to buy a hunting, fishing or fur-bearer license, you can always make a financial donation on a Game and Fish Department license form, which is available statewide.

Now let me tell you about the routine of a trapper. First, a trapper check his traps three to five times a day, depending on how many there are and their distance between one another, which is normally half a mile to 15 miles. Fur-trappers always make their last round at sunset to ensure that no animal is left overnight. When they arrive at a trap that contains a captured predator, they take a wooden stick or wood handle of a shovel and, at a safe distance, hit the predator on the end of the nose, which knocks the predator unconscious. They next proceed to kick the predator's heart, which is the same as reverse CPR, the animal does not feel a thing. During the procedure, there is very little blood loss, because if blood gets on the pelt, it would ruin its value, a value that has gone up in recent years.

On a level of cruelty, let's compare trapping to fishing. At first thought, there is no comparison, right? I have described trapping to you, now I would like to describe fishing to you.

First, you get a pole with a string and at the bottom of the string you put a sharp hook and then bait the hook. Second, you throw the string (with the hook on it) 20 to 30 yards into the water and snare the fish in the mouth with the hook; and then drag the fish back 20 to 30 yards; pull the fish out of the water, where it cannot breathe; pull the hook out of its mouth and throw it back in the water so the next person can do the same thing.

I did not write this letter to bash on fishing. I am an avid fisherman. I just wish people would look at all the facts before they start drawing conclusions about something they know nothing about and have never experienced.

Would the public rather see these predators in our backyards because they are overpopulated and starving? If states keep banning trapping and other traditional predation control methods, we're going to see the same problems that New Jersey and California have dealt with.

So would you, as an American, rather see trappers carrying on the traditions of their family roots or see a child get killed by a predator on a school playground?

Wesley Hill, *El Defensor Chieftain*, August 28, 2004

9. *U.S. House wants taxes, IRS to die—yeah, right*

Even by the lax standards governing political grandstanding, what the U.S. House did was particularly dumb.

As the lawmakers rushed to leave town on spring break, the Republicans pushed through a bill, 229–187, to abolish the federal tax code and the Internal Revenue Service on December 31, 2004.

The bill now goes to the Senate, where the measure's House backers assume it will die a quiet and certain death. If the Senate were malicious enough to enact it, the House would be forced into a hasty and embarrassing retraction, since the nation can't function without taxes and the means to collect them.

Voting to abolish the IRS was, of course, designed to give lawmakers something to boast about on Tax Day, Monday, on the assumption that the taxpayers back home are so dim they will somehow appreciate this gesture.

"We are again demonstrating to the American people, 'We are on your side,'" says House GOP leader Dick Armey of Texas. Sure you are.

Every April, Congress likes to pretend that the income tax and the IRS materialized out of nowhere. They denounce the tax laws for their avaricious complexity and the coldhearted bureaucrats who administer them.

However, the tax laws are the way they are, and the IRS is the way it is, because Congress wants them that way. A mischievous document called the Constitution gives

Congress, and specifically the House, the sole power to "lay and collect taxes."

And this inane bit of political grandstanding is nothing compared with the political contortions lawmakers will go through to get assigned to the House Ways and Means Committee, the very panel that oversees the IRS and writes the tax laws.

Editorial, *Albuquerque Tribune,* April 18, 2000

10. *Smokers die early, but it's not all bad*

The big tobacco organization [Philip Morris] recently hired the consulting organization of Arthur D. Little to prepare a piece of actuarial economic analysis that turned out to be remarkable, in its own way. The report was such good news, as seen by Philip Morris, that the corporate thinkers began distributing it through the Czech Republic as a grand PR tool.

Here's the good news that has Philip Morris bragging: The report concludes that smoking has produced "positive effects" for the Czech Republic's budget—due to revenue from taxes on cigarettes plus "health-care cost savings due to early mortality."

Do not adjust your bifocals. The Philip Morris-Arthur D. Little report not only says it but also has the numbers to prove it.

Big tobacco's good Euro-news: The premature demise of Czech smokers saved the Czech Republic between 943 million and 1.19 billion Czech koruna, which is $23.8 million to 30.1 million U.S. dollars, in 1999, the report says. That's because the Czech government didn't have to pay for long-term health care, pensions and housing for the elderly—because, of course, they were dead.

The organizational duo of Philip Morris and Arthur D. Little have more numbers to make their good news case. They have factored in the downside costs incurred by the government due to smokers, in terms of the government paying for the care of people who become ill due to smoking or second-hand smoke, plus the income tax revenue that is lost because of the death of working smokers. The combined corporate thinkers weighed the costs and benefits and still came up with a good news bottom line: In 1999, the Czech government had a net gain of 5.82 billion koruna ($147.1 million) due to smoking.

Philip Morris execs explained to the Wall Street Journal that they have been handing out the report to counter complaints from Czech officials that smoking had caused the government to incur large health care costs. Philip Morris cares—because it makes approximately 80 percent of the cigarettes smoked in the Czech Republic and owns 77.5 percent of the once state-owned Czech tobacco company.

Now the sticklers have begun to surface. Some anti-tobacco experts are saying that the Phillip Morris study is flawed, because it doesn't consider such things as the economic impact that would occur if those who were smoking simply stopped smoking and continued to pay taxes and buy goods—rather than opting out by prematurely dying.

I, however, take the Big Tobacco's best and brightest at their word. I recall the bad old days when all of the tobacco bigwigs sat in a line at a table in a congressional hearing room and swore before the U.S. Congress and the Almighty that tobacco was not addictive, let alone a killer weed.

Now Big Tobacco is stipulating that of course their weed is a killer. A mass murderer. Now they are simply saying that the good news is that there is a bottom line virtue in the mass killing caused by the cancer sticks that are their livelihood.

Just look at the good numbers.

The deadly duo of Philip Morris and Arthur D. Little have produced a line of reasoning that could cause lawyers for accused war criminals such as Yugoslavia's Slobodan Milosevic to rewrite their defense arguments.

Martin Schram, Scripps Howard News Service, July 25, 2001

11. *Nuclear waste to travel through Utah to N.M.*

The first of 4,900 shipments of radioactive waste is expected to roll through northern Utah on Tuesday headed from Idaho to New Mexico for disposal.

"We expect it to pass through the state without incident," Utah Division of Radiation Control Director Bill Sinclair [said] of the shipment of 42 drums of waste now at Idaho National Engineering and Environmental Laboratory.

Still, more than 900 Utah law-enforcement officers, firefighters and paramedics have been trained in how to deal with a possible traffic accident involving radioactive materials, said Sinclair. And, the Utah Highway Patrol has obtained specialized equipment to monitor for radiation leaks in case of an accident.

"(Motorists) shouldn't be any more concerned than when coming into contact with a gasoline truck, which is a greater hazard in my opinion," said Sinclair.

Cindy King, a member of the Utah Chapter of the Sierra Club's environmental health committee, said she has greater safety concerns. "One you glow and one you don't," she said of Sinclair's comparison. . . .

The first truck will contain clothing, tools, rags, debris and other disposable items contaminated with man-made radioactive elements used in the development of nuclear weapons. The material is less radioactive than spent fuel from nuclear power plants, but it remains toxic for thousands of years and requires special handling.

Associated Press, April 25, 1999

12. *Women distract from training. Inclusion at military colleges lowers standards.*

The essence of ground combat is to kill or capture the enemy by fire and maneuver. Sometimes this includes hand-to-hand fighting with bayonets and even bare knuckles.

Those who have never been in actual kill-or-be-killed combat cling to a wishful, even wistful, notion that our future combat leaders can be trained effectively in the same educational environment that produces poets and politicians. Strolling the halls of ivy, hand-in-hand with coeds, while talking of Yeats and Shelley isn't likely to produce many George Pattons.

The reality of actual combat requires an absolute and total focus on killing or capturing others whose mission is to kill or capture you. It is a business that does not permit distraction.

Historically, institutions such as The Citadel and Virginia Military Institute have produced some of the United States' best combat officers. Unless and until our nation totally loses its collective mind and puts women into the combat arms, we, like the Israelis, do not permit women to serve in front-line combat units. Front-line combat remains an all-male endeavor, and it should follow that the training environment designed to place males in the line of fire should not be diluted by the distractions inevitably presented by the presence of women.

Unfortunately, the courts have ruled that women must be allowed to study at publicly funded military colleges such as The Citadel and VMI. Such decisions are based, no doubt, on conceptions of civil law. Sadly, those decisions have not been based on the cruel and harsh realities of actual combat.

Moreover, the inclusion of women in military training, including our national service academies, has led to the lowering of physical standards for males and females alike. Someday, we may pay a high price for sacrificing effective combat training on the altar of women's rights.

Combat is a serious business. America should reconsider this matter and permit certain institutions to conduct all-male military education and training. But for now, we seem more interested in social experimentation than winning on the field of battle.

> William Hamilton, retired Army officer and syndicated columnist, served two years in combat with the 1st Air Cavalry Division in Vietnam. *USA Today,* May 7, 1999

13. *Prairie Dogs*

Just about every time the word "prairie dog" is mentioned anymore in Iron County, there is heated debate.

Biology professor Jim Bowns discussed prairie dogs during a meeting sponsored by the Color Country Chapter of People for the West in Cedar City Thursday night. Bowns is a professor for both Southern Utah University and Utah State University.

Prairie dogs are a threatened species in Southern Utah. There has been quite a bit of argument in Iron County over how to preserve the little critters without creating chaos.

Iron County is working on a Habitat Conservation Plan (HCP) otherwise known as the Prairie Dog Plan. The HCP will serve as a blanket application for people to safely remove prairie dogs from their land without all the red tape.

Bowns dissected the HCP page by page, voicing his concerns and explaining jargon to the audience. Several discussions ensued during the process.

Bowns said he is especially concerned with prairie dog habitat.

"Finding ideal habitat for prairie dogs is not simple," he said.

The prairie dogs usually have about a 6 percent survival rate, a 94 percent loss, he continued, reading from the HCP.

Lin Drake appeared unhappy at this statement. He is a developer and an officer for the Color Country Chapter of People for the West. If he lost 94 percent of his business, Drake explained that the bank sure wouldn't be accommodating. "Yet they're expecting Iron County to put millions of dollars into a project that is a losing cause," he said. . . .

Throughout the discussion, the topic of government distrust surfaced and resurfaced.

"Eighteen people came to me this week to talk about the plan," Jack Hill said. Hill is president of the Color Country Chapter of People for the West.

"They have a lack of faith in the federal government and they don't have any trust," Hill said. "The whole issue is with the government."

Drake agreed, saying the HCP appears to weaken his rights to his land. He would prefer the government back off and worry about more important things, he said.

"We've got fathers beating babies and drugs on the streets and we're spending money on this," Drake said. "Tell them to get the hell out of Iron County." . . .

Drake was disappointed at the turnout of the meeting. Only a dozen people attended, though the meeting was advertised adequately.

"They'll wake up when we don't have a community left," he said.

The Spectrum, April 18, 1997

(On June 26, 1997, Lin Drake was fined $15,000 by the U.S. Fish and Wildlife Service for putting a subdivision on a prairie dog habitat.)

14. *Sailors imprisoned for rape*

(Concerning the rape of a school girl by three U.S. sailors in Okinawa)

Letter to the editor:

Judging by your opinionated editorial about the Navy, it appears your paper is entirely governed by women for you do not have the slightest conception of what men are all about. But several points need emphasizing:

1. All human beings are animals, and sex is an integral part of their well-being.

2. When a man meets a woman, his thoughts go quickly past the beauty of her eyes and the color of her hair, certainly the capabilities of her brain. That comes later! In 1995, many women have the same thoughts about men.

3. Soldiers, especially sailors who have been at sea for a long time, have a libido that's healthy and must be sustained in order to function normally. Ask any veteran to confirm what precedes.

4. A prostitute has never been called a decent woman in any language. She is still a whore who gets paid for a job well-done. Thank you! It's her choosing, not that of the men at large.

Now, rape is another thing. It is strictly about sex but it is perpetrated by devious minds who could not care about whom they violate, man or woman. Subjugation of the female . . . my foot! What counts is sexual satisfaction, nothing else.

Admiral Macke was honest when he declared it was stupid of his sailors to have raped the Japanese girl when they could have afforded a girl for the price of the rented car. His remark was not unbelievable; it was just. It had nothing to do with the act itself. It was a statement of fact.

This society encourages hypocrisy. The admiral was right and brave enough to declare his assumption in public. He should have been commended for his fortitude in viewing the world the way it really is, not what it portrays.

Rene Vergught, *The Spectrum,* December 21, 1995

From Volume 1 of the *Bulletin of Advanced Reasoning and Knowledge*

The following four passages concern whether an acceptable solution to the problem of stray dogs in a city is to kill them. That solution had been proposed in Bucharest, Romania, where the problem of stray dogs was acute. But it had not been implemented because of an outcry by animal rights activists. The following article appeared shortly thereafter in newspapers:

At least three dozen dogs are being killed in Tehran every day in an effort to rid Iran's capital city of canines. The Qods daily reported that at least 1,000 dogs, which are regarded as impure in the Islam belief system, have been killed in the last month alone. The figure is a 50 percent increase over the previous month. There are no animal shelters in the country and roving canines are frequently seen going through sidewalk garbage cans looking for scraps. While many affluent city residents secretly keep dogs as pets, the animals are regularly denounced by the country's ruling clergy.

In discussions in the Advanced Reasoning Forum, I suggested that it was a sin to kill dogs. This is the exchange that ensued and was published in the journal of ARF.

15. *On why killing dogs is morally acceptable*

I don't mean to step on anybody's paws, but . . . if the dogs are digging scraps in garbage cans, they probably aren't enjoying life very much. While dogs are keen olfactors, and can remember signs of pleasant and painful stimuli, and can thus anticipate the very near future, I am unaware of evidence that suggests they form hopes for the far future. If that is so, they don't dread or grieve loss of life, and they don't have plans beyond the next meal or mounting that will be frustrated by early demise. On the other hand, as we know first hand, when not cared for as pets, they can be dangerous to people, who can suffer anxiety about this possible source of danger to themselves and their children over long periods of time. On balance, therefore, it seems morally acceptable to end the lives of dogs that are not being cared for as pets, especially in cities where humans are numerous and food is scarce. (There is, of course, no argument for doing this in any fashion other than the most painless available. Nor for clerics to indulge in insults or condemnations of Doghood as such, or of individuals that have formed particular human attachments.)

William S. Robinson, August 7, 2000

Very interesting argument indeed, except at least one premise is dubious. Ever see a dog waiting for his master at the door, or at a gate, hours after the master left through it? Mine waits for me at the gate, (apparently) hoping I'll come home and play with him when I'm away for a whole day in Albuquerque. I'm not claiming that this means he's planning ahead, but it gives us good reason to doubt your premise that he doesn't plan.

Richard L. Epstein, August 8, 2000

I have enjoyed the ethical exchange between [Epstein] and [Robinson] on dogs and Doghood. But I have a question about [Robinson's] argument, and the response. Is that argument using a premise like "Animals, human or non-human, are only to be protected if they cause no substantial harm to the well-being of humans, and they plan for the future."? Or is it, as I suspect, assuming a more complex premise about the nature and scope of the plans (and, to avoid the obvious reply that young infants are implicated, something about at least having the potential for such planning)?

I suspect that the line:

[Dogs don't] form hopes for the far future. If that is so, they don't dread or grieve loss of life . . .

is more important to the argument than the line:

They don't have plans beyond the next meal or mounting that will be frustrated by early demise.

Anyway, this kind of uncertainty about the structure and content of the argument is something we are all familiar with, except we tend to forget it when we do analysis of arguments with students (at least my tutors do).

Analysing arguments is an art. Fred Kroon, August 14, 2000

16. *William Robinson expanding on why killing dogs is morally acceptable*

I agree that I didn't give canine cognitive abilities their full due in my argument. They may pine for the return of [Epstein]. (I think this is actually included under remembering signs of pleasant and painful stimuli, but I should have made that explicit, and the time frame is longer than I implied.) I'm also convinced that they respond to signals in play in a way that must be considered symbolic. (Where did I learn this? Allen & Bekoff, *Species of Mind: The Philosophy and Biology of Cognitive Ethology.* I recommend the book, for those who are interested in abilities of nonhuman animals. (If you aren't already, you might become so by reading this book.)

However, I don't think these omissions undercut the essential point of the argument I was making. "And what was that argument?" asks Fred.—Two preliminaries: (a) As Fred can be taken to suggest, I don't think I was appealing to the first of the possible premises he mentions. (b) I agree that the absence of dread and grief is more important than the absence of plans. Plans become relevant in at least two (possible) ways: (i) One might dread failure of one's plans by premature interruption (which, of course, doesn't arise if one doesn't have plans). And (ii) There's a value that might be called "aesthetic," but which might be a value even for plans that aren't yours and that you don't like. Suppose someone is writing a book that you're sure defends a false view. You might still regard it as a bad thing if the work never comes to completion because the author dies in a crash—that is, you'd think it was awful in a way that is something additional to the regret at losing the author. Calling this kind of value "aesthetic" may risk making it sound like something not too serious, but I don't take it too lightly.—But yes, the dread and the grief weigh more.

So, what's the argument? As I was aiming for brevity, I spoke as a utilitarian. But I don't really premise that utilitarianism is true. I know about justice and rights issues against utilitarianism, and I'll return a bit to them. But the main drift is that those problems for utilitarianism don't overturn a utilitarian view *in this case*. The main drift, that is, is that (a) Canine abilities (to plan) and susceptibilities (to dread, grieve) are quite limited, (b) They're not having much pleasure, while (c) Human fears about attack are substantial and (d) There are actual pains due to actual attacks. The disvalues on the human side seem to me to *far* outweigh the values on the canine side—not because canines are a different species, but just because of the contingent facts about the capabilities and conditions of each species.

If I thought that word would get around among the dogs, and they'd be living in fear of their lives, my view would be different. As it is, I think conspiracy theories are beyond their imagination. I think there would be some "Where's Fido got to?" thoughts (well, actually, images of Fido accompanied by vague unease), but when it comes to "imagin(ing) the possibilities," I suppose the dogs are going to be quite limited.

But don't they have a right to life? This question opens a large topic; where do rights come from anyway? No, you're not going to get a treatise! At most a plausibility consideration. Namely, if they had such a right, then it would be unjust for us to violate it. On many views that would imply that (at least) it would be unfair to violate it. But putting the matter this way returns us to the kinds of factors already mentioned. For now we can ask: Wouldn't it be unfair to us to demand that we go out of our way to preserve the lives of dogs, given that there are the differences in abilities and susceptibilities already noted? It can't be fair to demand equal treatment for dogs and humans when they are so unequal in relevant respects. (I haven't argued that the respects are relevant, but I expect that view to recommend itself to you without argument.)

Now, this shows at most a reduced right to life (compared with humans), and so there'll be a question about how much the reduction is. But I think the argument will proceed along the lines above, i.e., the same factors I've identified will be the ones agreed to be relevant, and the large disparity will have the effect of reducing the right to life claim to a very small weight.

No one is going to let me off the hook without my saying something about infants. Imagine a species that's just like infants, except they never progress. Such a species would have less ability than dogs, and less claim on our consideration. So, yes, infants don't make it into a class we ought to protect by virtue of their actual abilities. But I don't see any attraction in the idea that we have to bring about potentialities, so I don't think it is mere potentiality that can justify protection for infants. I think the connection goes through parental love and correlative parental fear. Most parents want strong laws of protection for their children (to put it mildly). Of course, they expect them to grow up. Attitudes toward children would be quite different if people thought of them as never growing up. But it's the attitudes and fears, and not the mere potentiality, that justify the protection.

This view leads to the question of what to say about cases where a parent *doesn't* care about his or her infant. Well, it's not possible to maintain respect for law while making an exception of an infant's own parent. But, morally speaking, I don't see infanticide as so awful, IF (it's a big if) it's not going to result in a terrible sense of loss to one of the parents. (This would usually mean that it's the parents, or at least one parent, who did the infanticide.)

This may sound a little stark at first sight, but I think it's actually close to most people's sensibilities. Not many years ago there were two cases of infanticide within about a year of each other, both in East Coast states of the US. These were cases in which no one (except the father, in one of the cases) knew that the mothers were pregnant. (Amazing, but true.) One of them delivered alone in a campground, then abandoned the baby. The other went to a motel with her boyfriend (the father) and the two cooperated in disposing of the body in a dumpster. Of course, they were identified, prosecuted, and convicted. (I can't say on exactly what charge—it could have been manslaughter instead of murder, and murder in most US states comes in several degrees.) The point here is that the *sentences* were on the order of two or three years. I take this to reflect a kind of official judgment that infanticide is a considerably less serious offense than other murders. (There were also many expressions of pity for the perpetrators, who must have been wildly estranged from most social goods.)

The point of these cases is, of course, not to argue that the courts' judgments were right. I only mean to deflect an objection to the effect that my ruminations lead to a stance that severely diverges from everybody's actual moral sensibilities.

Well, this is more than I said before, but obviously not enough! What would be enough? *At least* a book! Probably two or three. But (as you may be glad to hear) this is all I'm going to write about it today.   William S. Robinson, August 16, 2000

17. *Newcomer stunned at local prices*

Letter to the editor:

I read an article recently in your paper regarding the apparent shortage of local tax dollars and just had to write.

Being a newcomer to your area and coming from one of the most expensive areas in the state, I was appalled at the price of some of the goods and services in this community. One does not need to be a brain surgeon to figure out that as long as some of these merchants continue to gouge people that come into their stores and/or request their services, tax dollars will probably continue to decline. I expect that you will see another decline in the coming year.

Trying to get folks to feel guilt about spending their hard earned money wherever they choose, is not going to correct the problem. Plus, I have the right to choose. This is still a free country. Why doesn't the author of the article address the real issue here and that is the overpricing of goods and services by some of the more greedy merchants? I will continue to drive 90 miles round trip to buy my groceries, and my beer, and my other items that I spend money on and not feel one tinge of guilt. I would love to be able to support some of the local merchants and will continue to buy at those stores that do not gouge me every time I walk in their door but the rest of them can and will do without my dollar in their pockets.

This is a very poor area and I feel sorry for those that cannot get away from the greed of some of our "outstanding" merchants. I am grateful that I can, at least, travel outside this area and get a little more value for my dollar and will continue to go outside this area to shop for any item that I need and or will need until the greedy merchants come down on their prices and start providing some service instead of just lip service.

New Mexico leads the nation in the number of hungry. Isn't that a great claim to fame? And our legislators continue to tax us on medicine and food, but that is another letter.   E. T. Moss, *El Defensor Chieftain*, December 4, 1999

18. *It's time to protect our farms and ranches, not government-fed wolves*

Just as predicted, the cattle-killing has spread from Arizona to New Mexico with a "grisly" attack (by a Mexican gray wolf) on a pregnant cow belonging to a family rancher. How much do the citizens of New Mexico and Arizona have to endure with this failed federal program? Forcing predators into an incompatible ecosystem is a certain recipe for disaster.

The latest attack, by the pen-raised government wolves, occurred on the Cross Y ranch and was witnessed by a U.S. Forest Service employee and a deputy sheriff. They stated that the wolves showed no fear of humans and plied their carnivorous traits on a defenseless animal with a sickening pack attack. This is why the people who came before us were so intent on eliminating this threat.

The disingenuous Defenders of Wildlife organization offers to reimburse ranchers for their killed cattle. We are very concerned that it's only a matter of time until a person is attacked by these misplaced predators. What then?

Let's look at the track record of the U.S. Fish and Wildlife Service in regard to this troublesome wolf program. It spent millions for a decade "studying" the possibility of putting these wolves in our backyards despite total opposition to the program by local communities. There were immediate conflicts with people and livestock. Wolves died and were shot for varmints.

The Fish and Wildlife Service, and their apologists in the radical environmental movement, immediately—without any proof—blamed local ranchers. Armed federal agents raided a legitimate business in Reserve, N.M. Menacing letters were sent to elk hunters who were in the area of the killed wolves. No one has been charged with any crime.

Now the radical environmentalists are clamoring for their stooges in Fish and Wildlife to dump a bunch of wolves in the Gila National Forest. Based on the current record, expanding this program is the ultimate folly.

Are these government-fed wolves worth one single life? The answer is no. Can the Defenders of Wildlife be trusted to pay for any livestock deaths? Our experience with them indicates that is not likely. The real forte of the group is distributing false information, jamming our phone lines and threatening people. The cow that was killed had much more value beyond its market price. No consideration is given to future calf-bearing years. So the offers are meaningless hype.

Consider this quote from the animal's owner, Bud Collins: "She ran two miles from the pasture to the line camp. They were chewing on her all the way, and she died close to the cabin. She was looking for protection. It was pretty grisly."

I hope the U.S. Fish and Wildlife Service employees are proud of themselves. The sad thing is, they probably are. And where are the normally vocal people in the so-called animal-rights movement? They are the ultimate hypocrites in their selective silence.

Collins also stated that the deer and elk populations are almost nonexistent in his area. When the cattle are gone, what is the next meal for the wolf? Hunters? Household pets? Horses? Where does it end? Are backpackers, fishermen and hunters willing to give up their rights for this boondoggle?

As the largest farm-and-ranch organization in the nation, we will continue to fight this wasteful, ill-advised and dangerous program in the courts of public opinion and litigation until it's just a bad memory. If you agree, please contact your congressional representatives and register your opposition.

The wolf program has been put above the people and beyond common sense, and it's time to halt the whole thing. Let's put these pampered federal bureaucrats out to pasture and protect the investment of our family farms and ranches. Let our people produce the food that feeds the nation without the oppressive hand of the "federal fish and wolf police" disrupting our lives and business.

You might also want to call or drop a line to the Defenders of Wildlife and ask what the going price is for a family pet or, for that matter, a child.

Norm Plank, *The Albuquerque Tribune,* January 5, 2000

Plank is the executive vice president of the New Mexico Farm and Livestock Bureau.

19. *The set-point theory*: *Why fad diets don't work*

There's probably not one of us who hasn't tried losing weight fast, *too fast,* through fad diets, fasting, overly restricting our caloric intake, and other such attempts at starving ourselves into thinness. There are two main problems with these all-too-common approaches to losing weight, however. First, they seriously jeopardize our health. And second, such dieting efforts are fundamentally counterproductive. Ultimately they don't work.

- We lose fat, yes, but also a large measure of muscle.
- We unintentionally lower our metabolism.
- We set the stage for gaining fat increasingly faster in the future when we come off the diet, and thereby get caught up in perpetual dieting.
- We receive inadequate nutrients in imbalanced combinations.
- We tax the entire body.

Prolonged fasting, for instance, causes important electrolytes like sodium, calcium, magnesium, and phosphate to be excreted. Weakness and fainting can occur due to dehydration and a reduction in the volume of blood. Congestive heart failure and even death have been reported in cases of fasting and extremely low caloric intake.

Fasting and very low calorie diets (diets below 500 calories) cause a loss of nitrogen and potassium in the body, a loss which is believed to trigger a mechanism in the body that causes us to hold on to our fat stores and to turn to muscle protein for energy instead. Scientists have speculated that within each of us is a unique "set-point mechanism" that regulates the amount of fat we carry. It's believed to be a survival mechanism of our species, a way of stocking up for times of famine and emergency. If the body perceives that it's starving, as it rightly does if we are *always* on a diet or if we suddenly *crash*-diet or *fast,* the set point is thought to kick into action, causing the body to keep a tenacious grip on its fat supply. In order to replenish itself, the body will first cause you to *crave food*—most commonly full-dense, high-caloried sugars and fats. If you successfully resist these cravings, the body's next line of defense will be to react by *slowing down the metabolism* in order to conserve calories. In the face of food deprivation, the body holds on to its fat tissue for dear life.

Given all this, you should immediately rule out such approaches to weight loss.

Jane Fonda's New Workout and Weight Loss Program

20. *Police chief's dumping a dumb deed by North Las Vegas*

North Las Vegas cannot afford to lose any IQ points—especially in the area of law enforcement—and that's exactly what happened with the forced retirement of city Police Chief Alan Nelson. A 25-year veteran, Nelson was arrested Friday on a drunken driving charge. Rather than battle it out in the courts and attempt to play politics with the North Las Vegas City Council, Mayor James Seastrand and City Manager Linda Hinson, Nelson cleared off his desk and turned in his badge.

That's a shame.

If I may be so presumptuous, the people of North Las Vegas—hard-working people who live in one of the nation's high-crime areas—need police officers of Nelson's experience and level. I'm not condoning driving while legally impaired—although it would be refreshing to read the department's official lab findings before seeing the Northtown political machine bury the chief's career without even playing "Taps."

It makes painfully little sense to force him out of office in the name of political correctness and image enhancement. Holding a top police officer to a higher standard is fine, but this presses the point to the extreme.

If the man has a drinking problem, he should be treated with compassion—not a pink slip. After all, it's not as if he is the first cop to drive drunk, if he did.

Fact is, if he were anyone but the chief and were arrested and later convicted of driving while intoxicated, Nelson probably would have received a 40-hour suspension and, like almost everyone else similarly situated, would have been ordered by the court to attend alcohol-awareness classes and seek rehabilitation.

Imagine the image Nelson might have enhanced had he been asked to cut a few public-service announcements for anti-DUI groups?

That's not possible now.

Nelson has plenty of critics these days, but he also has his share of friends. North Las Vegas Police Lt. Bob King is one of them. With nearly 26 years on the department, King is the Narcotics Division commander. He knows sticking up for his ousted comrade is unlikely to win him any points with the city's political hierarchy.

"He's not a high-profiler. He's one of those guys who has been in the trenches, kind of a worker bee," King says. "It just breaks my heart, the whole thing. He was really beginning to move the department forward. He was doing all these good things. And he has one transgression, if you will, four blocks from his house."

Be honest. If you were the top cop in one of the nation's roughest communities, wouldn't you be tempted to drink?

Arsenic.

That doesn't mitigate the seriousness of the offense, but neither should the offense wipe out a quarter century of hard work.

As chief, Nelson was implementing the progressive Safe Streets 2000 community policing program and, King says, was a fair-minded administrator who had a mature grasp of the budget realities the small department faced. He also understood the convoluted federal government grant-writing process, an essential component in the budget mechanism in many departments. North Las Vegas has fewer than 200 cops on the street.

"Those talents are gone," King says. "When he gave his word, you knew he was there for you. You knew exactly where he stood day to day. He has my respect, appreciation and admiration."

In an open letter, King adds, "I see a man whose entire 25-year professional career of personal contributions and accomplishments as both an outstanding policeman and administrator are totally overshadowed and will be measured by a single regrettable incident. . . . He neither asked for nor received any preferential treatment. He practiced and demonstrated this ethic his entire career. With eloquence and dignity he has left the job he dearly loves."

For all his human frailties, Chief Nelson was a hard-working cop who was dumped in the name of political correctness. In North Las Vegas, yet.

And that's just plain dumb.

John L. Smith, *Las Vegas Review-Journal,* March 20, 1997

21. *Dumb deed* (reply to the previous argument)

In his March 20 column ("Police chief dumping a dumb deed by North Las Vegas"), John L. Smith used sarcastic remarks to assess the situation pertaining to North Las Vegas and its former chief of police, Alan Nelson.

But the only "dumb deed" in North Las Vegas was created by its former police chief when he chose to drink and drive. And let's not forget the "dumb deed" was further enhanced by the fact he was driving a city vehicle. It is also dumb for people to minimize the seriousness of drinking and driving by singing the praises of a potential killer. How potential? If a driver's blood-alcohol level is .10 the risk of a fatal crash is increased by 300 percent. Mr. Nelson's chemical test revealed his BAC level to be at .12.

And consider this: The profile of a drunken driver includes the fact that DUI offenders drive drunk an average of 80 times per year.

The "dumb" continues—"He wasn't drunk," "It's only a misdemeanor," "A single regrettable incident," "He has one transgression" . . . these are the reasons I have heard and read in defense of Mr. Nelson. This mentality is nearly as frightening as the crime of DUI. "A single regrettable incident" and "one transgression" on the part of drinking drivers was all it took in 1996 to cause the death and injury of more than 1,600 people in Clark County.

Mr. Smith suggested certain IQ points were lost by North Las Vegas and he also alluded to that city's need for police officers of Mr. Nelson's experience. Based on the numerous calls I received from the citizens of North Las Vegas, I believe they want officers at that experience level to also possess an IQ that would not allow jeopardizing a 25-year career nor permit conduct that would endanger the citizens.

Mr. Smith agreed that holding "top police officers" to a higher standard is fine—but he said "political correctness" has gone too far in this instance. Political correctness? Has our society strayed so far from the realm of social, moral and ethical responsibilities that when these standards are utilized, they are scoffed at as "political correctness"?

As far as Mr. Nelson's "forced retirement" is concerned, I can only say that if I had dedicated a quarter of a century of my life to a career and was wrongly accused of a crime that would have a negative effect on that career, I would fight like hell to vindicate myself. Again, that is only if I were wrongly accused.

I question whether Mr. Smith's commentary would have been as generous and compassionate if he and his beautiful child whom he wrote so eloquently about not so long ago had been in the path of Mr. Nelson the night he was arrested (assuming they lived to write about it). Never forget there is only one thing that separates a felony from a misdemeanor—it's called luck.

Mr. Smith stated that if Mr. Nelson has a drinking problem he should be treated with compassion. If he has a "drinking problem," why wasn't it recognized by his friends and co-workers? How could he be treated if the stale, antiquated "drinking problem" excuse is deemed not to be applicable?

If you want to hear "Taps," Mr. Smith, come to our next DUI Victims Candlelight Vigil. You have attended before—however, it appears you may have forgotten the victims who were there. Let me refresh your memory. They were the people who were sobbing their guts out in memory of their loved ones who had been killed by people like Alan Nelson. Your seat is reserved.

Sandy Heverly, president of Stop DUI, a Nevada non-profit organization
Las Vegas Review-Journal, April 9, 1997

REASONING ABOUT

OUR EXPERIENCE

12 Reasoning by Analogy

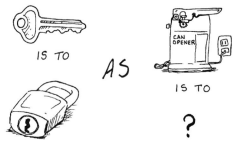

IS TO AS IS TO ?

A. What is Reasoning by Analogy?

We have a desire to be consistent in our lives, to see and apply general principles. "Why shouldn't I hit you? You hit me," says the first-grader, invoking the principle that whatever someone does to me that's bad, I'm justified in doing back to her.

Since it was O.K. there, it should be O.K. here. This situation is like that one. Since we concluded here, we can conclude there. That's arguing by analogy.

> We should legalize marijuana. After all, if we don't, what's the rationale for making alcohol and tobacco legal?

Alcohol is legal. Tobacco is legal. Therefore, marijuana should be legal. They are sufficiently similar.

> DDT has been shown to cause cancer in rats. Therefore, there is a good chance DDT will cause cancer in humans.

Rats are like humans. So if rats get cancer from DDT, so will humans. That's arguing by analogy.

Reasoning by analogy starts with a comparison. But not every comparison is an argument.

> ***Reasoning by analogy*** A comparison becomes reasoning by analogy when it is part of an argument: On one side of the comparison we draw a conclusion, so on the other side we should conclude the same.

"My love is like a red, red rose" is a comparison. Perhaps your English teacher called it an analogy. But it is not an argument—what conclusion is being drawn by Robert Burns?

Analogies, as we'll see, are often only suggestions for arguments. But they have to be taken seriously, for they are used in science, law, and ethics. You use them yourself every day—how often have you heard or said, "But last time . . ." ?

How can we tell if an analogy is good?

B. An Example

Example 1   (Country Joe MacDonald was a rock star who wrote songs protesting the war in Vietnam. In 1995 he was interviewed on National Public Radio about his motives for working to establish a memorial for Vietnam War soldiers in Berkeley, California, his home and a center of anti-war protests in the 60s and 70s. Here is what he said.)

"Blaming soldiers for war is like blaming firemen for fires."

Analysis   This is a comparison. But it's meant as an argument:

> We don't blame firemen for fires.
> Firemen and fires are like soldiers and wars.
> Therefore, we should not blame soldiers for war.

This sounds pretty reasonable.

But in what way are firemen and fires like soldiers and wars? They have to be similar enough in some respect for Country Joe's remark to be more than suggestive. We need to pick out important similarities that we can use as premises.

> *Firemen and fires are like soldiers and war.*
> wear uniforms
> answer to chain of command
> cannot disobey superior without serious consequences
> fight (fires/wars)
> work done when fire/war is over
> until recently only men
> lives at risk in work
> fire/war kills others
> firemen don't start fires—soldiers don't start wars
> usually drink beer

That's stupid: Firemen and soldiers usually drink beer. So?

When you ask "So?" you're on the way to deciding if the analogy is good. It's not just any similarity that's important. There must be some crucial, important way that firemen fighting fires is like soldiers fighting wars, some similarity that can account for why we don't blame firemen for fires that also applies to soldiers and war. Some similarities listed above don't seem to matter. Others we can't use because they trade on an ambiguity, like saying firemen "fight" fires.

We don't have any good guide for how to proceed—that's a weakness of the original argument. But if we're to take Country Joe MacDonald's remark seriously, we have to come up with some principle that applies to both sides.

The similarity that seems most important is that both firemen and soldiers are involved in dangerous work, trying to end a problem/disaster they didn't start. We don't want to blame someone for helping to end a disaster that could harm us all.

(‡)   Firemen are involved in dangerous work.
      Soldiers are involved in dangerous work.
      The job of a fireman is to end a fire.
      The job of a soldier is to end a war.
      Firemen don't start fires.
      Soldiers don't start wars.

But even with these premises added to the original argument, we don't get a good argument for the conclusion that we shouldn't blame soldiers for wars. We need a general principle, some glue. And we know it has to be prescriptive:

> You shouldn't blame someone for helping to end a disaster that could
> harm others if he didn't start the disaster.

This claim, this general principle seems plausible, and it yields a valid argument.

But is the argument good? Are all the premises true? This is the point where the differences between firemen and soldiers might be important.

The first two premises of (‡) are clearly true, and so is the third. But is the job of soldiers to end a war? And do soldiers really not start wars? Look at this difference:

> Without firemen there would still be fires.
> Without soldiers there wouldn't be any wars.

Without soldiers there would still be violence. But without soldiers—any soldiers anywhere—there could be no organized violence of one country against another ("What if they gave a war and nobody came?"—an anti-war slogan of the 1960s).

So? The analogy shouldn't convince. The argument has a dubious premise.

We did not prove that soldiers *should be* blamed for wars. As always, *when you show an argument is bad you haven't proved the conclusion false.* You've only shown that you have no more reason than before for believing the conclusion.

Perhaps the premises at (‡) could be modified, using that soldiers are drafted for wars. But that's beyond Country Joe's argument. If he meant something more, then it's his responsibility to flesh it out. Or we could use his comparison as a starting place to decide whether there is a general principle, based on the similarities, for why we shouldn't blame soldiers for war.

C. Judging Analogies

Why was the example of firemen and soldiers so hard to analyze? Like many analogies, all we had was a sketch of an argument. *Just saying that one side of the analogy is* like *the other is too vague to use as a premise.* Unless the analogy is very clearly stated, we have to survey the similarities and guess the important ones in order to find a general principle that applies to both sides. Then we have to survey the differences to see if there isn't some reason that the general principle might not apply to one side.

Example 2   Magic Johnson was allowed to play in the National Basketball Association and he was HIV-positive. So people who are HIV-positive should be allowed to remain in the military.

Analysis   This doesn't seem very convincing. What has the NBA to do with the military? We can list similarities (uniforms, teamwork, orders, winning, penalties for disobeying orders) and differences (great pay/lousy pay, game/not a game), but none of these matter unless we hit on the basis of the argument.

> The only reason for eliminating someone who is HIV-positive from a job
> is the risk of contracting HIV for others who work with that person.
> Magic Johnson was allowed to play basketball when he was HIV-positive.
> So in basketball the risk of contracting HIV from a fellow worker is
> considered insignificant.
> Basketball players have as much chance of physical contact and
> contracting HIV from one another as soldiers do (except in war).
> Therefore, the risk of contracting HIV from a fellow soldier should be
> considered insignificant.
> Therefore, people with HIV should be allowed to remain in the military.

Here it is not the similarities between basketball players and soldiers that are important. Once we spot the general principle (the first premise, which in this case is prescriptive), it is the differences that support the conclusion (basketball players sweat and bleed all over one another every day, soldiers normally do not, except in war). Whether the analogy is good depends on whether these premises are true, but it's certainly a lot better than it seemed at first glance.

Example 3

Tom: Homosexual marriage threatens the sanctity of marriage. We should outlaw it in order to protect children, since every child needs a mother and a father to raise it. A constitutional amendment will ensure that the same laws reign throughout this country.

Zoe: The same argument could be made against divorce. So Britney Spears should still be married, 'cause that one-day marriage she had was sure a slam against the "sanctity" of marriage. And we should have a constitutional amendment outlawing divorce. Perhaps also an amendment with severe penalties for out-of-wedlock births?

Analysis Zoe is showing that Tom's argument is bad by showing that another argument "just like" his has a conclusion that we would consider absurd. Whatever general principle that makes his argument work must also apply in the other case. So Zoe has refuted Tom—though that doesn't mean his conclusion is false.

>   *An analogy of one argument to another can be a powerful way to refute.* See also Zoe's refutation of Dick's argument about killing flies on pp. 149–150.

Example 4 It's wrong for the government to run a huge deficit—just as it's wrong for any family to overspend its budget.

Analysis We often draw analogies between individuals and groups. But the differences between individuals and groups are usually too great for such an analogy to be good. In this example, it's claimed that what is good for a person or family is also what is good for a country. But without more premises, this is unconvincing because of the enormous differences between a family and a country: a family doesn't have to repair roads, can't put up tariffs, nor can it print money. The *fallacy of composition* is to argue that what is true of the individual is therefore true of the group, or that what is true of the group is therefore true of the individual.

Evaluating an analogy

1. Is this an argument? What is the conclusion?
2. What is the comparison?
3. What are the premises? (one or both sides of the comparison)
4. What are the similarities?
5. Can we state the similarities as premises and find a general principle that covers the two sides?
6. Does the general principle really apply to both sides? Do the differences matter?
7. Is the argument strong or valid? Is it good?

D. Analogies in the Law

Most analogies are not made explicit enough to serve as good arguments. But in the law, analogies are presented as detailed, carefully analyzed arguments, with the important similarities pointed out and a general principle stated.

Laws are often vague, or situations come up which no one ever imagined might be covered by the law: Do the tax laws for mail-order purchases apply to the Internet? Similarities or differences have to be pointed out, general principles enunciated. Then those principles have to be respected by other judges. That's the idea of precedent or common law.

> The basic pattern of legal reasoning is reasoning by example. It is reasoning from case to case. It is a three-step process described by the doctrine of precedent in which a proposition descriptive of the first case is made into a rule of law and then applied to a next similar situation. The steps are these: similarity is seen between cases; next the rule of law inherent in the first case is announced; then the rule of law is made applicable to the second case.
>
> Edward H. Levi, *An Introduction to Legal Reasoning*

But why should a judge respect how earlier judges ruled? Those decisions aren't actually laws.

Imagine getting thrown in jail for doing something that's always been legal, and the law hadn't changed. Imagine running a business and suddenly finding that something you did, which before had been ruled safe and legal in the courts, now left you open to huge civil suits because a judge decided differently this week. If we are to live in a society governed by laws, the law must be applied consistently. It's rare that a judge can say that past decisions were wrong.

Only a few times has the Supreme Court said that all rulings on one issue, including rulings the Supreme Court made, are completely wrong. Brown vs. the Board of Education said that segregation in schools, which had been ruled legal for nearly a hundred years, was now illegal. Roe vs. Wade said that having an abortion, which had been ruled illegal for more than a century, was now legal. Such decisions are rare. They have to be. They create immense turmoil in the ways we live. We have to rethink a lot. And we can't do that regularly.

So what does a judge do when he's confronted by fifteen cases that were decided one way, the case before him falls under the general principle that was stated to cover those cases, yet his sense of justice demands that he decide this case the other way? He looks for differences between this case and those fifteen others. He tweaks the general principle just enough to get another principle that covers all those fifteen cases, but doesn't include the one he's deciding. He makes a new decision that now must be respected or overthrown.

Example 5 The Supreme Court has decided that it is a constitutional right for a doctor to terminate medical treatment that prolongs the life of a terminally ill or brain-dead person, so long as the doctor acts according to the wishes of that person (*Cruzan vs. Director, Missouri Department of Health,* 497 U.S. 261). Therefore, the Supreme Court should decide that assisting someone to commit suicide, someone who is terminally ill or in great suffering, as Dr. Kevorkian does, is a constitutionally protected right (*Compassion in Dying vs. State of Washington*).

Analysis   The question here is whether the two situations are similar. The court should decide with respect to the actual incidents in these cases. The court can decide narrowly, by saying this new case is not sufficiently like *Cruzan*, or broadly, by enunciating a principle that applies in both cases or else distinguishes between them. Or it can bring in more cases for comparison in trying to decide what general principle applies. (In the end the court was so divided that it ruled very narrowly, sidestepping the whole issue. You can look it up on the Internet.)

Summary   Comparisons suggest arguments. When we draw a conclusion from a comparison, we say we are reasoning by analogy: We can use the similarities to draw conclusions, so long as the differences don't matter.

Analogies are usually incomplete arguments. Often they are best treated as motive for finding a general principle to govern our actions or beliefs by surveying similarities and differences between two cases. When a general principle is made explicit, an analogy can be a powerful form of argument. When no general principle is made explicit, an analogy can be a good place to begin a discussion.

Exercises for Chapter 12

1.   Some words and phrases that suggest an analogy is being used are "like," "just as," and "for the same reason." List three more.

2.   What do you need to make a comparison into reasoning by analogy?

3.   Are analogies typically complete arguments? Explain.

4.   What should you do first in evaluating an analogy? Second?

Tom has caught on to the idea of how to evaluate analogies pretty well. Here are some of the exercises he did, with Dr. E's comments.

You should treat dogs humanely. How would you feel if you were caged up all day and experimented on? Or if you were chained to a stake all day? Or someone beat you every time you did something wrong?

Argument? (yes or no) Yes.

Conclusion (if unstated, add it): You should treat dogs humanely.

Comparison: I'm not certain, 'cause they stated most of it as questions. But it seems they're comparing being a dog and being treated badly with you being treated badly, like getting caged up all day, or chained to a stake all day, or someone beating you every time you did something wrong.

Premises: Most of this is unstated. We're just supposed to put down what's actually said here, which I guess would be:

    You shouldn't cage up a person all day.

    You shouldn't chain a person to a stake all day.

> You shouldn't beat someone every time she does something wrong.
> People are like dogs.
> So you shouldn't do any of that to dogs.

Similarities: I know we're supposed to pick out ones that'll give us a general principle. I've got to figure out how dogs and humans are similar. Well, dogs and humans are both mammals.

Additional premises (make the comparison explicit, add a general principle):
Dogs and humans are both mammals. You shouldn't mistreat any mammal.

Classify (with the additional premises): <u>valid</u>   strong ——————— weak

Good argument? (look for differences or ways the general principle could be false) I don't know. I guess the added premises are O.K. So probably it's pretty good.

Good. You've got the basis of the analogy right. You understand the method. You've picked out a general principle. But is it true? Isn't it too broad? After all, hyenas are mammals—does that mean we should treat them humanely? There's one clue you overlooked. They said, "How would you <u>feel</u> . . ." I can imagine how it would feel to be a dog and be mistreated, just as I can (sort of) imagine how it would feel to be you and be mistreated. How about:

> *We can imagine what it would be like to be a dog and be mistreated.*
> *We should treat humanely any creature that we can imagine what it would feel like to be mistreated.*

That's more plausible because it rules out bats. And it might include fish, which some people think should be treated humanely. But really, you did O.K. We're unsure how to repair the original argument because it's too sketchy.

It is easier for a camel to go through the eye of a needle than for a rich man to enter into the kingdom of God.

Argument? (yes or no) This is from the Bible, right? I think it's supposed to make us think that being rich is bad. But I'm not sure. I can't figure out a conclusion, so I better say it's not an argument.

Conclusion (if unstated, add it):

Comparison:

Premises:

Similarities: *Good work!*

Critical thinking is like learning to drive a car. It requires practice—you can't just learn it as theory. That's why I give you so many messy arguments to analyze.

Argument? (yes or no) Yes, but just barely.

Conclusion (if unstated, add it): You should have lots of messy arguments to analyze in doing critical thinking.

> *Comparison*: Critical thinking isn't at all like driving a car. Driving a car is a kind of physical skill, like playing basketball. Critical thinking is something you strain your brain over. Sure you need practice on hard stuff till it gets routine. But I don't see how messy arguments are anything like driving a car.
>
> *Premises*:
>
> *Similarities*:
>
> *Additional premises* (make the comparison explicit, add a general principle):
>
> *Classify* (with the additional premises): valid   strong ——————— weak
>
> *Good argument?* (look for differences or ways the general principle could be false) I think it's pretty bad. I can't figure out what general principle you'd want.
>
> *Good—you jumped to the punch line. There may be something in this comparison, but it's not clear yet, and you're justified in stopping here.*

Exercises 5–24 are comparisons for you to evaluate. Use the following outline. There may be more than one argument in an exercise.

> *Argument?* (yes or no)
>
> *Conclusion* (if unstated, add it):
>
> *Comparison*:
>
> *Premises*:
>
> *Similarities*:
>
> *Additional premises* (make the comparison explicit, add a general principle):
>
> *Classify* (with the additional premises): valid   strong ——————— weak
>
> *Good argument?* (look for differences or ways the general principle could be false)

5. You wouldn't buy a kitten at a pet store to give to your dog. Why, then, do you consider it acceptable to buy white rats for your boa constrictor?

6. All the world's a stage, and all the men and women merely players.

7. Zoe: It's outrageous that Wal-Mart won't sell the morning-after abortion pill or RU486. They carry the highly popular and profitable drug Viagra.

8. Zoe: (*while driving*) Don't throw that banana peel out the window.
    Dick: Don't worry, it's biodegradable.
    Zoe: So is horse manure.

9. Dick: Zoe, let's get married.
    Zoe: I've told you before, Dick, I won't get married until we sleep together.
    Dick: But that would be wrong. I won't sleep with you before we get married.
    Zoe: Would you buy a car without a test drive?
    Dick: Why buy the cow when the milk's free?

10. Dick: Congratulations on getting away with the shoplifting.
    Zoe: What are you talking about?
    Dick: Didn't you just install Adobe Photoshop on your computer from Tom's copy?

11. If killing is wrong, why do you punish murderers by killing them?

12. For at least three years in California, about every third teacher hired was brought aboard under an emergency permit, a provisional license that enables people who possess college degrees, but no teaching credentials, to work.

    "We wouldn't allow a brain surgeon to learn on the job," says Day Higuchi, president of the United Teachers Los Angeles, a 41,000-member teachers union. "Why is it OK to let someone who doesn't know what they're doing teach our kids?"

    USA Today, August 30, 1999

13. Suzy: This candy bar is really healthy. Look, on the label it says "All natural ingredients."

    Dick: Lard is all natural, too.

14. From an article in *Smithsonian*, vol. 32, no. 11, 2002, about irrigation of small farms in New Mexico:

    The practice of trading in water as a commodity, observes one activist, is like "selling sunshine."

15. Maria: Suppose someone came up to you and offered you a sure-fire method for finding $100 bills on the street, for which he'd charge you only $5.95. You'd be crazy to buy it from him. After all, he could just as easily pick up the $100 bills himself. Besides, we know there aren't any $100 bills lying around the street, since any time there's a $100 bill floating free you can be sure that someone will pick it up immediately. So why pay money to a stock analyst?

16. Downloading computer software from someone you don't know is like accepting candy from a stranger.

17. Flo's mother: It's just so hard raising Flo.

    Dick: How hard can it be to raise a kid? After all, I've trained two dogs.

18. Tom: I can't believe you're out demonstrating against the U.S. fighting in Iraq.

    Dick: I'm against war—all wars. I'm a pacifist.

    Tom: So, if someone came up to you on the street and hit you from behind, you wouldn't turn and hit him back?

19. We should take claims about extra-sensory perception seriously. Look, suppose no one in the world had a sense of smell except one person. He would walk along a country road where there is a high stone wall and tell his friend, "There are roses there." Or he would walk into a home and say, "Someone cooked onions here yesterday." These would seem extraordinary extra-sensory perceptions to his friends and acquaintances. Similarly, just because we don't understand and can't imagine a mechanism that would explain extra-sensory perception, we shouldn't stop the investigation.

20. Tom: Seat belts cause accidents.

    Dick: Are you crazy? Seat belts save lives. Everyone knows that.

    Tom: No, they cause accidents. They may prevent serious injury in some accidents, but there are more accidents now because people use seat belts.

    Dick: Why's that?

Tom: The threat of getting killed or seriously injured in an accident is much less if you're wearing a seat belt. Because people reckon they are safer, they're less careful and drive faster. So they get into more accidents. Some guy at the University of Chicago looked at the numbers in the 1970s and found that there are fewer deaths per accident, but more accidents, so that the actual number of people getting killed remained about the same after seat belts were required.

Dick: Well, if that's the case, we better not make any more improvements on cars. And we certainly shouldn't require motorcycle riders to wear helmets.

21. Letter to the editor in the *El Defensor Chieftain*, Socorro, NM, March 29, 2003:

This year's Legislative session and the bills against cockfighting have caused some heated arguments.

The opposition's reasoning is ridiculous, considering that many of them do not understand anything about cockfighting. The people that are trying to ban our sport are not affected by it in any way, shape or form.

A fellow cockfighter recently asked a lawyer, "How would you like it if we tried to take your license away?" Lawyers make their living practicing law; cockfighters make their living by buying, selling, raising and fighting roosters.

Our occupations may differ, but the fact that we both pay our bills and support our families, makes us a lot alike. Leave us alone!

We fight roosters and are proud of it. We are third-generation cockfighters and it has been in our family for over 50 years. Those of you who think no one actually makes a living this way are sadly mistaken—think again.

In conclusion, we are a family and we are just trying to survive in this society. We teach our children to have morals and value their upbringing. Please don't take that away—it is all we have.
                                                                                           Tara Parish

22. I know I can't really feel a pain you have. But because we're so much alike in so many ways, I'm sure that you feel physical pain in roughly the same way I do.

23. Dick: Our diet should be similar to that of cavemen—that's what our genes are programmed for.

    Zoe: You're nuts. Besides, it's *cave dwellers*, not "cavemen."

24. God must exist. The way everything works together in nature, the adaptation of means to ends, the beauty, resembles, but far exceeds, what humans do. Everything works together as a fine piece of machinery, like a watch. So there must be some maker with intelligence behind all of nature. That is, God exists and is similar to human mind and intelligence.

25. Voters in Arizona and California approved ballot measures Nov. 5 allowing prescriptions of marijuana and other controlled substances for certain patients.

The most prevalent use is to ease the suffering of terminal patients or to counteract the side effects of chemotherapy. . . .

The legal effect of the measures' passage is still up in the air, since the uses remain outlawed under federal statute. But retired General Barry McCaffrey, the White House's drug policy director, is quite certain about what the practical effect will be:

"Increased drug abuse in every category will be the inevitable result of the referenda," he said in a speech last week. "There could not be a worse message to young people than the provisions of these referenda. . . . They are being told that marijuana and other drugs are good, they are medicine."

Apply this logic to the general's primary area of expertise:

Does the necessity of maintaining a standing army and engaging in war to protect national interests send a message to teens to arm themselves and form street gangs? . . . There is a line between use and abuse of a necessary evil like lethal force or a powerful narcotic.

Social, economic and political circumstances justify the use of lethal force in war; medical circumstances justify the use of drugs.

But to think that teens or other forms of life lower on the food chain than generals are unable to differentiate between use and abuse may lead directly to the kind of logic under which students are expelled for possession of over-the-counter analgesics like Midol.

Editorial, *Albuquerque Journal,* November, 1996

a.   What is the conclusion?
b.   What analogy does the editorial make?
c.   How does it use the methods for evaluating analogies?
d.   Are there any slanters or bad argument types?
e.   Is the argument good?

26. a.   Suppose that tomorrow good, highly reliable research is announced showing that oil derived from tails removed without anesthetic from healthy cats when applied to human skin reduces wrinkles significantly. Would it be justifiable to do further research and manufacture this oil?

   b.   Same as (a) except that the oil is drunk with orange juice and significantly reduces the chance of lung cancer for smokers.

   c.   Same as (a) except the oil is mixed with potatoes and eaten and significantly reduces the chance of heart disease and lengthens the lives of women.

   d.   Same as (a) except that when drunk, the oil kills off all viruses harmful to humans.

27. Do Exercise 26 reading "dogs" for "cats."

Further Study   Analogies are discussed in courses in criminal justice, ethics, and health sciences, among others. The exercise Tom did about how we justify treating dogs humanely is typical of the sort of problem and reasoning you'd encounter in a course on ethics. Some philosophy classes on reasoning or philosophy of science look at the nature of analogies more deeply. In the *Science Workbook* for this text you can read about how scientists reason with models as analogies, and Science Analyses 4.8, 8, and 10.C deal with ESP.

Writing Lesson 10

You understand what reasoning by analogy is now. So write an argument *using an analogy* either for or against the following:

> *Just as alcohol and tobacco are legal, we should legalize the use of marijuana.*

Check whether your instructor has chosen a different topic for this assignment.

There are roughly three ways you can argue:

- Marijuana is no worse than alcohol or tobacco, so we should legalize it.
  (Arguing from similarities.)

- Marijuana is worse than alcohol and tobacco, so we should not legalize it.
  (Arguing from differences.)

- Marijuana is no worse than alcohol or tobacco, but it is a mistake to
  have those legal, and we should not make the situation worse by
  legalizing marijuana.
  (Arguing from similarities.)

Be sure to make explicit what prescriptive premises you are using.

Write your argument as a maximum *one page* essay. It should be clear and well structured, since you will have written out the claims first for yourself. You shouldn't have to do major research for this, but at least be sure your premises are plausible.

13   Numbers?

In this chapter we'll look at some ways you can get confused about numbers in claims. If your eyes are starting to glaze, if your mind is going blank with talk of numbers, relax. Numbers don't lie.

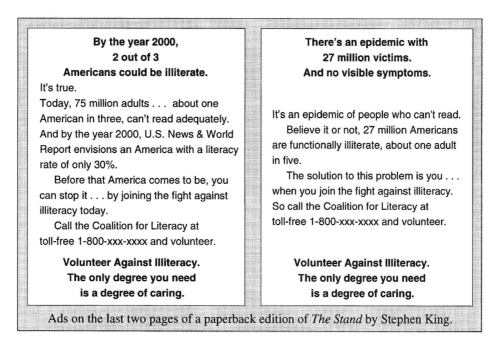

**By the year 2000,
2 out of 3
Americans could be illiterate.**

It's true.

Today, 75 million adults . . . about one American in three, can't read adequately. And by the year 2000, U.S. News & World Report envisions an America with a literacy rate of only 30%.

Before that America comes to be, you can stop it . . . by joining the fight against illiteracy today.

Call the Coalition for Literacy at toll-free 1-800-xxx-xxxx and volunteer.

**Volunteer Against Illiteracy.
The only degree you need
is a degree of caring.**

**There's an epidemic with
27 million victims.
And no visible symptoms.**

It's an epidemic of people who can't read.

Believe it or not, 27 million Americans are functionally illiterate, about one adult in five.

The solution to this problem is you . . . when you join the fight against illiteracy. So call the Coalition for Literacy at toll-free 1-800-xxx-xxxx and volunteer.

**Volunteer Against Illiteracy.
The only degree you need
is a degree of caring.**

Ads on the last two pages of a paperback edition of *The Stand* by Stephen King.

A. Misleading Claims with Numbers

Zoe has 4 apples and Dick has 2 oranges. Who has more? More *what*?

When numbers are used it looks exact, but a vague or meaningless comparison gets no better by having a few numbers in it.

> There were twice as many rapes as murders in our town.

Yes, that's a claim, but a misleading one. It seems to say something important, but what?

> It's getting really violent here. There were 12% more murders this year.

This is also a mistaken comparison. If the town is growing rapidly and the number of tourists is growing even faster, it would be no surprise that the *number* of murders is going up, though the *rate* (how many murders per 100,000 population) might be going down. I'd feel safer in a town of one million that had 20 murders last year than in a small town of 25,000 that had 6. A numerical comparison where it doesn't make sense to compare the items is called comparing **apples and oranges**.

Increases and decreases are comparisons, too:

> Attendance up 50% this week at performances of Othello!
> Tickets still available!

Great ad, but what was the attendance last week? 25? 250? 1,000? We call it **two times zero is still zero** when someone gives a numerical comparison that makes something look impressive but the base of the comparison is not stated. For example, a clothing store advertises a sale of sweaters at "25% off." You take it to mean 25% off the price they used to charge which was $20, so you'd pay $15. But the store could mean 25% off the suggested retail price of $26, so now it's $19.50.

Percentages can be misleading, too You see a stock for $60 and think it's a good deal. You buy it; a week later it's at $90, so you sell. You made $30—that's a 50% gain! Your buddy hears about it and buys the stock at $90; a week later it goes down to $60, so he panics $\quad 50\% \uparrow \begin{bmatrix} \$90 \\ \$60 \end{bmatrix} \downarrow 33\tfrac{1}{3}\%$ and sells the stock. He lost $30—that's a $33^1/_3\%$ loss. The same $30 is a different percentage depending on where you started.

And then there's the report that says unemployment is up 8%. That does not mean unemployment is *at* 8%. It means that if unemployment was 5%, it is now 5.4%. There is a difference between "up" and "up to." Here's another example:

> *X-Ray Cancer Risk Up to 3%*
> The risk of cancer from common X-rays and increasingly popular CT scans
> ranges from less than 1 percent to about 3 percent, according to a new study. . . .
>
> The new research indicates the cancer risk—ranging from 0.6 percent to
> 3.2 percent—varies depending on the frequency of X-rays and scans in 15
> countries surveyed. . . .

> Of the 15 countries surveyed, the cancer risk believed linked to X-rays
> was lowest in Britain, where they are used least frequently. They estimated that
> 0.6 percent of the cumulative British cancer risk for those 75 years old came
> from X-ray exposure, accounting for about 700 of the nation's annual cancer
> diagnoses.
> Beth Gardiner, Associated Press, January 30, 2004

Sounds good, except when they say that the cancer risk is 1 percent, what do they mean? With percentages, you always need to ask: *percentage of what*?

An article in the journal *Science*, vol. 292, uses percentages to assess risk in health care. Mammography screening, it says, can reduce the risk of breast cancer fatalities in women ages 50 to 74 by 25%. That seems like a real incentive for women of that age to get tested. But, the article points out, only 2 out of 1,000 women *without symptoms* are actually likely to die of breast cancer within the next 10 years. So reducing the risk by 25% just means that only 1 more woman in 1,000 who undergoes screening in the next 10 years would be saved. Yet the other women who won't benefit from screening are subjected to X-rays, false positive tests, or treatment for slow-growing cancers that could be left alone. To make choices about health care you need not only the percentages, but the actual numbers, too.

Still, it doesn't matter whether it's percentages or actual numbers if *there's no way they could know the number*. For example, on a National Public Radio news broadcast I heard:

> Breast feeding is up 16% from 1989.

How could they know? Who was looking in all those homes? A survey? Who did they ask? Women chosen randomly? But lots of them don't have infants. Women who visited doctors? But lots of women, lots of poor ones, don't visit their doctors. What does "breast feeding" mean? Does a woman who breast feeds one day and then gives it up qualify as someone who breast feeds? Or one who breast feeds two weeks? Six months? Maybe NPR is reporting on a reliable survey (in the next chapter we'll look at what that means). But what they said is so vague and open to doubt as to how they could know it that we should ignore it as noise.

Rich getting richer, except in Africa and Asia

The rich got richer in most parts of the world last year, except for Asia and Africa.

There were nearly 7.2 million people around the globe in 2000 who had at least $1 million in investable assets, an increase of 180,000 from 1999, said a study released Monday. Their total wealth was estimated at $27 trillion, up 6 percent from $25.5 trillion the previous year.

Albuquerque Tribune, May 15, 2001

Where did they get these seemingly unknowable figures? What study? Who wants to let people know they're rich? This is a worthless report.

B. Graphs

Graphs can be useful in making comparisons clearer. But we have to be careful when reading them because they can conceal claims, mislead, or just be wrong.

Example 1

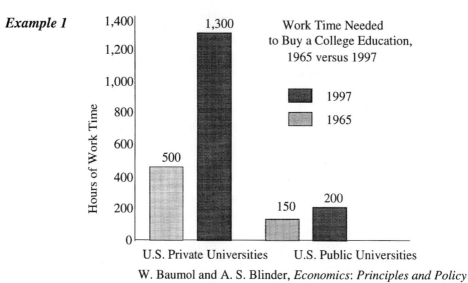

W. Baumol and A. S. Blinder, *Economics*: *Principles and Policy*

Analysis   You should check the information in a graph against your personal experience. The authors of this economics textbook say that the average hourly wage is about $13. So according to the graph the (average?) cost of a college education in 1997 at a U.S. public university was about $13/hour **x** 200 hours = $2,600. But that's unlikely to be enough for tuition and books for one year, much less housing and board—and certainly not for four years.

Example 2

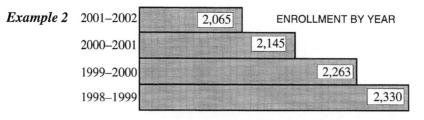

Socorro, N.M. Consolidated Schools Accountability Report, 2000–2001

Analysis   The numbers here are correct, but the graph greatly exaggerates the differences between years. The enrollment in 2001–2002 is 11.4% less than in 1998–1999, but the difference in the lengths of the bars representing those enrollments is 66%. Visually the difference appears even greater because we're comparing areas instead of lengths. *A graph is likely to distort comparisons if the baseline is not zero or if it uses bars.*

Example 3

Analysis Here we can see how the angle, the sharpness of increase and decrease, can be exaggerated greatly by the spacing of the scales on the axes. This affects our perception of the volatility and the amount of increase or decrease of prices.
A graph can create misleading comparisons by the choice of how the measuring points on the axes are spaced.

Example 4 An economics text gives the following graph and notes that from 1966 to 1982 the prices of stocks were generally going down.

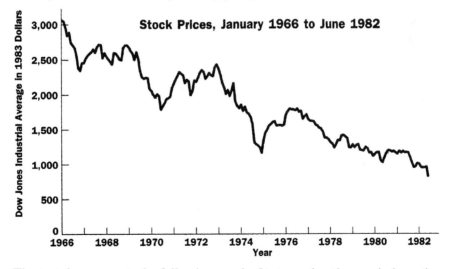

The text then presents the following graphs for two other time periods, noting in particular that from 1993 to 1998 stock prices were generally going up.

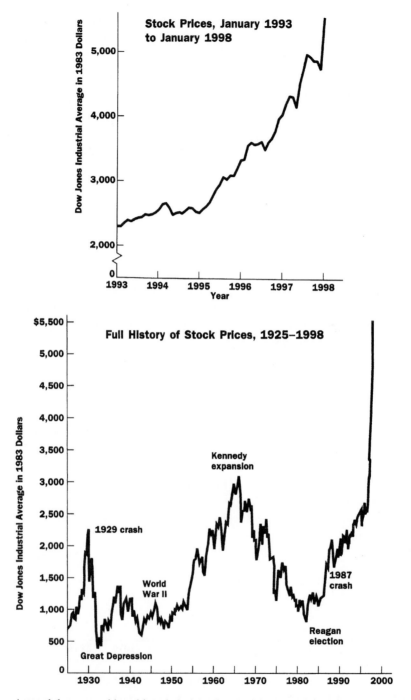

A much longer and less-biased choice of period (1925–1998) gives a less distorted picture. It indicates that investments in stocks are sometimes profitable and sometimes unprofitable.   W. Baumol and A. S. Blinder, *Economics*: *Principles and Policy*

Analysis Why is the longer period apt for comparison to the present day? If we looked at 1890 onwards, we'd have a different picture still ("Full History" is a bad label). Maybe the best comparison for an *analogy* about investing in stocks is with the later periods because of new regulations on buying and selling stocks. These graphs, however, do compensate for inflation by stating the values in 1983 dollars— if they didn't, the comparisons would be apples and oranges.

C. Averages

"It ought to be safe to cross here. I heard that the average depth is only two feet."

Beware: The average is not the maximum or most likely depth.

The ***average*** or ***mean*** of a collection of numbers is obtained by adding the numbers and then dividing by the number of items. For example,

> The average of 7, 9, 37, 22, 109 is calculated:
> > *Add* $7 + 9 + 37 + 22 + 109 = 184$
> > *Divide* 184 by 5 = 36.8, *the average*

An average is a useful figure to know if there isn't too much variation in the figures. For example, suppose the marks Dr. E gave for his course were:

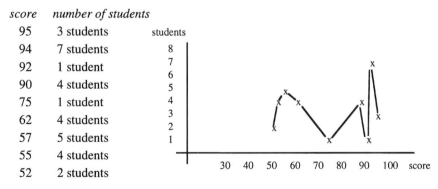

score	number of students
95	3 students
94	7 students
92	1 student
90	4 students
75	1 student
62	4 students
57	5 students
55	4 students
52	2 students

The grading scale was 90–100 = A, 80–89 = B, 70–79 = C, 60–69 = D, 59 and below = F. When Dr. E's department head asked him how the teaching went, he told her, "Great, just like you wanted, the average mark was 75%, a C."

But she knows Dr. E too well to be satisfied. She asks him, "What was the median score?" The **median** *is the midway mark: the same number of items above as below.* Again Dr. E can reply, "75." As many got above 75 as below 75.

But knowing how clever Dr. E is with numbers, she asks him what the mode score was. The **mode** *is the number most often obtained.* Dr. E flushes, "Well, 94." Now she knows something is fishy. When she said that she wanted the average score to be about 75, she was thinking of a graph that looked like:

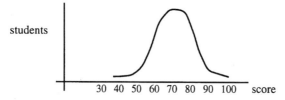

The distribution of the marks should be in a bell-shape, clustered around the median.

> Unless you have good reason to believe that the average is pretty close to the median and that the distribution is more or less bell-shaped, the average doesn't tell you anything important.

Sometimes people misuse the word "average" by confusing it with the mode or most, as in "The average American enjoys action movies."

> Get your class to stand up. Look around. Do you think the average height is the same as the median height? How can you tell? Come up with a *physical* way to determine the median height and the mode of the heights.
>   Suppose your class had just eight players from the men's basketball team and five women gymnasts. Do you think the median and the average would be the same?

Summary   Numbers are our way of measuring. They are important in our reasoning. But it's easy to be misled or use them wrong. A vague claim doesn't get any better by using numbers. Both sides of a comparison must be made clear. The numbers must represent quantities someone could actually know. And often it's not the average that's significant, but the median or the mode.

We also have to be careful in reading graphs, for they can mislead or conceal claims by not taking the base of the comparison to be zero, or by using bars, or by spacing the numbers on the axes in certain ways.

Key Words   apples and oranges   mean
                   two times zero is still zero   median
                   average   mode

Exercises for Chapter 13

1. Find an advertisement that uses a claim with percentages that is misleading or vague.

2. Find an advertisement that uses a claim with numbers other than percentages that is misleading or vague.

3. Compare a sundial on a sunny day with a digital watch that is set wrong.
   a. Which is more accurate at telling the time?
   b. Which is more precise?

4. Dick is contemplating getting a new printer. It's faster than his old one. He prints out a cartoon and finds that it takes 7 minutes. On his old printer it took 10 and a half minutes. Tom tells him he'll save 1/3 of his time. Dick says no, he'll save about 50% of his time. Who is right?

5. "The birth control pill is 99% effective." What does this mean?

6. Find the average, mean, median, and mode of the scores of Dr. E's students who took his critical thinking final exam: 92, 54, 60, 86, 62, 76, 88, 88, 62, 68, 81.

7. Estimate the average age of students in your class. Do you think it's the same as the median? As the mode?

8. The experts say that over the long term the stock market is the best place to invest. So you invested most of your retirement in stocks. You've just turned 70 and need cash to retire. But the market went down 15% last week. Evaluate those experts' advice now.

For Exercises 9–27 point out any use of numbers that is vague, misleading, or wrong.

9. [Advertisement] Our employees have a combined 52 years of experience!

10. [On a box of Texmati® rice]
    Serving size 1/4 cup (45g)
    Servings Per Package about 22

Amount per serving	
Calories 150	%DV*
Total Fat 0.5g	1%
Sodium 0mg	0%
Total Carb. 34g	11%
Protein 3g	

    * Percent Daily Values are based on a 2,000 calorie diet.

11. [From a glossy brochure "Why do I need a water softener?" by Pentair Water Treatment] The Bureau of Statistics found that between 17 and 20.8 cents of every dollar are spent on cleaning products. . . . The bottom line? Soft water can save you thousands of dollars.

12. [Advertisement for *3 Musketeers*® candy bars]
    The sweetest part is finding out how little fat it has.
    (45% less fat than the average of the 25 leading chocolate brands, to be exact.)*
        *Not a low-fat food. 8 fat grams per serving for single bar vs. 15 gram average for leading chocolate brands.

13. [Advertisement] Studies have shown that three cups of Cheerios® a day with a low-fat diet can help lower cholesterol.

14. Dick: Gee, cars are really expensive now. My uncle said he bought a new Ford Mustang in 1968 for only $2,000.

15. [On the box of a fan made by Lasco™ that Dr. E bought]
    NEW   WIND RING™   30% MORE Air Velocity

16. [Concerning the way the U.S. Census Bureau operates] In 1990, 65% of the questionnaires that were mailed were filled out and returned. Census counters went back to every household that didn't mail back a form. Even then, the bureau was able to count only 98.4% of the U.S. population.   *USA Today,* April 15, 1998

17. Less than 10% of women who get breast cancer have the gene for breast cancer. Therefore, if you have the gene, there's only a 10% chance you'll get breast cancer.

18. In America 7 out of 10 people believe that they are one of the 3 out of 10, whereas in Japan 7 out of 10 people believe they are one of the 7.
    Advanced Reasoning Forum, May, 2000

19. *Roadway Congestion*
    Cities with highest and lowest roadway congestion index. A value greater than 1.0 indicates significant congestion.

Highest	Index	Lowest	Index	
Los Angeles	1.57	Bakersfield, Calif.	0.68	
Washington	1.43	Laredo, Texas	0.73	
Miami-Hialeah	1.34	Colorado Springs	0.74	
Chicago	1.34	Beaumont, Texas	0.76	
San Francisco	1.33	Corpus Christi, Tex.	0.78	*USA Today,* 4/13/99

20. *New Mexico Lodging Report: May 2001*

	Available Room-Nights	Occupied Room-Nights	Occupancy	Average Rate
Albuquerque	190,373	125,780	66.1%	$67.84
Santa Fe	100,752	72,512	72.0%	$120.72
Farmington	18,197	12,667	69.6%	$57.66
Carlsbad	17,647	10,753	61.6%	$56.20
Las Cruces	29,884	19,218	64.3%	$57.32
Taos	25,345	12,250	48.3%	$68.04
Other	53,040	31,247	59.3%	$57.83
STATE	435,058	284,607	65.4%	$78.61

    Albuquerque Tribune, June 28, 2001

21. Dick: I read that drinking a shot of whiskey a day is good for your health. I didn't drink much last year, so I better make up for it tonight.

22. Dick: I read that on average, women think of sex about every 12 minutes.
    Zoe: Really? I guess some woman out there is thinking about sex only once a year.

23. [Advertisement] Mitsubishi is the fastest growing Japanese car company in America.

24. [Advertisement]
    Official Royal Flush Results!   Fiesta 2,115   Texas 1,735
    It's not even close
    Fiesta backs up its claim:

    "We Pay More Royal Flushes per Machine Than Any Other Casino Hotel in the World!"

    For the month of September, Texas [Casino] claimed that it paid out a total of 1,735
    Royals, with approximately 2,000 machines, but for that same period, Fiesta Casino paid
    out 2,115 Royal Flushes, with just 1,200 machines. Here's proof, once again, that
    Fiesta's Slots and Video Poker Machines are the loosest on Earth!

25. *The Vacancy Rate of Albuquerque Apartment Complexes*

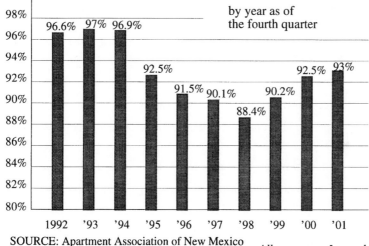

SOURCE: Apartment Association of New Mexico

Albuquerque Journal, March 3, 2002

26. *S. Korea declares war on leftovers*
    Because of the feeling of bounty and plenty that it gives, Koreans routinely cook more at
    home than they can eat, and restaurants serve more than any customer could reasonably
    consume. . . .

    "Koreans are used to thinking 'the more the better,'" said Koh, the restaurant
    manager.

    It's a philosophy the government is battling to change. In the latest round, the govern-
    ment announced Dec. 6 that it will make a major push in 1997 to cut food waste by half.

    Many Koreans say they are careful at home to eat leftovers the next day. But
    restaurant waste, which the government says accounts for 42 percent of food garbage, is
    a tougher problem. . . .

    The government says the country's 45 million people throw away nearly 48,000
    metric tons of garbage a day.   Pauline Jelinek, Associated Press, 11/23/96

27. *Artery narrowing can be reversed*

 A new study has shown what many researchers have thought all along—cardiovascular disease (i.e., narrowing of the arteries) can be moderately reversed.

 The well-known secret: lifestyle changes.

 In the study, heart patients who had coronary artery (heart) disease—diagnosed through angiograms (X-rays of the arteries)—were: 1) put on a vegetarian diet, 2) told to stop smoking, 3) started on a mild to moderate aerobic exercise program (three hours per week), and 4) told to practice stress management techniques (e.g., meditation) one hour a day.

 Five-year findings: In a *control* group of heart patients who had *not* made the above lifestyle changes, 45% had coronary narrowing that became worse; 50% showed no change; and 5% showed improvement.

 By comparison, 99% of the group who made significant lifestyle changes (see above) had healthier arteries (i.e., improved blood flow) or their condition remained stable.

 From the heart, Washoe Health System, Fall, 1996

Which of the following should be trusted to give you a good idea of the population as a whole? For which would you prefer to know the median or mode? Explain.

28. The average wage in the U.S. is $28,912.

29. The average wage in one rural county of Utah was $14,117.

30. The average wage of concert pianists in the U.S. is less than the average wage of university professors.

31. The average number of people in a household in Las Vegas is 2.1.

32. The average GPA of a graduating senior at this college in 2000 was 2.86, while in 1972 it was 2.41.

33. Dick: Which section of English Lit should I take, Zoe, Professor Zzzyzzx's or Professor Øllebød's?

 Zoe: It doesn't really matter. You can't understand either, and the department info on the sections said the average mark in both their classes was a C.

34. The average income of a woman in the U.S. was only 82% that of a man.

14   Generalizing

A. Generalizing

> I think I'll get a border collie. Every one I've met has been friendly and loyal.

> I'd better not visit your home. You've got a cat, and every time I've been
> around a cat I get a terrific sneezing fit and asthma.

We generalize every day, arguing from a claim about some to a claim about more.
It's how we make sense of our world: What's happened before is likely to happen
again. My experience is typical, until I learn otherwise. As we experience more, we
generalize better because we have more examples from which to generalize.

But it's not only our own experience. Poll takers and scientists generalize, too,
as when they say that the President's approval rating is 54%, or they report that 28%
of all people who smoke get cancer. Those are generalizations from the groups of
people that were interviewed or studied.

> ***Generalizing*** We are generalizing if we conclude a claim about a group, the ***population***, from a claim about some part of it, the ***sample***. To generalize is to make an argument.
>
>   Sometimes the general claim that is the conclusion is called the ***generalization***; sometimes we use that word for the whole argument. Plausible premises about the sample are called the ***inductive evidence*** for the generalization.

To evaluate whether a generalization is good, we need to see it as an argument. Strong arguments with plausible premises will be the best we're likely to get, since there will always be the possibility that there's an exception to a generalization.

Examples   Are the following generalizations? If so, what is the sample? What is the population?

Example 1 In a study of 816 people who owned sport utility vehicles in Cincinnati, Rigochi owners expressed the lowest satisfaction with their SUVs. So Rigochi owners are less satisfied with their cars than other SUV owners.

Analysis Here we know about the 816 people who were surveyed in Cincinnatti. They are the sample. The conclusion is about all SUV owners everywhere, and they constitute the population.

    Is the generalization good? That is, is the argument good? Unstated premises are needed about how the study was conducted. Is there any reason that we should think that these 816 people are like all SUV owners everywhere?

Example 2 I should build my house with the bedroom facing this direction to catch the morning sun.

Analysis We believe we know where the sun will rise in the future based on where we see it rise today. The sample is all the times in the past when the sun rose: We know that the point where the sun rises varies slightly from season to season, but is roughly east. The population is all times the sun has risen or will rise, which we think will be in roughly the same direction.

Example 3 Of potential customers surveyed, 72% said that they liked "very much" the new green color that Yoda plans to use for its cars. So about 72% of all potential customers will like it.

Analysis The sample is the group of potential customers interviewed, and the population is all potential customers.

    Sometimes the generalization we want and we're entitled to isn't "all," but "most," or "72%": The same proportion of the whole as in the sample will have the property. This is a ***statistical generalization***.

Example 4   Every time unemployment goes past 6% there's a call for restricting immigration. I read that the forecast is for unemployment to reach 6.2% this month. So I hope that Juan can get the visa for his wife real soon.

Analysis   Here the unstated conclusion is that there will be a call for restricting immigration. The reason given is in the past that's happened when there's been the same rate of unemployment. The sample is all times in the past that the unemployment rate rose above 6%, and the population is all times it has risen or will rise.

We need to know how to judge whether the examples are sufficient for the generalization: Do they have enough in common with the situation now? Are there enough examples?

Example 5   The doctor tells you to fast from 10 p.m. Then at 10 a.m. she gives you glucose to drink. Forty-five minutes later she takes some of your blood and has it analyzed. She concludes you don't have diabetes.

Analysis   The sample is the blood the doctor took. It's a very small sample compared to the amount of blood you have in your body, but the doctor is confident that it is representative of all your blood.

Example 6   You go to the city council meeting with a petition signed by all the people who live on your block requesting that a street light be put in. Addressing the city council, you say, "Everyone on this block wants a street light here."

Analysis   You're not generalizing here: There's no argument from some to more, since the sample equals the population.

Exercises for Section A

Here's some of Tom's work on identifying generalizations.

> **Lee: Every time I've gone to Luigi's, it's taken over 30 minutes to get our pizza. So let's not go there tonight because we're in a hurry.**
>
> *Generalization?* (yes/no)   Yes.
> *Sample*:   Every time Lee has gone to Luigi's and ordered a pizza.
> *Population*:   All the times anyone orders a pizza at Luigi's.
>   *Good work!*
>
> **You shouldn't go out with someone from New York. They're all rude and pushy.**
>
> *Generalization?* (yes/no)   Yes.
> *Sample*:   All the New Yorkers the person has met.
> *Population*:   All New Yorkers.
>
> *You're too generous. How do you know if the speaker has ever met a New Yorker? Maybe he's just spouting off a prejudice he acquired from his friends. It's not a generalization if you can't identify the sample.*

> **Should we try the new Mexican restaurant on Sun Street? I heard it was pretty good.**
>
> *Generalization*? (yes/no) Yes.
>
> *Sample*: People who told him it was good.
>
> *Population*: It will be good food for him, too.
>
> *A generalization is an argument, right. But the sample and the population <u>aren't</u> <u>claims</u>—they're groups. The sample here is the times that other people have eaten there (and reported that it was good). The population is all times anyone has or will eat there. It's a past to future generalization.*

For Exercises 1–13 answer the following questions:

Generalization? (yes/no)

Sample:

Population:

1. German shepherds have a really good temperament. I know, because lots of my friends and my sister have one.

2. Maria: Look! That dry cleaner broke a button on my blouse again. I'm going to go over there and complain.

3. Suzy: I hear you got one of those MP3 players from Hirangi.
    Maria: Yeah, and I wish I'd never gotten one. It's always breaking down.
    Suzy: Well, I won't get one then, since they're probably all the same.

4. Maria to Suzy: Don't bother to ask Tom to do the dishes. My brother's a football player and no football player will do the dishes.

5. Suzy: Guys are such nitwits.
    Zoe: What do you mean?
    Suzy: Like, they can't even tell when you're down. Emotionally, they're clods.
           Besides, they just want a girl for her body.
    Zoe: How do you know?
    Suzy: Duh, it's like a cheerleader like me isn't going to have a lot of dates?

6. Lee: Are you taking Spot for a walk?
    Dick: No. I'm getting the leash because I have to take him to the vet, and it will be hard to get him to go. Every time I take him to the vet he seems to know it before we get in the car.

7. Manuel: Are those refried beans?
    Maria: Yes.
    Manuel: I can't believe you'd cook those for dinner. Don't you remember I had terrible indigestion the last time you made them?

8. Maria: Do you know of a good dry cleaner other than Ricardo's?
    Zoe: The one in the plaza north of campus is pretty good. They've always done O.K. with the stuff I take them.

9. Don't go to Seattle in December. It rains there all the time then.

10. Dogs can be trained to retrieve a newspaper.

11. I want to marry a Japanese guy. They're hard-working and really family-oriented.

12. You don't have to worry about getting the women's gymnastic team in your van—I saw them at the last meet, and they're small enough to fit in.

13. From our study it appears that bald men are better husbands.

14. Write down three examples of generalizations you have heard or made in the last week and one example of a claim that sounds like a generalization but isn't. See if your classmates can pick out the one that isn't. For the generalizations, ask a classmate to identify the sample and the population.

B. What is a Good Sample?

1. How you can go wrong

Tom's sociology professor has assigned him to conduct a survey to find out the attitudes of students on campus about sex before marriage. "That's easy," Tom thinks, "I'll just ask some of my friends. They're typical, aren't they?"

So he asks all his friends he can reach on Tuesday whether they think sex before marriage is a great idea or not. Twenty of the twenty-eight say "Yes," while eight say "No." That was easy.

Tom takes the results to his professor and she asks why he thinks his friends are typical. "Typical? I guess they are," Tom responds. But aren't they mostly your age? And the same sex as you? How many are gay? How many are married? And is twenty-eight really enough to generalize from? And what about that question "Is sex before marriage a *great* idea or not?" A bit biased?

O.K., it wasn't such a good job. Back to the drawing board. Tom brainstorms with some of his friends and figures he'll ask 100 students as they leave the student union one question, "Do you approve of sexual intercourse before marriage?"

He goes to the student union at 4 p.m. on Wednesday, asks the students, and finds that 83 said "No," while 17 said "Yes." That's different from what he expected, but what the heck, this is science, and science can't be wrong. There was no bias in the question, and surely those 100 students are typical.

Tom presents the results to his professor, and she suggests that perhaps he should find out what was going on at the student union that day. . . . It seems the campus Bible society was having a big meeting there that let out about 4 p.m. Maybe this survey won't give a good generalization.

So Tom and two friends get together, and at 9 a.m., 1 p.m., and 6 p.m. they station

themselves outside the student union, the administration offices, and the big classroom building. Each is to ask the first 20 people who come by just two questions: "Are you a student here?" and "Do you approve of sexual intercourse before marriage?"

They get 171 people saying they are students, with 133 saying "Yes" and 38 saying "No" to the second question. That's a lot of responses with no evident bias in the sampling. Tom's sure his professor will be happy this time.

Tom tells his professor what they've done, and she asks, "Why do you think your sample is representative? Why do you think it's big enough?"

Tom's puzzled. It's big enough. Surely 170 out of 20,000 students is a lot, isn't it? How many could she expect us to interview? We're just human.

And representative? What does she mean? "We didn't do anything to get a bias," he says. "But are those students typical?" she asks. "Is not doing anything to get a bias enough to ensure your sample is representative?"

2. Representative samples

Tom's first two attempts to survey students about their attitudes towards sex before marriage used clearly unrepresentative samples. But his third attempt? Can we be sure he has a sample that is just like the population, one that is representative?

> **Representative sample** A sample is representative if no one subgroup of the whole population is represented more than its proportion in the population. A sample is **biased** if it is not representative.

Tom's method was **haphazard sampling**: Choosing the sample with no *intentional* bias. Possibly the sample is representative. Maybe not. But we don't have any good reason to believe that it is representative. There is, however, a way we can choose a sample that is very likely to get us a representative sample.

> **Random sampling** A sample is chosen randomly if at every choice there is an equal chance for any one of the remaining members of the population to be picked.

If you assign a number to each student, write the numbers on slips of paper, put them in a fishbowl, and draw one number out at a time, that's probably going to be a random selection. But there's a chance that slips with longer numbers will have more ink and fall to the bottom of the bowl when you shake it. Or the slips aren't all the same size. So typically to get a random selection we use tables of random numbers prepared by mathematicians. Most spreadsheet programs for home computers can now generate tables of random numbers. So for Tom's survey he could get a list of all students; if the first number on the table is 413, he'd pick the 413th student on the list; if the second number is 711, he'd pick the 711th student on the list; and so on, until he has a sample that's big enough.

Why is random sampling better? Suppose that of the 20,000 students at your school, 500 are gay males. Then the chance that *one* student picked at random would be a gay male is $500/_{20,000} = 1/_{40}$. If you were to pick 300 students at random, the chance that half of them would be gay is very small. It is very likely, however, that 7 or 8 ($1/_{40}$ of 300) will be gay males.

Or suppose that roughly 50% of the students at your school are female. Then each time you choose a student at random there's a roughly 50% chance the person will be female. And if you randomly choose a sample of 300 students the chance is very high that about 50% will be female.

The **law of large numbers** says, roughly, that if the probability of something occurring is X percent, then over *the long run* the percentage of times that happens will be about X percent. For example, the probability of a flip of a fair coin landing heads is 50%. So, though you may get a run of 8 tails, then 5 heads, then 4 tails, then 36 heads to start, in the long run, repeating the flipping, if the coin is fair, eventually the number of heads will tend toward 50%.

IT'S COME UP RED 12 TIMES IN A ROW. IT'S BOUND TO COME UP BLACK SEVERAL TIMES IN A ROW NOW.

Don't bet on it. The times it comes up red and the times it comes up black will even out in the *long run*. But if it came up red 100 times in a row, black could even out by coming up just one more time than red every 100 spins for the next 10,000 spins.

The **gambler's fallacy**: A run of events of a certain kind makes a run of contrary events more likely in order to even up the probabilities.

If you choose a large sample randomly, the chance is very high that it will be representative. That's because the chance of any one subgroup being over-represented is small—not nonexistent, but small. It doesn't matter if you know anything about the composition of the population in advance. After all, to know how many homosexuals there are, and how many married women, and how many Muslims, and how many . . . you'd need to know almost everything about the population in advance. But that's what you use surveys to find out.

With a random sample we have good reason to believe the sample is representative. A sample chosen haphazardly may give a representative sample— but you have no good reason to believe it will be representative.

Weak Argument	*Strong Argument*
Sample is chosen *haphazardly*. Therefore, The sample is representative.	Sample is chosen *randomly*. Therefore, The sample is representative.
Lots of ways the sample could be biased.	Very unlikely that the sample is biased.

The classic example that haphazard sampling needn't work, even with an enormous sample, is the poll done in 1936 by *Literary Digest*. The magazine mailed out 10,000,000 ballots asking who the person would vote for in the 1936 presidential election. They received 2,300,000 back. With that huge sample the magazine confidently predicted that Alf Landon would win. Roosevelt received 60% of the vote, one of the biggest wins ever. What went wrong? The magazine selected its sample from lists of it own subscribers and telephone and automobile owners. In 1936 that was the wealthy class. And the wealthy folks preferred Alf Landon. The sample wasn't representative of all voters.

In any case, we can't always get a perfectly representative sample. Of 400 voters in Mississippi that are chosen randomly, 6 are traveling out of the state, 13 have moved with no forwarding address, . . . you can't locate them all. Like being vague, the right question to ask is: Does the sample seem *too* biased to be reliable?

> Beware of *selective attention*:
> It seems that buttered toast always lands the wrong side down because you notice— or remember—when it does.

Exercises for Section B

1. What is a representative sample?

2. Explain why a good generalization is unlikely to be valid.

3. a. What is the law of large numbers?
   b. How does it justify random sampling as giving unbiased samples?

4. Why does the phone ring more often when you're in the shower?

5. Which of the following seem too biased to be reliable, and why?
    a. To determine the average number of people in your city who played tennis last week, interview women only.
    b. To determine what kind of cat food is purchased most often, interview only people who are listed in the telephone directory.
    c. To determine what percentage of women think that more women should be doctors, poll female students as they leave their classes at your school.
    d. To determine whether to buy grapes at the supermarket, pick a grape from the bunch you're interested in and taste it.

6. a. Suppose you want to find out whether people in your city believe that there are enough police officers. Give four characteristics of people that could bias the survey. That is, list four subgroups of the population that you would not want to have represented out of proportion to their actual percentages in the population.
    b. Now list four characteristics that you feel would not matter for giving bias.

7. A professor suggested the best way to get a sample is to make sure that for the relevant characteristics, for example, gender, age, ethnicity, income, . . . , we know that the sample has the same proportion as in the population as a whole. Why won't that work?

8. One of Dr. E's students was a blackjack dealer at a casino and heard a player say, "I ran a computer simulation of this system 1,000 times and made money. So why didn't I win today playing for real?" Can you explain it?

9. Is every randomly chosen sample representative? Explain.

C. When Is a Generalization Good?

1. Sample size

> I've got a couple of Chinese students in my classes. They're both hard-working and get good grades. I suppose that all Chinese are like that.

That's generalizing from *too small a sample*—the way stereotypes begin. It's a **hasty generalization** using **anecdotal evidence**.

But how big does a sample have to be? To estimate what percentage of students at your school approve of sex before marriage, is it enough to ask 5? 25? 150? Why is it that opinion polls regularly extrapolate to the preferences of all voters in the U.S. from sampling 1,500 or less?

Roughly, the idea is to measure how much more likely it is that your generalization is going to be accurate as you increase the number in your sample. If you want to find out how many people in your class of 300 sociology students are spending 15 hours a week on the homework, you might ask 15 or 20. If you interview 30 you might get a better picture, but there's a limit. After you've asked 100, you probably won't get a much different result if you ask 150. And if you've asked 200, do you really think your generalization will be different if you ask 250? It hardly seems worth the effort.

Often you can rely on common sense when small numbers are involved. But when we generalize to a very large population, say 2,000, or 20,000, or 200,000,000, how big the sample should be cannot be explained without at least a mini-course on statistics. In evaluating statistical generalizations, you have to expect that the people doing the sampling have looked at enough examples, which is reasonable if it's a respected organization, a well-known polling company, physicians, or a drug company that has to answer to the Food and Drug Administration. Surprisingly, 1,500 is typically adequate for the sample size when surveying all adults in the U.S.

2. Is the sample studied well?

Choosing a large enough representative sample is important, but it's not enough. The sample has to be investigated well.

The doctor taking your blood to see if you have diabetes won't get a reliable result if her test tube is contaminated or if she forgets to tell you to fast the night before. You won't find out the attitudes of students about sex before marriage if you ask a biased question. Picking a random sample of bolts won't help you determine if the bolts are O.K. if all you do is inspect them visually, not with a microscope or a stress test.

Questionnaires and surveys are particularly problematic. Questions need to be formulated without bias.

> At the bottom of the barrel: Issues entrepreneurs cared about least in the election
>   1. Electric utility deregulation, 2%
>   2. Superfund reform, 3%
>   3. Pension simplification and reform, 9%
>   4. Estate tax reform, 12%   List of the Week from
>   5. Product liability and tort reform, 24%   Arthur Andersen
>
> What questions did they ask? Wouldn't windshield wiper standardization laws have ranked lower?

Even then, we have to rely on respondents answering truthfully. Surveys on sexual habits are notorious for inaccurate self-reporting. Invariably, the number of times that women in the U.S. report they engaged in sexual intercourse with a man in the last week, or month, or year is much lower than the reports that men give of sexual intercourse with a woman during that time. The figures are so different that it would be impossible for both groups to be answering accurately.

3. Three premises needed for a good generalization

A generalization is an argument. You need to examine it as you would any argument: Does the argument rely on slanted or vague language? What unstated premises are missing? Do you have good reason to believe the premises? Does the conclusion follow from the premises? For some generalizations you will have to rely on "the experts" for whether to believe the premises, which include "The sample is representative," "The sample is big enough," "The sample was studied well," whether stated or not. Even if you have a degree in statistics, you will rarely have access to the information necessary to evaluate those premises.

Premises needed for a good generalization
- The sample is representative.
- The sample is big enough.
- The sample is studied well.

But you could choose a big enough representative sample, study it well, get a trustworthy generalization, and still have a lousy argument.

Dick: A study I read said that people with large hands are better at math.

Suzy: I guess that explains why I can't divide!

You don't need a study to know that people with large hands do better at math: Babies have small hands, and they can't even add. The collection of all people is the wrong population to study.

---

4. The margin of error and confidence level

It's never reasonable to believe exact statistical generalizations: 37% of the people in your town who were surveyed wear glasses, so 37% of all people in your town wear glasses. No matter how many people in your town are surveyed, short of virtually all of them, you can't be confident that exactly 37% of all of them wear glasses. Rather, "37%, more or less, wear glasses" would be the right conclusion.

That "more or less" can be made fairly precise according to a theory of statistics. The *margin of error* tells us the range within which the actual number for the population is likely to fall. How likely is it that they're right? The *confidence level* measures that. For example,

The opinion poll says that when voters were asked their preference, the incumbent was favored by 53% and the challenger by 47%, with a margin of error of 2%, and a confidence level of 95%. So the incumbent will win tomorrow.

From this survey they are concluding that the percentage of *all* voters who favor the incumbent is between 51% and 55%, while the challenger is favored by between 45% and 49%. The confidence level is 95%. That means there's a 95% chance it's true that the actual percentage of voters who prefer the incumbent is between 51% and 55%. If the confidence level were 60%, then the survey wouldn't be very reliable: There would be a 4-out-of-10 chance that the conclusion is false, given those premises.

The confidence level, then, *measures the strength of the generalization as an argument*. Typically, if the confidence level is below 95%, the results won't even be announced. To summarize for the example above:

> Margin of error ± 2% gives the range around 53% in which it is likely that the population value lies. It is part of the conclusion: Between 51% and 55% of all voters favor the incumbent.

> Confidence level of 95% says exactly how likely it is that the population value lies in that range. It tells you how strong the generalization is.

The bigger the sample, the higher the confidence level and the lower the margin of error. The problem is to decide how much it's worth in extra time and expense to increase the sample size in order to get a better argument.

So will the incumbent win? The generalization that a majority of voters at the time of polling favor the incumbent is strong. But to conclude the incumbent will win depends on what happens from the time of the polling to the voting. It depends on how fixed people are in their opinions and on a lot of other unstated premises.

5. Variation in the population

> Dick: It takes me forever to download anything on the Internet.
> Tom: But you've got a PowerMac G5 just like mine.
> Dick: Yeah, but I only have a dial-up connection.
> Tom: Get on to that high-speed service that Clurbach Internet is providing. I've got it and it's super fast. I can download a song from the Apple site in less than a minute.

Tom is generalizing. His conclusion is that any other computer like his on the same kind of Internet connection will be as fast. But isn't that a hasty generalization?

No. Tom's generalization is good, because any other computer like his (that's in running order) with the same Internet connection should perform exactly as his. They're all supposed to be the same.

How big the sample has to be depends on how much **variation** there is in the population. If there is very little variation, then a small sample chosen haphazardly will do. Lots of variation demands a very large sample, and random sampling is the best way to get a representative sample.

6. Risk

With a shipment of 30 bolts, inspecting 15 of them and finding all of them O.K. would allow you to conclude that all the bolts are O.K. But if they're for the space shuttle, where a bad bolt could doom the spacecraft, you'd want to inspect each and every one of them.

On the other hand, suppose that for the first time you try eating a kumquat.

Two hours later you get a stomachache, and that night and the next morning you have diarrhea. I'll bet you wouldn't eat a kumquat again. But the argument from this one experience that kumquats will always do this to you is pretty weak— it could have been something else you ate, or a twenty-four-hour flu, or . . . .

> Risk doesn't change how strong an argument you have, only how strong an argument you want before you'll accept the conclusion.

7. Analogies and generalizations

Analogies are not generalizations, but they often require a generalization as premise.

The analysis of analogies usually ends in our trying to come up with a general claim that will make a valid or strong argument. Analogies lead to generalizations. This car is like that one. They both had bad suspension. And here's another from the same manufacturer, which the owner says has bad suspension, too. So if you buy one of these cars, it will have bad suspension, too. From two or three or seventeen examples, you figure that the next one will be the same. That's an analogy, all right, but the process is more one of generalization, for it's the unspoken general claim that needs to be proved: (Almost) all cars from this manufacturer have bad suspension.

Summary We generalize all the time: From a few instances (the sample) we conclude something about a bigger group (the population). Generalizations are arguments. They need three premises to be good: the sample is representative; the sample is big enough; the sample is studied well.

Often we can figure out whether these premises are true. But it's harder for large populations with a lot of variation. The best way to ensure that a sample is representative is to choose it randomly. Haphazardly chosen samples are often used, but we have no reason to believe a sample chosen haphazardly is representative.

With polls and scientific surveys we usually have to decide whether to believe the experts. They should tell us the margin of error and confidence level. We can develop some sense of when a generalization is good or bad. Our best guide is to remember that a generalization is an argument, and all we've learned about analyzing arguments applies.

Key Words

generalization	random sampling
population	law of large numbers
sample	gambler's fallacy
inductive evidence	hasty generalization
statistical generalization	anecdotal evidence
representative sample	margin of error
biased sample	confidence level
haphazard sampling	variation in a population

> The popularity of American therapy movements might also explain why all the books mentioned in this review base much of their thinking on interviews and personal stories, or "narratives," as though American readers can no longer follow abstract arguments from ethical or economic or statistical premises. As a result, instead of constructive social policy based on statistical data, we have endless testimonials, diatribes, and spurious science from people who imagine that their personal experience, the dynamics of their particular family, sexual taste, childhood trauma, and personal inclination constitute universals.
>
> Diane Johnson, "What Do Women Want?"
> *The New York Review of Books,* vol. 43, no. 19.

Exercises for Chapter 14

1. Your candidate is favored by 56% to 44%, with a margin of error of 5% and a confidence level of 94%. What does that mean?

2. You read a poll that says the confidence level is 71%. Is the generalization reliable?

3. a. What do we call a weak generalization from a sample that is obviously too small?
    b. Can a sample of one ever be enough for a strong generalization?

4. The larger the _____ in the population, the larger the sample size must be.

5. What premises do we need for a good generalization?

6. a. You're at the supermarket trying to decide which package of strawberries to buy. Describe and evaluate your procedure as a sampling and generalizing process (of course you can't actually taste one).
    b. Now do the same supposing the package is covered everywhere but on top.

7. Suppose you're on the city council and have to decide whether to put a bond issue for a new school on the next ballot. You don't want to do it if there's a good chance it will fail. You decide to do a survey, but haven't time to get a polling agency to do it. There are 7,200 people in your town. How would you go about picking a sample?

8. The president of your college would like to know how many students approve of the way she is handling her job. Explain why no survey is going to give her any useful ideas about how to improve her work.

9. The mayor of a town of 8,000 has to decide whether to spend town funds on renovating the park or hiring a part-time animal control officer. She gets a reputable polling organization to do a survey.
    a. The results of the survey are 52% in favor of hiring an animal control officer and 47% in favor of renovating the park, with 1% undecided, and a margin of error of 3%. The confidence level is 98%. Which choice will make the most people happy? Should she bet on that?
    b. The results are 61% in favor of hiring an animal control officer and 31% in favor of renovating the park, with 8% undecided, and a margin of error of 9%. The confidence level is 94%. Which choice will make the most people happy? Should she bet on that?

10. A "Quality of Education Survey" was sent out to all parents of students at Socorro High School (Socorro, NM) for the school year 2000–2001. Of 598 forms sent out, 166 were returned. For one of the issues the results were:

    My child is safe at school   6% (10 forms) strongly agreed, 42.8% (71) agreed, 28.9% (48) disagreed, 13.9% (23) strongly disagreed, 7.8% (13) did not know, and 0.6% (1) left the question blank.

    What can you conclude?

11. Flo to Dick: I talked to all the people who live on this street, and everyone who has a dog is really happy. So if I get my mom a dog, she'll be happy, too.

    How should Dick explain to Flo that she's not reasoning well?

    Here are some of Tom's attempts to use the ideas from this chapter.

Maria: Every time I've seen a stranger come to Dick's gate, Spot has barked. So Spot will always bark at strangers at Dick's gate.

Generalization (state it; if none, say so): Spot will bark at every stranger who comes to the gate.

Sample: All the times Maria has seen a stranger come to the gate.

Sample is representative? (yes or no) Who knows?

Sample is big enough? (yes or no) No.

Sample is studied well? (yes or no) Yes—Maria knows if Spot barked when she was there.

Additional premises needed:

Good generalization? No. The sample isn't good.

You almost got it. The generalization shouldn't convince you—that's right. But the problem isn't that the sample isn't "good," but that Maria hasn't given any reason to believe that it's big enough and representative. Is "every time" once? Twice? 150 times? And are those times representative? It's enough that you have no reason to believe that the sample is representative to make this a bad generalization, that is, a bad argument.

In a study of 5,000 people who owned pets in Anchorage, Alaska, dog owners expressed higher satisfaction with their pets and their lives. So dog owners are more satisfied with their pets and their own lives.

Generalization (state it; if none, say so): Dog owners are more satisfied with their pets and their own lives.

Sample: The people surveyed.

Sample is representative? No.

Sample is big enough? Don't know.

Sample is studied well? Not sure—I don't know what questions were asked.

Additional premises needed:

Good generalization? No. The sample isn't good.

Right. Once you note that the sample isn't representative, you know immediately that the argument isn't good.

> **Every time the minimum wage is raised, there's squawking that it will cause inflation and decrease employment. And every time it doesn't. So watch for the same worthless arguments again this time.**
>
> *Generalization* (state it; if none, say so): Raising the minimum wage won't
>   cause inflation and decrease employment.
>
> *Sample:* Every time in the past that the minimum wage was raised.
>
> *Sample is representative?* Yes.
>
> *Sample is big enough?* Yes—it was all the times before.
>
> *Sample is studied well?* Yes—assuming the speaker knows what she's
>   talking about.
>
> *Additional premises needed:* None.
>
> *Good generalization?* Yes.
>
> *The sample is big enough, since it can't get any bigger. But is it representative? Is there any reason to think that the situation now is like the situations in the past when the minimum wage was raised? It's like an analogy: This time is like the past times. Until the speaker fills that in, we shouldn't accept the conclusion.*
>
> **Maria has asked all but three of the thirty-six people in her class whether they've ever used heroin. Only two said "yes." So she concluded that almost no one in the class has used heroin.**
>
> *Generalization* (state it; if none, say so): Almost no one in Maria's class has
>   used heroin.
>
> *Sample:* The thirty-three people Maria asked.
>
> *Sample is representative?* Yes.
>
> *Sample is big enough?* Yes.
>
> *Sample is studied well?* Yes.
>
> *Additional premises needed:*
>
> *Good generalization?* Yes.
>
> *Do you really think everyone who's used heroin is going to admit it to a stranger? The sample isn't studied well—you'd need anonymous responses at least. So the generalization isn't good.*

Evaluate Exercises 12–30 by answering the following.

Generalization (state it; if none, say so):

Sample:

Sample is representative? (yes or no)

Sample is big enough? (yes or no)

Sample is studied well? (yes or no)

Additional premises needed:

Good generalization?

12. It's incredible how much information they can put on a CD. I just bought one that contains a whole encyclopedia.

13. Socialized medicine in Canada isn't working. I heard of a man who had colon cancer and needed surgery. By the time doctors operated six months later, the man was nearly dead and died two days later.

14. Lee: Every rich person I've met invested heavily in the stock market. So I'll invest in the stockmarket, too.

15. Don't take a course from Dr. E. I know three people who failed his course last term.

16. Everyone I've met at this school is either on one of the athletic teams or has a boyfriend or girlfriend on one of the athletic teams. Gosh, I guess just about everyone at this school is involved in sports.

17. Dick: Hold the steering wheel.
    Zoe: What are you doing? Stop! Are you crazy?
    Dick: I'm just taking my sweater off.
    Zoe: I can't believe you did that. It's *so* dangerous.
    Dick: Don't be silly. I've done it a thousand times before.

18. Manuel to Maria: Lanolin is great for your hands—you ought to try it. It's what's on sheep wool naturally. How many shepherds have you seen with dry, chapped hands?

19. Lee: When I went in to the health service, I read some women's magazine that had the results of a survey they'd done on women's attitudes towards men with beards. They said that they received over 10,000 responses from their readers to the question in their last issue, and 78% say they think that men with beards are really sexy! I'm definitely going to grow a beard now.

20. My grandmother was diagnosed with cancer seven years ago. She refused any treatment that was offered to her over the years. She's perfectly healthy and doing great. The treatments for cancer are just a scam to get people's money.

21. Tom: Can you pick up that pro basketball player who's coming to the rally today?
    Dick: I can't. Zoe's got the car. Why not ask Suzy?
    Tom: She's got a Yoda hatchback. They're too small for someone over six foot tall.

22. (Overheard at a doctor's office) I won't have high blood pressure today because I got enough sleep last night. The last two times you've taken my blood pressure I've rested well the night before and both times it was normal.

23. Suzy: I've been studying this astrology book seriously. I think you should definitely go into science.
    Lee: I've been thinking of that, but what's astrology got to do with it?
    Suzy: I remember your birthday is in late January, so you're an Aquarius?
    Lee: Yeah, January 28.
    Suzy: Well, Aquarians are generally scientific but eccentric.
    Lee: C'mon. That can't be right.
    Suzy: Sure it is. Copernicus, Galileo, and Thomas Edison were all Aquarians.

24. Give the baby his pacifier so he'll stop crying. Every time I give him the pacifier he stops crying.

25. We will be late for church because we have to wait for Gina. She's always late. She's been late seven Sundays in a row.

26. Every time I or anyone else has looked into my refrigerator, the light is on. Therefore, the light is always on in my refrigerator.

27. Every time I or anyone I know has seen a tree fall in the forest, it makes a sound. Therefore, anytime a tree falls in the forest it makes a sound.

28. *Biology breeds grumpy old men*
Men lose brain tissue at almost three times the rate of women, curbing their memory, concentration and reasoning power—and perhaps turning them into "grumpy old men" —a researcher said Wednesday.

"Even in the age range of 18 to 45, you can see a steady decline in the ability to perform such (attention-oriented) tasks in men," said Ruben C. Gur, a professor of psychology at the University of Pennsylvania.

Gur said shrinking brains may make men grumpier because some of the tissue loss is in the left frontal region of the brain, which seems to be connected to depression.

"Grumpy old men may be biological," said Gur, who is continuing to study whether there is a connection.

However, one researcher not affiliated with the study said Wednesday that other recent studies contradict Gur's findings on shrinkage.

The findings, which augment earlier research published by Gur and colleagues, are the result of his studies of the brain functions of 24 women and 37 men over the past decade. He measured the brain volume with an MRI machine and studied metabolism rates. From young adulthood to middle age, men lose 15% of their frontal lobe volume, 8.5% of temporal lobe, he said. Women, while they have "very mild" shrinkage, lose tissue in neither lobe. For the brain overall, men lose tissue three times faster.

Gur found that the most dramatic loss was in men's frontal lobes, which control attention, abstract reasoning, mental flexibility and inhibition of impulses, and the temporal lobe [which] governs memory.

Associated Press, April, 1996

29. *Sex, lies, and HIV*
Reducing the risk of human immunodeficiency virus (HIV) transmission among sexually active teenagers and young adults is a major public health concern [reference supplied]. Young people are advised to select potential sexual partners from groups at lower risk for HIV [reference supplied], in part by asking about partners' risk histories [reference supplied]. Unfortunately, this advice overlooks the possibility that people may lie about their risk history [reference supplied].

In a sample of 18-to-25-year-old students attending colleges in southern California (n = 665), we found strong evidence that undermines faith in questioning partners as an effective primary strategy of risk reduction. The young adults, of whom 442 were sexually active, completed anonymous 18-page questionnaires assessing sexual behavior, HIV-related risk reduction, and their experiences with deception when dating.

Variable	Men (N = 196)	Women (N = 226)
History of disclosure	*percent*	
Has told a lie in order to have sex	34	10*
Lied about ejaculatory control or likelihood of pregnancy	38	14
Sexually active with more than one person	32	23‡
Partner did not know	68	59
Experience of being lied to		
Has been lied to for purposes of sex	47	60**
Partner lied about ejaculatory control or likelihood of pregnancy	34	46
Willingness to deceive***		
Would lie about having negative HIV-antibody test	20	4*
Would lie about ejaculatory control or likelihood of pregnancy	29	2*
Would understate number of previous partners	47	42
Would disclose existence of other partner to new partner		
Never	22	10*
After a while, when safe to do so	34	28*
Only if asked	31	33*
Yes	13	29*
Would disclose a single episode of sexual infidelity		
Never	43	34‡
After a while, when safe to do so	21	20‡
Only if asked	14	11‡
Yes	22	35‡

* $P < .001$ by chi-square test   ‡ $P < .05$ by chi-square test   ** $P < .01$ by chi-square test
*** Hypothetical scenarios were described in which honesty would threaten either the opportunity to have sex or the maintenance of a sexually active relationship.

We found that sizable percentages of the 196 men and 226 women who were sexually experienced reported having told a lie in order to have sex. Men reported telling lies significantly more frequently than women (Table). Women more often reported that they had been lied to by a dating partner. When asked what they would do in hypothetical situations, both men and women frequently reported that they would actively or passively deceive a dating partner, although again, men were significantly more likely than women to indicate a willingness to do so.

Although we cannot be certain that our subjects were fully forthcoming in their responses (e.g., they reported more frequent dishonesty from others than they admitted to themselves), one can probably assume that their reports of their own dishonesty underestimate rather than overestimate the problem. The implications of our findings are clear. In counseling patients, particularly young adults, physicians need to consider realistically the patients' capacity for assessing the risk of HIV in sexual partners through questioning them [reference]. Patients should be cautioned that safe-sex strategies are always advisable [references], despite arguments to the contrary from partners. This is particularly important for heterosexuals in urban centers where distinctions between people at low risk and those at high risk may be less obvious because of higher rates of experimentation with sex and the use of intravenous drugs and undisclosed histories of high-risk behavior.

Susan D. Cochran and Vickie M. Mays,
Letter to the Editor,
New England Journal of Medicine, vol. 322, pp. 774–775, © 1990,

30. *Sex unlikely to cause heart attacks*

Sexual intercourse is unlikely to trigger a heart attack, even among people who have already survived one, according to a study that is the first to examine this widespread fear.

Only 1 percent of heart attacks were triggered by sexual activity in a nationwide sample of nearly 900 heart attack survivors who said they were sexually active.

The odds of suffering a heart attack after engaging in sex are only about 2 in a million, the study found—about twice as high as the average hourly risk of heart attack among 50-year-old Americans with no overt sign of coronary artery disease.

"It's easy to get the message from movies, and even from Shakespeare, that sexual activity can trigger heart attacks," said Dr. James Muller of New England Deaconess Hospital in Boston, who led the study. "It's part of the mythology, and it's certainly in the minds of many cardiac patients and their spouses."

"What has been lacking in the past are actual numbers. Now the numbers are available, and the risk is quite, quite low."

Furthermore, regular exercise can substantially reduce the risk of a sex-triggered heart attack.

Patients who never engaged in heavy physical exertion, or got vigorous exercise only once a week, had a threefold risk of heart attack in the two hours after sexual activity. But the relative risk dropped to twofold among patients who exercise twice a week, and only 1.2 fold among those who exercised three or more times weekly.

The new figures, which appear in this week's Journal of the American Medical Association, suggest that sexual activity triggers 15,000 of the 1.5 million heart attacks that occur in this nation annually.

"Although sexual activity doubles the risk" of heart attack, the researchers noted, the effect on annual risk "is negligible because the absolute risk difference is small, the risk is transient and the activity is relatively infrequent."

For instance, for an individual without cardiac disease, weekly sexual activity would increase the annual risk of a heart attack from 1 percent to 1.01 percent.

Richard Knox, *Boston Globe,* May, 1996

31. Would you try this new procedure? Explain.

Chili peppers a red hot cure for surgical pain

When burning pain lingers months after surgery, doctors say there is a red-hot cure: chili peppers. In a study, an ointment made with capsaicin, the stuff that makes chili peppers hot, brought relief to patients with tender surgical scars, apparently by short-circuiting the pain.

Patients undergoing major cancer surgery, such as mastectomies or lung operations, are sometimes beset by sharp, burning pain in their surgical scars that lasts for months, even years. Sometimes the misery is so bad that sufferers cannot even stand the weight of clothing on their scar, even though it is fully healed.

The condition, seen in about 5 percent or fewer of all cases, results from damage to the nerves during surgery. Ordinary pain killers don't work, and the standard treatment is antidepressant drugs.

However, these powerful drugs have side effects. So in search of a better alternative, doctors tested a cream made with capsaicin on 99 patients who typically had suffered painful surgical scars at least six months.

Patients preferred capsaicin over a dummy cream by 3-to-1.

"The therapy clearly worked," said Dr. Charles L. Loprinzi, head of medical oncology at the Mayo Clinic. He released his data Monday at the annual meeting of the American Society for Clinical Oncology.

Capsaicin is believed to work by blocking substance P, a natural chemical that carries pain impulses between nerve cells. That same blocking effect may explain why people who eat hot peppers all the time develop a tolerance to the burn.

Dr. Alan Lyss of Missouri Baptist Medical Center in St. Louis called it "a creative, new and very inexpensive way to take care of some kinds of cancer pain."

Capsaicin is sold in drug stores without a prescription, and a tube that lasts a month costs about $16. . . .

In the study, the patients were randomly assigned to capsaicin cream or the look-alike placebo four times a day for eight-week intervals. Until the study was over, no one knew which was which.

Patients kept score of their pain. It went down 53 percent while using capsaicin but only 17 percent while on the placebo. About 10 percent said their pain disappeared completely.

The doctors followed the patients for two months after they stopped using capsaicin and found that pain did not come back. Longer follow-up will be necessary to see if the treatment relieves the pain permanently.　　　　Associated Press, May 21, 1996

For Exercises 32–34 identify the analogy and explain how a generalization is required.

32. Dick: What do you think about getting one of those Blauspot rice cookers?
    Zoe:　It's not a good idea. Remember, Maria got one and she had to return it twice to get it fixed.

33. Of chimpanzees fed one pound of chocolate per day in addition to their usual diet, 72% became obese within two months. Therefore, it is likely that most humans who eat 2% of their body weight in chocolate daily will become obese within two months.

34. Zoe:　Suzy invited us over to dinner tonight. We've got to be there at 6 p.m.
    Dick: I'm not going over there. The last time we went she served some concoction she'd read about in a cookbook, and I had the runs for two days.

Further Study　Courses on statistics explain the nature of sampling and generalizing. A course on inductive logic in a philosophy department will study more fully the topics of this chapter and the next. A course on philosophy of science will study the role of generalizations in science, which you can also read about in my *Five Ways of Saying "Therefore."* Many disciplines, such as sociology, marketing, or the health sciences give courses on the use of sampling and generalizing that are specific to their subject.

Two books about statistics in reasoning with lots of examples are *Flaws and Fallacies in Statistical Thinking*, by Stephen K. Campbell and *How to Lie with Statistics*, by Darrell Huff.

15 Cause and Effect

PAY UP.

CRACK!

6 6

Maria caused the accident. Smoking causes cancer. Gravity causes the moon to stay in orbit. These are *causal claims*. We make lots of them, though they may not always contain the word "causes" or "caused." For example, "Jogging keeps you healthy" or "Taking an aspirin every other day cuts the risk of having a heart attack." And every time someone blames you, you're encountering a claim that you caused something that was bad and, apparently, avoidable.

What does a claim about causes look like? How do we judge whether it's true?

A. What is the Cause?

1. Causes and effects

What exactly is a *cause*? Consider what Dick said last night:

> Spot caused me to wake up.

Spot is the thing that somehow caused Dick to wake up. But it's not just that Spot existed. It's what he was doing that caused Dick to wake up:

Spot's barking caused
Dick to wake up.

So barking is a cause and waking is an effect? What exactly is barking? What is waking? The easiest way to describe the cause is to say:

> Spot barked.

The easiest way to describe the effect is to say:

> Dick woke up.

Whatever causes and effects are, we can describe them with claims. And we know a lot about claims: whether they're objective or subjective, whether a sentence is too vague to be a claim, how to judge whether an unsupported claim is true.

So now we have:

$$\text{Spot barked} \xrightarrow[\text{caused}]{} \text{Dick woke up}$$

What is this relationship of being caused?

It has to be a very strong relationship. Once Spot barked, it had to be true that Dick woke up. There's no way (or almost no way) for "Spot barked" to have been true and "Dick woke up" to be false.

We know about that relationship—it's the relationship between the premises and conclusion of a valid or strong argument. But here we're not trying to convince anyone that the conclusion is true: We know that Dick woke up. What we can carry over from our study of arguments is how to look for all the possibilities—all the ways the premises could be true and the conclusion false—to determine if there is cause and effect. But there has to be more in order to say there's cause and effect.

2. The normal conditions

A lot has to be true for it to be (nearly) impossible for "Spot barked" to be true and "Dick woke up" to be false:

> Dick was sleeping soundly up to the time that Spot barked.
> Spot barked at 3 a.m.
> Dick doesn't normally wake up at 3 a.m.
> Spot was close to where Dick was sleeping.
> There was no other loud noise at the time. . . .

We could go on forever. But as with arguments, we state what we think is important and leave out the obvious. If someone challenged us, we could add "There was no earthquake at the time"—but we just assume things are the way they "normally" are.

> ***Normal conditions***   For a causal claim, the normal conditions are the obvious and plausible unstated claims that are needed to establish that the relationship between purported cause and purported effect is valid or strong.

3. Particular causes, generalizations, and general causes

Spot waking Dick is a ***particular cause and effect***. This happened once, then that happened once.

  To establish the causal claim, we have to consider all the possible ways Spot could have barked, under the normal conditions, and ask whether Dick would have woken up. With a physical situation like this we could even do experiments to look at some of the possible ways the cause could be true, say, getting Spot to bark at 3:23 a.m. on a cloudless night, or getting Spot to bark at 4:18 a.m. on an overcast night. We need that every time Spot barked, Dick woke up. There has to be a ***correlation***: Every time this happens, that happens. So to establish a particular cause and effect, we might try to establish a *generalization*.

  Alternatively, we could generalize from this particular cause and effect to any situation like it:

> Very loud barking by someone's dog near him when he is sleeping *causes* him to wake, if he's not deaf.

This is a ***general cause and effect*** claim: For it to be true, lots of particular cause and effect claims must be true. The normal conditions for this general claim won't be specific just to the one time Spot woke Dick, but will be general. Here, too, in trying to survey the possible ways that the cause could be true, we might want to establish a generalization: "Anytime anyone's encountered these conditions—the barking, the sleeper, etc.—the sleeper woke up."

Exercises for Sections A.1–A.3

For each exercise here, if appropriate rewrite the sentence as a *causal claim*, that is, one that uses the word "causes" or "caused." If it's a particular causal claim, describe the purported cause and the purported effect with claims. Here are two of Tom's exercises.

Your teaching made me fail this class.

Causal claim: Your teaching caused me to fail this class.
Particular or *general*? Particular.
Cause (stated as a claim): You taught badly.
Effect (stated as a claim): I failed.

You've got the idea. But why did you say the cause was "You taught badly"? Maybe it should be "You taught well, but didn't slow down for unprepared students." The problem is that the original sentence is <u>too vague</u>.

Drinking coffee keeps people awake.

Causal claim: Drinking coffee causes people to stay awake.
Particular or *general*? General.
Cause (stated as a claim): People drink coffee. *No.*
Effect (stated as a claim): People stay awake. *No.*

Remember that with a general causal claim there isn't <u>a</u> cause and effect, but lots of them. So there's no point in filling in after "cause" and "effect." When we try to figure out a particular causal claim that this general one covers, we see the real problem: Maria drank coffee yesterday, Maria stayed awake. How long did she stay awake? What would count for making this true? It's still too vague.

---

1. The police car's siren got me to pull over.

2. The speeding ticket Dick got made his auto insurance rate go up.

3. Speeding tickets make people's auto insurance rates go up.

4. Because you were late, we missed the beginning of the movie.

5. The onion's smell made my eyes tear.

6. Dogs make great pets.

7. I better not get the pizza with anchovies, because every time I do, I get heartburn.

8. Someone ringing the doorbell made Spot bark.

9. Your allowing me to take the final exam a day late made it possible for me to pass.

10. Coffee keeps me from getting a headache in the afternoon.

11. Penicillin prevents serious infection.

12. If it weren't for my boyfriend, I'd have no problems.

13. My hair looked nice today until I walked outside and the wind messed it up.

14. Our airplane took off from gate number thirteen. No wonder we're experiencing so much turbulence.

15. Tom: Hey, you want to be a ball player, you have to do better than that.
    Lee: It was the sun that made me drop the ball.

16. The cold makes people shiver.

4. The cause precedes the effect

We wouldn't accept that Spot's barking caused Dick to wake up if Spot began barking only after Dick woke up. The cause has to precede the effect. That is, "Spot barked" became true before "Dick woke up" became true.

For there to be cause and effect, the claim describing the cause has to become true before the claim describing the effect becomes true.

5. The cause makes a difference

We often need a correlation to establish cause and effect. But a correlation alone is not enough.

Dr. E has a desperate fear of elephants. So he buys a special wind chime and puts it outside his door to keep the elephants away. He lives in Cedar City, Utah, at 6,000 feet above sea level in a desert, and he confidently claims that the wind chime causes the elephants to stay away. After all, ever since he put up the wind chime he hasn't seen any elephants. There's a perfect correlation here: "Wind chime up on Tuesday, no elephants," Dr. E notes in his diary.

Why are we sure the wind chime being up did not cause elephants to stay away? Because even if there had been no wind chime, the elephants would have stayed away. Which elephants? All elephants. The wind chime works, but so would anything else. The wind chime doesn't *make a difference.*

For there to be cause and effect, it must be that *if the cause hadn't occurred, there wouldn't be the effect.* If Spot had not barked, Dick would not have woken. Checking that the cause makes a difference is how we make sure we haven't overlooked another possible cause.

6. Overlooking a common cause

Night causes day.

This is just wrong. There is a common cause of both "It was night" and "It's now day," namely, "The earth is rotating relative to the sun."

> Dick: Zoe is irritable because she can't sleep properly.
> Tom: Maybe it's because she's been drinking so much espresso that she's irritable and can't sleep properly.

Tom hasn't shown that Dick's causal claim is false by raising the possibility of a common cause. But he does put Dick's claim in doubt. We have to check the other conditions for cause and effect to see which causal claim seems most likely.

7. Tracing the cause backwards

So Spot caused Dick to wake up. But Dick and Zoe's neighbor tells them that's not right. It was because of a raccoon in her yard that shares the same fence that Spot started barking. So really, a raccoon entering her yard caused Dick to wake up.

But it was no accident that the raccoon came into their neighbor's yard. She'd left her trash can uncovered. So *really* the neighbor's not covering her trash caused Dick to wake up.

But really, it was because Spot had knocked over her trash can and the top wouldn't fit; so their neighbor didn't bother to cover her trash. So it was Spot's knocking over the trash can that caused Dick to wake up.

But really, ... This is silly. We could go backwards forever. We stop at the first step: Spot's barking caused Dick to wake up. We stop because *as we trace the cause back further it becomes too hard to fill in the normal conditions.*

Compare what happened to Dick yesterday:

Dick is just wrong. The purported cause—Spot lying next to where Dick walked—was too far away from the effect. But what does "too far away" mean? The astronomer is right when she says that a star shining caused the image on the photograph, even though that star is billions of miles away and the light took billions of years to arrive.

"Too far away in space and time" is just a sloppy way to say that we can't see how to fill in the normal conditions, the other claims that would make it obvious that it's (nearly) impossible for the claim describing the cause to be true and effect false.

8. Criteria for cause and effect

We can collect everything we've learned about cause and effect so far. These are necessary conditions for there to be cause and effect, once we *describe the cause and effect with claims.*

Necessary criteria for cause and effect

- The cause happened (the claim describing it is true).
- The effect happened (the claim describing it is true).
- The cause precedes the effect.
- It is (nearly) impossible for the cause to happen (be true) and the effect not to happen (be false), given the normal conditions.
- The cause makes a difference—if the cause had not happened (been true), the effect would not have happened (been true).
- There is no common cause.

---

9. Two mistakes in evaluating cause and effect

a. Reversing cause and effect

Consider what Tom said after the demonstration in front of the post office:

Tom: That ecology group is twisting their members' minds around.
Dick: Huh?
Tom: They're all spouting off about the project to log the forest on
     Cedar Mountain. All in lockstep. What do they do to those guys?

Tom's got it backwards. Joining the group doesn't cause the members to become concerned about the logging on Cedar Mountain. People who are already concerned about ecological issues join the group. He's *reversing cause and effect*.

Suzy: Sitting too close to the TV ruins your eyesight.
Zoe: How do you know?
Suzy: Well, two of my grade school friends used to sit really close,
      and both of them wear really thick glasses now.
Zoe: Maybe they sat so close because they had bad eyesight.

Even if Suzy had a huge sample instead of just anecdotal evidence, it would be just as plausible to reverse the cause and effect. That doesn't mean Suzy's claim is false. It just shows we have no good reason to believe that sitting too close to the TV ruins your eyesight.

b. Looking too hard for a cause

Every Tuesday and Thursday at 1:55 p.m. a tall red-headed lady walks by the door of Professor Zzzyzzx's classroom. Then he arrives right at 2 p.m. When Suzy says the lady walking by the door causes Professor Zzzyzzx to arrive on time at his class, she's jumping to a conclusion: It happened after, so that's the cause. We call that kind of reasoning *post hoc ergo propter hoc* (after this, therefore because of this).

Zoe belched loudly in the shower with the bathroom window open, and she and Dick haven't seen Spot since. He must have run away because she belched.

That's just *post hoc ergo propter hoc*. A possible cause is being overlooked:

Perhaps someone left the gate open, or someone let Spot out, or . . . . *Post hoc* reasoning is just not being careful to check that it's (nearly) impossible for the cause to be true and effect false. Jumping to conclusions about causes isn't a sign of a rich imagination. ("Gee, I'd never have thought the red-haired lady caused Professor Zzzyzzx to arrive on time.") It's a sign of an impoverished imagination.

We look for causes because we want to understand, to explain, so we can control our future. But sometimes the best we can say is that it's **coincidence**.

Before your jaw drops open in amazement when a friend tells you that a piano fell on her teacher the day after she dreamt that she saw him in a recital, remember the law of large numbers: If it's possible, given long enough, it'll happen. After all, most of us dream—say one dream a night for fifty million adults in the U.S. That's three hundred and fifty million dreams per week. With the elasticity in interpreting dreams and what constitutes a "dream coming true," it would be amazing if a lot of dreams didn't "accurately predict the future."

But doesn't everything have a cause? Shouldn't we look for it? For much that happens in our lives we won't be able to figure out the cause—we just don't know enough. We must, normally, ascribe lots of happenings to chance, to coincidence, or else we have paranoia and end up paying a lot of money to psychics.

> Suppose two million Parisians were paired off and set to tossing coins in a game of matching. Each pair plays until the winner on the first toss is again brought to equality with the other player. Assuming one toss per second for each eight-hour day, at the end of ten years there would still be, on the average, about a hundred-odd pairs; and if the players assign the game to their heirs, a dozen or so will still be playing at the end of a thousand years! The implications are obvious. Suppose that some business had been operating for one hundred years. Should one rule out luck and chance as the essence of the factors producing the long-term survival of the enterprise? No inference whatever can be drawn until the number of original participants is known; and even then one must know the size, risk, and frequency of each commitment.
>
> A. Alchian, "Uncertainty, Evolution, and Economic Theory,"
> *Journal of Economic Theory*, 1950

> *Sometimes our best response to a causal claim is*
> - Did you ever think that might just be coincidence?
> - Just because it followed doesn't mean it was caused by . . . .
> - Have you thought about another possible cause, namely . . . .
> - Maybe you've got the cause and the effect reversed.
> - Not always, but maybe under some conditions . . . .

Exercises for Section A

1. What criteria are necessary for there to be cause and effect?

2. Why isn't a perfect correlation enough to justify cause and effect? Give an example.

3. Comparable to the unstated premises of an argument, what do we call the claims that must be true for a causal claim to be true?

4. What real problem in establishing cause and effect is usually mis-stated as: "That's not close enough in space and time to be the cause"?

5. Dick makes a causal claim. Zoe says it's just *post hoc ergo propter hoc* reasoning. How can he show her that he's right?

6. Explain why it's not amazing that every day a few dream predictions come true.

7. When should we trust authorities rather than figure out a cause for ourselves?

B. Examples

We have necessary conditions for there to be cause and effect. What about sufficient conditions? In practice, all we can do is check that the necessary conditions hold, being careful not to make one of the obvious mistakes, even if we're not satisfied that we can exactly state sufficient conditions for there to be cause and effect.

Are the following examples of cause and effect?

Example 1

The cat made Spot run away.

Cause: What is the cause? It's not just "the cat." How can we describe it with a claim? Perhaps "A cat meowed close to Spot."

Effect: Spot ran away.

Cause and effect each happened: The effect is clearly true. The cause is highly plausible: Almost all things that meow are cats.

Cause precedes effect: Yes.

It is (nearly) impossible for the cause to be true and effect false: What needs to be assumed as "normal" here? Spot is on a walk with Dick. Dick is holding the leash loosely enough for Spot to get away. Spot chases cats. Spot heard the cat meow. We could go on, but this seems enough to guarantee that it's unlikely that the cat could meow near Spot and Spot not chase it.

The cause makes a difference: Would Spot have run away even if the cat had not meowed near him? Apparently not, given those normal conditions, since Dick seems surprised that he ran off. But perhaps he would have even if he hadn't heard the cat, if he'd seen it. But that apparently wasn't the case. So let's revise the cause to be "Spot wasn't aware a cat was near him, and the cat meowed close to Spot, and Spot heard it." Now we can reasonably believe that the cause made a difference.

Is there a common cause? Perhaps the cat was hit by a meat truck and lots of meat fell out, and Spot ran away for that? No, Spot wouldn't have barked. Nor would he have growled.

Perhaps the cat is a hapless bystander in a fight between dogs, one of whom is Spot's friend. We do not know if this is the case. So it is possible that there is a common cause, but it seems unlikely.

Evaluation: We have good reason to believe the original claim on the revised interpretation that the cause is "Spot wasn't aware a cat was near him, and the cat meowed close to Spot, and Spot heard it."

> *These are the steps we should go through in establishing a causal claim.*
If we can show that one of them fails, though, there's no need to check all the others.

Example 2 Maria caused the traffic accident.

Analysis We're interested in who or what was involved in the cause when we go about assigning blame or fault. But it's not just that Maria exists. Rather:

> *Cause*: Maria didn't pay attention.
> *Effect*: The cars collided.

Is this really cause and effect? Let's assume that these claims are true. It seems the cause preceded the effect. But did the cause make a difference? If Maria had been paying attention, would the cars still have collided? Since she was broadsided by a car running through a red light where a line of cars blocked her vision, we would say that it didn't matter that she was changing a CD at the time: The cars would have collided even if she had been paying attention, or so we all imagine. The purported cause didn't make a difference. It's not cause and effect.

Example 3 Lack of rain caused the crops to fail in the Midwest in 2000.

Analysis We've talked about causes as if something active has to happen. But almost any claim that describes the world could qualify as a cause.

Cause: There was no rain in the first part of the year 2000.

Effect: The crops failed.

Is this cause and effect? We better check the meteorological records and ask some farmers if there wasn't some other cause, perhaps locusts.

Example 4   Oxygen in the laboratory caused an explosion.

Analysis   This seems right, but what are the normal conditions? Harry works in a laboratory where there's not supposed to be any oxygen. The materials are highly flammable. He has to wear breathing gear. Harry knows that matches won't light in the laboratory.

But it certainly isn't "normal" that Harry carried matches with him into the laboratory for a joke with a friend and struck a match. Nor is it normal that there was a leak in his face mask.

When several claims together are taken *jointly* as the cause, we say that each is (describes) ***a cause*** or that each is a ***causal factor***.

Example 5   Running over nails causes your tires to go flat.

Analysis   This is a general causal claim. But it's false. Lots of times we run over nails and our tires don't go flat.

But sometimes they do. What's correct is:

Running over nails *can cause* your tires to go flat.

That is, if the conditions are right, running over a nail will cause your tire to go flat.

The difference between *causes* and *can cause* is the difference between the normal conditions. We'll look at how to evaluate claims like this in Section D.

Example 6   When more and more people are thrown out of work, unemployment results.

Calvin Coolidge

Analysis   You don't have to be smart to be President. This isn't cause and effect; it's a definition.

Example 7   Birth causes death.

Analysis   In some sense this is right. But it seems wrong. Why?

What's the cause? What's the effect? The example is a general causal claim covering every particular claim like "That this creature was born caused it to die."

We have lots of inductive evidence: Socrates died. My dog Juney died. My teacher in high school died. President Kennedy died. . . .

The problem seems to be that though this is true, it's uninteresting. It's tracing the cause too far back. Being born should be part of the normal conditions when we have the effect that someone died.

Example 8   Maria: Fear of getting fired causes me to get to work on time.
Analysis   How can we describe the purported cause with a claim?

> *Cause*: Maria is afraid of getting fired.
> *Effect*: Maria gets to work on time.

Is it possible for Maria to be afraid of getting fired and still not get to work on time? Certainly, but not, perhaps, under normal conditions: Maria sets her alarm; the electricity doesn't go off; there isn't bad weather; Maria doesn't oversleep; . . . . But there's something odd in calling these the normal conditions: Isn't it supposed to be because she's afraid that Maria makes sure these claims will be true, or that she'll get to work even if one or more is false?

In that case how can we judge whether the relationship between the purported cause and effect is valid or strong? That Maria gets to work regardless of conditions that aren't normal is what makes her consider her fear to be the cause.

Subjective causes are often a matter of feeling, some sense that we control what we do. They are often too vague for us to classify as true or false.

Example 9   Dick: Hold the steering wheel.
                Zoe: What are you doing? Stop! Are you crazy?
                Dick: I'm just taking my sweater off.
                Zoe: I can't believe you did that. It's *so* dangerous.
                Dick: Don't be silly. I've done it a thousand times before.
                      (crash . . . later . . .)
                Dick: You had to turn the steering wheel!? That made us crash.

Analysis   The purported cause: Zoe turned the steering wheel. The effect: The car crashed. The necessary criteria are satisfied.

But as they say in court, Zoe's turning the steering wheel is a ***foreseeable consequence*** of Dick making her take the wheel, which is the real cause. The normal conditions are not just what has to be true before the cause, but also what will normally *follow* the cause.

Example 10   Dick: Wasn't that awful what happened to old Mr. Grzegorczyk?
                  Zoe: You mean those tree trimmers who dropped a huge branch on him and killed him?

Dick: You only got half the story. He'd had a heart attack in his car and pulled over to the side. He was lying on the pavement when the branch hit him—he would have died anyway.

Zoe: But I heard his wife is going to collect from the tree company.

Analysis What's the cause of death? Mr. Grzegorczyk would have died anyway. So the tree branch falling on him wouldn't have made a difference.

But the tree branch falling on him isn't a foreseeable consequence, part of the normal conditions of his stumbling out of his car with a heart attack. As they say in court, it's an ***intervening cause***. Juries, usually made up of people like you, will be asked to decide what is the cause of Mr. Grzegorczyk's death. There's no clear answer, though these kinds of cases have been debated for centuries.

Example 11 Sunspots cause stock prices to rise.

Analysis Suppose your finance teacher tells you this general causal claim, and she backs it up with data showing a very good correlation between the appearance of large sunspots and rises in the Dow Jones index. But a correlation, though needed for a general causal claim, doesn't establish cause and effect by itself. It's hard to imagine a common cause, but coincidence can't be ruled out. If we look around the world long enough, we'll eventually find *some* phenomenon that can be correlated to the rise and fall in stock prices. Even if there were a very exact correlation between the size of the sunspots and the percentage of increase in the Dow Jones average two days later, we still want a theory—normal conditions that give us a way to trace how the sunspots cause the price rises—before we accept that this is cause and effect.

Example 12 The Treaty of Versailles caused World War II.

Analysis The cause: The Treaty of Versailles was agreed to and enforced. The effect: World War II occurred.

To analyze a conjecture like this an historian will write a book. The normal conditions have to be spelled out. You have to show that it was a foreseeable consequence of the enforcement of the Treaty of Versailles at the end of World War I that Germany would re-arm.

But was it foreseeable that Chamberlain would back down over Hitler's invasion of Czechoslovakia? More plausible is that the signing of the Treaty of Versailles is *a* cause, not *the* cause of World War II.

Example 13 Poltergeists are making the pictures fall down from their hooks.

Analysis To accept this, we have to believe that poltergeists exist. That's dubious. Worse, it's probably not *testable*: How could you determine if there are poltergeists? Dubious claims that aren't testable are the worst candidates for causes.

Exercises for Sections A and B

Here is an exercise Tom did on cause and effect.

I used Diabolic Grow on my roses and they grew great! I'll always use it.

Causal claim: (unstated) Diabolic Grow caused my roses to grow great.

Cause: The speaker put Diabolic Grow on his roses.

Effect: The roses grew great.

Cause and effect each happened? Apparently so.

Cause precedes effect? Yes.

It's (nearly) impossible for the cause to be true and effect false? Hard to say.

Cause makes a difference? It seems so, but did the cause really make a
difference? Maybe they would have grown great anyway. Some years
that happens when it rains at just the right time in the spring.

Common cause? For sure, no.

Evaluation: You'd need a lot more evidence to believe the claim.

Excellent! You're thinking critically.

For the exercises here, find the causal claim. Then evaluate it, explaining why it's plausible or clearly wrong, or whether you need more information to evaluate it by answering:

Causal claim:

Cause:

Effect:

Cause and effect each happened?

Cause precedes effect?

It's (nearly) impossible for the cause to be true and effect false?

Cause makes a difference?

Common cause?

Evaluation:

1. Maria: I had to slam on the brakes because some idiot pulled out in front of me.

2. Suzy: My feet hurt so bad the other day when I was cheerleading. My feet have never hurt at the other cheerleading events, but I was wearing new shoes. So it must have been my new shoes.

3. Dick: Ooh, my stomach hurts.
   Zoe: Serves you right. You really pigged out on the nachos and salsa last night. They always give you a stomachache.

4. Marriage is the chief cause of divorce.

5. I've got to go to the game. The only time I wasn't in the bleachers this season, they lost.

6. Hazards are one of the main causes of accidents. (OSHA, "Safety with Beef Cattle")

7. Zoe: The dark sky makes me really depressed today.

8. Dick: Boy, are you red.

   Zoe: Ouch! I got a terrible sunburn because the sun was so strong yesterday.

9. The emphasis on Hollywood figures in the media causes people to use drugs because people want to emulate the stars.

10. Maria: It's awful what's happened to Zeke.

    Lee: Why? What happened? I haven't seen him for ages.

    Maria: He started using drugs. It's because he was hanging out with that bad bunch.

11. Lou's college education helped him get a high-paying job the year after he graduated.

12. Dick: Every day I run up this hill and it's no big deal. Why am I so beat today?

    Zoe: It's 'cause you stayed out late and didn't get enough sleep.

13. Zoe: My life's a mess. I've never really been happy since all those years ago in high school you told Sally that I killed Puff. She believed your stupid joke, and made sure I wasn't a cheerleader. I'll never be a cheerleader. It's your fault I'm so miserable now.

    Dick: There, there.

14. Sex, drugs, and rock 'n roll are the causes of the decline in family values.

15. Suzy: Eating potato chips and sitting on the couch must be healthy. All the guys on the football team do it.

16. Lee: Yesterday my neighbor said this spring has been the worst season ever for allergies, but I told her I hadn't had any bad days. Then today I started sneezing. Darn it—if only she hadn't told me.

17. Dick: Normally my pulse rate is about 130 after exercising on this bike.

    Zoe: I can't believe you actually measure your heart rate! You're so obsessive.

    Dick: But for the past week or so it's been about 105. That's odd.

    Zoe: You stopped drinking coffee two weeks ago, remember?

18. He's stupid because his mother dropped him on his head when he was young.

19. A recent study shows that everyone who uses heroin started with marijuana. So smoking marijuana causes heroin use.

20. Dr. E: My students don't like the material at the end of this course. That's why so many have missed class the last two weeks of the course.

21. The swallows never come back to Capistrano except when there are a lot of people waiting to see them there at the festival they have each year. They must come back because they like the welcome.

22. Flo: Salad makes you fat. I know 'cause Wanda's really fat and is always eating salad.

23. (An advertisement by the Iowa Egg Council in the Des Moines International Airport)
    Children who eat breakfast not only do better academically, but they also behave better.
    Archives of Pediatric and Adolescent Medicine

24. *Gingrich: Liberalism led to Colorado massacre*

In his first speech since leaving Congress, former House speaker Newt Gingrich blamed the Littleton, Colo., school shootings on 35 years of liberalism.

In a speech Wednesday to about 500 Republican women, Gingrich said elimination of prayer and "the Creator" from schools, lack of teaching about the Constitution and a steady stream of violence in the movies and video games have produced teen-agers who are morally adrift. He blamed an overtaxing government for forcing parents to spend more time working, away from their children.

But Gingrich said attempts to make guns a scapegoat for last month's shootings at Columbine High School were "banalities." "I want to say to the elite of this country— the elite news media, the liberal academic elite, the liberal political elite," Gingrich told the Republican Women's Leadership Forum, "I accuse you in Littleton, and I accuse you in Kosovo, of being afraid to talk about the mess you have made, and being afraid to take responsibility for things you have done, and instead foisting upon the rest of us pathetic banalities because you don't have the courage to look at the world you have created." . . .

Gingrich was harsh in placing the blame for the murder of 12 students and a teacher in Littleton, Colo., by two classmates. He said the killers probably never realized they were robbing the "inalienable rights of life, liberty and the pursuit of happiness" of their victims because the schools never taught them the constitutional meaning of the words.

"For 35 years, the political and intellectual elites (and) political correctness have undermined the core values in American history, so the young people may not know who George Washington is, or they may not know who Abraham Lincoln is—but they know what MTV is," Gingrich said.

Gingrich said Republicans should lead a campaign to "expose" movie and video game makers to liability lawsuits, and to challenge "Democrats to cut off the fund-raising" from makers of violent movies.

Chuck Raasch, Gannett News Service, USA Today, May 13, 1999

C. How to Look for the Cause

I have a waterfall in my backyard in Cedar City. The pond has a thick rubberized plastic pond liner, and I have a pump and hose that carry water from the pond along the rock face of a small rise to where the water spills out and runs down more rocks with concrete between them. Last summer I noticed that the pond kept getting low every day and had to be refilled. You don't waste water in the desert, so I figured I'd better find out what was causing the loss of water.

I thought of all the ways the pond could be leaking: The hose that carries the water could have a leak, the valve connections could be leaking, the pond liner could be ripped (the dogs get into the pond to cool off in the summer), there could be cracks in the concrete, or it could be evaporation and spray from where the water comes out at the top of the fountain.

I had to figure out which (if any) of these was the problem. First I got someone to come in and use a high pressure spray on the waterfall to clean it. We took the rocks out and vacuumed out the pond. Then we patched every possible spot on the pond liner where there might be a leak.

Then we patched all the concrete on the waterfall part and water-sealed it. We checked the valve connections and tightened them. They didn't leak. And the hose wasn't leaking because there weren't any wet spots along its path.

Then I refilled the pond. It kept losing water at about the same rate.

It wasn't the hose, it wasn't the connections, it wasn't the pond liner, it wasn't the concrete watercourse. So it had to be the spray and evaporation.

I reduced the flow of water so there wouldn't be so much spray. There was a lot less water loss. The rest I figured was probably evaporation, though there might still be small leaks.

In trying to find the cause of the water leak I was using the method scientists often use:

> Conjecture possible causes, and then by experiment eliminate them until there is only one. Check that one:
>> Does it make a difference? If the purported cause is eliminated, is there still the effect? Could there be a common cause?

Not much spray, not much water loss. I couldn't be absolutely sure, but it seemed very likely I had isolated the cause.

The best prophylactic against making common mistakes in reasoning about causes is experiment. Often we can't do an experiment, but we can do an imaginary experiment. That's what we've always done in checking for validity: Imagine the possibilities. But note: This method will help you find the cause only if you've guessed it among the ones you're testing.

Exercises for Section C

1. Come up with a method to determine whether there's cause and effect:
    a. Pressing the "Door Close" button in the elevator causes the doors to close.
    b. Zoe's belching caused Spot to run away.
    c. Reducing the speed limit to 55 m.p.h. saves lives.
    d. The red-headed lady walking by the classroom causes Professor Zzzyzzx to arrive at class on time.

2. Flo: Isn't it amazing that of all the houses in this town, I was born in one where the people look so much like me!
    What is Flo overlooking?

3. Dick: (*Bending over, sweating and cursing*) There's something wrong with my bike.
    Zoe: What?
    Dick: Something's going "click, click, click" all the time.

Zoe: Must be something that's moving.

Dick: Duh. Here, hold it up while I turn the pedals. (*click, click, click, . . .*)

Zoe: Yup, there it is.

Dick: It must be in the pedals or the wheels.

Zoe: Stop pedaling. . . . It's gone away.

Dick: It must be in the pedals, then.

Evaluate how Dick and Zoe have tried to isolate the cause here.

Tom was asked to bring in a causal claim he made recently and evaluate it. Here's his work.

The only time I've had a really bad backache is right after I went bicycling early in the morning when it was so cold last week. Bicycling never bothered me before. So it must be the cold weather that caused my back to hurt after cycling.

Causal claim: The cold weather caused my back to hurt after cycling.

Cause: It was cold when I went cycling.

Effect: I got a backache.

Cause and effect true? Yes.

Cause precedes the effect? Yes.

Valid or strong? I think so.

Cause makes a difference? Sure seems so.

Common cause? None.

Evaluation: The criteria seem to be satisfied. But now I'm wondering if I haven't overlooked some other cause. I also had an upset stomach. So maybe it was the flu. Or maybe it was tension, since I'd had a fight with Suzy the night before. I guess I'll have to try cycling in the cold again to find out.

Good. But you're still looking for the cause, when it may be a cause. Another possible cause: Did you warm up first? Another possibility: You'll never know for sure.

---

4. Write down a causal claim that you made recently and evaluate it. Have a classmate critique your evaluation.

5. Make up three causal claims and trade with a classmate to analyze.

6. Judge: I find that Nancy sustained serious injuries in this accident. There is sufficient evidence that the defendant ran a red light and broadsided her car, causing the injuries. But I hold that Nancy was partly responsible for the severity of her injuries in that she was not wearing a seat belt. Therefore, Nancy shall collect only 50% of the costs associated with this accident.

Explain the judge's decision in terms of normal conditions and foreseeable consequences.

7. Mickey has taken his four-wheel-drive Jeep out into the desert to explore on this hot sunny Sunday. But his two cousins want to see him dead. Bertha has put poison in Mickey's five-gallon canteen. Richard, not knowing of Bertha's plans, has put a very small hole in the canteen.

Mickey's car breaks down. He's getting hot and thirsty. His cellular phone doesn't work because he forgot to recharge it. He goes to get some water and finds the canteen empty. . . .

Overcome by guilt later in the year, both Bertha and Richard confess. Who should be blamed for causing Mickey's death?

D. Cause and Effect in Populations

When we say "Smoking causes lung cancer," what do we mean? If you smoke a cigarette, you'll get cancer? If you smoke a lot of cigarettes this week, you'll get cancer? If you smoke 20 cigarettes a day for 40 years, you'll get cancer?

It can't be any of these, since we know smokers who did all that yet didn't get lung cancer. And the cause always has to follow the effect. So what do we mean?

Cause in populations is usually explained as meaning that given the cause, there's a higher probability that the effect will follow than if there were not the cause. In this example, people who smoke have a much higher probability of getting lung cancer than non-smokers.

That's how it's explained. But really we are talking about cause and effect just as we did before. Smoking lots of cigarettes over a long period of time will cause (inevitably) lung cancer. The problem is that we can't state, we have no idea how to state, nor is it likely that we'll ever be able to state the normal conditions for smoking to cause cancer. Among other factors, there's diet, where one lives, exposure to pollution and other carcinogens, and one's genetic inheritance. But *if we knew exactly*, we'd say: "Under the conditions _____, smoking _____ (number of) cigarettes every day for _____ years will result in lung cancer."

Since we can't specify the normal conditions, the best we can do is point to the evidence that convinces us that smoking is a cause of lung cancer and get an argument with a statistical conclusion: "People who continue to smoke two packs of cigarettes per day for ten years are ___% more likely (with a margin of error of ___ %) to get lung cancer."

What kind of evidence do we use?

1. Controlled experiment: cause-to-effect

This is our best evidence. We choose 10,000 people at random and ask 5,000 of them never to smoke and 5,000 of them to smoke 25 cigarettes every day. We have two samples, one composed of those who are administered the cause, and one of those who are not, the latter called the *control group*. We come back 20 years later to check how many in each group got lung cancer. If a lot more of the smokers got lung cancer, and the groups were representative of the population as a whole, and we can see no other *common thread* amongst those who got lung cancer, we'd be justified in saying that smoking causes lung cancer. The point of using a control group is to show that, at least statistically, the cause makes a difference.

But we don't do such an experiment. It would be unethical. It's not acceptable to do an experiment on humans that has a (major) potential for doing them harm.

So we use some animals sufficiently like humans that we feel are "expendable," perhaps rats. We fit them with little masks and have them breathe the equivalent of 25 cigarettes per day for a few years. Then if lots of them get lung cancer, while the ones who don't smoke are still frisky, we can conclude with reasonable certainty that smoking causes cancer in laboratory rats.

So? We then argue that since rats are sufficiently similar to humans in their biological processes, we can extrapolate to say that smoking can cause cancer in humans. We argue by analogy.

2. Uncontrolled experiment: cause-to-effect

Here we take two randomly chosen, representative samples of the general population for which we have factored out other possible causes of lung cancer, such as working in coal mines. One of the groups is composed of people who say they never smoke. One group, comparable to the control group for controlled experiments, is composed of people who say they smoke. We follow the groups and 15–20 years later check whether those who smoked got lung cancer more often. Since we think we've accounted for other common threads, smoking is the remaining common thread that may account for why the second group got cancer more often.

This is a *cause-to-effect* experiment, since we start with the suspected cause and see if the effect follows. But it is uncontrolled: Some people may stop smoking, some may begin, people may have quite variable diets—there may be a lot we'll have to factor out in trying to assess whether it's smoking that causes the extra cases of lung cancer.

3. Uncontrolled experiment: effect-to-cause

Here we look at as many people as possible who have lung cancer to see if there is some common thread that occurs in (almost all) their lives. We factor out those who worked in coal mines, those who lived in high pollution areas, those who drank a lot, ... If it turns out that a much higher proportion of the remaining people smoked than in the general population, we have good evidence that smoking was the cause.

This is uncontrolled because how they got to the effect was unplanned, not within our control. And it is an *effect-to-cause* experiment because we start with the effect in the population and try to account for how it got there.

How do we "factor out" other possible causes? How do we determine whether the sample of people we are looking at is large enough to draw conclusions about the general population? How do we determine if the sample is representative? How do we decide how many more cases of the effect—lung cancer—have to occur before it can be attributed to some cause rather than just to chance? These are the problems that arise whenever we generalize (Chapter 14), and only a course on statistics will make these issues clearer.

Until you do take such a course and have access to actual write-ups of the experiments—not just the newspaper or magazine accounts—you'll have to rely on "the experts." If the experiment was done by a reputable group, without bias, and what we read passes the obvious tests for a strong generalization, a good analogy, and a good causal argument, then we can assume that the researchers know statistics well enough to conduct proper experiments—at least until some other reputable group challenges their results.

Example 14 Reginald smoked two packs of cigarettes each day for thirty years. Reginald now has lung cancer. Reginald's smoking caused his lung cancer.

Analysis Is it possible for Reginald to have smoked two packs of cigarettes each day for thirty years and not get lung cancer? We can't state the normal conditions. So we invoke the statistical relation between smoking and lung cancer to say it is unlikely for the cause to be true and effect false.

Does the cause make a difference? Could Reginald have gotten lung cancer even if he had not smoked? Suppose we know that Reginald wasn't a coal miner, didn't work in a textile factory, and didn't live in a city with a very polluted atmosphere—all conditions that are associated with a higher probability of getting lung cancer. Then it is possible for Reginald to have gotten lung cancer anyway, since some people who have no other risks do get lung cancer. But it is very unlikely, since very few of those people do.

We have no reason to believe that there is a common cause. It may be that people with a certain biological make-up feel compelled to smoke, and that that biological make-up also contributes to their getting lung cancer independently of their smoking. But we have no evidence of such a biological factor.

So assuming a few normal conditions, "Reginald's smoking caused his lung cancer" is as plausible as the strength of the statistical link between smoking and lung cancer, and the strength of the link between not smoking and not getting lung cancer. We must be careful, though, that we do not attribute the cause of the lung cancer to smoking just because we haven't thought of any other cause, especially if the statistical links aren't very strong.

Example 15 Zoe: I can't understand Melinda. She's pregnant and she's drinking.
        Dick: That's all baloney. I asked my mom, and she said she drank when she was pregnant with me. And I turned out fine.
        Zoe: But think how much better you would have been if she hadn't.

Analysis Zoe doesn't say but alludes to the cause-in-population claim that drinking during pregnancy causes birth defects or poor development of the child. That has been demonstrated: Many cause-in-population studies have been done that show there is a higher incidence of birth defects and developmental problems in children born to mothers who drink than to mothers who do not drink, and those defects and problems do not appear to arise from any other common factor.

Dick, however, makes a mistake: He confuses a cause-in-population claim with a general causal claim. He is right that his mother's experience would disprove the general causal claim, but it has no force against the cause-in-population claim.

Zoe's confusion is that she thinks there is a perfect correlation between drinking and physical or mental problems in the child, so that if Dick's mother had not drunk he would have been better, even if Zoe can't point to the particular way in which Dick would have been better. But the correlation isn't perfect, it's only a statistical link.

> The problem of *selection bias* in cause-in-population studies:
>
> No matter how carefully studies are made on the effectiveness of different contraceptives, they will be only marginally useful in helping women choose which method to use. That's because women who most want to avoid pregnancy choose the contraceptive they think will be most effective. So the women using the pill, which is currently touted as the most effective of the common ways to avoid pregnancy, will be more motivated to follow the instructions for its use and always use it, while those who use contraceptive foam are likely to be more lax in following the method. And, according to the scientists who devise these studies (see the article "Data called misleading in rating contraceptives," *New York Times*, December 1, 1987), there doesn't seem to be any way to correct for this bias in the analysis of the data.

Exercises for Section D

Describe what evidence you have for the claims in Exercises 1–5 and what experiments you would devise to try to prove or disprove them. (Don't do the experiments yourself!)

1. Universities cause students to become smarter.

2. Hedonistic lifestyles cause premature death.

3. Money brings happiness.

4. Drinking alcohol causes promiscuous behavior.

5. Unprotected sex causes disease.

Explain what's wrong in Exercises 6–9.

6. Tom: Don't feed those chicken bones to Spot. Don't you know that a dog can choke and die on one of those?
   Dick: Don't be silly, I've been giving Spot chicken bones for years.

7. Suzy: Vegetarians get cancer much less than meat-eaters.
    Manuel: Oh, yeah, so how come Linda McCartney, a well-known vegetarian, died from cancer when she was only in her 50s?

8. Dick: Hey, Zoe. Listen to this. A Roper survey said wine drinkers are more successful than those who don't drink. Frequent wine drinkers, it says, earn about $67,000 a year, while occasional drinkers earn about $40,000. Those who don't drink at all earn a little more than $30,000.
             You want to be successful, don't you?
    Zoe: You're not going to get me to start drinking wine that way.

9. Maria: Wives of servicemen suffer domestic abuse at the rate of 2 to 5 times that of other women.
    Suzy: Boy, I sure hope Tom doesn't join the army.

10. One of Dr. E's dogs gets loose. He comes back the next day. He's coughing and hacking, and he vomits a couple times. Dr. E thinks maybe he ate something bad. Three days later that dog is O.K., but his other dog, who hasn't left the yard, is coughing and hacking, and vomits. Dr. E concludes that his dogs have had a flu or some illness.

    Explain why you think Dr. E is right or why he is wrong.

Analyze the following passages by answering these questions:

What causal claim is at issue?
Which type of cause-in-population experiment, if any, was done?
Evaluate the evidence for the causal claim.
How would you further test the claim?

11. *Two new studies back value of high-fiber diet*
    New research has revived the notion that a high-fiber diet may protect against colon cancer. Long-standing recommendations for high-fiber diets have taken a hit over the last few years after a handful of carefully conducted studies failed to find a benefit.

    But experts say two major studies published this week in The Lancet medical journal—one on Americans and the other on Europeans—indicate previous research may not have examined a broad enough range of fiber consumption or a wide enough variety of fiber sources to show an effect.

    "These two new findings show that the fiber hypothesis is still alive," said the leader of the American study, Ulrike Peters of the U.S. National Cancer Institute.

    Figuring out the relationship between nutrition and disease has proved difficult, but experts say fiber is particularly complicated because there are various types and they all could act differently.

    Fiber is found in fruits, vegetables and whole grains. Americans eat about 16 grams a day, while Europeans eat about 22 grams. The new studies indicate fiber intake needs to be about 30 grams a day to protect against colon cancer.

    There are 2 grams of fiber in a slice of whole meal bread. A banana has 3 grams and an apple has 3.5 grams, the same as a cup of brown rice. Some super-high fiber breakfast cereals have as much as 14 grams per half cup.

In the American study, investigators compared the daily fiber intake of 3,600 people who had precancerous growths in the colon with that of around 34,000 people who did not. People who ate the most fiber had 27 percent lower risk of precancerous growths than those who ate the least.

In the European study, the largest one ever conducted on nutrition and cancer, scientists examined the link in more than 500,000 people in 10 countries.

Those who ate the most fiber, about 35 grams a day, had about a 40 percent lower risk of colorectal cancer compared with those who ate the least, about 15 grams a day, the study found.

"In the top quintile (group) they were eating 15 grams of cereal fiber, which is equivalent to five or six slices of whole meal bread, plus they were eating seven portions of fruit and vegetables a day, which is basically the Mediterranean levels," said the study's leader, Sheila Bingham, head of the diet and cancer group at Cambridge University's human nutrition unit. Associated Press, May 2, 2003

12. [Bernard] Goldberg documents the steady decline in the behavioral, emotional and physical health of America's kids that has taken place as the percentage of latchkey and day-care children has increased. Some examples:

• From 1979 to 1988 (a period that coincides with a sizable increase in two-income families), the suicide rate for girls 10–14 rose 27 percent, while for boys it rose 71 percent.

• In 1970, only one in 20 American girls under 15 had had sex; today, one in three is having sex, and 3 million teenagers are infected with sexually transmitted diseases every year.

• A study of 5 million eighth-graders found that children who are left home alone more than 11 hours a week are three times more likely than kids with after-school adult supervision to abuse drugs, alcohol or tobacco.

• A study by the National Institute of Child Health and Human Development published in 2001 found that toddlers in full-time day care tended to be more aggressive toward other children and defiant toward adults. This, the institute found, regardless of the quality.

Goldberg acknowledges that not all the evidence is bad. Some studies on day care have found it's not bad at all. (When one considers only studies conducted by people or groups without apparent bias, however—as is the case with the above study—the results always paint a not-so-pretty picture.) And he's clear that he's talking about parents who choose to work outside the home, not those who effectively have no choice. John Rosemond, "Parenting," *Albuquerque Journal*, March 7, 2002

13. *Vitamin E in moderation may protect heart*
Eating a moderate amount of food rich in vitamin E, such as nuts, vegetable oils and margarine, reduces the risk of death from heart disease, says a study in today's *New England Journal of Medicine*.

This supports a growing body of evidence that links vitamin E to a healthy heart.

Researchers surveyed 34,486 postmenopausal women about their eating habits in

1986 and followed up about seven years later. They studied women but say the results apply to men, too.

They found women with the diets highest in vitamin E-rich foods had half the risk of death from heart disease compared with those eating diets low in these foods. The highest group got more than 10 IUs of vitamin E from food daily, the equivalent of about an ounce of almonds. Those in the lowest group got about half that amount.

Margarine and salad dressings are high in fat and calories, so people should use common sense when eating them. "I wouldn't go overboard with these things, but I wouldn't necessarily cut them out entirely," says the study's lead author, Lawrence H. Kushi of the University of Minnesota School of Public Health. The women who did the best in the research did not eat "outrageous amounts" of vitamin E foods.

Dr. Walter Willett, Harvard School of Public Health, says "one of the unfortunate parts of the fat phobia is that people eliminate major sources of vitamin E in their diets."

This study didn't come to a definitive conclusion on supplements, but other studies indicate they are beneficial.

Other rich sources of vitamin E: hazelnuts, sunflower seeds, wheat germ, mayonnaise, peanut butter, avocados.

Nanci Hellmich, USA Today, 1996

14. *Academy Award winning actors and actresses*

(from the transcript for National Public Radio's *All Things Considered,* May 15, 2001)
ROBERT SIEGEL, host: An article reached us today with the title Survival in Academy Award-winning Actors and Actresses. It is not about casting or contracts. It's actually in the Annal of Internal Medicine, and it's about survival. Dr. Donald Redelmeier and his colleague Sheldon Singph found that actors and actresses who have won Oscars live, on average, 3.9 years longer than other performers who have never won Oscars. Dr. Redelmeier is in Toronto and joins us now.

Dr. Redelmeier, how did you conduct this study?

Dr. DONALD REDELMEIER: What we did is, we identified every actor and actress who's ever been nominated for an Academy Award in either a supporting role or a leading role over the full history of the Academy Awards since 1929.

SIEGEL: What does this tell you? What do you think is the cause of the greater longevity among those actors and actresses who won Academy Awards.

Dr. REDELMEIER: One possible theory is that winning an Academy Award improves a person's self-esteem and gives them a much greater resilience to the normal stressors that confront us on a day-to-day basis. And that, in turn, causes changes in the hypothalamic, pituitary, adrenal glands of the body or the immunological systems, and so that much less damage occurs over the years.

SIEGEL: If this is true, do you think we should find then that, say, the Academy Award winners among the film editors or the special effects people would also outlive their colleagues or do you think it requires the adulation that only star actors and actresses get to add the extra 3.9 years to a life span.

Dr. REDELMEIER: Well, more research is always needed. Another possibility is that it isn't due to a person's internal biology, but it reflects their external behavior—i.e., that stars live lives under continuous scrutiny, and so because of that, they need to sleep properly every night, eat a balanced diet at every meal, exercise regularly every day in order to preserve their glamorous image. And so it's those external behaviors rather than the internal peace of mind that confers a much greater survival benefit than is generally appreciated.

15. *Study: Better primary care increases hospitalization*
Researchers set out to show that giving sick people better access to family doctors keeps them out of the hospital. But to the surprise of everyone involved, the study found just the opposite.

Doctors apparently end up diagnosing more ills, including ones that probably would otherwise go unnoticed.

"I went in knowing that primary care could help keep these patients out of the hospital. That was my passion. I was exactly wrong," said Dr. Eugene Z. Oddone of the Veterans Affairs hospital in Durham, N.C.

He and Dr. Morris Weinberger of the VA hospital in Indianapolis had thought the experiment would prove the obvious: Better primary care keeps people healthier, reducing hospital admissions by about one-third and saving money.

Working with nine VA hospitals, they offered poor, seriously ill veterans the kind of care available in most HMOs—ready access to a nurse, a family doctor in charge of their case, reminders of appointments and follow-up calls.

After six months of this attention, hospitalizations actually rose by one-third.

"We were more surprised than anybody," Weinberger said.

The doctors said their study, published in Thursday's issue of the *New England Journal of Medicine*, illustrates one of the difficulties of refashioning the health care system: Even common-sense ideas need to be tested to make sure they work.

Furthermore, for some, it raises doubts about an article of faith among doctors— that catching and treating diseases early will make people healthier in the long run.

In an accompanying editorial, Dr. H. Gilbert Welch of Dartmouth Medical School said the study forces doctors to consider a "heretical view."

"Instead of conferring benefit, closer scrutiny of the patients simply led to more medical care and perhaps to harm," he said. "We can no longer assume that early intervention is always the right thing to do." Associated Press, May 30, 1996

16. *Bad hair can give self-esteem a cowlick, study says*
People's self-esteem goes awry when their hair is out of place, according to a Yale University researcher's study of the psychology of bad-hair days.

People feel less smart, less capable, more embarrassed and less sociable, researchers said in the report released Wednesday.

And contrary to popular belief, men's self-esteem may take a greater licking than women's when their hair just won't behave. Men were more likely to feel less smart and less capable when their hair stuck out, was badly cut or otherwise mussed.

"The cultural truism is men are not affected by their appearance," said Marianne LaFrance, the Yale psychology professor who conducted the study. "(But) this is not just the domain of women."

The study was paid for by Proctor & Gamble, which makes hair-care products. The Cincinnati-based company would not discuss how much the study cost or what they planned to do with their newfound knowledge about the psychology of hair.

Janet Hyde, a psychology professor at the University of Wisconsin at Madison who studies body image and self-esteem, said personal appearance can have an enormous effect on people, especially adolescents.

But Hyde said she was surprised to hear bad hair had a stronger effect on men than on women in some cases.

For the study, researchers questioned 60 men and 60 women ages 17 to 30, most of them Yale students. About half were white, 9 percent were black, 21 percent were Asian and 3 percent were Hispanic.

The people were divided into three groups. One group was questioned about times in their lives when they had bad hair. The second group was told to think about bad product packaging, like leaky containers, to get them in a negative mind-set. The third group was not asked to think about anything negative.

All three groups then underwent basic psychological tests of self-esteem and self-judgment. The people who pondered their bad-hair days showed lower self-esteem than those who thought about something else. . . .

LaFrance, who has also studied the psychology of smiles, facial expressions and body language, said she would continue to look into the effects of bad hair. "We all do research that at first pass might seem quite small," she said. "Yes, some of my colleagues said, 'That's interesting, ha, ha.' But then, when we talk about it, people are interested."

Associated Press, January 27, 2000

17. In the mid-1970s a team of researchers in Great Britain conducted a rigorously designed large-scale experiment to test the effectiveness of a treatment program that represented "the sort of care which today might be provided by most specialized alcoholism clinics in the Western world."

The subjects were one hundred men who had been referred for alcohol problems to a leading British outpatient program, the Alcoholism Family Clinic of Maudsley Hospital in London. The receiving psychiatrist confirmed that each of the subjects met the following criteria: he was properly referred for alcohol problems, was aged 20 to 65 and married, did not have any progressive or painful physical disease or brain damage or psychotic illness, and lived within a reasonable distance of the clinic (to allow for clinic visits and follow-up home visits by social workers). A statistical randomization procedure was used to divide the subjects into two groups comparable in the severity of their drinking and their occupational status.

For subjects in one group (the "advice group"), the only formal therapeutic activity was one session between the drinker, his wife, and the psychiatrist. The psychiatrist told the couple that the husband was suffering from alcoholism and advised him to abstain from all drink. The psychiatrist also encouraged the couple to attempt to keep their marriage together. There was a free-ranging discussion and advice about the personalities and particularities of the situation, but the couple was told that this one session was the only treatment the clinic would provide. They were told in sympathetic and constructive language that the "attainment of the stated goals lay in their hands and could not be taken over by others."

Subjects in the second group (the "treatment group") were offered a year-long program that began with a counseling session, an introduction to Alcoholics Anonymous, and prescriptions for drugs that would make alcohol unpalatable and drugs that would alleviate withdrawal suffering. Each drinker then met with a psychiatrist to work out a continuing outpatient treatment program, while the social worker made a similar plan with the drinker's wife. The ongoing counseling was focused on practical problems in the areas of alcohol abuse, marital relations, and other social or personal difficulties. Drinkers who did not respond well were offered in-patient admissions, with full access to the hospital's wide range of services.

Twelve months after the experiment began, both groups were assessed. No significant differences were found between the two groups. Furthermore, drinkers in the treatment group who stayed with it for the full period did not fare better than those who dropped out. At the twelve-month point, only eleven of the one hundred drinkers had become abstainers. Another dozen or so still drank but in sufficient moderation to be considered "acceptable" by both husband and wife. Such rates of improvement are not significantly better than those shown in studies of the spontaneous or natural improvement of chronic drinkers not in treatment.

Herbert Fingarette, *Heavy Drinking: The Myth of Alcoholism as Disease*

Summary We encounter cause and effect claims every day. The best way to begin to evaluate them is to describe the purported cause and effect with claims. Then we can use much of what we know about how to reason with claims.

For there to be cause and effect, it must be (nearly) impossible for the claim describing the cause to be true and effect false. That's the same relation as between premises and conclusion of a valid or strong argument, except that here these claims should already be plausible. As with arguments, we often need additional premises, what we call the "normal conditions," to show that the inference is valid or strong. Among those additional premises will often be a generalization establishing a correlation.

Checking that the cause makes a difference is how we rule out other possible causes. In addition, the cause has to precede the effect, and there must be no common cause. Once we've checked that all these necessary conditions for cause and effect hold, there's not much more we can do except make sure we haven't made one of the common mistakes of reversing cause and effect or arguing *post hoc ergo propter hoc* (after this, therefore because of this).

When we can't specify the normal conditions for a general causal claim, we rely on statistical arguments to establish that there is some causal link. Three kinds of experiments are important for those arguments: controlled cause-to-effect, uncontrolled cause-to-effect, and uncontrolled effect-to-cause.

Key Words

causal claim	coincidence
cause	causal factor
effect	foreseeable consequence
normal conditions	intervening cause
particular cause and effect	cause in population
general cause and effect	control group
correlation	common thread
common cause	controlled cause-to-effect experiment
reversing cause and effect	uncontrolled cause-to-effect experiment
post hoc ergo propter hoc	uncontrolled effect-to-cause experiment

Further Study   To read about cause and effect in scientific explanations, see the *Science Workbook* for this text. For a fuller discussion of how to reason about cause and effect, including reasoning in the sciences, see my *Five Ways of Saying "Therefore,"* also published by Wadsworth, which has many more examples and a history of the subject back to Aristotle.

Writing Lesson 11

Below are two pairs of arguments. Each pair involves some causal claim. Choose one of the pairs and prepare a full analysis in outline form of both arguments. Then present the analyses in an essay, either agreeing with one of the arguments or explaining why you should suspend judgment.

    This will take all the skills you've learned in this course. For guidelines, see "The steps in analyzing complex arguments" on p. 229 and the section "Evaluating Reasoning" on p. 341 below.

1. *Power lines and leukemia*

A. *Power lines and leukemia: beware of scientists bearing glad tidings*
    "No Adverse Health Effects Seen From Residential Exposure to Electromagnetic Fields," said the press release from the National Academy of Sciences (NAS). "Study Fails to Link EMFs With Illnesses," repeated the *Los Angeles Times*. "Panel Sees No Proof of Health Hazards From Power Lines," "Electromagnetic research review finds no danger," "Power lines cleared as cause of cancer," "Power Line Hazard Called Small," echoed the *New York Times, Boston Globe, San Francisco Examiner,* and *Washington Post.*

    Feel better now? No need to worry about buying or renting a home near high-voltage electric power lines. Forget the scare stories about your children getting leukemia (cancer of the blood), and worry about real problems like the kids being abducted by aliens.

    But the headlines lie. Digging a bit deeper reveals that the study issued last October by a panel of 16 distinguished experts does not exonerate power lines, nor electromagnetic fields (EMFs), from being a danger to human health. In fact, the report itself (as opposed to the press release) summarizes the many existing epidemiological studies as saying that proximity to high-voltage lines raises a child's chances of contracting leukemia by 50%—hardly a negligible figure.

    While making this admission, the report goes on to emphasize that childhood leukemia is "a rare disease." This means about one case per 30,000 children in a year, says committee vice-chair David Savitz of the University of North Carolina. Since about one-quarter of homes are exposed to power lines, a bit of arithmetic shows that raising this rate by 50% could cause hundreds of additional deaths per year in the United States!

    Perhaps not as frightening as destruction of the ozone layer, but far worse than some other current scares, such as passenger-side air bags. How to reconcile the headlines with the 50% increase? It seems that although statistical studies of humans demonstrate an *association* between EMF strength and cancer, laboratory research has not found the mechanism by which EMFs actually cause cancer. So while the epidemiologists believe there is a problem, the physicists don't buy it.

The report, rather than focusing on this association, instead centers on the lack of physical proof: "No clear, convincing evidence exists to show that residential exposure to electric and magnetic fields are a threat to human health." Yet in a dissenting statement three committee members point out that, "Even in the case of cigarette smoking, it took nearly 50 years after the demonstration of a statistical association with lung cancer for scientists to define a cellular mechanism by which compounds in smoke could definitely cause the cellular changes associated with lung cancer."

The report's executive summary, and chair Charles Stevens, argue that the association of power lines with cancer could be pure coincidence. Other factors, such as "age of home, housing density, and neighborhood traffic density," could be the cause of the higher rates of leukemia.

But epidemiologists say that these other factors have been investigated and no relationship has been found. "There is no good evidence to suggest that it is something else [other than EMFs]—socioeconomic status, traffic density, or the type of neighborhood," says committee member Larry Anderson of Pacific Northwest Labs. And member Daniel Driscoll of the New York State Department of Public Services agrees.

By adopting an extremely high standard of proof to reach a conclusion of "guilty" the committee ensured that it would exonerate the defendant, says Louis Slessin, editor of *Microwave News*. Stevens also used "the oldest trick in the book," by issuing a press release that did not reflect the more balanced comments in the full report, adds Slessin.

Whose interests would be threatened by a conclusion that EMFs cause leukemia? The conventional view, seconded by Larry Anderson, is that the electric utilities have the most at risk, since their power lines criss-cross the nation, entering every community.

But, claims Slessin, "We are talking about all the technologies of the 21st century. The number one interest group is the military." The modern military, he argues, is fully dependent on electromagnetic fields, for weapons, reconnaissance and communications. Physicists, such as those on the committee, whose work is heavily funded by the military, "are doing the work of the Department of Defense, either consciously or unconsciously," says Slessin.

So don't believe the reassurances from the National Academy of Sciences. Until further notice, if you can avoid living near a power line, do so. And while you're at it, stay away from military bases.

Resources: Possible Health Effects of Exposure to Residential Electric and Magnetic Fields, National Research Council (National Academy of Sciences), October, 1996; "NAS Finds No EMF-Cancer Link; Report Stirs Controversy," *Microwave News,* Nov/Dec 1996.

Marc Breslow, *Dollars & Sense,* May/June 1997

B. *Power lines not a cancer risk for children*
Children who live near high-voltage power lines appear to be no more likely to get leukemia than other kids, doctors report today in the most extensive study of the controversial issue ever done. Researchers in nine states studied 629 children with leukemia and 619 healthy children. No child was admitted to the study unless the

investigators could measure the electromagnetic fields (EMF) in homes where the children had lived 70% of the time. In addition, the researchers:

• Measured EMF in all homes where children under 5 had lived more than 6 months.

• Measured the EMF in homes where the mothers of 460 children—half of whom had cancer—lived for 5 months of their pregnancy.

• Placed dose meters in the children's bedrooms for a day.

They found that children without cancer were exposed to the same levels of electromagnetic energy as children with cancer, effectively ruling out EMF as a cause.

"Overall, I believe this study demonstrates that exposure to electromagnetic fields does not increase a child's risk of leukemia," says Leslie Robinson, of the University of Minnesota and a co-author of the report in today's *New England Journal of Medicine.*

The study, sponsored by the National Cancer Institute, is the latest of hundreds to examine EMF and cancer. Parents nationwide have been alarmed and concerns have cost the nation an estimated $1 billion a year in diminished real estate prices and stalled power-transmission projects.

All of the studies, including the 1979 report that triggered these worries had drawbacks. Indeed, the National Research Council, an arm of the National Academy of Sciences, reported eight months ago that 500 studies over 17 years yielded no conclusive evidence that household EMF causes cancer.

The overall finding comes with a caveat. A handful of children exposed to moderately elevated EMF appeared to be 1.7 times more likely to develop cancer. In contrast, smokers face a 20-fold increase in cancer risk.

However, the children's risk increase was so small—14 of the 19 had cancer—that researchers believe it's a matter of chance.

Even more telling was evidence indicating that children exposed to much more powerful energy fields faced no risk.   *USA Today,* July 3, 1997

2. ***Should AIDS exhibit be OK'd as school field trip?***
   (This pair of arguments is from the *Las Vegas Sun,* March, 1996)

A. *Yes: Information is not false; trustees should reconsider their decision*
   Sandra Thompson, managing editor of the *Las Vegas Sun*

   The message is written in a teenage scrawl: "A friend of mine is always having unprotected sex. I hope she doesn't have AIDS."

   One of many comments in a book at the AIDS exhibit in the Lied Discovery Children's Museum, it sums up one of the purposes of the exhibit: To inform people that if they have sex, they can get AIDS.

   And that message is causing a ruckus in the community.

   The School Board—without having seen the exhibit—on February 13 voted against approving it as a field trip for students. Members may reconsider their decision at a March 12 board meeting since several have seen the exhibit since their vote.

   All members should see the exhibit for themselves and then approve it as a field-trip option.

The operative word here is "option."

By its vote, the School Board in effect made the decision for every parent. Critics counter that parents still have the choice—they can take their kids to the museums themselves.

Sure. And they could do other things with them, spend time with them and get involved in their education and extracurricular activities.

The reality is that many parents don't even attend their own children's school activities let alone take them to a museum.

I agree with Nevada Concerned Citizens that parents should take a more active role in their children's lives, especially education. They should know what their children are learning.

The furor over students seeing the traveling national AIDS exhibit centers on a perception that it does not stress abstinence, and talks about the risks of unprotected sex. Nevada Concerned Citizens objects to wording in the exhibit literature that says to protect yourself against AIDS, don't share needles and wear a condom during sex.

Members say that's misinformation because just doing that won't protect you, won't prevent AIDS. After all, condoms break.

The objection is based on semantics. The exhibit does not say taking such precautions will protect you 100 percent. And several times it mentions abstinence as the safest and best way to avoid AIDS.

I'm a great believer in youths abstaining from sex. But look around you: Kids are sexually active. They need information contained in the exhibit. They need to know what can happen if they fool around.

The exhibit does not promote sex. Nor does it promote a certain lifestyle connected with AIDS such as homosexuality, promiscuity or drug use.

"Whenever you deal with issues like this you set up alarms," Emily Newberry says of the "What About AIDS?" exhibit. "These are touchy issues. It's not the easiest topic to bring up."

Newberry is the public affairs coordinator for the Lied Discovery Children's Museum. She says the exhibit, which opened Feb. 3, is a national touring exhibit that does not contain any misinformation. A local advisory board of health-care professionals, educators and others reviewed the exhibit to ensure that.

"We got this exhibit because we were the only science museum in the state," she says, adding that it contains strong science content "with a compassionate side."

If school field trips were approved for the AIDS exhibit, Newberry says students would be accompanied by teachers and a school nurse who could clear up any perceived misinformation.

High school students should see the exhibit. And just because it's a field trip does not mean ALL students should attend. Parents who don't want their children to view such an exhibit should have the option to say no. Likewise, those parents who do should have the option to say yes.

B. *No: Amid questions about HIV virus, trustees were right to reject trip*
   (Kris Jensen of Nevada Concerned Citizens)
   Contrary to accusations, the School Board acted responsibly and wisely when it voted
   not to allow the AIDS exhibit to be a school-sponsored field trip. The five board
   members each had individual concerns which were all valid reasons as to why they
   would not endorse the AIDS exhibit and send busloads of school children to the
   museum.

   Nevada Concerned Citizens had attended meetings and had fully reviewed the
   materials (all 65 pages), when finally provided in the School Board back-up material.
   Within the panels on display in the exhibit is a statement that we found to be untruthful
   and were concerned about given the fact that they were seeking permission for Clark
   County School District students to view this display on school time.

   It reads: *"HIV is spread only by sexual intercourse, contact with blood or from a
   pregnant mother to her unborn child. By not sharing needles and not having sexual
   intercourse without a condom, we can protect ourselves from infection with HIV."*
   This is a blatant lie. Risk may be reduced, but there is no 100 percent assurance that
   we will be protected from infection by using a condom. What would happen when the
   first student who read and believed that statement contracted AIDS?

   After we read this statement, we raised the concern to the School Board that this is
   inaccurate information and that we need to be totally honest with the students. There is
   no room for error in contracting AIDS, it is 100 percent fatal. We must be completely
   straight and say that the *only safe* way for protection from infection is abstinence. Other
   methods may reduce risk, but don't tell people that they are protected and imply they are
   safe.

   Perhaps the fact that 230 million AIDS viruses can fit on the head of a pin and
   certain condoms allow passage should tell us that there is no fail-safe way to protect
   ourselves from infection with HIV other than abstinence.

   Condoms leak. Perhaps the fact that dentists double and even triple glove when
   dealing with AIDS patients, and their actions are nowhere near as risky, should send us a
   message. So don't lead Clark County school kids down the primrose path with a false
   assurance.

   Former Secretary of Education William Bennet stated: ". . . 'safe sex' or even 'safer
   sex' was no way to prevent AIDS, that people had to re-learn the value of traditional
   morality or play a dangerous game."

   Dr. Theresa Cranshaw, former member of the Presidential AIDS Commission, said:
   "Saying that the use of condoms is 'safe sex' is in fact playing Russian roulette. A lot of
   people will die in this dangerous game."

   What about the three women out of 18 who contracted AIDS from their husbands
   while using condoms during intercourse in Dr. Margaret Fischl's extensive study (that's
   a 17 percent failure rate)!

   Best yet, there's the report how an Australian man's sperm, frozen for months at
   temperatures that would kill other viruses, infected four of the eight women
   impregnated.

   The point is that the jury is still out as to the "only" methods of transmission of

AIDS. Why would we put children at greater risk by telling them half-truths and giving them false assurances?

We commend the five School Board members who had a concern with misinformation that could cost a student his/her life and voted not to lend their endorsement. We encourage them to hold firm for the protection of Clark County school children.

Furthermore, we challenge the Lied Discovery Children's Museum and the National Aids Exhibit Consortium to give their patrons honest and accurate information. Don't ask the School Board to endorse false statements and contradictory information. Do not risk lives by spreading inaccurate information that could have deadly results.

Cartoon Writing Lesson E

For each cartoon below there is a sentence that can be understood as a causal claim. Argue either for or against that causal claim, based on what you see in the cartoon and your general knowledge. Check that the necessary conditions for cause and effect are satisfied and that you have not made any of the common mistakes in reasoning about cause and effect. Compare Example 1 of Chapter 15, p. 310.

1.

The falling apple knocked Dick unconscious.

2.

The wasps chased Professor Zzzyzzx because he hit their nest.

3.

Dick got burned because he put too much lighter fluid on the barbecue.

4.

Suzy failed because she stayed up late dancing.

5.

Dick crashed because of the turtle.

6.

Dick had to hitchhike because he didn't get gas.

Review Chapters 12–15

In Chapters 1–5 we established the fundamentals of critical thinking. In Chapters 6–8 we looked at the structure of arguments. In Chapters 9–11 we considered ways that people make bad arguments. In this section we looked at particular ways to reason from experience.

Generally, when we reason from experience we cannot get certainty. Judging arguments is more often weighing up the possibilities.

Analogies are common: We note similarities and draw conclusions. Often that's all that's done, and then an analogy is more a suggestion for discussion than an argument. To take an analogy seriously as an argument, the similarities have to be spelled out clearly and a general principle drawing the conclusion from those similarities is needed.

Analogies lead to generalizations. We generalize when we start with a claim about some and conclude a claim about more. Generalizations often involve numbers, and we looked at a few common problems when using numbers in arguments. Then we saw that though we don't always know the details of how a generalization was made, we can often judge whether the generalization is good by reflecting on whether the sample is big enough, whether the sample is representative, and whether the sample is studied well.

How big the sample needs to be and whether it is representative both depend on the variation in the population. When there is a lot of variation, random sampling—not to be confused with haphazard sampling—is the best way to get a representative sample. With polls and surveys an estimate of the likelihood of the conclusion being right and the margin of error should be given.

Analogies and generalizations play a role in perhaps the most important kind of reasoning we do every day, figuring out cause and effect. We can set out necessary conditions for there to be cause and effect. And we can survey some of the common mistakes made when reasoning about cause and effect. The most pernicious is *post hoc ergo propter hoc* reasoning (after this, therefore because of this). Often the best we can say with our limited knowledge is that it's a coincidence.

When we reason about cause and effect in populations with large variation, it's hard, if not impossible, to specify the normal conditions. Typically a statistical causal link is established. Considering the three main kinds of experiments used for those arguments, we can see that, as with generalizations, a little common sense allows us to make judgments about the truth of the conclusion.

Review Exercises for Chapters 12–15

1. What is an argument?

2. What three tests must an argument pass to be good?

3. What is the difference between a valid argument and a strong argument?

4. Is every valid or strong argument with true premises good? Explain.

5. What is reasoning by analogy?

6. What are the steps in evaluating an analogy?

7. Define, for a collection of numbers:
   a. The average.
   b. The mean.
   c. The median.
   d. The mode.

8. What is a "two times zero is still zero" claim? Give an example.

9. a. What is a generalization?
   b. What do we call the group being generalized from?
   c. What do we call the group being generalized to?

10. What is a representative sample?

11. Is every randomly chosen sample representative? Explain.

12. Is it ever possible to make a good generalization from a sample of just one? Give an explanation or example.

13. A poll says that the incumbent is preferred by 42% of the voters with a margin of error of 3% and confidence level of 97%. What does that mean?

14. What three premises are needed for a good generalization?

15. What do we call a weak generalization from a sample that is obviously too small?

16. List the necessary conditions for there to be cause and effect.

17. Why is a perfect correlation not enough to establish cause and effect? Give an example.

18. List two common mistakes in reasoning about causes and give an example of each.

19. List the three common types of experiments used to establish cause in populations and give an example of each.

20. Why is it better to reason well with someone even if you could convince him or her with bad arguments?

21. a. What did you find most valuable in this course?
    b. What did you find least valuable in this course?
    c. Would you recommend this course to a friend? Why?

Evaluating Reasoning

Here is a summary of all the methods of evaluating reasoning we have studied.

Arguments

1. Read the entire passage and decide if there's an argument. If so, identify the conclusion, then number every sentence or clause that might be a claim.

2. For each numbered part, decide:
   a. Is it too vague or ambiguous to be a claim?
   b. If it's vague, could we clear that up by looking at the rest of the argument? Are the words implicitly defined?
   c. If it's too vague, scratch it out as noise.
   d. If it uses slanters, reword it neutrally.

3. Identify the claims that lead directly to the conclusion.

4. Identify any subarguments that are meant to support the claims that lead directly to the conclusion.

5. See if the obvious objections have been considered.
   a. List ones that occur to you as you read the passage.
   b. See if they have been answered.

6. Note which claims in the argument are unsupported, and evaluate whether they are plausible.

7. Evaluate each subargument as either valid or on the strong–weak scale.
   a. Note if the subargument is a valid type or one of the fallacies we've seen.
   b. If it is not valid or strong, can it be repaired?
   c. If it can be repaired, do so and evaluate any added premises.

8. Evaluate the entire argument as either valid or on the strong–weak scale.
   a. Note if the argument is a valid type or one of the fallacies we've seen.
   b. If it is not valid or strong, can it be repaired?
   c. If it can be repaired, do so and evaluate any added premises.

9. Decide whether the argument is good.

Analogies

1. Is this an argument? What is the conclusion?
2. What is the comparison?
3. What are the premises (one or both sides of the comparison)?
4. What are the similarities?
5. Can we state the similarities as premises and find a general principle that covers the two sides?
6. Does the general principle really apply to both sides?
   Do the differences matter?
7. Evaluate the entire argument using the procedure for arguments.

Generalizing

1. Is this an argument? What is the conclusion?
2. Identify the sample and the population.
3. Are the three premises for a generalization plausible?
   a. The sample is representative.
   b. The sample is big enough.
   c. The sample is studied well.
4. Evaluate the generalization using the procedure for arguments.

Cause and Effect

1. Identify what appears to be the causal claim.
   If it is not too vague, describe each of the cause and effect with a claim.
2. Decide whether the purported cause and effect happened (the claims are true).
3. Decide whether the purported cause precedes the effect.
4. Evaluate whether it is (nearly) impossible for the claim describing the cause to be true and the claim describing the effect to be false, relative to normal conditions that you could provide.
5. Decide whether the cause makes a difference: If there were no cause, would the effect still have happened?
6. Decide whether there is a common cause.
7. Make sure that none of the obvious mistakes are made:
   a. Cause and effect are not reversed.
   b. It's not *post hoc ergo propter hoc*.
   d. It's not tracing the cause too far back.
8. Decide whether you can conclude that there's a cause and effect relationship.

Cause in Populations

1. Identify the kind of experiment that is used to support the conclusion: controlled or uncontrolled; cause to effect, or effect to cause.
2. Decide whether you should accept the results of the experiment.
   a. Was it conducted well?
      (Use the methods for evaluating generalizations.)
   b. Does it really support the conclusion?
      (Use the steps for evaluating arguments and cause and effect.)
3. Decide whether the argument is good.

Composing
Good Arguments

By now you've learned a lot about how to compose an argument. Here is a summary of some of the main points.

- *If you don't have an argument, literary style won't salvage your essay.*

- *If the issue is vague, use definitions or rewrite the issue to make a precise claim to deliberate.*

- *Don't make a clear issue vague by appealing to some common but meaningless phrase, such as "This is a free country."*

- *Beware of questions used as claims. The reader might not answer them the way you do.*

- *Your premises must be highly plausible, and there must be glue, something that connects the premises to the conclusion. Your argument must be impervious to the questions: So? Why?*

- *Don't claim more than you actually prove.*

- *There is often a trade-off: You can make your argument valid or strong, but perhaps only at the expense of a rather dubious premise. Or you can make all your premises clearly true, but leave out the dubious premise that is needed to make the argument valid or strong. Given the choice, opt for making the argument valid or strong. If it's weak, no one should accept the conclusion. And if it's weak because of an unstated premise, it is better to have that premise stated explicitly so it can be the object of debate.*

- *Your reader should be able to follow how your argument is put together. Indicator words are essential.*

- *Your argument won't get any better by weaseling with "I believe that" or "I feel that." Your reader probably won't care about your feelings, and they won't establish the truth of your conclusion.*

- *Your argument should be able to withstand the obvious counter-arguments. It's wise to consider them in your essay.*

- *For some issues, the best argument may be one which concludes that we should suspend judgment.*

- *Slanters turn off those you might want to convince—you're preaching to the converted. Fallacies just convince the careful reader that you're dumb or intending to mislead.*

- *If you can't spell, if you can't write complete sentences, if you leave words out, then you can't convince anyone. All the reader's effort will be spent trying to decipher what you intended to say.*

You should be able to distinguish a good argument from a bad one. Use the critical abilities you have developed to read your own work. Learn to stand outside your work and judge it, as you would an exercise in this text.

If you reason calmly and rationally you will earn the respect of others, and may learn that others merit your respect, too.

Cartoon Writing Lesson F

For each of the following write the best argument you can that has as its conclusion the claim that accompanies the cartoon. List only the premises and conclusion. If you believe the best argument is only weak, explain why.

1.

Manuel is angry.

2.

Lee is allergic to bee stings.

3.

Professor Zzzyzzx is trying to lose weight.

4.

Harry's rabbit was pregnant.

5.

Dr. E grew a beard.

6.

A. The man at the car in the parking lot is the person who ran over the bicycle.

B. The man in the car knew he ran over the bicycle and purposely didn't stop.

Writing Lesson 12

Let's see how much you've learned in this course. Write an argument for or against the following.

Student athletes should be given special leniency when the instructor assigns course marks.

Making Decisions

The skills you've learned in this course can help you make better decisions.

Making a decision is making a choice. You have options. When making a decision you can start as you would on a writing exercise: Make a list for and against the choice—all the pros and cons you can think of. Make the best argument for each side. Then your decision should be easy: Choose the option for which there is the best argument. Making decisions is no more than being very careful in constructing arguments for your choices.

But there may be more than two choices. Your first step should be to list all the options and give an argument that these really are the only options, and not a false dilemma.

Suppose you do all that, and you still feel there's something wrong. You see that the best argument is for the option you feel isn't right. You have a gut reaction that it's the wrong decision. Then you're missing something. Don't be irrational. You know that when confronted with an argument that appears good yet whose conclusion seems false, you must show that the argument is weak or a premise is implausible. Go back to your pro and con lists.

Now at the end of this course your reasoning has been sharpened, you can understand more, you can avoid being duped. And, I hope, you will reason well with those you love and work with and need to convince. And you can make better decisions. But whether you will do so depends not just on method, not just on the tools of reasoning, but on your goals, your ends. And that depends on virtue.

Exercises on Making Decisions

1. Decide whether you should cook dinner at home tonight.

2. Decide whether and what kind of dog you should get.

3. Decide whether you should buy a car during this next year.

4. Decide whether you should recommend this course to a friend.

5. If you don't have a job, decide whether you should get one next semester.
   If you have a job, decide whether you should quit.

6. Decide what career you should have.

7. If you're not married, decide whether you should ever get married.
   If you are married, decide whether you should get divorced.

8. If you have children, decide whether you should have more.
   If you don't have children, decide whether you ever should.

9. If you're doing drugs, decide whether you should stop.

10. If you have slept with your friend's lover, decide whether you should tell your friend.

11. Decide whether you should be honest for the rest of your life.

12. Decide whether you should believe in God.

13. Decide whether you should keep this book or sell it back at the end of the term.

Key Words   virtue
                   the love of wisdom

APPENDICES

Using Examples in Reasoning

A. Examples for Definitions and Methods

When I defined "valid argument" in Chapter 3, I gave an example of a valid argument. So there really are such things. Then I showed that not every argument is valid by giving another example. So the definition wasn't vacuous: Some arguments fit the definition, some don't.

Then I gave examples so you could see the difference between valid arguments and similar notions, such as strong arguments and good arguments.

We need examples when we make definitions in order to be sure we've got the right definition. Compare the attempt to define "school cafeteria" on p. 30.

We need examples with definitions to:

• Show that something fits the definition.

• Show that not everything fits the definition.

• Show the difference between the definition and other notions we already know.

The first two points are essential when the term we're defining, like "school cafeteria," is one we supposedly all understand. We want to be sure the definition fits our usual way of talking. Getting definitions of ordinary words is very important in insurance policies and courts of law.

On the other hand, suppose we want to make a vague term precise:

A *classic car* is one that was built before 1959 and is in mint condition.

So a 1956 Chevy Bel Air in mint condition would be a classic car. A 1965 Corvette in perfect condition would not be a classic car by this definition, even if some people might call it one. And a classic car might not be an *antique,* for no car built in the

50s would normally count as an antique. Nor would a 1932 Ford in lousy condition, which is an antique, be called a classic car.

I've shown that there are classic cars that aren't antiques, and antiques that aren't classic cars. That is, I showed that neither definition included the other.

Note what I did after listing the three reasons for using examples with definitions above: I showed how to use the method. I showed that the method made sense and gave you an idea how to use it *by giving an example.* Whenever I've introduced a new method in this book, I've given you an example of how to use it.

B. Showing a General Claim is False

> Dick: All dogs hate cats.
> Zoe: No way. Remember Zelda on Elm Street when we were growing up? She had a dog and cat that got along fine.

Zoe has shown that Dick's general claim is false by providing an example.

> Harry: No car built before 1992 had an airbag.
> Tom: That's not right. My buddy's 1991 Volvo has an airbag.

Tom's example shows that Harry's general claim is false.

> Suzy: Almost all students at this university live on campus.
> Harry: No they don't. I know lots of guys who go to night classes who don't.
> Suzy: Well, anyway, all my friends live on campus.

For Harry to show that Suzy's "almost all" claim is false he has to give not one, but a lot of examples.

People often generalize badly, too quickly from too few examples. You can bring them back to earth with well-chosen examples.

C. Showing an Argument is Not Valid

How do we show an argument is invalid? Consider:

> Dick is a bachelor.
> Therefore, Dick was never married.

We could say, no, that's not valid because Dick could be divorced, and we call a divorced man a bachelor. That's giving an example of a *possible* case where the premises are true and the conclusion false.

Or we could say the argument's not valid because I know someone, Ralph, who's a bachelor and he was married. And his name could have been "Dick." That's giving an *actual* example (with the names changed).

When we want to show an argument is not valid we give a possible or actual example in which the premises are true and the conclusion false.

We do the same when we want to show that an argument is not strong.

> Zoe and Dick have each gone out for the day. Dick returns, sees that Zoe is gone, and finds that there's a roast cooking in the oven. So (he thinks) Zoe has started dinner.

Viewing the first three sentences as premises, we can say that Dick's argument is not valid: A burglar might have broken in and left a roast in the oven. That's extremely unlikely, but it will do to show that the argument isn't valid.

But is the argument strong? Well, Dick's friend Jose has been visiting for a week, and maybe he decided to help out and started dinner. That's an example of a possibility that isn't so unlikely. So we conclude the argument is weak. That's how we show an argument is weak: We look for one or more (possible) examples that aren't unlikely where the premises are true and the conclusion false.

Summary   We've reviewed some of the ways we can use examples in reasoning:

- To make sure we've given a good definition and to clarify how to use the definition.
- To show how to use a new method.
- To show that a general claim is false.
- To show that an argument is not valid.
- To show that an argument is weak.

You should get good at using examples, because theory without examples isn't understood—it's unusable, and sometimes just plain wrong.

Exercises on Examples

1. Detail how examples were used in making the definition of "argument" in Chapter 1 (look at the three reasons for using examples with definitions).

2. Define "professional athlete." Use examples to contrast professional athletes with college athletes who receive scholarships, and amateur athletes, who are supported by governments to participate in the Olympics.

3. Define "student financial aid" and use examples to make your definition clear.

4. Detail how examples were used in Chapter 4 to show how to use the Guide to Repairing Arguments.

5. Show that the following are false or at least dubious:
   a. All dogs bark.
   b. All sheep are raised for meat.
   c. Nearly everyone who is at this college is on financial aid.
   d. No teacher at this school gives good lectures.
   e. No fast-food restaurant serves healthy food.

For each argument below, if it is meant to be valid but is invalid, give an example to show that. If it's meant to be strong but it's weak, give enough examples to show that. If the argument is valid but not good, give an example to show why.

6. All good teachers give fair exams. Professor Zzzyzzx gives fair exams. So Professor Zzzyzzx is a good teacher.

7. If this course were easy, the exams would be fair. The exams are fair. So this course is easy.

8. President Clinton didn't inhale marijuana. So President Clinton never got high from marijuana.

9. Almost all teachers at this school speak English as their first language. So the mathematics professor you're going to have for calculus next semester speaks English as his or her first language.

10. Professor Zzzyzzx was late for class. He's never been late for class before. He's always conscientious in all his duties. So he must have been in an accident.

11. Dick: I'm telling you I'm not at fault. How could I be? She hit me from the rear. Anytime you get rear-ended it's not your fault.

Truth-Tables

A. Symbols and Truth-Tables

The ancient Greek philosophers were the first to analyze arguments using compound claims. From then until the mid-19th century the analysis of compound claims wasn't much different from what you saw in Chapter 6, though many more valid and invalid argument forms had been catalogued, with Latin names attached.

In the early 1900s a simple method was devised for checking whether an argument form using compound claims is valid. Using it we can easily justify the validity and invalidity of the argument forms we studied in Chapter 6.

We can analyze many arguments using compound claims by concentrating on how compound claims can be built up from just four English words or phrases:

>   and,   or,   not,   if . . . then . . .

These words are used in many different ways in English, too many for us to investigate every possible way they could be used in arguments. We will concentrate on just one aspect of them: *How compound claims that use them depend on the truth or falsity* (truth-value) *of the claims from which they are built*. We won't care how plausible a claim is, or how we might happen to know it, or its subject matter, or any other aspect of it. We make the following assumption.

> **The classical abstraction** The only aspects of a claim we'll pay attention to are whether the claim is true or false, and how it is compounded from other claims.

So long as the argument we are analyzing makes sense in terms of this assumption, the methods we develop here will allow us to check for validity. To remind us that we're making this assumption, we're going to use special symbols to represent the words we're interested in.

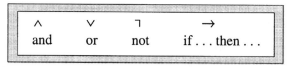

∧	∨	⌐	→
and	or	not	if . . . then . . .

Now we can be precise about how we will understand these words in arguments, relative to the classical abstraction. Let's start with "and".

Spot is a dog and Puff is a cat.

When is this true? When both "Spot is a dog" is true and "Puff is a cat" is true. That's the only way it can be true. Let's summarize that in a table, where A and B stand for any claims:

A	B	A∧ B
T	T	T
T	F	F
F	T	F
F	F	F

> A *conjunction* (∧-claim) is true (T) when both parts are true. Otherwise it is false (F).

Now we'll look at "not".

Spot is not a dog.

This is true if "Spot is a dog" is false, and false if "Spot is a dog" is true. That's simple to formalize:

A	⌐A
T	F
F	T

> A *negation* (⌐-claim) is true if its part is false; it is false if its part is true.

How about "or"?

London is the capital of England or Paris is the capital of France.

Is this true? There's going to be disagreement. Some say it isn't, because "London is the capital of England" and "Paris is the capital of France" are both true. Others say the compound is true. The question is whether an "or" claim can be true if both parts are true.

It turns out to be simplest to use ∨ to formalize "or" in the *inclusive* sense: One or the other or both parts are true. Later we'll see how to formalize "or" in the *exclusive* sense: One or the other but not both parts are true.

A	B	A ∨ B
T	T	T
T	F	T
F	T	T
F	F	F

> A *disjunction* (∨ -claim) is false if both parts are false. Otherwise it is true.

Finally, we have "if . . . then . . .". These words have so many connotations and uses in English that it's hard to remember that we're going to pay attention only to whether the parts of the compound claim are true or false. The following table is the one that's best:

A	B	A → B
T	T	T
T	F	F
F	T	T
F	F	T

> A *conditional* (→ -claim) is false if the antecedent is true and consequent false. Otherwise it is true.

Why do we choose this table? Let's look at it row by row.

We said the direct way of reasoning with conditionals is valid:

If A then B,   A,   so B.

So if A→B is true, and A is true, then B is true (*the first row*).

Suppose A is true and B is false (*the second row*). In a valid form we can't get a false conclusion (B) from true premises. Since there are only two premises, it must be that A→B is false.

But why should A→B be true in the last two rows? Suppose Dr. E says to Suzy,

If you get 90% on the final exam, you'll pass this course.

It's the end of the term. Suzy gets 58% on the final. Dr. E fails her. Can we say that Dr. E lied? No. So the claim is still true, even though the antecedent is false and the consequent is false (*the fourth row*).

But suppose Dr. E relents and passes Suzy anyway. Can we say he lied? No, for he said "if", not "only if". So the claim is still true, even though the antecedent is false and the consequent is true (*the third row*).

The formalization of "if . . . then . . ." in this table is the best we can do when we adopt the classical abstraction. We deal with cases where the antecedent "does not apply" by treating the claim as vacuously true.

B. The Truth-Value of a Compound Claim

With these tables to interpret "and", "or", "not", and "if . . . then . . ." we can calculate the truth-value of a compound claim fairly easily. For example,

> If Dick goes to the movies and Zoe visits her mother, then no one will walk Spot tonight.

We can formalize this as:

> (Dick goes to the movies ∧ Zoe visits her mother) →
> no one will walk Spot tonight

I had to use parentheses to mark off the antecedent. They do the work that commas should do in ordinary English.

When is this claim true? Let's look at the form of it:

> $(A \wedge B) \rightarrow C$

We don't know which of A, B, and C are true and which are false. We have to look at all possibilities to decide when the compound claim is true. We can construct a table:

A	B	C	A∧B	(A∧B)→C
T	T	T	T	T
T	T	F	T	F
T	F	T	F	T
T	F	F	F	T
F	T	T	F	T
F	T	F	F	T
F	F	T	F	T
F	F	F	F	T

In the table we first list all possible values for A, B, and C. Then we calculate the value of A∧B. With the truth-value of A∧B we can use the truth-value of C (to its left in the table) to calculate the truth-value of (A∧B)→C.

We can see now that the original claim can be false only if both "Dick goes to the movies" is true, and "Zoe visits her mother" is true, and "No one will walk Spot tonight" is false. For example, if Dick doesn't go to the movies (A is F) and Zoe doesn't visit her mother (B is F), then the whole claim is true—the antecedent of (A∧B)→C is false, so the claim is vacuously true.

Perhaps you could have figured out when this claim was true without using a table. But it's equally routine to analyze a complex claim with the complicated form (¬(A∧B)∨C) → (¬B∨(C∧¬A)).

Some compound claims are true for every way that their parts are true or false. For example:

Ralph is a dog or Ralph isn't a dog.
A ∨ ⅂A

A	⅂A	A ∨ ⅂A
T	F	T
F	T	T

It doesn't matter whether A is true or false. Any claim with the form A ∨ ⅂A is true.

> **Tautology**   A compound claim is a tautology if it is true for every possible assignment of truth-values to its parts.

The form (A ∨ B) → (B ∨ A) is a tautology, which reflects that the order of the parts of an "or" claim doesn't matter.

A	B	A ∨ B	B ∨ A	(A ∨ B) → (B ∨ A)
T	T	T	T	T
T	F	T	T	T
F	T	T	T	T
F	F	F	F	T

> A claim is a tautology if in the table for its form
> *the last column of the table has only* T.

Using tables we can also verify the equivalences of informal claims we noted in Chapter 6. Recall that two claims are equivalent if they are both true or both false in every possible circumstance.

A → B   is equivalent to   ⅂B → ⅂A   *contrapositive*

⅂(A → B) is equivalent to   A ∧ ⅂B   *the contradictory of a conditional*

⅂A ∨ B   is equivalent to   A → B   *conditional form of an "or" claim*

For example, no matter what truth-values A and B have, A → B is going to have the same truth-value as ⅂B → ⅂A. They have the same tables:

A	B	A → B	⅂B	⅂A	⅂B → ⅂A
T	T	T	F	F	T
T	F	F	T	F	F
F	T	T	F	T	T
F	F	T	T	T	T

Exercises for Sections A and B

1. What are the four fundamental English words or phrases that we will analyze in studying compound claims?

2. What is the first big assumption about claims we made when we decided to use the symbols ∧, ∨, ⌐, → ?

3. What is a tautology?

4. What is the method for checking whether a claim is a tautology?

5. Explain the method for checking whether two forms of claims are equivalent.

Here's an example of a method Tom devised to check whether a claim is a tautology. It's a little long-winded, but it made it clear to him.

Decide whether $(A \wedge B) \to \lnot(A \vee B)$ **is a tautology.**

A	B		A	∧	B		⌐	(A	∨	B)		(A∧B)	→	⌐(A∨B)
T	T		T	T	T		F	T	T	T		T	F	F
T	F		T	F	F		F	T	T	F		F	T	F
F	T		F	F	T		F	F	T	T		F	T	F
F	F		F	F	F		T	F	F	F		F	T	T
1	2		3	4	5		6	7	8	9		10	11	12

Columns 1 and 2 are all the possible combinations of truth-values of the claims.
Columns 3 and 5 are just 1 and 2 repeated to see how to get column 4
    (the table for A∧B).
Columns 7 and 9 are just 1 and 2 repeated so as to see how to get column 8
    (the table for A∨B).
Then column 6 is the table for ⌐ applied to column 8, which gives the table
    for ⌐(A∨B).
Column 10 is just column 4 repeated. And column 12 is just column 6 again.
    That lets us see how to get column 11 using the table for →.
Column 11 gives the truth-values for (A∧B)→⌐(A∨B). Since there's an F in
that column, this isn't the form of a tautology.

Use truth-tables to show that the following are tautologies:

6. ⌐⌐A → A

7. ⌐(A∧⌐A)

8. ((A→B) ∧ (⌐A→B)) → B

9. ⌐(A∧B) → (⌐A∨⌐B)

Decide whether the following are tautologies using truth-tables. Then explain your answer in your own words.

10. A → (A∨B)

11. ((A∨B) ∧ ¬B) → A

12. (A∨B) → (A∧B)

13. ((A→B) ∧ ¬B) → ¬A

14. (¬(A∧B) ∧ ¬A) → B

15. ((A→B) ∧ (¬A→C)) → (B∨C)

Using truth-tables, show that the following are equivalent.

16. ¬(A→B) is equivalent to A∧¬B

17. A→B   is equivalent to ¬A∨B

18. ¬(A∧B) is equivalent to ¬A∨¬B

19. ¬(A∨B) is equivalent to ¬A∧¬B

C. Representing Claims

To use truth-tables we have to be able to represent ordinary claims and arguments.

Examples Can the following be represented in a form that uses ¬, →, ∧, ∨ ?

Example 1 Spot is a dog or Puff is a cat and Zoe is not a student.
Analysis What's the form of this? (A∨B)∧¬C ? or A∨(B∧¬C) ? Without a context, we have to guess. We analyze the argument on one reading, then on the other, and see which is better. Our formal analyses help us see ambiguities.

Example 2 Puff is a cat or someone got swindled at the pet store.
Analysis This one's easy: Puff is a cat ∨ someone got swindled at the pet store.

Example 3 London is in England or Paris is in France.
Analysis We can represent this using *exclusive* "or":

(London is in England ∨ Paris is in France) ∧
¬(London is in England ∧ Paris is in France)

In Exercise 1 I ask you to show:

(A∨B) ∧ ¬(A∧B) is true when exactly one of A is true or B is true.

Example 4 Harry is a football player if he plays any sport at all.
Analysis We're used to rewriting conditionals. This one is:

If Harry plays any sport at all, then Harry is a football player.

Harry plays any sport at all → Harry is a football player

Example 5   Zoe loves Dick although he's not a football player.

Analysis   This is a compound claim, with parts "Zoe loves Dick" and "Dick is not a football player." But "although" isn't one of the words we're formalizing.

When is this compound claim true? If we stick to the classical abstraction, then "although" doesn't do anything more than "and." It shows that the second part is perhaps surprising, but that isn't what we're paying attention to. We can formalize the claim as:

Zoe loves Dick ∧ Dick is not a football player

If all we're interested in is whether the argument in which this appears is valid, this representation will do.

There are a lot of words or phrases that can sometimes be represented with ∧:

and	even if	even though
but	although	despite that

Sometimes, though, these serve as indicator words, suggesting the roles of the claims in the overall structure of the argument. "Even though" can indicate that the claim is going to be used as part of a counterargument. We can represent these words or phrases with ∧, or we can just represent the parts of the sentence as separate claims. That's what we did in Chapter 6, and we can do that because the table for ∧ says that the compound will be true exactly when both parts are true.

Example 6   Spot thinks that Dick is his master because Zoe doesn't take him for walks.

Analysis   Can we represent "because" using ∧, ∨, ⌐, →? Consider the following two claims:

Spot is a dog because Las Vegas is in the desert.

Spot is a dog because Las Vegas is not in the desert.

Both of these are false. Spot is a dog, and that's true whether Las Vegas is or is not in the desert. The truth-value of "Las Vegas is in the desert" is irrelevant to the truth-value of the whole compound. Yet all we've got to work with in representing "because" are compounds that depend on whether the parts are true or false. We can't represent this example as a compound claim.

Example 7   Zoe took off her clothes and went to bed.

Analysis   We shouldn't represent this compound as:

Zoe took off her clothes ∧ Zoe went to bed

That has the same truth-value as:

Zoe went to bed ∧ Zoe took off her clothes

Example 7 is true most nights, but "Zoe went to bed and took off her clothes" is false. In this example "and" has the meaning "and then next," so that *when* the claims become true is important. But if we use these symbols we can only consider whether the claims are true, not when they become true. So we can't represent this claim.

Example 8   (On the playground): Hit me and I'll hit you.

Analysis   We don't represent this as: You hit me ∧ I hit you. The example is a conditional, and we represent it as:

> You hit me → I hit you

> We can't blindly represent every use of "and", "or", "not", and "if . . . then . . ." as ∧, ∨, ⌐, →. We have to ask what the words mean in the way they're used. Does the use accord with the classical abstraction?

Exercises for Section C

1. Make up the table for (A∨B) ∧ ⌐(A∧B) and show that it is true when exactly one of A, B is true.

For each of the following, either represent it using ∧, ∨, ⌐, →, or explain why it can't be represented.

2. If critical thinking is hard, then mathematics is impossible.

3. If you don't apologize, I'll never talk to you again.

4. Dick prefers steak, while Zoe prefers spaghetti.

5. Dick was shaving while Zoe was preparing dinner.

6. Either Dick loves Zoe best, or he loves Spot best.

7. Even if you do whine all the time, I love you.

8. Spot is a good dog even though he scared the living bejabbers out of your cat.

9. Spot is a good dog because he scared the living bejabbers out of your cat.

10. We're going to go to the movies or go out for dinner tonight.

11. Since 2 + 2 is 4, and 4 times 2 is 8, I should be ahead $8, not $7, in blackjack.

12. If Dick has a class and Zoe is working, there's no point in calling their home to ask them over for dinner.

13. If it's really true that if Dick takes Spot for a walk he'll do the dishes, then Dick won't take Spot for a walk.

14. If Dick goes to the basketball game, then he either got a free ticket or he borrowed money from somebody.

15. Either we'll go to the movies or visit your mom if I get home from work by 6.

16. Whenever Spot barks like that, there's a skunk or raccoon in the yard.

17. I'm not going to visit your mother and I'm not going to do the dishes, regardless of whether you get mad at me or try to cajole me.

18. Every student in Dr. E's class is over 18 or is taking the course while in high school.

19. No matter whether the movie gets out early or late, we're going to go out for pizza.

20. Suggest ways to represent:

a.	A only if B	d.	A if and only if B
b.	A unless B	e.	B just in case A
c.	When A, B	f.	Neither A nor B

D. Checking for Validity

An argument is valid if for every possible way the premises could be true, the conclusion is true, too. So suppose we have an argument of the form:

$A \rightarrow B$, $\neg A \rightarrow B$, So B.

For an argument of this form to be valid, it has to be impossible that $A \rightarrow B$ and $\neg A \rightarrow B$ are both true, and B is false. We need to look at all ways that $A \rightarrow B$ and $\neg A \rightarrow B$ could be true:

A	B	$A \rightarrow B$	$\neg A$	$\neg A \rightarrow B$
T	T	T	F	T
T	F	F	F	T
F	T	T	T	T
F	F	T	T	F

We list all the values of A and B. Then we calculate the truth-values of $A \rightarrow B$ and $\neg A \rightarrow B$. In the first row both of those are true, and so is the conclusion, B. Ditto for the third row. In the second row $A \rightarrow B$ is false, and we don't care about that. In the last row $\neg A \rightarrow B$ is false, and we can ignore that. So whenever both $A \rightarrow B$ and $\neg A \rightarrow B$ are true, so is B. Any argument of this form is valid.

> *Valid argument form*   An argument form is valid if every argument of that form is valid.
>
> We can show that an argument form is valid by making a table that includes all the premises and the conclusion. If in every row in which all the premises are true, the conclusion is true, too, then the form is valid.

Let's look at the indirect way of reasoning with conditionals:

$$A \rightarrow B, \ \neg B$$
$$\overline{\qquad \neg A \qquad}$$

I've drawn a line to indicate the conclusion, rather than write "so" or "therefore."

Again, we have to look at every way the premises could be true.

A	B	A→B	¬B	¬A
T	T	T	F	F
T	F	F	T	F
F	T	T	F	T
F	F	T	T	T

Only in the last row are both premises A→B and ¬B true. There we find that ¬A is true, too. So every argument of this form is valid.

The third row of this table also shows that, in contrast, denying the antecedent is invalid:

$$A \rightarrow B, \ \neg A$$
$$\overline{\qquad \neg B \qquad}$$

Both A→B and ¬A are true, but ¬B is false. It is possible to have the premises true and the conclusion false.

Reasoning in a chain provides a more complicated example:

$$A \rightarrow B, \ B \rightarrow C$$
$$\overline{\qquad A \rightarrow C \qquad}$$

We have the table:

A	B	C	A→B	B→C	A→C
T	T	T	T	T	T
T	T	F	T	F	F
T	F	T	F	T	T
T	F	F	F	T	F
F	T	T	T	T	T
F	T	F	T	F	T
F	F	T	T	T	T
F	F	F	T	T	T

I've circled the rows in which both premises are true. In each of them the conclusion is also true. So every argument of this form is valid.

This last table also shows that the following form isn't valid:

$$\frac{A \rightarrow B, \ A \rightarrow C}{B \rightarrow C}$$

The third row from the bottom has both $A \rightarrow B$ and $A \rightarrow C$ true, with $B \rightarrow C$ false.

So far this has been just a game, playing with symbols. It's only when we can apply these tables to real arguments that we're doing critical thinking. Consider:

> If Tom knows some logic, Tom is either very bright or he studies hard.
> Tom is bright. Tom studies hard. So Tom knows some logic.

First we represent these claims. Only the first is a compound claim:

> Tom knows some logic $\rightarrow$ (Tom is very bright $\vee$ Tom studies hard)

So this argument has the form:

$$\frac{A \rightarrow (B \vee C), \ B, \ C}{A}$$

A	B	C	B∨C	A→(B∨C)
T	T	T	T	T
T	T	F	T	T
T	F	T	T	T
T	F	F	F	F
F	T	T	T	T
F	T	F	T	T
F	F	T	T	T
F	F	F	F	T

I've circled a row in which all of $A \rightarrow (B \vee C)$, B, and C are true, yet the conclusion A is false. So the argument isn't valid.

That alone does not make it a bad argument. We still have to see if it could be strong. But this argument isn't even strong: Though Tom is very bright and studies hard, and the first premise is true too, it's not at all implausible that Tom could have been majoring in art history and knows no logic at all.

You might not have needed a table to figure out this last one. But you will for some of the exercises. Have fun.

Exercises for Section D

1. What does it mean to say an argument form is valid?

2. If an argument has a form that is not valid, is it necessarily a bad argument?

Use truth-tables to decide whether the following argument forms are valid.

3. $\dfrac{A \rightarrow B, \ B}{A}$

4. $\dfrac{A \rightarrow B, \ A \rightarrow \neg B}{\neg A}$

5. $\dfrac{A, \ \neg A}{B}$

6. $\dfrac{A \vee B}{A \wedge B}$

7. $\dfrac{A \vee B, \ \neg A}{B}$

8. $\dfrac{B \vee D, \ B \rightarrow C, \ D \rightarrow E}{C \vee E}$

9. $\dfrac{A \rightarrow \neg B, \ B \wedge \neg C}{A \rightarrow C}$

10. $\dfrac{A \rightarrow \neg\neg B, \ \neg C \vee A, \ C}{B}$

Represent the arguments in the following exercises and decide whether they are valid. Use truth-tables or not as you wish.

11. If Spot is a cat, then Spot meows. Spot is not a cat. So Spot doesn't meow.

12. Either the moon is made of green cheese or $2 + 2 = 4$. But the moon is not made of green cheese. So $2 + 2 = 4$.

13. Either the moon is made of green cheese or $2 + 2 = 5$. But the moon is not made of green cheese. So $2 + 2 = 5$.

14. The students are happy if and only if no test is given. If the students are happy, the professor feels good. But if the professor feels good, he won't feel like lecturing, and if he doesn't feel like lecturing, he'll give a test. So the students aren't happy.

15. If Dick and Zoe visit his family at Christmas, then they will fly. If Dick and Zoe visit Zoe's mother at Christmas, then they will fly. But Dick and Zoe have to visit his family or her mother. So Dick and Zoe will travel by plane.

16. Tom is not from New York or Virginia. But Tom is from the East Coast. If Tom is from Syracuse, he is from New York or Virginia. So Tom is not from Syracuse.

17. The government is going to spend less on health and welfare. If the government is going to spend less on health and welfare, then either the government is going to cut the Medicare budget or the government is going to slash spending on housing. If the

government is going to cut the Medicare budget, the elderly will protest. If the government is going to slash spending on housing, then advocates of the poor will protest. So the elderly will protest or advocates of the poor will protest.

Summary   By concentrating on just whether claims are true and the structure of arguments that involve compound claims, we can devise a method for checking the validity of arguments. We introduced symbols for the words "and", "or", "not", and "if . . . then . . ." and made precise their meaning through truth-tables. We learned how to use the symbols and tables in representing claims. Then we saw how to use truth-tables to check whether the structure of an argument relative to the compound claims in it is enough to guarantee that the argument is valid.

Key Words   classical abstraction   conjunction
                 truth-table   negation
                 $\wedge$ disjunction
                 $\neg$ conditional
                 $\vee$ tautology
                 $\rightarrow$ valid argument form

Further Study   For a fuller study of the formal logic of reasoning with compound claims, see my *Propositional Logics*, also published by Wadsworth.

Aristotelian Logic

A. The Tradition

Aristotle, over 2,300 years ago in his *Prior Analytics*, focused his study on arguments built from claims of the forms:

All S are P.   No S is (are) P.

Some S is (are) P.   Some S is (are) not P.

The following argument, for example, uses only claims of these forms:

No police officers are thieves.
Some thieves are sent to prison.
So no police officers are sent to prison.

Aristotle developed a method for determining whether such an argument is valid by inspection of its *form*. From then until the early 1900s his work was the basis for most argument analysis. That tradition, called *Aristotelian logic*, was very broad, and in the Middle Ages—especially from about 1100 to 1400—it was made into a very subtle tool of analysis of reasoning.

In the late 1500s scholars became more interested in studying informal reasoning, inspired also by the work of Aristotle. They ignored the complexities of the formal logic of the medievals and were content with just the rules and forms of Aristotelian logic, rote exercises and puzzles for students. That simplified tradition of Aristotelian logic, current since about 1600, is what I'll present here. It is worth studying because many writers from that time to today have used its terminology. It also makes a contrast with modern formal logic. But it is only in the work of the medievals, which has begun to be rediscovered, translated, and discussed only in the last hundred years, that the Aristotelian tradition can offer us much in the way of a serious study of arguments in terms of their form.

B. Categorical Claims

> ***Categorical claims*** A categorical claim is one that can be rewritten as
> an equivalent claim that has one of the following *standard* forms:
>
>   All S are P.   Some S is P.   No S is P.   Some S is not P.

For example,

> All dogs are mammals.
> No nurse is a doctor.
> Some newspaper is written in Arabic.
> Some snow is not white.

Most of the claims we reason with in daily speech aren't in any of these forms.
But, Aristotelians suggest, we can rewrite many of them to show that they are
categorical. For example, using "≡" to stand for "is equivalent to", we can rewrite:

> All dogs bark. ≡ All dogs are things that bark.
> No horse eats meat. ≡ No horse is a thing that eats meat.
> Some cats eat birds. ≡ Some cat is a thing that eats birds.
> Some dogs don't chase cats. ≡ Some dog is a thing that doesn't chase cats.

Somewhat more colloquially, or at least avoiding the constant use of the phrase
"thing that," we might rewrite these as:

> All dogs are barkers.
> No horse is a meat eater.
> Some cat is a bird eater.
> Some dog is not a cat chaser.

It might seem that categorical claims are concerned only with things and
collections of things. But the following argument uses only categorical claims:

> All snow is white.
> All that is white is visible.
> So, all snow is visible.

And snow, whatever it is, isn't a thing or collection of things, like dogs or pencils.
Snow is spread out everywhere across many times and places. It is a mass, like gold
or mud, and Aristotelian logic is useful for reasoning about masses, too.

It's often difficult to rewrite claims to "show" their categorical form, and there
are no general rules for how to do so. That's because so many different kinds of
words for so many different kinds of things and substances and classes can be used

for the S or P in the forms. In this appendix we'll concentrate on words that stand for classes or collections of things in order to make the discussion easier. We'll also adopt the Aristotelian assumption that the S and P *stand for things that actually exist.* So "All dodos are flightless birds" is not a categorical claim, because there are no dodos.

Recall (Chapter 8) that "All S is not P" is equivalent to "No S is P." So claims of the form "All S are P" and "No S is P" are called ***universal*** claims. Aristotelians call claims of the form "Some S is P" and "Some S is not P" ***particular*** claims, since they are about some particular things, even if those are not picked out. In order to make their logic more applicable, they also say that claims of the form "a is P" or "a is not P" are *universal* categorical claims, where "a" stands for a name, as in:

Maria is Hispanic.
Spot is not a cat.

Claims of the form "All S are P" and "Some S is P" are called ***affirmative,*** and claims of the form "No S is P" and "Some S is not P" are called ***negative.*** So, for example, "All dogs are mammals" is a universal affirmative claim, while "No dog is a feline" is a negative universal claim. Whether a claim is universal or particular denotes its ***quantity***; whether a claim is affirmative or negative denotes its ***quality***.

In a categorical claim, the *term* (word or phrase) that replaces the letter S is called the ***subject*** of the claim. The term that replaces the letter P is called the ***predicate*** of the claim. These words are not used in the way we use them in grammar. In "All dogs are mammals" your English teacher would say that the predicate is "are mammals," while in Aristotelian logic the predicate is "mammals."

Exercises for Section B

1. What is a categorical claim?

2. What assumption about the existence of things do we make about the terms used in categorical claims?

3. What is a universal categorical claim?

4. What is a particular categorical claim?

5. What is an affirmative categorical claim?

6. What is a negative categorical claim?

7. What does the quantity of a categorical claim designate?

8. What does the quality of a categorical claim designate?

On the following two pages are some of Tom's exercises, as graded by Dr. E.

All students are employed.

Categorical? Yes. Already in standard form.

Subject: Students.

Predicate: Employed.

Quantity: Universal.

Quality: Affirmative.

Good, except that since we've decided to view all subjects and predicates as either things or collections of things, let's take the predicate here to be "employed people."

Not even one art student is enrolled in calculus.

Categorical? Yes. "No art student is enrolled in calculus."

Subject: Art students.

Predicate: Enrolled in calculus.

Quantity: Universal.

Quality: Negative.

Good, except take the predicate here to be "people enrolled in calculus" or "calculus enrollees."

Someone who likes Picasso also likes Monet.

Categorical? Yes. "Some people who like Picasso are people who like Monet."

Subject: People who like Picasso.

Predicate: People who like Monet.

Quantity: Particular.

Quality: Affirmative.

Good work.

Dr. E's students all pass.

Categorical? Yes. "All students of Dr. E pass."

Subject: Students of Dr. E.

Predicate: Pass.

Quantity: Universal.

Quality: Affirmative.

Almost. But you haven't given a categorical form for the claim. Where is "is a" or "is not a" or "are"? We need "All students of Dr. E are people who pass." Then the predicate is "people who pass."

Very few dogs chase mice.

Categorical? Yes. "No dog chases mice."

Subject: Dogs.

Predicate: Mice chasers.

Quantity: Universal.

Quality: Negative.

No. "Very few" does not mean the same as "No," which means the same as "None." Don't try to force every claim into one of these forms.

Some football players don't take steroids.

Categorical? Yes. "Some student who is a football player is not someone who takes steroids."

Subject: Students who are football players.

Predicate: People who take steroids.

Quantity: Particular.

Quality: Negative.

Almost—just delete the words "student who is a": "Some football player is not someone who takes steroids." Your claim isn't equivalent, because it could be true and the original false if a professional football player takes steroids.

Some student at this school is majoring in football or there is a student who will not get a degree.

Categorical? No. This is a compound claim, and I can't figure out how to get it into a standard form.

Subject: Students.

Predicate: Football players and people who get degrees.

Quantity: Particular.

Quality: Affirmative and negative.

I don't think this exercise is very funny, Dr. E. We football players work hard at school and sport.

You're right that if it's a compound it isn't a categorical claim. But then why did you fill in after the other parts? Were you on automatic pilot? Only categorical claims have subjects and predicates, quantity and quality.

You're also right that I should be more sensitive about the examples. In the future I'll talk about basketball players.

For each of the following answer:

Categorical? (If yes, and it is not already in one of the standard forms, rewrite it.)
Subject:
Predicate:
Quantity:
Quality:

9. All dogs are carnivores.

10. Some cat is not a carnivore.

11. Tom is a basketball player.

12. No fire truck is painted green.

13. Donkeys eat meat.

14. There is at least one chimpanzee who can communicate by sign language.

15. Every border collie likes to chase sheep.

16. No one who knows critical thinking will ever starve.

17. Nearly every college graduate is employed at a full-time job.

18. All dogs bark or Spot is not a dog.

19. There is a teacher of critical thinking at this school who gives all A's to her students.

20. Heroin addicts cannot function in a 9–5 job.

21. Some people who like pizza are vegetarians.

22. Not every canary can sing.

23. Dr. E does not have a cat.

24. If Zoe does the dishes, then Dick will take Spot for a walk.

25. Of all the teachers at his school, none is as good as Dr. E.

26. Maria has a part-time job.

27. Waiters in Las Vegas make more money than lecturers at the university there.

28. In at least one instance a professor at this school is known to have failed all the students in his class.

29. Make up five claims, three of which are categorical and two of which are not. Give them to a classmate to classify.

C. Contradictories, Contraries, and Subcontraries

Recall that two claims are ***contradictory*** if in every possible circumstance they have opposite truth-values. We say that two claims are ***contrary*** if there is no way in which they both could be true. So if two claims are contradictory, they're also contrary, but not vice-versa. For example, "All dogs bark" and "No dogs bark" are contrary (they can't both be true), but they're not contradictory: Since "dogs" must refer to some object when it's used here, they can both be false.

We say that two claims are ***subcontrary*** if there is no possible way for them both to be false. So contradictories are also subcontraries, but not vice-versa. For example, "Some dogs bark" and "Some dogs don't bark" can't both be false, since to use the term "dogs" in a categorical claim is to assume there are such things. But both of these claims could be true.

In order to discuss these relationships when they apply to pairs of categorical claims, it is traditional to name the forms with letters:

"All S are P."	**A**
"No S is P."	**E**
"Some S is P."	**I**
"Some S is not P."	**O**

From Chapter 8 we already know that "All S are P" and "Some S is not P" are contradictory. So any A claim and O claim using the same S and P are contradictory. Also "No S is P" and "Some S is P" are contradictory: any E claim and I claim using the same S and P are contradictory.

On the other hand, "All S are P" and "No S is P" are contraries (they can't both be true). And "Some S is P" and "Some S is not P" are subcontraries (they can't both be false), since to use S as a subject term there must be something that is an S.

There is a further relationship that Aristotelians noted. From "All dogs bark" we can conclude "Some dogs bark." Since using a term S as subject in a categorical claim requires that there be at least one thing that is an S, we have generally:

- If an A claim is true, the I claim using the same S and P is true.

Similarly, from "No S is P" we can conclude "Some S is not P," because "No S is P" is equivalent to "All S is not P," and the use of S comes with the assumption that there is at least one S. That is:

- If an E claim is true, the O claim using the same S and P is true.

Going the other direction works, too, except that it's falsity that's inherited:

- If an I claim is false, then the corresponding A claim is also false
- If an O claim is false, then the corresponding E claim is false.

The Aristotelians summarized these relationships by saying that A and I claims using the same subject and predicate are **subalternates**, and E and O claims using the same subject and predicate are subalternates. Here is how they diagrammed these relationships:

The Square of Opposition

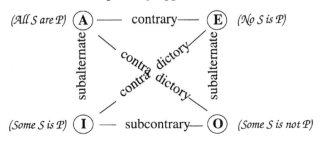

For nearly a thousand years students were expected to commit this diagram to memory. But don't bother. Even if you don't remember the definitions, it's not hard to spot that "All basketball players at this school are on scholarship" and "Some basketball player at this school is not on scholarship" are contradictory, or that "No employee of this school is enrolled in a health-care plan" and "All employees at this school are enrolled in a health-care plan" can't both be true.

Exercises for Section C

1. What is the contradictory of a claim?

2. a. What does it mean to say that two claims are contrary?
    b. Give an example of two claims that are contrary but not contradictory.

3. a. What does it mean to say that two claims are subcontrary?
    b. Give an example of two claims that are subcontrary but not contradictory.

4. a. What does it mean to say that "All dogs bark" and "Some dogs bark" are subalternate?
    b. What does it mean to say that "No cats bark" and "Some cats do not bark" are subalternate?

5. a. What is an A claim? Give an example.
    b. What is an E claim? Give an example.
    c. What is an I claim? Give an example.
    d. What is an O claim? Give an example.

6. Show that for claims that use the same subject and predicate:
    a. If the I claim is false, then the A claim is false.
    b. If the O claim is false, then the E claim is false.

For each pair of claims below state which of the following terms apply:

    contradictory   contrary   subcontrary   subalternate   none

7. All dogs bark.
    Some dogs do not bark.

8. No Russians are Communists.
    All Russians are Communists.

9. Maria is a widow.
    Maria was never married.

10. No animals with horns are carnivores.
    Some animals with horns are carnivores.

11. All uranium isotopes are highly unstable substances.
    Some uranium isotopes are highly unstable substances.

12. Some assassinations are morally justifiable.
    Some assassinations are not morally justifiable.

13. Dick and Tom are friends.
    Dick and Tom can't stand to be in the same room together.

14. Not even one zebra can be trained to jump through fire.
    Every zebra can be trained to jump through fire.

15. Homeless people don't like to sleep on the street.
    Some homeless people don't like to sleep on the street.

16. Dick almost always washes the dishes after dinner.
    Dick almost never washes the dishes after dinner.

17. Very few cats will willingly take a bath.
    Very few cats won't willingly take a bath.

D. Syllogisms

We said that the arguments for which Aristotelian logic was devised contain only categorical claims. Many of those can be reduced to arguments of a special kind.

> *Categorical syllogism*   A categorical syllogism is an argument composed of three categorical claims (two premises and a conclusion). The three claims use three terms as subject or predicate, each of which appears in exactly two of the claims.

The first argument we considered in this chapter is a categorical syllogism:

No police officers are thieves.
Some thieves are sent to prison.
So no police officers are sent to prison.

Here the terms are "police officers," "thieves," "people sent to prison." Each appears in exactly two of the claims.

Aristotelians identify the predicates and subjects in syllogisms by the roles they play in determining whether the argument is valid.

> *Major*, *minor*, and *middle terms* of a categorical syllogism
>
> | | | |
> |---|---|---|
> | *major term* | = | predicate of the conclusion |
> | *minor term* | = | subject of the conclusion |
> | *middle term* | = | the term that appears in both premises |
> | *major premise* | = | premise that contains the major term |
> | *minor premise* | = | premise that contains the minor term |

For example, in the last argument the major term is "people sent to prison." The minor term is "police officers." The middle term is "thieves." The major premise is "Some thieves are sent to prison." The minor premise is "No police officers are thieves."

The main focus of Aristotelian logic, as traditionally presented, is to show that we can mechanically determine of any given categorical syllogism whether it is valid or invalid. One way to do that is by inspecting its form. We list all possible forms of syllogisms in *standard form*: All the claims are in standard form, and the major premise comes first, then the minor premise, then the conclusion. For example, "No S is M; All M are P; so No S is P" has form EAE. We determine for each form whether it is valid or invalid; this one is valid. Given any categorical syllogism, we can first rewrite it in standard form and then check whether it is one of the valid forms.

But instead of listing all the forms, Aristotelians have shown how we can start with knowing whether a few are valid or invalid, and then convert any other form into one of those by a detailed reduction procedure.

Alternatively, we can take any categorical syllogism, rewrite it in standard form, and then use the method of diagrams presented in Chapter 8 to determine whether it is valid. Or we can use one of several other well-known diagram methods, similar to but distinct from the methods of Chapter 8.

Once we've checked for validity, we still have to decide whether the syllogism is a good argument. We know that a valid argument need not be good, for a premise could be false, or the premises may not be more plausible than the conclusion. Indeed, many valid Aristotelian syllogisms beg the question. For example, with "All dogs eat meat. Spot is a dog. So Spot eats meat.", it's more plausible that Spot eats meat than that all dogs do. Categorical syllogisms, as originally used by Aristotle, are really a logic of explanations, not arguments. In an explanation the conclusion is supposed to be more plausible than the premises, as when someone tries to explain why "The sky is blue" is true. (The *Science Workbook* for this text teaches how to reason about explanations.)

In any case, in ordinary speech we first have to decide how the person giving the argument intends "all" and "some" to be understood, and many times those readings won't be compatible with the assumptions of Aristotelian logic. Even if those readings are compatible, we often have to do a lot of work to rewrite the claims into standard categorical form. Then we have to check against a (memorized?) list of valid Aristotelian forms. Then we have to ask about the plausibility of the premises to determine whether the syllogism is a good argument. Even then, many simple arguments using "some" or "all" can't be analyzed as categorical syllogisms, such as "Some dogs like cats; some cats like dogs; so some dogs and cats like each other."

For hundreds and hundreds of years students and scholars preoccupied themselves with the methods of Aristotelian logic as the primary focus of their analysis of reasoning. They could rely on standard methods and checkable rules. But that tradition missed most of the important work in critical thinking that has been incorporated into the foundations of reasoning analysis only in the last 150 years, even though much of that can also be traced to Aristotle.

For reasoning in your daily life, being able to listen and analyze as you read and speak, the methods and work we did in Chapter 8 will be more useful than the formal methods of Aristotelian logic. To decide whether a categorical syllogism is valid, do what we've always done: See if there is a possible way for the premises to be true and the conclusion false.

Exercises for Section D

1. What is a categorical syllogism?

2. What is the major term of a categorical syllogism?

3. What is the minor term of a categorical syllogism?

4. What is the middle term of a categorical syllogism?

5. What is the major premise of a categorical syllogism?

6. What is the minor premise of a categorical syllogism?

7. What is the standard form for a categorical syllogism?

Which of the forms of categorical syllogisms in Exercises 8–15 are forms of arguments that must be valid? The forms are presented by giving the letter name of the standard form of the major premise, then the minor premise, then the conclusion.

8. EAE (No S is M; all M are P; so no S is P.)

9. AAA

10. AEO

11. IAO

12. III

13. AEE

14. AOO

15. AAI

For each of the following arguments, either rewrite it in the standard form of a categorical syllogism and identify the form, or explain why it cannot be rewritten that way. In either case, determine if the argument is valid.

16. All students at this school pay tuition. Some people who pay tuition at this school will fail. So some students at this school will fail.

17. There aren't any wasps that will not sting. Some bumblebees will not sting. So some bumblebees aren't wasps.

18. Badly managed businesses are unprofitable. No oyster cultivating business in North Carolina is badly managed. So some oyster cultivating business in North Carolina is profitable.

19. Most critical thinking books do not teach Aristotelian logic. Chemistry textbooks never teach Aristotelian logic. So most chemistry books are not critical thinking textbooks.

20. Nothing that's smarter than a dog will cough up hair balls. Cats cough up hair balls. So cats are not smarter than dogs.

21. Dick will not visit Tom tonight if Zoe cooks dinner. Zoe didn't cook dinner. So Dick visited Tom tonight.

22. No pacifists will fight in a war. Dick is a pacifist. So Dick will not fight in a war.

23. Police chiefs who interfere with the arrest of city officials are always fired. People who are fired collect unemployment. So some police chiefs who interfere with the arrest of city officials collect unemployment.

24. Some temporary employment agencies do not give employee benefits. All employees of Zee Zee Frap's restaurant get employee benefits. So no employee of Zee Zee Frap's is hired through a temporary employment agency.

Key Words

categorical claim	A claim
standard form of a categorical claim	E claim
	I claim
universal categorical claim	O claim
particular categorical claim	subalternate
affirmative categorical claim	Square of Opposition
negative categorical claim	categorical syllogism
quantity of a categorical claim	major term
quality of a categorical claim	minor term
subject of a categorical claim	middle term
predicate of a categorical claim	major premise
contradictory	minor premise
contrary	standard form of a categorical syllogism
subcontrary	

Further Study   There are many textbooks that present the "traditional" Aristotelian logic with lots of diagrams and a listing of all valid and invalid forms of categorical syllogisms. But to see the real power of the Aristotelian tradition, you need to study medieval logic in the work of Buridan, Duns Scotus, Peter of Spain, and others. There are some good translations and expositions of the work of those logicians, but you're best off taking a philosophy course on the history of logic.

Diagramming Arguments

A. Diagrams

This appendix is a supplement to the section Complex Arguments for Analysis. It provides a way to visualize the structure of complex arguments. For example:

Spot chases rabbits. *1*
Spot chases squirrels. *2*
Therefore, Spot chases all small animals. *3*

To picture this argument, we number the premises and conclusion. Then we ask which claim is meant to support which other. Here *support* just means that it's a reason to believe the other claim.

> If a claim A is meant to support another claim B then we draw an arrow from A to B, putting A above B.

The conclusion will have to be at the bottom, since all the premises are supposed to support it. And both do. The picture we'll draw is:

Neither *1* supports *2*, nor does *2* support *1*. So there is no arrow from one to the other. But both support *3*, so we have arrows there. That's simple.
Now consider:

Dogs are mammals. *1*
Cats are mammals. *2*
Some dogs hate cats. *3*
Therefore, some dogs hate mammals. *4*

We number the claims. It's easy to see which is the conclusion (it's labeled with the word "therefore"). Which claims are meant to support which others? We need *2* and *3* to get the conclusion *4*. But what's *1* doing? Nothing. The argument doesn't get any better by adding it, since it doesn't support any of the other claims. So our picture is:

We also need a way to represent premises that are *dependent*, that is, they are meant together to support another claim, in the sense that if one is false, the other(s) do not give support.

> In a diagram we indicate that premises are dependent by putting '+' between them and drawing a line under them.

Dogs are loyal. *1*
Dogs are friendly. *2*
Anything that is friendly and loyal makes a great pet. *3*
Hence, dogs are great pets. *4*

$$\underline{1 \;+\; 2 \;+\; 3}$$
$$\downarrow$$
$$4$$

Recall now the argument discussed on pp. 221–222:

Whatever you do, don't take the critical thinking course from Dr. E. *1*
He's a really tough grader *2*, much more demanding than the other professors that teach that course. *3*   You could end up getting a bad grade. *4*

We rewrote *1* as "You shouldn't take the critical thinking course from Dr. E." And we rewrote *3* as "He's much more demanding than the other professors that teach that course." It wasn't clear which claim was supposed to support which other. We had two choices:

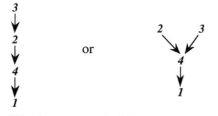

We chose to repair this argument with:

If you take critical thinking from someone who's more demanding than other professors who teach that course and who is a really tough grader, then you could end up getting a bad grade. *a*

That makes the second diagram a better choice, though we still need to get from *4* to *1*. We can use:

You shouldn't take any course where you might get a bad grade. *b*

We can see that the argument is only as good as the unsupported premise *b*.

Let's see how adding a series of unstated premises can affect the picture. Consider:

My buddies John, Marilyn, and Joe all took Dr. E's critical thinking class and did well. *1* So I'm going to sign up for it, too. *2* I need a good grade. *3*

First, we need to rewrite *2* as a claim "I should sign up for Dr. E's critical thinking class." I take this to be the conclusion (try the other possibilities, asking where you could put "therefore" or "because"). Initially we might take the diagram:

But we need some glue for this to be even moderately strong. To begin with, why do *1* and *3* yield *2* ? A (fairly weak) assumption might be:

Usually if John, Marilyn, and Joe all do well in a class, I'll do well. *a*

But even that plus *3* won't give us *2*. We need some further assumption like:

I should sign up for classes in which I know I'll get a good grade. *b*

Then the argument becomes:

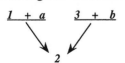

Still, there's something missing. We need:

I'll do well in Dr. E's course. *c*

And that changes the picture entirely:

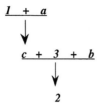

We have a strong argument, in which we see a dependence between *3* and what we get from *1*. Whether this is a good argument depends on whether the premises are plausible.

Exercises for Section A

For each of the following, if it is an argument, diagram it, repairing as necessary.

1. Dr. E is a teacher. All teachers are men. So Dr. E is a man.

2. No one under sixteen has a driver's license. So Zoe must be at least sixteen.

3. Sheep are the dumbest animals. If the one in front walks off a cliff, all the rest will follow him. And if they get rolled over on their backs, they can't right themselves.

4. I'm on my way to school. I left five minutes late. Traffic is heavy. Therefore, I'll be late for class. So I might as well stop and get breakfast.

5. Pigs are very intelligent animals. They make great pets. They learn to do tricks as well as any dog can. They can be housetrained, too. And they are affectionate, since they like to cuddle. Pigs are known as one of the smartest animals there are. And if you get bored with them or they become unruly, you can eat them.

6. Smoking is disgusting. It makes your breath smell horrid. If you've ever kissed someone after they smoked a cigarette you feel as though you're going to vomit. Besides, it will kill you.

7. You're good at numbers. You sort of like business. You should major in accounting—accountants make really good money.

8. Inherited property such as real estate, stocks, bonds, etc. is given a fresh start basis when inherited. That is, for purposes of future capital gains tax computations, it is treated as though it were purchased at its market value at the time of inheritance. Thus, when you sell property which was acquired by inheritance, tax is due only on the appreciation in value since the time it was inherited. No tax is ever paid on the increase in value that took place when the property belonged to the previous owner.

1994 Tax Guide for College Teachers

B. Counterarguments

Recall the conversation between Dick and Zoe we looked at in Chapter 7:

> We ought to get another dog. *1*
> (objection) We already have Spot. *2*
> The other dog will keep Spot company. *3*
> (objection) Spot already has us for company. *4*
> We are gone a lot. *5*
> He is always escaping from the yard. *6*
> He's lonely. *7*
> We don't give him enough time. *8*
> He should be out running around more. *9*
> (objection) It will be a lot of work to have a new dog. *10*
> (objection) We will have to feed the new dog. *11*
> (objection) It will take a lot of time to train the new dog. *12*
> Dick will train him. *13*
> We can feed him at the same time as Spot. *14*
> Dog food is cheap. *15*

We can diagram this if we have a way to represent that a claim is an objection, not support, for another claim.

To diagram the argument, then, note that it seems that Dick intends but never says:

> Spot needs company. *a*

That with *3* will be what gets the conclusion.

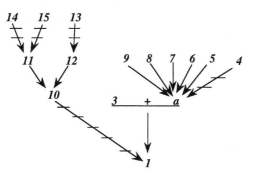

Claim *4* is an objection to *a*. That is, it's an attempt to show that a crucial premise of Dick is false. It must be answered. And Dick answers it by amassing enough other evidence for *a*. Claim *10* is a direct challenge to the conclusion. If it is true, the conclusion is in doubt. So it must be answered. Dick doesn't try to show that it is false directly. Rather he shows that the two claims Zoe uses to support *10* are false. So there is no reason to believe *10*.

When we finish diagramming we can see at a glance whether the argument has left some objection to a premise or objection to the conclusion unanswered. Either the objection is knocked off with a counterclaim above the support for it (as with *13–15* against *10*) or other claims are amassed as evidence (as with *5–9* against *4*). Of course you'll still need to evaluate whether the various claims are plausible.

Exercises for Section B

Diagram and evaluate the following arguments:

1. You should not take illegal drugs. They can kill you. If you overdose, you can die. If you share a needle, you could get AIDS and then die. If you don't die, you could end up a vegetable or otherwise permanently incapacitated. By using drugs you run the risk of getting arrested and possibly going to jail. Or at least having a hefty fine against you. Although some think the "high" from drugs is worth all the risks, the truth is that they are addicted and are only trying to justify supporting their habit.

2. Zoe: I think sex is the answer to almost everyone's problems.
   Dick: How can you say that?
   Zoe: It takes away your tensions, right?
   Dick: Not if you're involved with someone you don't like.
   Zoe: Well, anyway, it makes you feel better.
   Dick: Not if it's against your morals. Anyway, heroin makes you feel good, too.
   Zoe: But it's healthy, natural, just like eating and drinking.
   Dick: Sure, and you can catch terrible diseases. Sex should be confined to marriage.
   Zoe: Is that a proposal?

3. Dick: Nixon was a crook.
   Zoe: No he wasn't. Remember that famous "Checkers" speech where he said so?
   Dick: That was just political evasion. Anyway, you can't just take someone's word that he's not a criminal, especially if he's a politician. He directed the break-in at the Democratic Party Headquarters.
   Zoe: They never showed that he did that.
   Dick: That's because his accomplices like Haldemann were covering up. That's why they got pardoned. And he used the FBI against his enemies. He was a criminal. It was stupid for Clinton to make a speech honoring him when he died.
   Zoe: Maybe Clinton was doing it so that when he dies someone will make a speech for him, too.

Glossary

Terms used only in an appendix are not listed here, but may be found in the Index.

Affirming the consequent Reasoning in the form: If A, then B; B; so A. Usually weak.

All Usually means "every single one, no exceptions." Sometimes "all" is best understood as "every single one, and there is at least one."

Alternatives The claims that are the parts of an "or" claim.

Ambiguous sentence A sentence that can be understood in two or a very few obvious ways.

Analogy, reasoning by A comparison becomes reasoning by analogy when it is part of an argument: On one side of the comparison we draw a conclusion, so on the other side we should conclude the same.

Anecdotal evidence Claims about a sample of one or very few used as evidence for a generalization. The claims about the sample in a hasty generalization.

Antecedent The claim A in a conditional claim "If A, then B."

Appeal to authority An argument that uses or requires as premise: (Almost) anything that _____ says about _____ is true.

Appeal to common belief An argument that uses or requires as premise: If (almost) everyone else (in this group) believes it, then it's true.

Appeal to emotion An argument that uses or requires as premise: You should believe or do _____ if you feel _____ . (e.g., fear, pity, spite, . . .)

Apple polishing A feel-good argument that appeals to vanity.

Apples and oranges A meaningless comparison.

Arguing backwards Reasoning that the premises of an argument are true because the conclusion is true and the argument is valid or strong. *See also* Affirming the consequent.

***Arguing backwards with* all** Reasoning in the form: All S are P; *a* is P; so *a* is S. Usually weak.

***Arguing backwards with* almost all** Reasoning in the form: Almost all S are P; *a* is P; so *a* is S. Usually weak.

***Arguing backwards with* no** Reasoning in the form: All S are P; no Q is S; so no Q is P. Usually weak.

Argument An attempt to convince someone (possibly yourself) that a particular claim, called the *conclusion*, is true. The rest of the argument is a collection of claims called *premises*, which are given as the reasons for believing the conclusion is true.

Assertion   A claim that is put forward as true.

Average (*or mean*) *of a collection of numbers*   The number obtained by adding all the values and then dividing by the number of items.

Begging the question   An argument that uses a premise that is no more plausible than the conclusion.

Biased sample   A sample that is not representative.

Calling in your debts   An argument that uses or requires as premise: You should believe or do _____ if you owe _____ a favor.

Causal claim   A claim that is or can be rewritten as "— causes (or caused) —."

Causal factor   One of several claims that jointly qualify as describing the cause.

Cause   *See* Necessary criteria for cause and effect.

Cause in a population   A claim that if the cause is present, there is a higher probability the effect will follow than if the cause were not present.

Claim   A declarative sentence used in such a way that it is either true or false (but not both).

Composition, fallacy of   Reasoning that what is true of (or good for) the individual must also be true of (or good for) the group, or vice-versa.

Compound claim   A claim composed of other claims, but which has to be viewed as just one claim.

Conclusion   The claim whose truth an argument is intended to establish.

Conditional claim   A compound claim that can be rewritten as an "if . . . then . . ." claim that must have the same truth-value.

Confidence level   The percentage of the time that the same sampling method would give a result that is a true generalization. The strength of the generalization.

Confusing objective and subjective   Calling a claim objective when it is really subjective, or vice-versa.

Consequent   The claim B in a conditional claim "If A, then B."

Content fallacy   An argument that uses or requires for repair a particular kind of (generic) premise that, if false or dubious, classifies the argument as a fallacy.

Contradictory of a claim   A contradictory of a claim is one that has the opposite truth-value in all possible circumstances. Sometimes called a *negation* of a claim.
- Contradictory of "A or B" is "Not A and not B."
- Contradictory of "A and B" is "Not A or not B."
- Contradictory of "If A, then B" is "A but not B."

Contrapositive   The contrapositive of "If A, then B" is "If not B, then not A." The contrapositive is true exactly when the original conditional is true.

Control group   *See* Controlled experiment: cause-to-effect.

Controlled experiment: cause-to-effect An experiment to establish cause in a population. Two randomly chosen samples are used. One is administered the cause, and the other, called the *control group,* is not administered the cause. *See also* Uncontrolled experiment.

Criteria for Accepting or Rejecting a Claim In the order in which they should be applied:

Accept: We know the claim is true from our own experience.

Reject: We know the claim is false from our own experience.
(Exceptions: We have good reason to doubt our memory or our perception; the claim contradicts other experiences of ours; and there is a good argument against the claim.)

Reject: The claim contradicts other claims we know to be true.

Accept: The claim is made by someone we know and trust, and the person is an authority on this kind of claim.

Accept: The claim is made by a reputable authority we can trust as an expert about this kind of claim who has no motive to mislead.

Accept: The claim is put forward by a reputable journal or reference source.

Accept: The claim is in a media source that's usually reliable and has no obvious motive to mislead, if the source is named.

Critical thinking Evaluating whether we should be convinced that some claim is true or some argument is good, as well as formulating good arguments.

Definition An explanation or stipulation of how to use a word or phrase. A definition is not a claim. *See also* Good definition; Persuasive definition.

Denying the antecedent Reasoning in the form: If A, then B; not A; so not B. Usually weak.

Descriptive claim A claim that says what is. *Compare* Prescriptive claim.

***Direct way of reasoning with* all** Reasoning in the form: All S are P; *a* is S; so *a* is P. Valid.

***Direct way of reasoning with* almost all** Reasoning in the form: Almost all S are P; *a* is S; so *a* is P. Usually strong.

Direct way of reasoning with conditionals Reasoning in the form: If A, then B; A; so B. Valid. Also called *modus ponens.*

***Direct way of reasoning with* no** Reasoning in the form: All S are P; no Q is P; so no Q is S. Valid.

Direct ways of refuting an argument *See* Refuting an argument directly.

Disjunctive syllogism *See* Excluding possibilities.

Downplayer A word or phrase that minimizes the significance of a claim.

Drawing the line fallacy A type of bad argument which assumes that if you can't make the difference precise, then there is no difference.

Dubious claim *See* Implausible claim.

Dysphemism   A word or phrase that makes something sound worse than a neutral description. *See also* Euphemism.

Effect   *See* Necessary criteria for cause and effect.

Euphemism   A word or phrase that makes something sound better than a neutral description. *See also* Dysphemism.

Evidence   A claim or claims that give some reason to believe another claim.

Excluding possibilities   Reasoning in the form: A or B; not A; so B (can use more alternatives). Valid. Also called *disjunctive syllogism.*

Fallacy   An argument of one of the types that have been agreed to be so bad as to be unrepairable. *See also* Content fallacy; Structural fallacy.

False dilemma   A use of excluding possibilities, but the "or" claim isn't plausible. Sometimes the false or dubious "or" claim itself is called the "false dilemma."

Feel-good argument   An argument that uses or requires as premise: You should believe or do _____ if it makes you feel good.

Foreseeable consequence of a cause   A claim that becomes true after the actual cause, yet because it is a consequence of that cause is not counted as part of the cause.

Gambler's fallacy   An argument that uses or requires as premise: A run of events of a certain kind makes a run of contrary events more likely in order to even up the probabilities.

General cause and effect   A causal claim that is true if and only if many particular cause and effect claims are true. *See also* Particular cause and effect.

General claim   A claim that asserts something in a general way about all or a part of a collection.

Generalizing   Concluding a claim about a group, the *population*, from a claim about some part of it, the *sample*. To generalize is to make an argument. Sometimes the general claim is called the *generalization*; sometimes that word is used for the whole argument. The knowledge of the sample is called the *inductive evidence* for the generalization. *See also* Premises needed for a good generalization.

Good argument   *See* Tests for an argument to be good.

Good definition   A definition in which (1) The words doing the defining are clear and better understood than the word or phrase being defined, and (2) The word or phrase being defined and the words doing the defining can be used interchangeably.

Guide to Repairing Arguments   Given an (implicit) argument that is apparently defective, we are justified in adding a premise or conclusion if it satisfies all three of the following:
  • The argument becomes stronger or valid.
  • The premise is plausible and would seem plausible to the other person.
  • The premise is more plausible than the conclusion.
If the argument is then valid or strong, we may delete a premise if doing so does not make the argument worse. *See also* Unrepairable arguments.

Haphazard sampling Choosing a sample with no intentional bias. Not usually reliable for generalizing. *Compare* Random sampling.

Hasty generalization Generalizing from a sample that is much too small.

Hyperbole An extreme version of an up-player; a gross exaggeration.

If and only if "A if and only if B" means "If A, then B; and if B then A."

Impersonal standards *See* Objective claim.

Implausible claim A claim that we do not have good reason to believe is true.

Implying *See* Inferring and implying.

Inductive evidence *See* Generalizing.

Indicator word A word or phrase added to a claim telling us the role of the claim in an argument or what the speaker thinks of the claim or argument. Not part of a claim.

Indirect way of reasoning with conditionals Reasoning in the form: If A, then B; not B; so not A. Valid. Also called *modus tollens*.

Inferring and implying When someone leaves a conclusion unstated, he or she is implying the conclusion. When you decide that an unstated claim is the conclusion, you are inferring that claim. We also say someone is implying a claim if in context it's clear he or she believes the claim. In that case we infer that the person believes the claim.

Innuendo A concealed claim that is párticularly unpleasant.

Intersubjective claim A subjective claim about which (nearly) everyone agrees on.

Intervening cause A claim that becomes true after the cause and before the effect that is not a foreseeable consequence of the original cause and which qualifies as a cause, too.

Invalid argument An argument that is not valid. Usually classified from strong to weak.

Irrelevant premise A premise that can be deleted from an argument without making the argument any weaker. *See also* Relevance.

Issue A claim that is being debated.

Judging claims (three choices we can make about whether to believe a claim is true)
  • Accept the claim as true.
  • Reject the claim as false.
  • Suspend judgment.

Law of large numbers If the probability of something occurring is X percent, then over the long run the number of times that happens will be about X percent.

Loaded question A question that conceals a dubious claim that should be argued for rather than assumed.

Margin of error In a generalization, the range within which the actual number for the population is claimed to fall.

Mark of irrationality   If you recognize that an argument is good, then it is irrational not to accept the conclusion.

Mean   *See* Average.

Median *of a collection of numbers*   The midway mark: the number in the collection such that there are as many items above it as below it in the collection.

Mistaking the person for the argument   An argument that uses or requires as premise: (Almost) any argument that _____ gives about _____ is bad.

Mistaking the person for the claim   An argument that uses or requires as premise: (Almost) anything that _____ says about _____ is false.

Mode *of a collection of numbers*   The number that appears most often in the collection.

Modus ponens ("way of putting")   *See* Direct way of reasoning with conditionals.

Modus tollens ("way of taking")   *See* Indirect way of reasoning with conditionals.

Necessary criteria for cause and effect
- The cause happened (the claim describing it is true).
- The effect happened (the claim describing it is true).
- The cause precedes the effect.
- It is (nearly) impossible for the cause to happen (be true) and the effect not to happen (be false), given the normal conditions.
- The cause makes a difference—if the cause had not happened (been true), the effect would not have happened (been true).
- There is no common cause.

Necessary and sufficient conditions   A is *necessary* for B means that "If not A, then not B" is true. A is *sufficient* for B means that "If A, then B" is true.

Negation of a claim   *See* Contradictory of a claim.

No-matter-what argument   Reasoning in the form: If A, then B; if not A, then B; so B. Valid.

Normal conditions   For a causal claim, the obvious and plausible unstated claims that are needed to establish that the relationship between purported cause and purported effect is valid or strong.

Objective claim   A claim whose truth-value does not depend on what someone (or something) thinks, believes, or feels. An objective claim invokes *impersonal standards*.

Only   "Only S are P" is equivalent to "All P are S."

Only if   "A only if B" is equivalent to "If not B, then not A." It is also equivalent to "If A, then B."

Particular cause and effect   A claim that this particular cause caused this particular effect. *See also* General cause and effect.

Perfectionist dilemma An argument with (possibly unstated) premise: Either the situation will be completely perfect if we do this, or we shouldn't do it.

Personal standards *See* Subjective claim.

Persuasive definition A claim masquerading as a definition. An attempt to close off debate by stating the issue as a definition.

Phony refutation Concluding that an argument is bad because the person who made the argument has done or said something that shows he or she (apparently) does not believe one of the premises or the conclusion of the argument. A fallacy.

Plausible claim A claim that we have good reason to believe is true.

Population *See* Generalizing.

Post hoc ergo propter hoc ("After this, therefore because of this.") Claiming that there is cause and effect solely because this happened after that.

Premises The claims in an argument that are meant to establish that the conclusion is true.

Premises needed for a good generalization
  • The sample is representative.
  • The sample is big enough.
  • The sample is studied well.

Prescriptive claim A claim that says what should be. *Compare* Descriptive claim.

Principle of Rational Discussion We assume that the other person who is discussing an issue with us or whose arguments we are reading:
  • Knows about the subject under discussion.
  • Is able and willing to reason well.
  • Is not lying.

Proof substitute A word or phrase that suggests the speaker has a proof, but no proof is actually offered.

Qualifier A word or phrase that restricts or limits the meaning of other words.

Random sampling Choosing a sample so that at every choice there is an equal chance for any of the remaining members of the population to be picked. *Compare* Haphazard sampling.

Reasoning in a chain with **all** Reasoning in the form: All S are P; all P are Q; so all S are Q. Valid.

Reasoning in a chain with **almost all** Reasoning in the form: Almost all S are P; almost all P are Q; so almost all S are Q. Usually weak.

Reasoning in a chain with conditionals Reasoning in the form: If A, then B; if B, then C; so if A, then C. Valid. *See also* Slippery slope argument.

Reasoning in a chain with **some** Reasoning in the form: Some S are P; some P are Q; so some S are Q. Usually weak.

Reasoning from hypotheses   If you start with an assumption or hypothesis A that you don't know to be true and make a good argument for B, then what you have established is "If A, then B."

Reducing to the absurd   Proving that at least one of several claims is false or dubious, or collectively they are unacceptable, by drawing a false or unwanted conclusion from them.

Refuting an argument   Showing an argument is bad.

Refuting an argument directly
- Show that at least one of the premises is dubious.
- Show that the argument isn't valid or strong.
- Show that the conclusion is false.

Relevance   To say that the premises of an argument are irrelevant just means that the argument is so bad you can't see how to repair it.   *See also* Irrelevant premise.

Repairing arguments   *See* Guide to Repairing Arguments, Unrepairable arguments.

Representative sample   A sample in which no one subgroup of the whole population is represented more than its proportion in the population.

Sample   *See* Generalizing.

Shifting the burden of proof   Saying that the other person should disprove your claim, rather than proving it yourself.

Slanter   Any literary device that attempts to convince by using words that conceal a dubious claim.

Slippery slope argument   An argument that uses a chain of conditionals, at least one of which is false or dubious. A bad form of reducing to the absurd.

Some   Often taken to mean "at least one." Sometimes "some" is best understood as "at least one, but not all."

Sound argument   A valid argument with true premises.

Statistical generalization   A generalization that says that the same proportion of the whole as in the sample will have the property under discussion.

Strawman   An attempt to refute a claim or argument by arguing against another claim that's easier to show false or an argument that's easier to show weak. Putting words in someone's mouth.

Strong and weak arguments   Invalid arguments are classified on a scale from strong to weak. An argument is *strong* if it is possible but unlikely for the premises to be true and the conclusion false (at the same time). An argument is *weak* if it is possible and likely for the premises to be true and the conclusion false (at the same time).

Structural fallacy   An argument whose form alone guarantees that it is a bad argument.

Subjective claim   A claim whose truth-value depends on what someone (or something) thinks, believes, or feels. A subjective claim invokes *personal standards*.

Subjectivist fallacy Arguing that because there is a lot of disagreement about whether a claim is true, it is therefore subjective.

Sufficient condition *See* Necessary and sufficient conditions.

Support A claim or claims that gives some reason to believe another claim.

Tests for an argument to be good
- The premises are plausible.
- The premises are more plausible than the conclusion.
- The argument is valid or strong.

Truth-value The quality of being true or false.

Two times zero is still zero A numerical comparison that makes something look impressive, but the basis of comparison is not stated.

Unbiased sample *See* Representative sample.

Uncontrolled experiment: cause-to-effect An experiment to establish cause in a population. Two randomly chosen samples are used. In one the cause is (apparently) present, in the other (apparently) not, and they are followed over time.

Uncontrolled experiment: effect-to-cause An experiment to establish cause in a population. A sample of the population in which the effect is present is examined to see if the cause is also present and other possible causes are not present.

Unrepairable arguments We don't repair an argument if any of the following hold:
- There's no argument there.
- The argument is so lacking in coherence that there's nothing obvious to add.
- A premise it uses is false or dubious and cannot be deleted.
- Two of its premises are contradictory, and neither can be deleted.
- The obvious premise to add would make the argument weak.
- The obvious premise to add to make the argument strong or valid is false.
- The conclusion is clearly false.

Up-player A word or phrase that exaggerates the significance of a claim.

Vague sentence A sentence for which there are so many ways to understand it that we can't settle on one of those without the speaker making it clearer.

Valid argument An argument in which it is impossible for the premises to be true and the conclusion false (at the same time).

Weak argument *See* Strong and weak arguments.

Weaseler A claim that is qualified so much that the apparent meaning is no longer there.

Wishful thinking A feel-good argument used on oneself.

Answers to Selected Exercises

Chapter 1
1. Convincings/arguments.
3. We can convince others; others can convince us; we can convince ourselves.
4. a. Yes.
   b. Yes, but truth-value depends on who says it (looking forward to Chapter 2).
   e. No, a command.
   g. I could never figure out who was supposed to be in need. It's too unclear for me to classify it as a claim.
   i. Yes.
   k. Yes, but it might not have the same truth-value as (j).
   n. Depends on your view of what "true" means. Some might say "No," thinking that there's no way we could ever determine whether it is true or false. Others will argue that it is true or false, independently of us. That's philosophy.
7. To convince (establish) that a claim, called the "conclusion," is true.
8. *Given an argument,* the *conclusion* is the claim that someone is attempting to establish is true, while the *premises* are the claims that are used in trying to establish that.
9. Commands, threats, entreaties ("Dr. E, Dr. E, please, please let me pass this course"), etc., are not arguments.
12. Depends on whether she's talking to herself. We can't tell. Arguments use language.
14. *Argument?* Yes.
    Conclusion: You shouldn't eat at Zee-Zee Frap's restaurant.
    Premise: I heard they did really badly on their health inspection last week.
    NOTE: The premise isn't "They did really badly on their health inspection last week."
    Someone hearing that it's so and its being so aren't the same claim.
16. *Argument?* No.
20. *Argument?* No. No conclusion is stated (though it's implicit—we'll talk about when we're justified in supplying a missing conclusion in Chapter 4).
27. **Virtue.**

Chapter 2
Section A
2. b. O.K.
   d. O.K. Just because *you* don't know what the entire cost is doesn't mean it's vague.
   h. O.K. It's just a funny way of saying "Jane is really attractive."
   j. Too vague.
   l. Too vague (but see the next section).
4. It's an example of the drawing the line fallacy.
7. b. Ambiguous. Rumsfeld himself lacks intelligence. Intelligence agencies don't have enough information.
   c. Americans—individually or collectively? Compare Example 3, p.16.
   g. Each player on the team had a B average. The average of all the grades of the members of the team was B.
   i. Vague, not ambiguous.

10. c. Ambiguity due to the words "protect" and "valuable": Anything that's commercially valuable should be kept from harm or loss.
11. This appears to be an example of a drawing the line fallacy. But it's not. The mistake here is that there is a simple way to draw the line: It's excessive force if the suspect is hit when he is no longer resisting.
12. Ms. Hathaway is (implicitly) arguing that she was justified in allowing her 7-year-old daughter to fly across the country. You might believe her, until you realize she is trading on the vagueness of the words "freedom," "choice," and "liberty" (try to pin down what you think those words mean).

Section B

1. a. Subjective = Its truth-value depends on what someone or something thinks/believes/feels.
   b. Objective = Its truth-value does *not* depend on what anyone or anything thinks/believes/feels (= not subjective).
   c. No.
4. When describing our own feelings we don't have awfully precise language to use. So "It's hot" may be the best we can do in describing how we feel. But it's inadequate as an objective claim.
6. a. Objective.
   d. Subjective (even though Dr. E thinks it's objective and true).
   i. Objective in the Middle Ages, when people believed demons existed. Now probably understood as demons in the mind, so subjective.
   j. Objective, since "insane" is now a technical term of the law.

Section C

2. *Prescriptive or descriptive?* Prescriptive, since we shouldn't do what is evil. *Standard needed?* Yes. But it's not clear what's intended, so we shouldn't accept it as a claim until one is given.
3. *Prescriptive or descriptive?* Descriptive. *Standard needed?* No.
4. *Prescriptive or descriptive?* Prescriptive. *Standard needed?* Yes. Either one of Exercise 3 or 4 will do, but until one is chosen we shouldn't view it as a claim.
11. *Prescriptive or descriptive?* Descriptive. *Standard needed?* No, it's just a subjective value judgment. Unless the clerk happens to be an art history major or ex-art history professor, . . . in which case see the answer to Exercise 12.
12. *Prescriptive or descriptive?* Not clear until a standard is given. *Standard needed?* Yes. Is this meant as objective, and that you should like Picasso better than Rembrandt? Or is it meant as just a subjective value judgment?

Section D

1. c. Persuasive definition.
   d. Definition. No longer classifies correctly, but it once did.
   f. Not a definition.
4. The definition and the original phrase can be used interchangeably, and the words in the definition are clear and better understood than the words doing the defining.
5. Because they settle a debate before it's started. They are concealed claims.

Exercises for Chapter 2

1. All the possibilities are:
   claim + objective
   claim + subjective
   definition + not a claim

   ambiguous or too vague + not a claim
   persuasive definition + claim + objective
   persuasive definition + claim + subjective
3. Definition, not a claim.
7. Objective claim.
12. Too vague, not a claim.

Chapter 3

Sections A–C

4. No. The premises could be false. Even if the premises are true, they might be less plausible than the conclusion.

5. a. Come up with a (possibly imagined) situation in which the premises are true and the conclusion false.

   b. Come up with a (possibly imagined) *likely* situation in which the premises are true and the conclusion false.

7. Nothing.

14. No. A false conclusion shows the argument is bad. But the argument could still be valid (it would have at least one false premise then).

16. No. *Invalid* arguments are classified from strong to weak.

17. Bad. (Not necessarily weak—it could be valid.)

19. d.   20. d.   21. c.   22. d   23. d.   24. c.

Exercises for Chapter 3

1. Nothing.

4. No. See the parakeets example in Section B.

6. *Conclusion*: Flo got a haircut.
   Premises: Flo's hair was long. Now Flo's hair is short. ("So" is not part of the conclusion.)
   Invalid: Flo might have gotten her hair caught in a lawn mower. But it's strong. Good if premises are plausible.

10. Valid and good.

12. Weak, bad. Spot could be a penguin or a cockroach.

16. This is bad because it's begging the question.

17. Not an argument.

18. Weak, bad. They might want to hire conservatives for balance. Or conservatives are hired, but they become liberal over time. Or Maria just hasn't met enough professors.

19. Valid and good if premises are plausible. (Maybe Dick bought it on credit? Then the first premise is false.)

23. Weak. Professor Zzzyzzx may have changed his grading, or the school may have required him to become harder, or he may just never have had a student as bad as Suzy.

Chapter 4

Sections A–D

8. Nothing.

10. a.   i. premise, ii. premise, iii. premise, iv. conclusion
    b.   i. conclusion, ii. premise, iii. premise, iv. premise
    f.   i. premise, ii. premise, iii. conclusion

11. Deleting it doesn't make the argument weaker, and no obvious way to link it to the conclusion.

The most common errors in the following exercises

• Repairing arguments that are unrepairable.

• Adding premises that don't make the argument better or make a whole new argument.

• Adding a premise and then marking the argument moderate or weak. The only reason to add a premise is to make the argument valid or strong.

• Marking both "valid" and "strong" or both "valid" and "weak."

• Marking an argument "weak" when it's bad (valid or strong with a dubious premise).

In many answers only premise(s) that are needed are given. When a premise is added, the argument is good (if the premises are plausible), unless noted otherwise.

12. *Conclusion*: Dr. E is a man.   *Premises*: Dr. E is a teacher. All teachers are men.
    Valid, bad, unrepairable: The second premise is false.

13. "Anything that walks like a duck, looks like a duck, and quacks like a duck, is a duck" or
    "If it walks like a duck, looks like a duck, and quacks like a duck, it's a duck."

16. *Conclusion*: You didn't get the flu from me.
    "The person who shows symptoms of the flu first got the flu first. If you get the flu first, you
        can't have gotten it from someone who didn't have it." Valid.
    The first added premise is probably false, but it's the only way the argument could be repaired.
    So the argument is unrepairable.

    You *can't* add "The person who shows symptoms of the flu first *probably* got the flu first."
    The word "impossible" indicates the speaker thinks he/she is making a valid argument, so you
    can't repair it as a strong argument.

18. This is an argument: You can't ignore what the speaker intends, and "so" shows the speaker
    meant it as an argument. Can't be repaired (see Example 2).

19. Too much missing. Can't be repaired without making a new argument entirely. But it is an
    argument. See the comments for Exercise 18.

20. "Ralph barks." Good argument if this is plausible.

21. "(Almost) the only way you can inherit blue eyes is if both your parents are blue-eyed" is the
    obvious premise to add to make the argument valid. But that's false. So it's unrepairable.

25. *Conclusion*: The burgers are better at Burger King. *Premises*: "The bigger the burgers the
    better the burgers." "The burgers are bigger at Burger King." The latter is not obviously true,
    and anyway, bigger than what? Bigger than at other fast-food places? Which ones? Too vague.
    Even if true, whether the argument is good depends on whether you agree with the first premise,
    which is subjective.

28. Not an argument. If you try to interpret it as an argument, it's hopelessly bad, and that should
    convince you not to think of it as an argument.

31. *Conclusion*: "Cigarettes are not a defective product that causes emphysema, lung cancer, and
    other illnesses." The premises in the quote contradict each other, so the argument is bad.

Section E

1. a. The guy she's talking to is fat.   b. She thinks I'm fat.

6. She was driving within a couple miles from her home—even though she had macular
    degeneration, Parkinson's disease, and Alzheimer's! [And that should scare you a lot!]

Chapter 5

Sections A *and* B.1

2. Accept as true, reject as false, suspend judgment.

3. Because it's impossible for the premises to be true and the conclusion false.

6. No. It's just the experience of other people.

9. We have good reason to doubt our memory, or the claim contradicts experiences of ours and there
    is a good argument (theory) against the claim. Also, beware of confusing memory with
    deductions from experience.

15. Our memory.

16. Nothing.

17. The same attitude we had before we heard the argument. An argument with a false premise tells
    us nothing about the conclusion.

Section B

3. The criteria go from ones closest to our own experience to those furthest.

16. Clearly biased: "masking their greed under a cloak of politics." Suspend judgment on all of it.

22. You're being foolish if you buy the root extract. There's no reason to believe the clerk knows anything about the subject; most likely he or she is just parroting what they've heard. And the "Well, it can't hurt" line is just plain false: Lots of quack cures sold at health-food stores can hurt you. You could end up spending thousands of dollars following quack cures before you do something useful for yourself. On the other hand, you might want to get a second opinion.

25. a. Reject (common knowledge that it's false).
    b. Reject—if you know anything about toads and warts. Change doctors.
    c. Reject (personal experience. You *did* notice it rises in the East?).
    f. Accept if you haven't been looking at your speedometer, or if you have and you know you were speeding. Reject if you've been monitoring your speed, saw the speed limit sign, and you weren't speeding. (But don't sass back.)
    g. Suspend judgment (biased source).
    j. Accept!! You can't reject this on personal experience, since no personal experience you have will tell you who got sick worst from which pets in the U.S. during the last year. Cats can transmit a disease to pregnant women that causes birth defects, and they also cause untold cases of severe asthma each year. And that's not even counting the infections from clawing.
    m. Suspend judgment (contradictory claims).

Section C

7. Donation? See Exercise 1.

8. Why would anyone who can make $250,000 per year playing craps share his secret with you? Good reason to reject the claim on the first line.

Section D

1. Noting that the conclusion of the argument is true, the person thinks there's good reason to believe the premises.

6. It may smack of hypocrisy, yet not really be a contradiction. Just because the person who states the argument apparently doesn't believe the conclusion, that doesn't mean the argument is bad.

9. Suzy really blew it! She's taking the word of an authority over her own experience. Above all you should trust your own experience.

13. Suzy is right! She says that she has no good reason to believe me, since I'm not an expert on virtue (I'm a logician, after all). She's not suggesting that I'm wrong, but only that she has no reason to accept the claim. (Of course, if Suzy knew me better, she'd revise her opinion.)

19. Just a comment on the speaker's *apparent* inconsistency.

Review Exercises for Chapters 1–5

1. A collection of claims intended to show that one of them, the conclusion, is true.

2. A declarative sentence used in such a way that it is true or false.

3. a. A claim whose truth-value does not depend on what anyone or anything thinks/believes/feels.

4. Yes, depending on the context.

5. a. A claim that says what should be (versus a descriptive claim which says what is).

6. No. A definition is an instruction for how to use a word or words.

7. a. A claim masquerading as a definition.

8. An argument that uses as a (stated or unstated) premise: If you can't make the difference precise, then there is no difference.

9. The premises are plausible.
    The premises are more plausible than the conclusion.
    The argument is valid or strong.

10. a. A valid argument is one in which it is impossible for the premises to be true and the conclusion false (at the same time).

11. a. A strong argument is one in which it is very unlikely for the premises to be true and the conclusion false (at the same time).

12. Yes. See the answer to Exercise 9.

13. Give a likely example where the premises are true and the conclusion false.

14. No. From a false premise you can prove anything.

15. Nothing.

16. No. It could beg the question. Or a premise could be false or dubious.

17. No. See the parakeets example in Chapter 3.

18. We assume that the other person who is discussing with us or whose arguments we are reading:
    (1) Knows about the subject under discussion, (2) Is able and willing to reason well, and
    (3) Is not lying.

19. Someone recognizes that an argument is good but does not believe the conclusion.

20. Given an (implicit) argument that is apparently defective, we are justified in adding a premise or conclusion if: 1. The argument becomes stronger or valid, and 2. The premise is plausible and would seem plausible to the other person, and 3. The premise is more plausible than the conclusion. If the argument is valid or strong, yet one of the premises is false or dubious, we may delete the premise if the argument remains valid or strong.

21. The obvious premise to add to make the argument strong or valid is false.
    The obvious premise to add would make the argument weak.
    A premise it uses is false or dubious and cannot be deleted.
    Two of its premises are contradictory and neither can be deleted.
    The argument is so lacking in coherence that there's nothing obvious to add.
    There's no argument there.
    The conclusion is clearly false.

22. a. A word or phrase added to a claim telling us the role of the claim in an argument or what the speaker thinks of the claim or argument.
    b. No.

23. Our personal experience.

24. Accept as true; reject as false; suspend judgment.

25. We know the claim is true from personal experience.
    The claim is made by someone we know and trust and who is an authority on this kind of claim.
    The claim is made by a reputable authority whom we can trust as being an expert about this kind of claim and who has no motive to mislead.
    The claim is put forward in a reputable journal or reference source.
    The claim is in a media source that's usually reliable and has no obvious motive to mislead, and the original source is named.

26. We know the claim is false from personal experience.
    The claim contradicts other claims we know to be true.

27. When we do not have good reason to believe a claim, and we do not have good reason to think that the claim is false.

28. He or she believes the premises are true because the argument is valid or strong and the conclusion is true.

29. He or she says an argument is bad just because of who said it.

30. Never.
31. Never.
32. Rejecting an argument because the speaker's actions or words suggest that he/she does not believe the conclusion of his/her own argument.

Chapter 6

Sections A.1 and A.2

1. A claim composed of other claims, but which has to be viewed as just one claim.
2. Alternatives.
6. Because each has to be true anyway for the argument to be good.
7. *Alternatives*: Inflation will go up. Interest rates will go up.
   Neither will inflation go up nor will interest rates go up.
11. *Alternatives*: You're for me. You're against me.
   You're neither for me nor against me.
15. Not a claim.

Section A

6.

9. *Argument*? Yes.
   Conclusion: Lee will vote for the Republican.
   Premises: Either you'll vote for the Republican or the Democratic candidate for president. Lee won't vote for the Democrat.
   Additional premises needed: None.
   Classify: Valid.
   Good argument? No. It's a false dilemma. There are other choices for Lee (the candidate for the Reform Party, the Green Party, . . .).

10. *Argument*? Yes.
   Conclusion: Manuel and Tom went to the basketball game.
   Premises: Manuel and Tom went to the basketball game if they didn't go to the library.
      (= Manuel and Tom went to the basketball game or they went to the library.) They didn't go to the library.
   Additional premises needed: None.
   Classify: Valid.
   Good argument? Good if the premises are true.

Section B.1

1. a. A claim that can be rewritten as an "if . . . then . . ." claim that always has the same truth-value. b. Yes.
5. Here are two samples. Come up with your own.
   Don't come home and there'll be hell to pay.
   When you get married it means that you can no longer date anyone else.
6. A, but not B.

7. a. Suzy studies hard, but she doesn't pass Dr. E's class.
    b. Both (b) and (*) could be true (if Dr. E has a kind heart).
    c. Both (c) and (*) could be true.
    d. Both (d) and (*) could be true in the case that Suzy doesn't study hard, since neither tells us what happens then.

9. *Conditional?* (yes or no) Yes.
    Antecedent: Maria goes shopping.
    Consequent: Manuel will cook.
    Contradictory: Maria goes shopping, but Manuel will not cook.

10. *Conditional?* (yes or no) Yes.
    Antecedent: Dick will help Lee with his English exam.
    Consequent: Lee will take care of Spot next weekend.
    Contradictory: Dick will help Lee with his English exam, but Lee will not take care of Spot next weekend.

14. *Conditional?* (yes or no) No. An argument. No contradictory.

15. *Conditional?* (yes or no) Yes.
    Antecedent: You'll get me some cake mix.
    Consequent: I'll bake a cake.
    Contradictory: You get me some cake mix, but I won't bake a cake.

18. *Conditional?* (yes or no) Yes.
    Antecedent: If Dick takes Spot for a walk, Dick will do the dishes.
    Consequent: Dick won't take Spot for a walk.
    Contradictory: If Dick takes Spot for a walk Dick will do the dishes, and Dick did take Spot for a walk.

Section B.2

1. a. If Flo doesn't have to take a bath, then she didn't play with Spot.
2. a. If Suzy didn't go with Tom to the library, then he didn't get out of practice by 6.
3. a. Neither necessary nor sufficient. c. (i) is sufficient for (ii).
7. a. If Zoe gets a transcript, then she paid her library fines.
    Or: If Zoe doesn't pay her library fines, then she won't get her transcript.
8. a. If Maria buys a new dress, then she got a bonus this month. A necessary condition for Maria to buy a new dress is that she gets a bonus this month.

Section B.3

6. Flo came over early to play. (direct way)
7. Spot didn't bark. (indirect way)
11. None. Appears to be affirming the consequent.

Exercises for Chapter 6

1. Excluding possibilities, the direct way of reasoning with conditionals, the indirect way of reasoning with conditionals, reasoning in a chain with conditionals, (and in an exercise: no matter what).
2. Affirming the consequent, denying the antecedent.
3. Affirming the consequent, denying the antecedent, false dilemmas, slippery slope arguments, (in an exercise: perfectionist dilemma).
6. If you get a credit card, you'll be tempted to spend money you don't have.
    If you're tempted to spend money you don't have, you will max out on your card.
    If you max out on your card, you'll be in real debt.

If you're in real debt, you'll have to drop out of school to pay your bills.
If you drop out of school, you'll end up a failure in life.
So if you get a credit card, you'll end up a failure in life.
But (unstated premise) you don't want to end up a failure in life.
So you shouldn't get a credit card.

7. a. If Dr. E isn't rich, then he didn't win the lottery.
        If Dr. E isn't rich, then his book didn't sell a million copies.
        If Dr. E isn't rich, then he didn't marry a rich woman.
    b. Dr. E won the lottery, but he isn't rich.
        Dr. E's book sold a million copies, but he isn't rich.
        Dr. E married a rich woman, but he isn't rich.
    d. Dr. E winning the lottery is sufficient for Dr. E to be rich.
        Dr. E's book selling a million copies is sufficient for Dr. E to be rich.
        Dr. E marrying a rich woman is sufficient for Dr. E to be rich.
    e. Dr. E being rich is necessary for Dr. E winning the lottery.
        Dr. E being rich is necessary for Dr. E's book selling a million copies.
        Dr. E being rich is necessary for Dr. E marrying a rich woman.

9. *Argument*? Yes.
    Conclusion: Suzy won't break up with Tom.
    Premises: If Suzy breaks up with Tom, then she'll have to return his letter jacket. Suzy won't give up that jacket.
    Additional premises needed: None.
    Classify : Valid.
    Form of argument: Indirect way.
    Good argument? Yes.

11. *Argument*? Yes.
    Conclusion: If you take issue with current Israeli policy, you're an anti-Semite.
    Premises: If you take issue with current Israeli policy, then you're criticizing Israel. If you criticize Israel, then you're anti-Israel. If you're anti-Israel, you're an anti-Semite.
    Additional premises needed: None.
    Classify: Valid.
    Form of argument: Reasoning in a chain with conditionals.
    Good argument? No. Unrepairable: Slippery slope. Last premise in particular is false.

13. *Argument*? Yes.
    Conclusion: It's the ebola virus (in Uganda).
    Premises: People in Uganda are dying of some fever where they hemorrhage a lot. If people in Uganda are dying of hemorrhagic fever, then it's the ebola virus.
    Additional premises needed: None.
    Classify: Valid.
    Form of argument: Direct way.
    Good argument? Yes, if premises are true.

14. *Argument*? Yes.
    Conclusion: I should not allow questions in my class.
    Bad argument. Slippery slope.

17. *Argument*? Yes.
    Conclusion: Columbus didn't discover America.
    Premises: Only if Columbus landed in a place with no people in it could you say he discovered

it. The Americas, especially where he landed, were populated. Columbus met natives.

Additional premises needed: If Columbus met natives, then where he landed was populated.

Classify: Valid.

Form of argument: Indirect way (rewrite the "only if" claim as an "if . . . then . . ." claim).

Good argument? Yes.

19. *Argument*? Yes.

Conclusion: If you lock up someone, he should be locked up forever.

Premises: Every criminal either is already a hardened repeat offender or will become one. Criminals learn to be hardened criminals in jail. We don't want any hardened criminals running free on our streets.

Additional premises needed: *First argument*: If a criminal is not a hardened repeat offender and goes to jail, then he will learn to be a hardened repeat offender.* If a criminal goes to jail, then he will be a hardened repeat offender. Every criminal who is locked up will become a hardened repeat offender.

Second argument: If we don't want any hardened criminals running free on our streets, then if we lock up a criminal, we should lock him up forever.

Classify: *First argument*: Valid—no-matter-what. *Second argument*: Valid–direct way.

Good argument? No. Premises are dubious, especially *. It's a false dilemma.

20. *Argument*? Yes.

Conclusion: Mary Ellen went on the Jane Fonda workout plan.

Premises: If Mary Ellen goes on the Jane Fonda workout plan, she'll lose weight. Mary Ellen lost weight.

Additional premises needed: None.

Classify: Weak.

Form of argument: Affirming the consequent.

Good argument? No.

21. *Argument*? Yes.

Conclusion: (unstated) Tom will get a dog.

Premises: Dick heard that Tom is going to get a pet. The only pets allowed in this town are dogs or cats or fish. Tom can't stand cats. Tom doesn't like a pet that you just contemplate. Tom won't get a fish.

Additional premises needed: If Dick heard that Tom is going to get a pet, then Tom is going to get a pet. (1st conclusion) Tom is going to get a pet. If Tom gets a pet, then it will have to be a dog or cat or fish. (2nd conclusion) Tom will get a dog or cat or fish. If Tom can't stand cats, then he won't get a cat. (3rd conclusion) Tom won't get a cat. If Tom doesn't like a pet that you just contemplate, then Tom won't get a fish. (4th conclusion) Tom won't get a fish. (5th conclusion) Tom will get a dog.

Classify: Valid.

Form of argument: Direct way (four times) and excluding possibilities.

Good argument? Possibly. Arguments are valid or strong and premises are plausible except for one unstated: "If Dick heard that Tom's going to get a pet, then Tom is going to get a pet."

22. *Argument*? No. Zoe is just trying to show her Mom is wrong by stating the contradictory. But she gets the contradictory wrong.

Chapter 7

1. No. All I've shown is that the student is (apparently) being irrational.
2. Raising objections to parts of an argument to show the argument is bad.

3. Nothing.

4. Answer the objections by showing that they are false or do not destroy the support for your conclusion. OR you could say, "I hadn't thought of that. I guess you're right." OR you could say, "I'll have to think about that."

7. Sex is the answer to almost everyone's problems.

> *Unsubstantiated claim. Dick's "Why?" asks for support. It's an invitation to Zoe to give an argument.*

It takes away your tension.

> *Zoe offers support for her conclusion.*

It doesn't if you're involved with someone you don't like.

> *Dick shows her support is false or dubious.*

Sex makes you feel better.

> *Zoe gives up on that support and offers another.*

It doesn't if it's against your morals. Heroin makes you feel good.

> *Dick's first comment shows Zoe's claim is dubious. His second comment shows that the relation of Zoe's claim to the conclusion is weak (he's challenging the unstated premise "If it feels good, it's good to do").*

It's healthy and natural, just like eating and drinking.

> *Zoe gives one last try to support her conclusion.*

You can catch terrible diseases. Sex should be confined to marriage.

> *Dick shows that support is dubious, too. Then he asserts his own view, which is somewhat supported by his previous claims.*

10. Unrepairable.

11. Showing that at least one of several claims is false or dubious, or collectively they are unacceptable, by drawing a false or unwanted conclusion from them.

13. Ridicule is not an argument.

15. It's a bad argument.

16. a. Putting words in someone's mouth. Refuting an argument or claim that the other person didn't really say.

19. Reducing to the absurd. Whether it's effective depends on what unstated premises are added to make it valid or strong. If the other person accepts capital punishment, it might be effective.

20. Tom's presented a strawman. Lee is for equal rights, not preferences. Tom has a common misconception, identifying equal rights laws with affirmative action programs. Doesn't refute.

21. This shows how important it is to master the material in this chapter if you want to be a good CEO. We can classify this hopelessly bad attempt at a refutation as *blustering*.

Chapter 8

Section A

1. Dogs eat meat. Every dog eats meat. Everything that's a dog eats meat.

2. At least one cat swims. There is a cat that swims. There exists a cat that swims.

5. Everything that flies is a bird.

6. No one who is a police officer is under 18 years old. All police officers are not under 18 years old. Not even one police officer is under 18 years old. Nothing that's a police officer is under 18 years old.

7. Dogs and only dogs are domestic canines.

8. Nothing that's a pig can fly. Pigs can't fly.

9. c. Don't confuse this with "Some textbooks fall apart after one semester." You cannot know this from your personal experience unless you've worked for a publisher.

d. False. I've seen Crest in some stores.

10. (There are other correct answers.)
    a. Some student doesn't like to study.
    b. Some woman is a construction worker.
    c. Some CEO of a Fortune 500 company is not a man.
    d. This exam will not be given in some of the sections of critical thinking.
    e. Some exam is suitable for all students.
    f. All exams really test a student's knowledge.
    g. All drunk drivers get in accidents.
    h. Some donkeys don't eat carrots.
    i Some people who die young aren't good.
    j. Someone who is a teacher is not allowed to grade exams or someone who grades exams is not a teacher.
    k. Something both barks and meows.
    l. Tom is not suspended, and he will not start some football game.
    m. There is a football player who is a vegetarian and his coach doesn't hate him. (See Chapter 6.)
    n. Some decisions about abortions should not be left to the woman and her doctor.
    o. Some cowboy had a friend named "Tonto," and the cowboy wasn't the Lone Ranger.

11. a. Sometimes when Dr. E is irritated with his students he doesn't give an exam.
    b. Sometimes it rains in Seattle in July.
    c. Spot will always chase Puff.
    d. There are flocks of birds along the river at times other than in the winter.

Section B

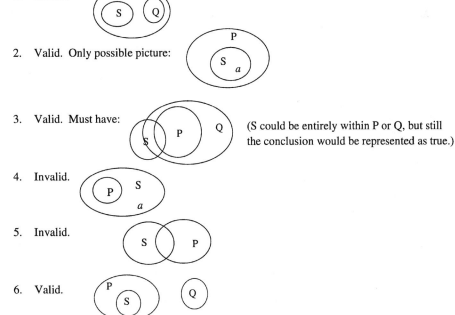

1. Invalid.

2. Valid. Only possible picture:

3. Valid. Must have: (S could be entirely within P or Q, but still the conclusion would be represented as true.)

4. Invalid.

5. Invalid.

6. Valid.

7. c.   9. c.   11. d.   13. d.

8. d.   10. c.   12. d.   14. d.

15. Invalid. Lee could be one of the ones who does attend lectures. Not every ≠ every not.

16. Not valid.

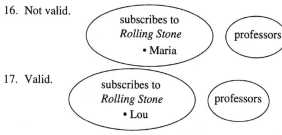

17. Valid.

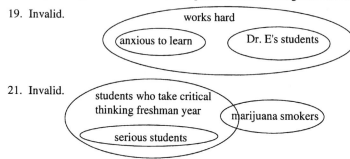

18. Invalid. No picture, but it could be that dogs bite only postal workers who are cowardly and would never bite back, and the postal workers who bite dogs are so tough they never get bitten. So there's no postal worker and dog that bite each other.

19. Invalid.

20.

21. Invalid.

23. Invalid. George could be mute.

25. Invalid.

26. Invalid. The premise is *not* "All hogs grunt." Don't mistake your knowledge of the world for what's actually been said. It's reasoning in a chain with "some."

30. Valid. No picture. Dr. E has a dog. That dog must love its master. So that dog loves Dr. E. So Dr. E is loved.

31. Invalid. Only janitors have access does not mean that all janitors have access. Paul could be one of the day janitors who doesn't have access.

33. For example,

   a. If it's a cat, then it coughs hair balls.
   b. If something is a donkey, then it eats hay.
   c. If something is made of chocolate, it's good to eat.
   d. If it's a duck, then it likes water.

Section C

1. All but a very few teenagers listen to rock music. Nearly every teenager listens to music. Only a very few teenagers don't listen to rock music.

2. Almost all adults don't listen to rock music. Very few adults listen to rock music. Almost no adult listens to rock music.

3. Strong.
4. Not strong. Arguing backwards with "very few."
5. Not strong. Here's a picture drawn to scale. ⟶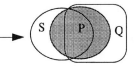
6. Strong.
7. Strong.
8. Strong.
9. Strong.
12. Weak, reasoning in a chain with "almost all."
13. Strong.

Review Exercises for Chapters 6–8

1. An argument is a collection of claims, one of which is called the "conclusion," and the others of which, called the "premises," are meant to establish or prove that the conclusion is true.
2. The premises are plausible. The premises are more plausible than the conclusion. The argument is valid or strong.
3. A valid argument is one for which it is impossible for the premises to be true and the conclusion false (at the same time).
4. A strong argument is one for which it is almost impossible for the premises to be true and the conclusion false (at the same time).
5. No. The premises could be false or it could beg the question. You should provide an example of a bad valid argument.
6. Provide a likely example where the premises are true and the conclusion false.
7. No. It could beg the question. You should provide an example.
8. A compound claim is one that is made up of other claims, but which has to be viewed as just one claim.
10. a. The contradictory of a claim is another claim that must have the opposite truth-value.
11. Yes.
12. A false dilemma is an "or" claim that seems to be true but isn't, because there is another possibility that it does not state.
13. Yes.   15. No.
14. Yes.   16. No.
17. No. It could be a slippery slope argument.
18. a. "A is a necessary condition for B" means that "If B, then A" is true.
19. It helps you avoid making your argument weak, and it shows others that you have considered the other side.
20. Show that one of the premises is dubious; show that the argument isn't valid or strong; show that the conclusion is false.
21. Only if the additional premises you have used are all true and the argument is valid. If the additional premises are only plausible, or the argument is only very strong, you've only shown that it's very likely that one of the original premises is false or collectively they lead to an absurdity.
22. A slippery slope argument is bad and doesn't refute.
23. Ridicule is not an argument.
31. Excluding possibilities.   The direct way of reasoning with "all."
    The direct way of reasoning with conditionals.   Reasoning in a chain with "all."
    The indirect way of reasoning with conditionals.   The direct way of reasoning with "no."
    Reasoning in a chain with conditionals.

32. Affirming the consequent.   Reasoning in a chain with "some."
    Denying the antecedent.   The direct way of reasoning with "almost all."
    Arguing backwards with "all."   Arguing backwards with "almost all."
    Arguing backwards with "no."   Reasoning in a chain with "almost all."

Chapter 9

14. Weaseler: Zoe didn't apologize!
16. This implies but does not state that in our part of the world people don't react with emotions and wouldn't be so easily manipulated as the Arabs, which is false.
19. There is no slanter in this highly disparaging remark about foreign-exchange dealers. It's all upfront ridicule.
21. Hyperbole: The whole forest?
23. Weaseler: He didn't say it *was* the most important message, but *if* . . . .
24. "Despite" is an up-player. Why "despite"?
26. "Gaming" is a euphemism for "gambling." Sure you'd say, "Honey, let's go out gaming tonight."
33. Euphemism: unspoiled wilderness area = uninhabited area.
35. Weaseler: This is not an apology for interfering with his course, but an attack on the professor's standards: He's the cause of the problem because he's male.
38. Implies without proof that junkies, rape, and bad families are "real life." But no slanters.
40. Qualifier: at present.
41. Euphemisms: resettled = forcibly moved to *and* internment camps = prison camps (it's a dysphemism to call them "concentration camps").   Innuendo: at last.
44. Concealed claim: seat belts protect from injury / she was lucky not to be injured when not wearing a seat belt. But in this case the concealed claim is true.

Chapter 10

8. Zoe's argument: appeal to pity. Premise: You shouldn't experiment on animals if you feel sorry for the dogs.
   Dick's argument: appeal to spite. Premise: You should experiment on cats if they make me sneeze.
9. Feel-good argument. Bad.
14. Appeal to patriotism (subspecies of feel-good argument). Generic premise: You should believe that democracy is the best form of government if you love the U.S. (and think it's the greatest country). Bad argument.
17. Appeal to fear. You might think it's O.K. because a senator is supposed to worry about how his votes will be perceived by his constituents. But it's bad: We have a *representative* democracy, so a senator is supposed to vote as he or she thinks best. And the children whose votes the writer is threatening the senator with aren't voters yet.
19. Appeal to fear. Without more premises it's bad.
20. Wishful thinking. Bad. That way of thinking may be useful, though, to motivate the person to lose weight.

Chapter 11

1. The argument must be valid or strong; we must have good reason to believe its premises; the premises must be more plausible than the conclusion.
4. No. It could beg the question, or a premise could be implausible even though true.
5. Only if the false premise can be eliminated and the argument remains strong.
6. Nothing.

7. Our own experience.

8. The argument has a valid form. It's just that some of the premises are false or collectively too dubious.

9. It's a valid argument form. But the "or" claim is false or dubious.

10. An attempt to reduce to the absurd is pretty clearly an argument. With ridicule there's no argument at all.

29. A strawman is putting words in someone's mouth, attempting to refute an argument by refuting a different one.

30. Because they are also clearly bad ways to convince, though they aren't arguments.

Short Arguments for Analysis

These are just sketches of answers, enough for you to see how to fill them out.

2. Shifting the burden of proof. Bad. But you probably knew that even before reading it.

4. Dick's response to Zoe's comments looks like an attempt to reduce to the absurd; but not enough argument is given, so it's just ridicule.

5. Not an argument; there's no attempt to convince.

7. Tom's argument has a prescriptive conclusion: You should get a small pig. Everything he says may be true, but it won't get him the conclusion unless he has some prescriptive premise. You figure out what that should be and if it's plausible.

    Dick makes an argument that Lee shouldn't accept Tom's argument. Dick is mistaking the person for the argument.

9. Conclusion: Maria's alarm didn't go off. Premise: She's still asleep. Unstated premise: If Maria's still asleep, her alarm clock didn't go off. Direct way of reasoning with conditionals. Good.

12. Shifting the burden of proof: The candidate who's speaking has to show inflation is a serious risk.

14. Powell is making an argument with conclusion (unstated/reworded), "Working with toxic chemicals is not exceptionally dangerous." This leads into Chapter 12, since it depends on a very faulty analogy. Bad, possibly wishful thinking.

16. Lee is refuting Tom's argument by reducing to the absurd. Good refutation.

19. It looks like Zoe is concluding that these cookies will be awful. If so, it's reasoning in a chain with "some," and it's bad.

20. Conclusion: You should employ Mr. Abkhazian as your lawyer.
    Premise: He's been doing accident cases for 20 years.
    Unstated premises: If he's been doing accident cases for 20 years, he's good at doing that. You should go to someone who's good at accident cases.
    Bad argument. First unstated premise is dubious.

22. Suzy draws a conclusion from Zoe's comment: You don't care about people.
    Weak and no way to make it stronger. Bad.

23. Strawman (Ms. F is putting words in the student's mouth). Bad.

28. Premises: Israel had 23 casualties. The combat took a long time.
    Conclusion: Great efforts were made by the IDF to conduct the operation carefully in an effort to bring to an absolute minimum the number of Palestinian civilian casualties.
    Unstated premises: Israel has a huge military advantage. Israel could just heavily bomb the refugee camp at Jenin. If a military operation in an urban setting takes a long time and the strong attacking force has a number of casualties, then a great effort was made to keep civilian casualties to a minimum.
    The last premise is implausible (a conditional form of a false dilemma), unless "great effort" means doing anything other than bombing a refugee camp flat. Since we can assume that the

people in the IDF can reason, this appears to be evidence that they don't adhere to the Principle of Rational Discussion.

31. Appeal to pity. With an unstated prescriptive premise, it's good.

32. Bad appeal to authority. The attorney general has motive to mislead. It's just too much to think that a political appointee never lies and always investigates thoroughly. But that's not to say the conclusion is false!

33. This conspiracy theory illustrates that possibility ≠ plausibility. The Interior Minister has given no reason to believe anything he's said. This is so bad that it's either an attempt to confuse people, or it shows that the Saudi minister can't reason. Either way, don't bother to engage him in rational discussion.

40. With appropriate unstated premises, it's excluding possibilities, and it's good.

42. Ridicule. Bad. Or it's reducing to the absurd, and good, depending on what Lee believes.

43. Begging the question.

44. Bad. Reasoning backwards with "all": Only tenants have a key = All people who have a key are tenants. Harry might be one of the tenants who doesn't have a key.

45. DOGS ARE GOOD. CATS ARE BAD.

46. Conclusion: Suzy or one of her friends will get a contract. Reasoning in a chain with "some." Bad.

48. Implied but unstated: Women heads of credit unions are not qualified—otherwise, Headlee would see that there are plenty of women in Utah who are qualified. Convincing without an argument with innuendo. Bad.

49. We can make this argument fairly strong by adding premises: "Society should do what it can to prevent young people from engaging in sexual activities before they are emotionally prepared and before they understand the health risks." "Young people who know about the mechanics of sex will not be as likely to engage in risky sexual activities." "Teaching young people to refrain from sexual intercourse will lessen the likelihood that they will engage in sexual intercourse before they are emotionally prepared."

    All these are plausible. But what about the third premise of the original argument? The unstated premise needed to link it to the conclusion is something like "Society should do what it can to prevent young women from becoming pregnant before they are 20" and/or "Becoming pregnant before age 20 is bad." Those are at best dubious (in parts of the U.S. it is considered a religious duty to start a family right after high school).

    Though the original premise is not itself dubious, trying to incorporate it into the argument will make the argument worse. Since we already have a moderately strong argument, we delete this premise, just as we would a false premise that isn't essential to the strength of the argument. If the speaker feels it is crucial, then he or she will have to link it to the conclusion.

50. Appeal to fear. (Do you really think Suzy's committed to self-immolation?) Bad.

51. Bad appeal to authority. It's the reverse of "If you're so smart, why aren't you rich?"

52. Bad argument. Proved the wrong conclusion! (Compare the last sentence to the first one.) Also bad generalizations, which we'll study in Chapter 14.

54. Lee is reasoning backwards with "no." Also, first premise is dubious. Bad.

57. Perfectionist dilemma, or bad appeal to common practice. ("If I were to stop making noise, that wouldn't solve the problem. So I shouldn't stop making noise.") Bad.

61. Good argument with unstated premises which you can add. (Prescriptive conclusion, so it'll need a prescriptive premise.)

62. Bad. Affirming the consequent.

63. Good. Direct way of reasoning with "no."

64. They're debating a vague sentence that has no truth-value. (Maybe Suzy thinks that arriving on time means within an hour, like most Brazilians.) Or they're trying to make a subjective claim objective.

65. Bad. Reasoning backwards with "all": "Only A are B" is equivalent to "All B are A." Sam might be one of the managers not allowed behind the bar because he doesn't have a bartender's license as he normally only works with food.

66. Maria's argument is pretty good with the added claim: If the factory farms are awful, you shouldn't eat meat. But that's too vague: What does she mean by "awful"? Maybe what's awful for her isn't awful to Suzy. Suzy responds with the "ostrich technique": If I don't see it, it's not there. She doesn't fulfill the Principle of Rational Discussion.

69. Weak argument—horse manure also has a lot of vitamins and protein in it. Unrepairable. Conclusion is also false. Bad. (As stated it's not wishful thinking.)

71. Bad. Maybe Dr. E went out with Ms. Fletcher who has a cat.

72. Conclusion: We have saved hundreds of thousands of lives.
    Premises: It took only 20 terrorists to kill 3,000 people. We've killed hundreds of people in an offensive against Al-Qaida fighters.
    Unstated premises: All, or at least the great part, of the people we killed were Al-Qaida fighters (and not innocent villagers boosting the death toll). Everyone who is an Al-Qaida fighter could be a terrorist who could kill 150 or more people, like the terrorists who flew the planes into the World Trade Center. Hundreds of people killed times 150 per person is hundreds of thousands of people.
    Each of the unstated premises is clearly false or highly dubious. In particular, the last unstated premise shows that Maj. Bryan Hilferty not only can't reason, he can't do simple arithmetic, either. Bad argument.

Complex Arguments for Analysis

Exercises on Structure of Arguments

1. My neighbor should be forced to get rid of all the cars in his yard. *1* People do not like living next door to such a mess. *2* He never drives any of them. *3* They all look old and beat up, *4* and (they) leak oil all over the place. *5* It is bad for the neighborhood, *6* and it will decrease property values. *7*
    Argument? Yes.
    Conclusion: *1*
    Additional premises needed? If someone drives a car occasionally, he'd have the right to keep it on his property. *a* So he doesn't have a right to keep the cars on his property. *b* Cars that leak oil on the land are an environmental hazard. *c* Environmental hazards should not be allowed to continue. *d* If a person has something on his property that his neighbors do not like, that is an environmental hazard, that he does not have a right to keep in his yard, and which decreases property values, then he should get it off his property. *e*
    Identify any subargument: *3* and *a* support *b*. *5* and *c* support *d*. Then *2, 7, c,* and *e* yield *1*. Note that *4* can be deleted. And *6* is too vague.
    Good argument? Claim *7* is not clearly true—it depends on the neighborhood (it could be an industrial area). Everything rides on claim *e,* which on the face of it looks pretty plausible. In that case the argument is valid and good.

2. I'm on my way to school. *1* I left five minutes late. *2* Traffic is heavy. *3* I'll be late for class. *4* I might as well stop and get breakfast. *5*
    Argument? Yes.
    Conclusion: *5*

Additional premises needed? Whenever I'm on my way to school and I'm 5 minutes late and traffic is heavy, I will be late for my class. *a* If I'm late for class, I might as well be very late or miss the class. *b*

Identify any subargument: *1, 2, 3,* and *a* support *4.* Then *4* and *b* support *5.*

Good argument? Depends on whether *b* is true.

3. Las Vegas has too many people. *1* There's not enough water in the desert to support more than a million people. *2* And the infrastructure of the city can't handle more than a million *3* the streets are overcrowded *4* and traffic is always congested; *5* the schools are overcrowded *6* and new ones can't be built fast enough. *7* We should stop migration to the city by tough zoning laws in the city and county. *8*

Argument? Yes.

Conclusion: 8

Additional premises needed? (You must know what "infrastructure" means to make sense of this argument.) Las Vegas has close to a million people. *a* If streets are crowded and schools are crowded, then the infrastructure is inadequate. *b* If infrastructure is inadequate and there is not enough water for more people, there are too many people. *c* If there are too many people, new migration to the city should be stopped. *d* The best way to stop migration is by tough zoning laws. *e* (Can't add: The *only* way to stop migration to the city is by tough zoning laws—you could arm gangs, or raise building fees.)

Identify any subargument: *4, 5, 6, 7,* and *b* are dependent as support for *3.*
    2, a, 3, and *c* support *1.* *1, d,* and *e* support *8.*

Good argument? Everything is plausible with the exception of *e.* If that can be shown to be true, it's good.

Chapter 12

2. We need to draw a conclusion based on the comparison.

3. No. They typically lack a statement of a general principle that would cover both (or all) cases.

4. First, state the conclusion. Second, look for similarities that suggest a general principle.

6. This is a comparison, not an argument. What conclusion could we draw?

The following are just sketches of answers.

8. Zoe is refuting Dick's argument that it's O.K. to throw a banana peel out the window by showing the same argument would work for horse manure.

11. This is not really an analogy. It's questioning whether the person believes the general principle he/she espouses.

12. This is an argument, with conclusion (stated as a rhetorical question) that it isn't O.K. to let someone who isn't trained as a teacher teach. Higuchi has, however, assumed the further premise "If someone doesn't have a teacher's credential, then he doesn't know what he's doing teaching," which is dubious. The comparison of a brain surgeon with a teacher has too many dissimilarities to be convincing: If a brain surgeon screws up, the patient dies or is mentally crippled, but if a teacher screws up a class, students will still likely learn, and by the end of the term he or she is likely to be teaching more or less competently, and the students won't do worse than with any bad teacher.

14. We can fill this out to be an argument: We don't sell sunshine. Trading water is like selling sunshine. So we *shouldn't* sell water.

    It's a very bad analogy. First, we do sell sunshine: In some big cities, there are laws and various covenants about blocking windows/views when building. Second, we *can't* sell sunshine in the same way we sell water, allocating a supply. And the prescriptive premise that's needed here is unclear.

18. Tom is committing the fallacy of composition: What is good for the individual is good for the group. But there are major differences: spontaneous vs. organized violence is the most obvious. There are too many differences between being against all wars and unwilling to participate in wars, and being unwilling to respond to personal violence.

19. This analogy breaks down. The person with the sense of smell will be right most of the time, in many different situations, and clearly so. No magician is going to find him out. Eventually, using brain scans and physical examinations, we could determine to some extent the mechanism behind his predictions, even if we ourselves couldn't experience them. But to date, claims about ESP can't be duplicated, even by the person claiming to have the powers; they are often debunked; they aren't right almost always, but just a bit more than average. It's not just that we have lost motivation to investigate ESP because of so many false claims about it. We haven't even found a good candidate to study.

20. Dick seems to be inferring that Tom is concluding we shouldn't use seat belts. But Tom doesn't say that, and it's not clear he believes that. In that case, Dick gives us food for thought, but not much more than unjustified ridicule.
    The research was done by Sam Peltzman of the University of Chicago.

21. This analogy relies on the unstated prescriptive premise: If people do something for a living, and they need that living to pay their bills and support their families, and they teach their children morals, then they should be allowed to get along with earning their living and not having that means of earning a living outlawed. That's a dubious principle, for it would justify any kind of murderous, immoral way of earning money, contract killing, for instance. Note that Parish does not say that the reason she should be allowed to continue is that it's a *sport* or that it *harms no one*. That would be a very different argument.

22. Challenge: If this isn't a good argument, how would you convince someone that others feel pain? And if you can't, what justification would you have for not torturing people? (We know that torture can elicit information or behavior we want.)

24. A bad analogy because of the differences. We determine that a watch was made by someone because it *differs* from what we find in nature that is not crafted, such as rocks or trees. And we can deduce from its construction that it has a purpose. We can't do that for all of nature.

26. If you said "yes" for some and "no" for others, what differences are there? If you said the same for all, did you reason by analogy? What general principle did you use?

27. Did you answer this the same as Exercise 26? If so, what was your reason? Are you arguing by analogy? What is your general principle?

Chapter 13

5. It means that for every 100 women who use the contraceptive *for one year*, one will become pregnant. (See the explanation on p. 340 of the *Workbook*.)

6. average: 74.27   mean: 74.27   median: 76   mode: 88 *and* 62

8. Well, the experts are right. All you have to do is wait until the stock market goes back up again —unless you die first. It's like doubling your bet on black with roulette every time you lose. You're sure to win in the long run. Unless you go broke first.

11. What dollars are they talking about? When you consider the trillions of dollars spent by the government on debt and the military—which isn't for cleaning products—you can see that this can't be right. And there's no reason to believe that so much money is spent on cleaning products by individuals. And there's no government agency called "The Bureau of Statistics."

12. It's 45% lower than the average of the other brands, but 24 of those other brands could actually have less fat than this candy bar if there's just one of them that has a huge amount of fat. And what are those "leading" brands? Leading where? In Brazil?

14. This is apples and oranges, because it doesn't correct for inflation: $2,000 in 1968 is equivalent to what in current dollars?

17. Wrong. It's just backwards. It should be: If you have breast cancer, there's less than a 10% chance you have the gene.

18. This is just a way to say that Americans think of themselves as nonconformists, and Japanese think of themselves as conformists. The numbers are meaningless.

21. Don't do it, Dick. One per day ≠ average of one per day.

27. Funny how they break down the figures in the next-to-last paragraph, but not in the last one. It could be that of the 99%, only 1% actually improved.

28. Meaningless: Too much variation from one area to another. Median or mode won't be much more use.

29. A fair indication, since there's not much variation.

30. Terrible comparison: There's little variation in university professors' salaries (almost all earn between $30,000 and $75,000), but there's a huge variation in concert pianists' income ($15,000 vs. $2,000,000). The mode would be more informative.

32. Curious, but not much you can conclude from it. Could be that it's easier to get good grades now, or the students are smarter, or students are taking a different mix of courses than before, or . . . .

Chapter 14

Section A

1. Generalizing. *Sample*: The German shepherds the speaker has met.
   Population: All German shepherds.

3. Generalizing. *Sample*: The MP3 player that Suzy has.
   Population: All Hirangi MP3 players.

6. Generalizing. *Sample*: The times Dick has taken Spot to the vet before.
   Population: All times Dick has or will take Spot to the vet.

8. Generalizing.   *Sample*: The times that Maria has taken her clothes to be cleaned at Ricardo's.
   Population: All times anyone will take their clothes to that dry cleaner.

9. Possibly generalizing, but could be just repeating a general claim he's heard. We can't identify the sample, so don't treat it as a generalization until the speaker elaborates.

10. A general claim, but no generalizing is going on, since there's no argument.

11. Hard to say if it's generalizing. Has the speaker met Japanese guys? Or is she just repeating a stereotype she's heard?

Section B

1. One in which no subgroup of the population is represented more than its proportion in the population.

2. There is always a possibility that the members of the population which you haven't studied are different from the ones you have studied.

3. a. If the probability of something occurring is X percent, then over the long run the number of occurrences will tend toward X percent.
   b. The probability of getting a sample that isn't representative is very small.

7. You can't know in advance what the "relevant" characteristics are. If you could, you wouldn't need to do a survey/experiment. You're biasing the sample towards the characteristics you think in advance are important. See Exercise 6.

9. No. Indeed, the law of large numbers predicts that eventually a randomly chosen sample of 20 students at your school will consist of just gay men. But the likelihood of a randomly chosen sample not being representative is small.

Exercises for Chapter 14

1. There is a 94% chance that between 51% and 61% of the entire population of voters actually favors your candidate.

2. No.

3. a. A hasty generalization using anecdotal evidence.
   b. Yes, see the example in Section C.5. There would have to be very little variation in the population.

4. Variation.

5. 1. The sample is big enough.
   2. The sample is representative.
   3. The sample is studied well.
   Note well: The second premise is *not* "The sample is chosen randomly." That claim can support the second premise, but isn't always needed. See the answer to Exercise 3.b.

8. Such a survey would be nonsense because most students don't know what the president of a college does—or can do. Do you approve of the way they're sweeping the streets in Timbuktu?

12. *Generalization*: All CDs can hold an encyclopedia's-worth of information.
    Sample: The CD that the speaker just bought.
    Sample is representative? Yes, no variation in population (if it's broken, it doesn't count).
    Sample is big enough? Yes, no variation in population.
    Sample is studied well? Yes, the speaker has seen it on his/her computer.
    Good generalization? Yes.

14. This is a confused attempt to generalize. Perhaps Lee thinks that the evidence he cites gives the conclusion that if you invest in the stock market, you'll get rich(er). But that's arguing backwards, confusing (1) "If you invest in the stock market, you'll get rich" with (2) "If you're rich, then you will have invested in the stock market." The population for (1) is all investors in the stock market, not just the rich ones. It's a case of selective attention.

15. *Generalization*: (unstated) Lots of people fail Dr. E's course.
    Sample: The three people the speaker knows.
    Sample is representative? No reason to believe so.
    Sample is big enough? More like anecdotal evidence.
    Sample is studied well? Yes, they failed.
    Good generalization? No.
    Unstated premise and conclusion: You shouldn't take a course you might fail. You shouldn't take Dr. E's course.

19. *Generalization*: (unstated) A high percentage of women think men with beards are sexy.
    Sample: The women who responded to the survey.
    Sample is representative? No reason to believe so. Lee doesn't even have reason to think the sample is representative of the women who read that magazine. After all, they may have got only 10,000 out of 200,000 sent out, and mostly women who like men with beards responded.
    Sample is big enough? Yes, if only we had reason to believe it is representative.
    Sample is studied well? Probably.
    Good generalization? No.

21. Tom is not making a generalization; he's using one. Almost all pro basketball players are over six feet tall, and people that tall won't fit into Suzy's car. Therefore, (unstated) You shouldn't use Suzy's car to pick up the basketball player. Needs an unstated premise: You shouldn't pick up someone in a car he can't fit into. Pretty good argument.

23. *Generalization*: Aquarians are scientific but eccentric.
    Sample: Copernicus, Galileo, and Thomas Edison.

Sample is representative? No.
Sample is big enough? No.
Sample is studied well? Probably O.K.
Good generalization? No.

24. *Generalization:* The pacifier will stop the baby from crying.
    Sample: All the times the speaker has given the pacifier to the baby.
    Sample is representative? Who knows?
    Sample is big enough? We don't know how often they've done it.
    Sample is studied well? Possibly, or possibly bad memory.
    Additional premises needed? None.
    Good generalization? Weak, but there's little risk in that course of action.

29. *Generalization:* Questioning partners about their sex lives is not an effective strategy for reducing the risk of acquiring AIDS for young people.
    Sample: 665 students attending colleges in California, aged 18–25.
    Sample is representative? No.
    Sample is big enough? Don't know.
    Sample is studied well? Only if you trust the responses people give to questions about their sexual history and what they'd do to get sex.
    Good generalization? Not as bad as it may seem. Remember, the authors are trying to disprove a generalization, rather than prove their own!

32. The analogy is comparing Maria's rice cooker to the one that Zoe wants to buy. The generalization needed is: (Almost) all Blauspot rice cookers will have a serious defect. Though the generalization is only anecdotal evidence, Zoe might decide that the risk is enough to go with that weak argument.

33. The analogy is between chimpanzees and humans. It requires a a generalization that (almost) all chimpanzees will become obese if fed one pound of chocolate per day in addition to their regular diet. The analogy depends on the similarity of chimpanzee physiology to human physiology, and assumes that the equivalent of one pound of chocolate for a chimpanzee to 1% of body weight for a human. And how much exercise did they get? A pretty poor argument: The conclusion is more plausible than the premises.

Chapter 15

Sections A.1–A.3

1. *Causal claim:* The police car's siren caused me to pull over.
   Particular or *general?* Particular.
   Cause (stated as a claim): The police car had its siren going near me.
   Effect (stated as a claim): I pulled over.

2. *Causal claim:* Dick getting a speeding ticket caused his insurance rates to go up.
   Particular or *general?* Particular.
   Cause (stated as a claim): Dick got a speeding ticket.
   Effect (stated as a claim): Dick's insurance rates went up.

3. *Causal claim:* People getting speeding tickets causes their insurance rates to go up.
   Particular or *general?* General—generalizing over all examples like Exercise 2.

4. *Causal claim:* Your being late caused us to miss the beginning of the movie.
   Particular or *general?* Particular. *Cause* (stated as a claim): You were late.
   Effect (stated as a claim): We missed the beginning of the movie.

6. Not a causal claim. (Sometimes "make" means "causes," and sometimes not.)

7. Not a causal claim. Inductive evidence is offered for a generalization that might be used in establishing a general causal claim.

8. *Causal claim*: Someone ringing the doorbell caused Spot to bark.
   Particular or *general*? Particular.
   Cause (stated as a claim): Someone rang the doorbell.
   Effect (stated as a claim): Spot barked.

10. *Causal claim*: Drinking coffee causes me not to get a headache in the afternoon.
    Particular or *general*? General. Perhaps too vague: How much coffee?

Section A

3. The normal conditions.

4. We can't see how to fill in the normal conditions. It's just like when we say a premise isn't relevant to the conclusion of an argument.

7. Reread Chapter 5.

Sections A *and* B

1. *Causal claim*: Someone pulling in front of Maria caused her to slam on her brakes.
   Cause: Someone pulled in front of Maria.
   Effect: Maria slammed on her brakes.
   Cause and effect true? Apparently so.
   Cause precedes effect? Yes.
   It's nearly impossible for the cause to be true and effect false? Yes, given some plausible normal conditions.
   Cause makes a difference? It seems so, but we need to know more about what was happening at the time. Was Maria paying attention?
   Common cause? Possibly, if the other driver was trying to avoid hitting someone.
   Evaluation: Plausible if nothing else unusual was happening at the time.

2. *Causal claim*: Wearing new shoes caused Suzy's feet to hurt when she was cheerleading.
   Cause: Suzy wore new shoes cheerleading.
   Effect: Her feet hurt.
   Cause and effect true? Apparently so. Suzy ought to know.
   Cause precedes effect? Yes.
   It's nearly impossible for the cause to be true and effect false? We need to know the normal conditions. Was everything like it usually is when Suzy is cheerleading? Apparently so, from what she says.
   Cause makes a difference? Suzy says it did, by comparing it to all the other times when she didn't have sore feet.
   Common cause? None apparent.
   Evaluation: Pretty plausible.

3. *Causal claim*: Dick pigging out on nachos and salsa caused his stomachache.
   Cause: Dick pigged out on nachos and salsa last night.
   Effect: Dick has a stomachache.
   Cause and effect true? Apparently so, but Zoe could be exaggerating.
   Cause precedes effect? Yes.
   It's nearly impossible for the cause to be true and effect false? We need to know more.
   Cause makes a difference? Can't say without knowing more.
   Common cause? No.
   Evaluation: Suspend judgment.

4. *Causal claim*: Marriage causes divorce. General causal claim.
   Evaluation: This is tracing too far back: Getting married is part of the normal conditions for getting a divorce.

5. *Causal claim*: (unstated) My not going to the game causes the team to lose. It's a general causal claim.
   Evaluation: Anecdotal evidence. *Post hoc* reasoning. No reason to believe it.

6. This isn't cause and effect, it's a definition.

7. *Causal claim*: The dark sky caused Zoe to be depressed.
   Cause: The sky was dark.
   Effect: Zoe got depressed.
   Cause and effect true? Apparently so.
   Cause precedes effect? Yes.
   It's nearly impossible for the cause to be true and effect false? Can't say. We'd need to know a lot more about Zoe's psyche, or else rely on a generalization that Zoe gets depressed every time it's dark in similar circumstances.
   Cause makes a difference? Perhaps, but we need to know what happened to Zoe before that might have made her depressed.
   Common cause? None.
   Evaluation: Suspend judgment until we know more.

8. *Causal claim*: The sun being strong yesterday caused me to get a sunburn.
   Cause: The sun was strong yesterday.
   Effect: I got a sunburn.
   Cause and effect true? Apparently so.
   Cause precedes effect? Yes.
   It's nearly impossible for the cause to be true and effect false? Depends on what we call the normal conditions.
   Cause makes a difference? Yes.
   Common cause? None.
   Evaluation: This is a good candidate for *a* cause, not *the* cause. Zoe being outside with her skin exposed for a long period of time is not a normal condition.

11. *Causal claim*: Lou's getting a college education is *a* cause of his getting a high-paying job the year after he graduated.
    Cause: Lou graduated college.
    Effect: Lou got a job the next year.
    Cause and effect true? Apparently so.
    Cause precedes effect? Yes.
    It's nearly impossible for the cause to be true and effect false? Unlikely.
    Cause makes a difference? Don't know. What are the normal conditions? Does Lou's dad own the factory where he got the job?
    Common cause? Perhaps Lou's parents are wealthy.
    Evaluation: Plausible as *a* cause, if the normal conditions are right.

13. *Causal claim*: Dick telling Sally that Zoe killed Puff caused Zoe to be miserable now.
    Cause: Dick told Sally that Zoe killed Puff.
    Effect: Zoe is unhappy now.
    Cause and effect true? Apparently so. Dick doesn't deny it!
    Cause precedes effect? Yes.
    It's nearly impossible for the cause to be true and effect false? Can't tell.
    Cause makes a difference? Can't tell.

Common cause? None apparent.

Evaluation: Tracing the cause too far back. A psychiatrist might say Zoe's right. But spelling out what she believes are the normal conditions might show she's wrong. It's like the Treaty of Versailles example, and on top of that it's subjective. Just have broad shoulders, Dick.

19. *Causal claim*: (General) Smoking marijuana causes heroin use.

    Evaluation: First, at best it's *can cause* not *causes,* since we all know examples of people who smoke marijuana and don't use heroin. But it's also *post hoc* reasoning. They probably all drank milk, too.

23. Clear possibility of common cause: Their parents are richer and/or spend time with them, which is why they get breakfast and do better.

Section C

2. There isn't a causal claim here. Rather, Flo is overlooking one. Perhaps coincidence is just our ignorance of real cause and effect. To be sure, our knowledge is limited. But not commonly as limited as with children.

3. *Causal claim*: The pedals are making a clicking sound on Dick's bike.

   Cause: The pedals are defective. ??   *Effect*: There is a clicking sound.

   Evaluation: Good method, but a false dilemma starts it. The clicking could also come from the gears. Have Zoe put her ear close to the pedals when Dick is turning them.

Section D

9. Suzy thinks that being in the army causes men to abuse their wives. But there's a possible common cause that hasn't been ruled out: Men who are prone to abuse their wives like violence and hence are more likely to join the army.

11. *Causal claim*: A high-fiber diet *can cause* less colon cancer.

    Type of cause-in-population experiment: Uncontrolled: cause-to-effect.

    Evaluate the evidence: Clear correlation. Not clear if sample is representative, though large. No mechanism given for explaining why there is the correlation. Equally likely is the reverse cause and effect: People eat more fruit and fiber because their digestion is good. Until that is ruled out, there's no reason to believe the claim.

    Further tests? Controlled studies seem in order to rule out the reverse cause and effect. Try to find an explanation for the correlation.

12. *Causal claim*: Suggests without saying it ("Some studies on day care have found it's not bad at all"): Day care causes behavioral, emotional, and physical health problems for children.

    Type of cause-in-population experiment: The first two bulleted items are not studies at all, just *post hoc* observations. The third bulleted item appears to be an uncontrolled cause-to-effect study, but it's hard to say, since not enough information is given. The fourth bulleted item appears to be an uncontrolled cause-to-effect study.

    Evaluate the evidence: All this is just *post hoc ergo propter hoc.* There's no reason to think there isn't a common cause of parents putting their children in day care and children's problems, namely, parents are too busy to give time to their kids. Or parents who leave their children in day care—on the whole—have pressures that make them not parent well. Or bad parents prefer to put their children in day care. Or . . . There's no reason to believe the causal claim based on what's said here.

    Further tests? Uncontrolled studies that factor out common threads. Controlled studies.

15. *Causal claim*: Giving sick people better health care causes them to be hospitalized more.

    Type of cause-in-population experiment: Controlled cause-to-effect. The control group is composed of those patients at those hospitals before the experiment, apparently. Or perhaps those that weren't given better care. It's not made explicit.

Evaluate the evidence: (1) The experiment can't be generalized to anyone other than poor, seriously ill veterans. Very dubious to generalize to all people. Especially dubious to generalize to people who are in good health to begin with.

(2) Overlooks other possible causes, such as normal deterioration in the patients' health during that period. (They were seriously ill to begin with.) Or the doctors, knowing the patients didn't have to pay, were more willing to hospitalize them.

Overall, there's not much you can conclude from this experiment.

Further tests? Do the same experiment with other populations throughout the country, ensuring that the samples are taken randomly. Choose control groups better. Assign doctors randomly and don't tell them the health care is free.

16. *Causal claim*: Having bad hair causes people to lack self-confidence.

Type of cause-in-population experiment: Sort of a cause-to-effect controlled experiment, except the subjects weren't interviewed on days they actually had bad hair, but about times when they had bad hair.

Evaluate the evidence: Hopelessly badly done. No reason to think the sample is representative even of that small age group. No reason to think that the subjects remembered correctly. Possibly reversing cause and effect. Research is sponsored by a company that benefits from the results that were obtained, so the authority of the researcher is called into question (possible conscious or unconscious bias of the researcher).

Further tests? I can't even begin to imagine any. It's a waste of time and money (except for Proctor & Gamble).

Review Exercises for Chapters 12–15

1. A collection of claims that are intended to show that one of them, the conclusion, is *true*.
2. The argument must be valid or strong, the premises must be plausible, and the premises must be more plausible than the conclusion.
3. For a valid argument it is impossible for the premises to be true and the conclusion false. For a strong argument it is unlikely the premise could be true and the conclusion false at the same time.
4. No. It could have a dubious premise or beg the question.
5. A comparison becomes reasoning by analogy when a claim is being argued for. On one side of the comparison we draw a conclusion, so on the other side we should conclude the same.
6. 1. Is this an argument? What is the conclusion?
   2. What is the comparison?
   3. What are the premises? (one or both sides of the comparison)
   4. What are the similarities?
   5. Can we state the similarities as premises and find a general principle that covers the two sides?
   6. Does the general principle really apply to both sides? What about the differences?
   7. Is the argument strong or valid? Is it good?
7. a. Add all the numbers in the collection. Divide by the number of items in the collection.
   b. Same as the average.
   c. The midway number: As many numbers in the collection are greater than it as are less than it.
   d. The number that appears most often in the collection (there may be more than one mode in a collection).
8. A comparison where the base is unknown.
9. a. A generalization is an argument concluding a claim about a group from a claim about some part of the group.
   b. The sample.   c. The population.

10. One in which no one subgroup of the population is represented more than its proportion of the population as a whole.

11. No. You could get a very biased sample by chance, but the likelihood of that happening is very, very small.

12. Yes. The computer example in Section C.5 of Chapter 14, p. 290.

13. There is a 97% chance that between 39% and 45% of the voters favor that candidate.

14. The sample is big enough. The sample is representative. The sample is studied well.

15. A hasty generalization. The claims about the too-small sample are called "anecdotal evidence."

16. *Describing the purported cause and effect with claims*:

    The cause happened (the claim describing it is true).

    The effect happened (the claim describing it is true).

    The cause precedes the effect.

    It is (nearly) impossible for the cause to happen (be true) and the effect not to happen (be false), given the normal conditions.

    The cause makes a difference—if the cause had not happened (been true), the effect would not have happened (been true).

    There is no common cause.

17. You still have to establish that the cause makes a difference.

18. Reversing cause and effect. *Post hoc ergo propter hoc* (looking too hard for a cause).

    Tracing the cause too far back.

19. Controlled cause-to-effect. Uncontrolled cause-to-effect. Uncontrolled effect-to-cause.

20. Because arguing or persuading badly:

    Undermines your own ability to reason well.

    Helps destroy democracy.

    In the long run doesn't work as well as reasoning well.

Appendix: Using Examples in Reasoning

5. a. Basenjis don't bark.

   e. Most Wendy's restaurants have a salad bar.

7. Even if the first premise is true, the argument is bad. This course is a counterexample: The exams are fair, but it's not easy.

8. Unstated premise: You have to inhale marijuana to get high from it. Valid. But that premise is false: You could eat it.

10. Unstated premise: Almost any professor who's never been late before and is very conscientious and is late for the first time has been in an accident. Unlikely. He could have been ill, and the secretary forgot to tell the class. Unstated premise is dubious. Without that premise it's not valid or strong. So it's unrepairable.

Appendix: Truth-Tables

Sections A and B

1. "and," "or," "not," "if . . . then . . ."

2. The only aspects of claims that we will pay attention to are whether the claim is true or false and how it may be compounded out of other claims.

3. A tautology is a compound claim that is true regardless of the truth-values of its parts.

4. Represent the claim using $\wedge$, $\vee$, $\neg$, $\rightarrow$. Replace the claims with letters. Make a truth-table with the last column the formal claim. If all the entries in that column are T, then it's a tautology. If even one is F, it's not a tautology.

5. Form the table for each. They are equivalent if for every row they are both true or both false.

6.

A	¬¬A	¬¬A→A
T	T	T
F	F	T

8.

A	B	A→B	¬A	¬A→B	(A→B)∧(¬A→B)	((A→B)∧(¬A→B))→B
T	T	T	F	T	T	T
T	F	F	F	T	F	T
F	T	T	T	T	T	T
F	F	T	T	F	F	T

11. Tautology.

A	B	A∨B	¬B	(A∨B) ∧ ¬B	((A∨B) ∧ ¬B) → A
T	T	T	F	F	T
T	F	T	T	T	T
F	T	T	F	F	T
F	F	F	T	F	T

12. Not a tautology.

A	B	A∨B	A∧B	(A∨B) → (A∧B)
T	T	T	T	T
T	F	T	F	F
F	T	T	F	F
F	F	F	F	T

14. Not a tautology.

A	B	A∧B	¬(A∧B)	¬A	¬(A∧B)∧¬A	(¬(A∧B)∧¬A)→B
T	T	T	F	F	F	T
T	F	F	T	F	F	T
F	T	F	T	T	T	T
F	F	F	T	T	T	F

15. Not a tautology.

A	B	C	A→B	¬A	¬A→C	(A→B)∨(¬A→C)	B∨C	((A→B)∨(¬A→C))→(B∨C)
T	T	T	T	F	T	T	T	T
T	T	F	T	F	T	T	T	T
T	F	T	F	F	T	T	T	T
T	F	F	F	F	T	T	F	F
F	T	T	T	T	T	T	T	T
F	T	F	T	T	F	T	T	T
F	F	T	T	T	T	T	T	T
F	F	F	T	T	F	T	F	F

16.

A	B	A→B	¬(A→B)	¬B	A∧¬B
T	T	T	F	F	F
T	F	F	T	T	T
F	T	T	F	F	F
F	F	T	F	T	F

18.

A	B	A∧B	¬(A∧B)	¬A	¬B	¬A∨¬B
T	T	T	F	F	F	F
T	F	F	T	F	T	T
F	T	F	T	T	F	T
F	F	F	T	T	T	T

Section C

1.

A	B	A∨B	A∧B	¬(A∧B)	(A∨B)∧¬(A∧B)
T	T	T	T	F	F
T	F	T	F	T	T
F	T	T	F	T	T
F	F	F	F	T	F

4. Dick prefers steak ∧ Zoe prefers spaghetti   ["While" doesn't mean "at the same time" here.]

5. "While" does mean "at the same time," and when a claim is true can't matter when we use the symbols. So the claim can't be represented.

7. Not compound, just two claims. Or: You whine all the time ∧ I love you

10. We're going to the movies tonight ∨ we're going out for dinner tonight. However, if you think the "or" is exclusive then follow Example 3.

13. (Dick takes Spot for a walk→Dick will do the dishes) → ¬(Dick will take Spot for a walk)

16. Spot barks → (there's a skunk in the yard ∨ there's a raccoon in the yard)

17. How you formalize this will depend on how you understand "regardless." Here's one interpretation:

   [(You get mad at me)→¬(I will visit your mother)] ∧ ¬(You get mad at me)→
   ¬(I will visit your mother) ∧   (You cajole me)→¬(I will visit your mother)
   ∧ ¬(You cajole me)→¬(I will visit your mother)

18. Can't represent it. It's *not*: Every student in Dr. E's class is over 18 ∨ every student in Dr. E's class is taking the course while in high school. That could be false and the original true.
   [Compare: Every student is male or female.]

20. a. A→B
    b. ¬B → A (This is the same as ¬A→B.)
    c. A→B "when" doesn't mean "at that time."
    d. (A→B) ∧ (B→A)
    e. B→A
    f. ¬A ∧ ¬B

Section D

1. Every argument that has that form is valid.

2. Not necessarily. It might have another valid argument form. Or it might be a strong argument. For example: All cats meow. Puff is a cat. So Puff meows. Truth-tables won't show that this is valid.

4. Valid

A	B	A→B	⌐B	A→⌐B	⌐A
T	T	T	F	F	F
T	F	F	T	T	F
F	T	T	F	T	T
F	F	T	T	T	T

(The rows F T and F F are circled, including the A→B column and the ⌐A column.)

5. Valid. It's not possible for the premises to be true and the conclusion false at the same time.

6. Invalid. Either circled row shows that.

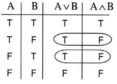

A	B	A∨B	A∧B
T	T	T	T
T	F	T	F
F	T	T	F
F	F	F	F

8. Valid. Argue that if C∨E were false, then both C and E would be false. Since B→C and D→E are true, both B and D would have to be false. But B∨D is true. So one of B or D is true. A contradiction. So one of C or E is true.

9. Valid.

A	B	C	⌐B	A→⌐B	⌐C	B∧⌐C	A→C
T	T	T	F	F	F	F	T
T	T	F	F	F	T	T	F
T	F	T	T	T	F	F	T
T	F	F	T	T	T	F	F
F	T	T	F	T	F	F	T
F	T	F	F	T	T	T	T
F	F	T	T	T	F	F	T
F	F	F	T	T	T	F	T

10. Valid.

A	B	C	⌐B	⌐⌐B	A→⌐⌐B	⌐C	⌐C∨A
T	T	T	F	T	T	F	T
T	T	F	F	T	T	T	T
T	F	T	T	F	F	F	T
T	F	F	T	F	F	T	T
F	T	T	F	T	T	F	F
F	T	F	F	T	T	T	T
F	F	T	T	F	T	F	F
F	F	F	T	F	T	T	T

11. Spot is a cat → Spot meows, ⌐ (Spot is a cat)
    So ⌐(Spot meows)

    $\dfrac{A→B, \ ⌐A}{⌐B}$ Not valid. Denying the antecedent.

12. The moon is made of green cheese ∨ 2 + 2 = 4
    ⌐(the moon is made of green cheese)
    So 2 + 2 = 4

    $\dfrac{A∨B, \ ⌐A}{B}$ Valid. Excluding possibilities.

13. Valid, same as Exercise 12. Sure, the conclusion is false. It's valid, not good.

14. (The students are happy → no test is given) ∧ (no test is given → the students are happy)

The students are happy → the professor feels good

The professor feels good → ⌐(the professor will feel like lecturing)

⌐(the professor feels like lecturing) → the professor will give a test

So ⌐(the students will be happy)

[Identify "the professor will give a test" with "a test is given."]

(A→⌐B) ∧ (⌐B→A) , A→C, C→⌐D, ⌐D→B
　　　　　　　　　⌐A

First note that the last three premises yield, via reasoning in a chain, A→B.

So we've reduced it to: (A→⌐B) ∧ (⌐B→A) , A→B
　　　　　　　　　　　　　　　　⌐A

Thus we have both A→B and A→⌐B. And so from Exercise 4 we have ⌐A. So it's valid.

15. Dick and Zoe visit his family at Christmas → they will fly

Dick and Zoe visit Zoe's mother at Christmas → they will fly

Dick and Zoe visit his family at Christmas ∨

　　Dick and Zoe visit Zoe's mother at Christmas

So they will fly. [Identify "They will fly"

with "Dick and Zoe will travel by plane."]

A→B, C→B, A∨C
　　B　　　　　　Valid.　　　　Valid

A	B	C	A→B	C→B	A∨C
T	T	T	T	T	T
T	T	F	T	T	T
T	F	T	F	F	T
T	F	F	F	T	T
F	T	T	T	T	T
F	T	F	T	T	F
F	F	T	T	F	T
F	F	F	T	T	F

16. ⌐(Tom is from New York ∨ Tom is from Virginia)

Tom is from Syracuse → (Tom is from New York ∨ Tom is from Virginia)

So, ⌐(Tom is from Syracuse)　["Tom is from the East Coast" isn't needed.]

⌐(B∨C) , D→(B∨C)　　Valid.
　　　　⌐D

If it were possible to have ⌐D false, and so D true, with these premises true, then by the direct way of reasoning with conditionals, B∨C would be true. But the first premise gives us that ⌐(B∨C) is true. A contradiction. So D is false. So ⌐D is true.

17. The government is going to spend less on health and welfare.

The government is going to spend less on health and welfare → (the government is going to cut the Medicare budget ∨ the government is going to slash spending on the elderly)

The government is going to cut the Medicare budget → the elderly will protest

The government is going to slash spending on the elderly → advocates of the poor will protest

So: The elderly will protest ∨ advocates of the poor will protest

A, A→(B∨C), B→D, C→E　　Valid.
　　　　D∨E

From the first two premises we get B∨C. Then if we want we can do a table. Or we can argue as follows. Suppose D∨E were false. Then both D and E are false. So by the indirect way of reasoning with conditionals, both B and C would have to be false. So B∨C would have to be false. But we already have that B∨C is true. So D∨E isn't false.

Appendix: Aristotelian Logic

Section B

2.   To use a term in a categorical syllogism, there must be at least one thing that term stands for.

7.   Whether the claim is universal or particular.

8.   Whether the claim is affirmative or negative.

10. *Categorical?* Yes.
     Subject: Cats.
     Predicate: Carnivores.
     Quantity: Particular.   *Quality*: Negative.

11. *Categorical?* Yes.
     Subject: Tom.
     Predicate: Football players.
     Quantity: Universal.   *Quality*: Affirmative.

13. *Categorical?* Yes. All donkeys are meat eaters.
     Subject: Donkeys.
     Predicate: Meat eaters.
     Quantity: Universal.   *Quality*: Affirmative.

16. *Categorical?* Yes (though it's a stretch). No knowers of critical thinking are things that will ever starve.
     Subject: Knowers of critical thinking.
     Predicate: Things that will ever starve.
     Quantity: Universal.   *Quality*: Negative.

17. *Categorical?* No. Nearly every ≠ all. Nearly every ≠ some.

18. *Categorical?* No. It's a compound.

23. *Categorical?* Yes. Dr. E is not a cat owner.
     Subject: Dr. E.
     Predicate: Cat owners.
     Quantity: Universal.   *Quality*: Negative.

25. *Categorical?* No. You can't make comparisons in categorical claims, or at least not in a way that's useful for reasoning.

28. *Categorical?* Yes. Some professor at this school is a person known to have failed all students in his class.
     Subject: Professors at this school.
     Predicate: People known to have failed all students in his class.
     Quantity: Particular.
     Quality: Affirmative.

Section C

2.   a. In no possible circumstance can they both be true, though they can both be false.

3.   a. In no possible circumstance can they both be false, though they can both be true.

4.   a. If "All dogs bark" is true, then "Some dogs bark" is true. If "Some dogs bark" is false, then "All dogs bark" is false.
     b. If "No cats bark" is true, then "Some cats do not bark" is true. If "Some cats do not bark" is false, then "No cats bark" is false.

5.   a. A claim equivalent to one in the form "All S are P."
     b. A claim equivalent to one in the form "No S is P."
     c. A claim equivalent to one in the form "Some S is P."
     d. A claim equivalent to one in the form "Some S is not P."

8. Contrary.
9. Contrary, but not via categorical form.
10. Contradictory.
11. Subalternate.
12. Subcontrary.
16. Contrary, but neither are categorical.

Section D
4. The term that appears in both premises.
5. The premise that uses the major term.
6. The premise that uses the minor term.
8. Invalid. Reasoning backwards with "no."
9. All S are M. All M are P. So all S are P. Valid. Reasoning in a chain with "all."
10. All S are M. No M is P. So some S is not P. Valid.
11. Some S is M. All M are P. So some S is not P. Invalid.
12. Some S is M. Some M is P. So some S is P. Invalid. Reasoning in a chain with "some."
13. All S are M. No M are P. So no S are P. Valid.
14. All S are M. Some M is not P. So some S is not P. Invalid.
15. All S are M. All M are P. So some S are P. Valid.
17. All wasps are stingers (A). Some bumblebees are not stingers (O).
    So some bumblebee is not a wasp (O).   Valid.
18. No badly managed business is profitable (E).
    No oyster cultivating business in North Carolina is badly managed (E).
    So some oyster cultivating business in North Carolina is profitable (I).
    Invalid.
19. Not categorical because "most" ≠ "all" and "most" ≠ "some." Invalid, but strong.
20. No straightforward way to view this as categorical. But valid.
21. Not categorical, because compounds aren't categorical. Invalid, weak, affirming the consequent.
22. EAE. Valid.
23. Police chiefs who interfere with the arrest of city officials are always fired. (A)
    People who are fired are people who collect unemployment. (A)
    So some police chiefs who interfere with the arrest of city officials are people who collect
        unemployment (I).
    Valid.
24. No obvious rewrite as categorical. But valid.

Appendix: Diagramming Arguments

Section A

The answers here are not definitive. When an argument is incomplete and doesn't have enough indicator words, there are likely to be different ways to repair it.

1.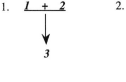

2. No one under sixteen has a driver's license. *1*
    So Zoe must be over sixteen. *2* Zoe has a driver's license. *a*

3.   If an animal is such that *2* and *3*, then it is the dumbest animal in the world. *a*   <u>2</u> + <u>3</u> + <u>a</u>

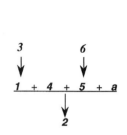

4.   I'm on my way to school. *1* I left five minutes late. *2* Traffic is heavy. *3* I'll be late for class. *4* I might as well stop and get breakfast. *5* Whenever I'm on my way to school and I'm five minutes late and traffic is heavy, I will be late for my classes. *a* If I'm late for classes, I might as well be very late or miss the class. *b*   <u>1</u> + <u>2</u> + <u>3</u> + <u>a</u>

5.   Pigs are very intelligent animals. *1* They make great pets. *2* They learn to do tricks as well as any dog can. *3* They can be housetrained. *4* And they are affectionate *5*. They like to cuddle. *6* Pigs are known as one of the smartest animals there are. *7* If you get bored with them or they become unruly, you can eat them. *8*   Anything that is intelligent, can be housetrained, and is affectionate is a great pet. *a*

6.   Smoking is disgusting. *1* It makes your breath smell horrid. *2* If you've ever kissed someone after they smoked a cigarette you feel as though you're going to vomit. *3*   Besides, it will kill you. *4*   You should not do anything that is disgusting and can kill you. *a*   You should not smoke. *b*

7.   You're good at numbers. *1* You sort of like business. *2* You should major in accounting *3*— accountants make really good money. *4* If you're good at numbers and sort of like business, you'll be good at accounting. *a* If you're an accountant you'll make good money. *b* You should major in something that you'll enjoy, be good at, and make good money at. *c* Accounting is the *only* thing that you'll enjoy, be good at, and make good money at. *d*

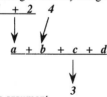

8.   Not an argument.

Section B

1.   You should not take illegal drugs. *1*   They can kill you. *2*   If you overdose, you can die. *3* If you share a needle, you could get AIDS. *4*   If you get AIDS, then you die. *5* If you don't die (not *3*), you may end up a vegetable or otherwise permanently incapacitated. *6*

By using drugs you run the risk of getting arrested and possibly going to jail or having a hefty fine against you. *7*

Some think the "high" from drugs is worth all the risks. *8*   They are addicted. *9*

They are only trying to justify supporting their habit. *10*

You shouldn't do anything that has a high risk of killing you or permanently incapacitating you or putting you in jail or having a fine against you. *a*

People who are addicted to drugs and are trying to justify their habit shouldn't be believed. *b*

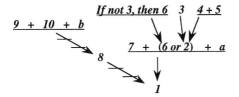

2. Sex is the answer to almost everyone's problems. *1*

It takes away your tensions. *2*

It doesn't if you're involved with someone you don't like. *3*

Sex makes you feel better. *4*

It doesn't if it's against your morals. *5*   Heroin makes you feel good. *6*

It's healthy, natural, just like eating and drinking. *7*

You can catch terrible diseases. *8* Sex should be confined to marriage. *9*

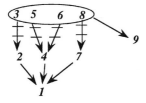

Just looking at the diagram, we can see that Zoe has not established her conclusion: Every one of her premises has been brought into doubt (by a plausible claim).

This is an example in which the counterargument is intended to do more than throw doubt on the conclusion: It's meant to establish another claim. (Though it's missing premises for that.)

3. Nixon was a crook/criminal. *1* He said he wasn't in the famous "Checkers" speech. *2*

That was just political evasion. *3*   You can't just take someone's word that he's not a criminal, especially if he's a politician. *4*

He directed the break-in at the Democratic Party Headquarters. *5*

They never showed that he did that. *6*

His accomplices like Haldemann were covering up. *7*

That's why they got pardoned. *8*

Nixon used the FBI against his enemies. *9*

It was stupid for Clinton to make a speech honoring Nixon when Nixon died. *10*

Clinton was doing it so that when he dies someone will make a speech for him. *11*

It is stupid to make a speech honoring someone who was a criminal. *a*

(Don't add "Clinton is a criminal." There's no reason to believe that Zoe thinks that's plausible.)

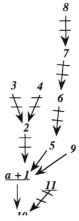

Index

Italic page numbers indicate a definition.